THE
LITTLE
MEN

'I was in Musa Qala for a month with the brave men of 5 Scots. Most of that time was spent on the front line fighting the Taliban. On average, we would get eight contacts before 8 o'clock in the morning. They referred to 5 Scots as The Little Men. They may have been small in stature, but they fought like giants.'

Ross Kemp

THE
LITTLE
MEN

AN AFGHANISTAN DIARY

GEORGE McCAFFERTY
AND ROBERT CAMERON

AMBERLEY

First published 2023

Amberley Publishing
The Hill, Stroud
Gloucestershire, GL5 4EP

www.amberley-books.com

British Library Cataloguing in Publication Data.
A catalogue record for this book is available from the British Library.

ISBN 978 1 3981 1403 6 (hardback)
ISBN 978 1 3981 1404 3 (ebook)

1 2 3 4 5 6 7 8 9 10

Typeset in 10.5pt on 14pt Sabon.
Typesetting by SJmagic DESIGN SERVICES, India.
Printed in the UK.

Contents

Contents

Acknowledgements

Firstly, I would like to thank my good friend Robert Cameron, whose knowledge of the literary world and experience of publishing would be invaluable in assisting me with this project as my co-author, his faith in me will hopefully be rewarded by this book.

My father George McCafferty Sr, the soldier I wish I had been and the man in whose footsteps I would eventually follow, finishing in the same Battalion as he did. His demons are now gone and all I can say is, now I understand.

My family, my wife Joanna, my stepson Jac and my daughter Georgina, born halfway through Op Herrick 13. This is what daddy did in the war. I love the three of you, always.

The real thank you goes to the brave and brilliant young men of 12 Platoon. A group of warriors from all walks of life and regiments, thrown together to make a hard-fighting unit. Without their dedication, skill and courage, I would not be here to tell this story. You are part of a great unsung generation who, surviving against the odds, matured and grew not only as soldiers but as men.

Thank you, brothers.

Prologue

In 2008 I kept a diary during my first tour of duty of Helmand Province, Afghanistan. It was never in my mind to publish it as a book, I did not see myself as an Ernest Hemingway or Rudyard Kipling, for me it was all about posterity as there would be a time when my war, like so many others, would be forgotten by everyone except those who had fought in it. I wanted a record of my first real combat tour as an infantry soldier so that in years to come when my children and grandchildren were older and they would see the medals, the faded desert shirt with its badges and wonder why every 11 November grandpa would sometimes get a little teary-eyed, there would be an answer, something tangible, something real that they could relate to.

I was persuaded by a friend that perhaps this might be worth getting into print and the more I thought about it, the more it made sense to me. The ink in my diary is fading and with it some of the memories of the tour – other than those moments of extreme violence, which come back to me with such clarity it's as though they happened yesterday. We are a part of our country's history and that service and sacrifice should never be forgotten.

This book is not meant to embarrass anyone or glorify anything I did in Afghanistan, it is simply a story I felt needed to be told because already, fifteen years after Op Herrick 8 ended, it is fast becoming a forgotten war. The story of the young men of Delta Company, 5 SCOTS and my own 12 Platoon needs to be told.

Going on my diary that I kept out there, time has not been good to the old grey matter and if there are mistakes in this book, the fault lies solely with me. I have tried to be as accurate as possible; however, some conversations have had to be manufactured for contextual reasons and may not have gone quite as written, but I hope it does convey some of what 12 Platoon, Delta Company, 5 SCOTS went through in that deadly summer of 2008.

Foreword

When I sat down to read *The Little Men*, I was unsure what to expect as there have been any number of excellent factual accounts written about the war in Afghanistan, from both sides of the Atlantic. One wondered what more there was to say. But as I began to immerse myself into the story, I found this to be a compelling depiction of the conflict – revelatory; gripping; shockingly-real – one written from the view of a rifle platoon sergeant in the British Army immersed in the very heart of battle.

From the outset that man, Sergeant George McCafferty, brings the war alive in vivid blow-by-blow detail, and with excellent recollection and recall, when you consider that the events occurred in 2008. Indeed, the book reads as if those very events are burned into his memory and consciousness, never to be forgotten – and as if this book is George McCafferty's unburdening of the most searing of recollections, hence the narrative power of the story's telling.

Of course, having spoken to veterans from many different units while writing my own books on the Afghan conflict, I was aware that this is not an unusual or solitary phenomenon: war tends to bring to the fore the most visceral, dramatic, traumatic and lasting of experiences and memories. If you were able to talk to a Roman or Greek soldier from ancient times, many of them would be able to recount the battles they had fought in with absolute clarity, for those seconds when you are closest to death are the moments that will live with you forever.

It is an odd but accurate truism that life never feels so very, very precious and valuable as when it has almost been taken away from you – whether that be by an accident, an illness, or, as in this case, by an enemy fighter.

This is not a tale about Special Forces operators conducting lightning raids against enemy strongholds or capturing high-value targets. Many of those stories have been written, including my own accounts of such operations. Instead, this is a tale of a unit of ordinary young men who are just trying to survive their six months of combat in Afghanistan and to go home to their loved ones alive, and hopefully un-maimed – in body, as well as in mind. In that sense, this is an Everyman story and it is one that I believe so many readers will be able to relate to so closely.

NATO declared that the 'fighting season' of the summer of 2008 was the deadliest of the war in Afghanistan, and while turning the pages of this book I could fully understand why. But what this compelling tale also highlights is just how resilient and hardy was – and is – the British soldier. Time and time again, these young men kitted up and patrolled out into the badlands of Helmand Province, not knowing whether they would return alive, but their raw courage and their undying respect for one another made them step out into the heat and the nightmare, driven on by the very basic understanding which is the very bedrock of the British military – *that you do not let your brother soldiers down.*

The men of D Company, 5 SCOTS, like their adversaries, were tribal, unyielding, toughened and they did not shrink from the fight when the battle was thrust upon them, just as their predecessors did not at Waterloo, Balaklava, Magersfontein and Gallipoli.

Reading about the men of 12 Platoon, George McCafferty's band of brothers, I got to know and understand just what it is like to be a soldier engaged in this most hellish of conflicts. George's writing brought the sights, the sounds, the pulse-pounding emotion and the smell of war into my very home. For those who have never served in the military or experienced frontline combat, *The Little Men* offers a vivid and compelling glimpse into the brutally intense and fierce nature of the fighting. As I read, I was transported into Helmand's densely vegetated, claustrophobic 'Green Zone', where the combat tended to coalesce, plus the isolated villages and the surrounding sun-blasted, barren desert, that repeatedly became the scene of close, terrifying and bloody combat for these brave young men.

From George's gripping eyewitness testimony I learned just how close this band of brothers became throughout their gruelling six-month tour, and how they made do with that typical can-do British squaddie attitude, enduring the primitive conditions, lack of food, sub-optimum kit and equipment and the constant threat of death, and how they faced all of that with the humour and stoicism that the British Tommy – or Jock – is rightfully renowned for.

Although no battle honours are yet stitched onto the colours of the British Regiments who served in Afghanistan, their efforts should never be forgotten nor diminished, for they are a credit to their country, their regiments and the British Army.

Once you have picked this book up, you will not put it down. And I guarantee, you – like me – will never forget the men of 12 Platoon, Delta Company, 5 SCOTS.

Damien Lewis

(*Damien Lewis is a former war reporter, an acclaimed and award-winning writer topping bestseller lists worldwide. He is the author of* The Flame of Resistance: American Beauty, French Hero, British Spy *and* Bloody Heroes: British Special Forces under Siege in Afghanistan *and many other titles.*)

Things to Come

My hands started to shake; they were covered in blood. I tried to wipe them clean but the blood simply smeared, some of it was dry and was ingrained on my skin. Drying in the edges of my fingernails. The Evac Helicopter had left and the atmosphere returned to an eerie quiet. I looked around at who was left with me; everyone had the same look on their faces. A state of shock.

The adrenaline that had just been coursing through my veins started to dissipate. The exhaustion that had been forgotten about during the contact was returning. I started to notice small injuries that I had taken during the firefight. Minor cuts, bruises and pressure wounds began to hurt. My hands started to shake as the adrenaline left my system.

I took a deep breath, held it and then let it out through parched lips. I rolled my eyes and took in another lungful of dry, dusty air. I needed oxygen to feed my weary muscles. My legs started to shake along with my hands, I lowered myself down onto one knee. My elbow rested on my thigh, holding me upright.

I had just seen some of my closest friends and colleagues wounded in the most horrific way. We had been in a firefight for our very lives whilst simultaneously providing major first aid and evacuating the most seriously wounded. It dawned on me that it could have easily been me. I had simply been lucky.

This was just the start of things to come.

Day 1

Thursday 10th April: Kandahar Air Base, Kandahar, Afghanistan

The order filtered down the isle of the privately chartered American airliner to put on our body armour. I was struck by the unreality of arriving in Afghanistan in this way. Here we were, hundreds of heavily armed, highly trained combat infantrymen from the British Army's rapid reaction air assault brigade, preparing to start a summer operational tour in the most dangerous country on earth (at that time). I watched as the tall, well-groomed ladies with American accents moved gracefully down the aisles flashing smiles displaying perfect white teeth, wishing us all a safe tour and thanking us for our service. Then the head of the cabin crew said something over the intercom which brought me back to the moment.

"Stay safe ladies and gentlemen and I hope to see you all safe and sound back with us in six months' time." I looked around and couldn't help wondering which seats would be empty on the return home. Would mine? Would any of the boys' seats be vacant? I could see a mixture of emotions written across people's faces, apprehension, excitement and those whose minds were still firmly at home in the UK. I was brought out of my trance by somebody tapping me on the shoulder.

"Move Ya tadger, I want tae get aff this fucking thing afore somebody uses it fer target practice!" I laughed and grabbed my daysack from the overhead storage bin. This could easily have been a flight to Benidorm or Malia. but instead of bags and laptops coming out of the lockers, body armour, patrol packs festooned with carabiners and grenade pouches were slung over shoulders. Name tags and addresses for lost baggage were replaced with blood groups and casualty zap numbers. I looked at my own kit and my eyes danced across digits scrawled in black Sharpie: 'MC6164 A POS NKA'.

I slung my daysack over both shoulders and turned to file down the aisle with the rest of the troops on the flight. A sea of helmeted heads in desert camouflage shuffled towards the door like a chain gang. As I approached the door, the flight attendant caught my eye. A pretty woman, around late thirties, her brown hair pinned up in a bun at the back of her blue uniform hat. Her ruby lips curled into a smile and a genuine look of warmth entered her eyes.

"Stay safe soldier, thank you for your service." She said in a clear mid-western US accent. All I could muster was a smile and a subdued "Thank you," before stepping out into the warm darkness of Southern Afghanistan. I turned once to see her shape distorted by the bright light of the interior cabin and under my breath I muttered "Hopefully see you in six months."

We were herded across the airfield towards a waiting Hercules. Our equipment shot past us in trolleys pulled by military airfield vehicles. We all looked behind us when we heard the engines of the civilian airliner throttle up. It was off. It didn't want to be here longer than it had to be.

While we waited for Crab Air to sort its life out, some of the boys took the chance to have a last smoke before we got onto the Herc. I looked around at the surrounding airhead station and was struck by how light it was, floodlights blazed around the airfield and red landing lights blinked slowly, almost lazily in the darkness.

I remembered back to everything I had read and heard about Afghanistan during the Soviet occupation and the rise of the Taliban. Kandahar was the birthplace of the Taliban and was currently the Area of Operations for Canadian, US and Afghan troops. From our Brigade (16 Air Assault) 3rd Bn The Parachute Regiment would form an Ops Battalion to go where units needed reinforcing.

We climbed into the C130, the tail ramp was down and waiting for us. Its four turbo-prop engines turned waiting to pull the airframe forward. We took our seats and our equipment was loaded into the tail ramp of the aircraft. Royal Air Force Loadmasters clambered all over the equipment like ants, securing it to the flooring with giant netting.

Shoulder to shoulder we sat down in the webbing strap seats and buckled ourselves in. The seats lined the sides of the aircraft, I strained round to look out the window behind me. Nothing but darkness. The huge motors pulling the metal tail ramp up, closing us in the belly of the airframe.

The engines revved; the breaks strained under the pull of the propellers. One of the Loadies moved around the cabin with a screwdriver opening panels and doing something inside them. The huge aircraft rumbled along the runway until the noise of the wheels on tarmac disappeared. The undercarriage raised with a thud leaving us with only the sound of the turbo-prop engines.

"They're your boys, are they no?" Said Goody (Goodall) elbowing me in the ribs. He motioned over to Dave Poderis and Davey McGhee. They were sat directly opposite us and were chatting away to each other.

"Aye," I said. "The two Daveys. They're good lads." Dave 'Pods' Poderis, was a Territorial Army soldier. Probably one of my most experienced soldiers in the aircraft. He simply went from operational tour to operational tour. Most likely when he ran out of money, he volunteered to go on another one. He was a tall, skinny lad, mid-thirties with missing teeth. He was a funny guy, but with his thick Glasgow accent even we sometimes struggled to understand him.

I chuckled thinking about the day Davey Pods arrived in Canterbury; he along with the other Reservists had stood outside the Company Sergeant Major's office ready to have a welcome chat. Dave was stood shaking like a dog and when he got in to the CSM's office, he slammed his tabs in and nearly fell over. As the discussion progressed the CSM couldn't help but notice Private Poderis shaking.

"Dinnae worry son, there's nay need to be feart, yer in a good company here! We'll look efter ye oot there." The CSM had said proudly. Davey nodded and upon dismissal he returned to the clerk's office and sagged into a chair, sweating profusely and looking not too healthy.

"What's wrong wi ye?" I asked him. Davey looked up and flashed me his soon to become trademark gap-toothed smile.

"The Sarn't Major hinks ah wiz fear teh gon tae Afghan! Naw man, ahm still pished, ah jist didnae want him tae stick me on extra duties this weekend!"

"Whit aboot wee Davey McGhee?" enquired Goody. I nodded, thinking of the best way to describe Davey.

"Dependable," I said. "He's a great wee laddie, he's keen. He's got a professional attitude. He's a wee bit on the quiet side, but I think he'll be aw right efter we get settled in." I'd given him the role of Minimi machine gunner, he'd carry one of our key section weapons.

"He's gonnie burn like a bastard," said Goody. I laughed.

"I've indented for an asbestos suit and a welder's mask for him, failing that factor fifty-seven sunscreen." He had pale skin and fair hair. Could easily have been given the nickname Casper. I was fond of the lad; he was small and skinny. but was very likable and confident.

Bastion was only a short flight from Kandahar, but it felt like it was never-ending. Inside the plane, the space that was actually cavernous seemed constricting, the red cabin lights giving out a dull glow that you could barely read by. As I looked through the blood -red gloom, I could make out lads asleep or at least pretending to be asleep, helmeted heads resting on the shoulders of their buddy. Others stared at the ceiling, feet tapping a rapid unheard beat on the metal floor of the C-130. Some tried to read books where others sat in quiet contemplation, lost in thoughts of home and family, or the task we had ahead of us. Training was 'almost' done now; this would be the real thing.

As I glanced around, I caught the eye of Pete Breen, one of my section 2i/c's. He grinned and made a funny face at me, which made me smile. We started our descent, I just wanted to be on the ground, I wanted out of this aircraft. I always hated being crammed in these things. As we came down to land, a drip coming from somewhere above me splashed onto my knee.

Goody shook his head and grinned his trademark smile. 'Great,' I thought, 'That's all I need, this thing to fall apart in the air before the Taliban even get a crack at me.' The wheels touched down smoothly, better than the first flight and the aircraft comfortably rolled to ground speed. The C130 lazily drove to its unloading area before dropping its tail ramp.

We all unclipped our seat belts and traipsed off the ramp onto the runway of Camp Bastion. I looked around and marvelled how it took Kandahar to a different level, it was lit up like a Christmas tree. There were lights everywhere and the dust thrown up by vehicles and personnel floated in large clouds caught by the lamp light, giving it an eerie, misty look.

It had the feel of a huge city. There were people all over the place, rushing about on their own business. We stood in awe, disorientated. It was fast approaching midnight and there was a chill in the air. I could tell it had been a hot day as the heat was still trapped in the tarmac. It was slowly dissipating.

We were led to a group of minibuses driven by LECs (locally employed civilians). As soon as we were crammed in, the driver ground the gears until he found the right one and headed off at breakneck speed, dust flying everywhere.

I couldn't help but thinking how ironic it would be if I was killed in Camp Bastion in an RTC because some Jinglie[1] couldn't drive. Thankfully, the drive was mercifully short and rather than debus, we all just fell out in a tangle of limbs, baggage and weapons.

We arrived at a huge hangar, the sheer size of it was incredible. It was full of bunk beds stacked three high. We were told this is where we would be spending the night. Tomorrow morning the briefings would start. We each claimed our bunks by throwing our daysacks onto a mattress. Small groups

---

1. The military contracted for host nation delivery trucks, known as "jingle trucks" because of the decorative metal tassels hanging from the bottom of the truck frames that jingled when the trucks moved.

started to congregate, we felt out of place and needed the comfort of our group. The lads were walking around, checking out who we were sharing the hangar with. I looked at some of the Paras' kit that was stacked at the end of beds, their SA80A2s had ACOG sights, rails and all kinds of Gucci kit.

"Fuck me, well seen we're the ginger bastard step-kids of this Brigade!" I announced. Even the Royal Irish lads in the brigade were issued with the same kit we were, no mod cons, nothing.

"It's fuckin shite," said Goody. "We dae the same fuckin job as they dae and they're pish."

"Ah well mate, we dinnae need any eh that shite," I said. "It's the way it'll always be." Goody silently agreed with a nod. He looked tired; he'd had a long day. The higher the rank, the more responsibilities you have. Sometimes I envied the young Jocks, just turn up and get on with it. "Heads up mate, here comes the Boss."

Major Nick Calder made his way over to us, stopping to talk to other groups of men hanging around in gaggles. Nick was a great leader of men. Decisive yet compassionate. He was tall and skinny. Intelligent and well spoken, all he cared about was getting us all home in one piece.

"Goody, Sergeant Mac," he said when he got around to us, "welcome to Bastion. How was your trip out?"

"Aye, all right Boss," said Goody with unusual restraint. "What's the crack?"

"Just get your heads down," said Nick. "Tomorrow's going to be a long day. We start our reception, staging and onwards integration training in the morning."

"That sounds like a lot of PowerPoint Boss," I said.

"To be honest," continued Nick. "The instructors are advisors in their particular field and have done well to avoid long, boring PowerPoint presentations. It's a long day but some of the presentations are a bit of a shock. You'll be interested in the medics input." The Boss knew I was keen on my battlefield first aid.

"How lang are we gonna be here?" said Goody crossing his arms. "In Bastion I mean."

"About a week," said Nick. "We need to acclimatise; it gets bloody hot out there. Then we'll be out at one of the FOBs." From the look on Nick's face I could tell he knew we were both tired. "Get your heads down guys, you've done enough today." Nick patted Goody on the shoulder and moved off towards another group of men.

Exhausted, we shuffled off to our respective bunks. I clambered into mine but stayed sitting. I looked around, I wanted to see that the other guys were getting some shuteye instead of standing around talking. Slowly, everyone made their way to their bunks and the floor of the hangar quietened down. I saw Tam Meighan climb into the top bunk a few rows away from me. He was a young Lance Corporal and was newly a dad. He was a nice lad, very polite in nature. He was short but stocky, his protruding ears and freckles made him look a little goofy. He was a capable soldier but lacked confidence in his abilities. I knew, however, I could always rely on him.

Even though I had been in the army fifteen years, and this wasn't my first operational tour. I, like some of the boys under my watch, had never been in a contact. I looked around for the rest of my team. I had a lot of young lads in my Platoon and I felt an overriding sense of responsibility to make sure they all got home in one piece.

Nick had the whole Company to bring home. Even though I didn't want to see anyone hurt, I desperately wanted to bring just my small section home. I noticed, a couple of bunks down, Pete Breen was clambering onto one of the rubberised mattresses, another new father. He had been a junior soldier only four years ago. I had trained him back at Army Training Regiment Bassingbourn. In a short time, he had risen to second in command of a rifle section, a highly demanding job. The saying goes that the rank of Lance Corporal is the hardest to earn, but the easiest to lose. His rise through the ranks in such a short space of time spoke for itself. Another short and stocky guy like Tam. But Pete had baby features and always had a naughty child look about him.

He was a good and dependable young NCO. I felt pleased and somewhat proud to be a part of this small team. We just have to keep our wits about us and we'll all get home safe. I lay down and pulled my Ranger blanket around my shoulders and closed my tired yes. But sleep didn't come straight away.

I was anxious about what was to come. The summer was approaching and they were notoriously bad tours. Summer was fighting season for The Taliban. I took a deep breath and sighed in an attempt to calm myself down.

I reached over and rubbed the injection sites on my arm. We had all been inoculated for all sorts of things before we left and the needle marks were still irritating, I felt like a fucking dart board and I really had no idea what I was getting inoculated for. Also, we had given blood for some kind of experiment. We were to give samples before and after the tour for the boffins to play around with. God only knew what they were looking for.

Day 10

Saturday 19th April: FOB Keenan, Upper Gereshk Valley

Hesco shelters ringed the Forward Operating Base (FOB), scattered sangers contained set up firing positions and sentry locations. A permanent Helicopter Landing Site was positioned in the centre. This was where we landed in a cloud of sand thrown up by the Chinook's rotor blades.

Situated to the north of the town of Gereshk, this company-sized FOB had been home to The Coldstream Guards for most of their tour. Over that time, they had been extending their patrols out to ten or so kilometres. They had pushed the enemy out and secured the area, returning governance to it. We would be taking over this duty and pushing out even further.

The elevated position, situated on the top of a sandy hill, was surrounded by other smaller compounds. Some occupied, some not. It had probably been owned by someone with money as it had hard standing buildings rather than dilapidated shacks.

Gereshk itself, further to our south was a small market town, hardly worth fighting for. It was the home to the Danish battle group HQ, FOB Price. At the bottom of the hill, guarding the bridge over a small river, was Patrol Base Bridgehead. This was one of our ways in and out of our FOB. It was a quick cross over between us and The Coldstream Guards. We got off the chopper, they got on.

"Good luck getting out of here in one piece," I heard as we crossed paths with the Guards. "Be careful not to burn in the sun you ginger Jock bastards." This was of course met with a volley of friendly insults back. My boys could give back as good as they got.

We all thought we would have to hit the ground running. Enemy presence was high in this area.

"Welcome to FOB Keenan," said Nick conducting one of his OC walk arounds. "Right," he continued. "First thing I feel I need to say is there are no cooking facilities."

"Aye," said Goody chipping in. "As ye kin see, the Guards've been cooking their scoff in these." He waved his hand over a line of empty H83 ammo containers. "And it's ten-man rat packs annaw, fresh scoff comes in noo and again wi' the Danish replen."

I looked around the small group of Sergeants being given the tour, everyone's eyes rolled at the news. Bruce Ewart looked over at me and shook his head. I had known Bruce for many years, he was even in a relationship with my now sister-in-law. To me, he felt like family.

Bruce was one of the toughest men I have ever known. He had grown up in the Borders of Scotland where his father was a gamekeeper. He was a country boy through and through and his fieldcraft skills were of the highest standards. He was a born soldier and that's why he was given one of the hardest and demanding jobs there was.

Bruce was our Joint Tactical Air Controller. He would be responsible for calling in fast air strikes and artillery on the enemy, sometimes so close to our position we would feel the impact. You wanted someone precise and calm under pressure, or things could go badly wrong. We couldn't have asked for anyone better than Bruce for that job.

"But we do have plenty of Irn Bru," said Nick, lightening the mood. He led the group away from the makeshift kitchen hoping to move the tour on and not dwell on the food situation. "The Guards thought it would be funny to stock up on that for us."

Nick and Goody continued the tour, slowly making their way up to the perimeter wall. As we passed the shit pits, I saw some graffiti spraypainted on a wall. 'Only the dead have seen the end of war' was sprayed over the toilet area. I was surprised the Coldstream Guards knew any Plato; I suspected it was more to do with the start of the film *Black Hawk Down*.

Nick gathered us on the perimeter wall and began pointing out areas of interest. I felt a trickle of sweat down my back, it was afternoon and still hot. Forty degrees plus.

"We have ten guys down on the bridgehead," said Nick. "But if they need help, our QRF will get down there in minutes to bump up their numbers."

"Who else is aroond Sir?" asked one of the Platoon Sergeants.

"FOB Armadillo, the Danes have tanks there if we need them. But that's about it."

"This place is heavin' wae Taliban," said Goody. "The Guards said they were Ghosts. Ghosts ma fuckin arse!"

"One thing we have going for us," said Nick. "Is that it's still spring. Fighting season hasn't begun yet, but it's on the way. Things will start to heat up on this tour. So, to that end I want to start as we mean to go on. Security patrols will go out immediately, out to half a K at first then push out."

"We're tae dominate and deter," said Goody. "10 Platoon are gearing up noo, they'll be headin' oot soon." We looked down into the compound from our elevated position on the wall. The patrol was almost ready to leave. They were gathered round their Platoon Commander who was giving a quick brief and confirming that everyone was aware of his plan.

I wished I was going with them. Even though this patrol was just a short skirt around the compound, it was the first one and I wanted to get stuck in. This was what I lived for. I was a soldier; I had always wanted to be ever since I was a young boy. We used to play war as a kid, my friends were all soldier's sons, so it seemed to be an occupational hazard of that kind of childhood. I was part of a highland warrior tradition. My dad had been a soldier in the Argylls, serving in Northern Ireland during the worst periods of the Troubles. He and I would patrol the same stretches of breathtaking Irish countryside, but decades apart. And my great-grandad had been a Private in the Cameron Highlanders during the great war; enlisting in 1914 and fighting through some of the most pivotal battles, surviving the war but forever changed by it.

Ever since I could stand, walk and talk it became an obsession. I ate slept and breathed soldiering. Every toy I ever owned was of a military nature, all my favourite films and TV shows were about war of some kind. I couldn't wait for the day I was old enough to join the Army. I had worked in a factory in the little town of Bonnyrigg, just outside Edinburgh. I was determined that I wouldn't do my A-levels or go to university, for me, my university was going to be basic infantry training. I told my supervisor in no uncertain terms that I was "only doing this until I could join up".

Sure enough, on 10th May 1993, I enlisted at the Armed Forces Career Office at Hanover Street in Edinburgh as a Private soldier in the 1st Battalion The Royal Scots. At that time, the only operational areas were Northern Ireland and after the dissolution of Yugoslavia, Bosnia. I couldn't wait to join my Battalion, I wanted action and I wanted it now. But the old adage ran true then, the same as it does now. 'Be careful what you wish for, you might just get it.'

Phase 1 training at Glencorse Barracks had flown by in a flurry of beastings and abuse, preparing us for our role as Scottish infantry soldiers. All our instructors were Op Granby Gulf war veterans and were extremely tough on us trainees. But the way I saw it, I had joined the infantry and was being prepared for war. There was a lot of shouting, collective punishment, unexplained bullshit and the occasional smack just to let you know you were a crow bag.

After leave, I reported to Infantry Training Battalion Ouston, near Newcastle. Our phase 2 training would be the very meat of our job, infantry tactics, weapons training, live firing and a lot of field work. The beastings did not stop, rather only intensified. Of the four Royal Scots recruits to start training, two of us would finish as fully trained infantry soldiers.

I enjoyed phase 2 training, even though most of it was conducted at Otterburn training area, which is notorious for its own weather system. Our final exercise was two weeks of wet and miserable weather during October/November 1993. I can still remember to this day the weather changing to shit as you drove up the road to the training area and crossed that cattle grid.

On the last phase, we were 'bugged out' again and I had to carry a camouflage net that was normally used to cover tanks and Armoured Personnel Carriers. What I didn't realise was that it had been raining quite hard and this netting had accumulated a lot of water and was now extremely heavy. As we were force-marched again and again, up and down hillsides, I began to fatigue quite badly, as a nine-stone soaking wet teenager carrying well over his own body weight would. I began to drop back from the rest of my Platoon, I watched as they disappeared ahead of me into the misty rain of Otterburn.

As I took a break and tried to relax my shoulders, which by now were burning as my bergan straps cut into me, I watched one of my Platoon Corporals approach me. I felt relief that perhaps he had come to assist me. Relief was cut short however, as the look of rage on his face came into focus.

"Git a grip!" He growled at me. "Ya wee fanny!" When I opened my mouth to explain why I had dropped back so far, I was rewarded with a punch to the face which broke my nose. Spitting blood, snot and blinking back tears, I decided not to say anything. I lifted my Light Support Weapon and staggered on.

Shouted at and cajoled by the Corporal, struggling under the weight of my kit, I must have looked a terrible sight. As I was pushed to the front of the Platoon the lads all looked at me in shock and disbelief. The sleeve of my combat smock was soaked with blood and it was drying on my chin and cheeks. But I made it through, somehow you always find the strength.

The rest of the exercise went by in a blur and before I knew it, we were preparing to pass out as fully trained infantrymen and head out to our Battalions. My Battalion had not long returned from a tour of duty in South Armagh in Northern Ireland. And I arrived in the sombre atmosphere of a Battalion who had lost one of their own on this tour,

Lance Corporal Lawrence Dickson having been killed by a sniper on St Patrick's Day.

My time in the Royal Scots had its ups and downs. I arrived at C Company in November 1993 at Fort George in Inverness. I got to visit some amazing places around the world and did my first operational tour of South Armagh in 1995. The Battalion moved from Inverness to Colchester where we would form part of 24 Airmobile Brigade, the British Army's rapid reaction unit.

'Here's the place,' I convinced myself. 'If I'm going to see any action, it's with this Brigade.' We were told that when anything happened in the world, we would be the first ones sent. This of course, turned out to be absolute bollocks. I would see Northern Ireland again twice.

Three months of that tour I would spend in Fermanagh, which was possibly the worst time in my life. I was a newly promoted Lance Corporal with no idea what I was doing, I couldn't map-read my way to the shower and floundered massively. During this time, my reputation would take a serious beating. Then, my young wife would leave me taking my eighteen-month-old daughter with her. So, all in all, a pretty fucking awesome time.

In 1999, as a more experienced Lance Corporal, I commanded a team in Forkhill South Armagh. During this tour I managed to improve my reputation and at the same time, my morale. Then, on our return from South Armagh, I received the news we were returning to Northern Ireland. This time for two years.

I was asked if I wanted to join the Reconnaissance Platoon, which would be forming the nucleus of the Battalion's Close Observation Platoon. This covert intelligence gathering team would help defeat terrorism in our areas by gathering intel for use by other outside agencies.

But then one grey cold day in September 2001, all that would change. Whilst on leave I was sat back in a friend's living room in Colchester watching Spongebob Squarepants when a friend called me.

"Are you watching the news? Put it on now!" he said, hanging up the phone. I changed the channel over to the news just in time to see a passenger aircraft crashing into the side of the World Trade Center in New York. Like the death of JFK and the moon landings, everyone remembers where they were the day the world changed forever. All I remember was confusion. Was this an accident? How could an accident of this magnitude happen? What had gone wrong?

The world itself asked the same questions I was asking myself. Replays and more information came in, rather than a tragic accident it was a planned and calculated attack on the United States. An attack that would change the course of history and the lives of many people. Terrorists affiliated to a group called Al Qaeda, or 'The Base', had just conducted the biggest terrorist atrocity the world had ever seen. I knew at that very moment that my job was about to get a whole lot more interesting. Nothing would be the same again.

Day 11

Sunday 20th April: FOB Keenan, Upper Gereshk Valley

I looked around at my Platoon, the boys were buzzing. Full of the nervous energy of any soldier heading out into an uncertain environment. We were all running possible scenarios through our heads, anything could happen out there and we were expecting a rough tour.

Our Company Commander Nick Calder had told us the Company expected to have five killed in action and double, possibly three times that number wounded. That was what the statisticians had come up with and it was a bloody sobering thought.

As a military history buff, I had been reading about what we were in for, both from our perspective and from the Russian invasion of Afghanistan, such as *The Bear Went over the Mountain*. If you don't learn from history, you are doomed to repeat it. I wanted to arm myself with as much information as I could so as not to do that.

Stories from previous tours had filtered down to us and we were all understandably nervous. We expected our time here to be an extremely busy one. On the other hand, the opium poppies had not yet been cultivated. This meant that the enemy would still be busy with the harvest until at least the end of July or even the start of August. They had to fund their war somehow. There was still no room for complacency, the lads were spread out around the helipad of FOB Keenan, still laughing and joking but with enough room between groups, just in case the Taliban decided to start the fighting season early this year and welcome us by chucking a few mortars our way.

As the boys were checking each other over I caught the eyes of my troops and got nods, winks and nervous grins. The thought of one of the boys being killed horrified me. I looked around at lads I had trained with, those I had even trained as young recruits and men I had drunk with back in Canterbury. I could not imagine any of my boys being killed, but I was reminded of the ones I had known who had died here on previous tours. Their faces flashed into my mind's eye, and the circumstances of our meeting. I promised myself I would do anything I could to ensure we beat the odds. After all, one of my tasks as Platoon Sergeant was to deal with the dead and wounded. Ours, theirs, allies and civilians. It was work I'd like to avoid.

We still hadn't fully acclimatised yet and were all bright red from the sun. The Guards had joked about us Jocks burning, I hated to admit it, but they had been right. We sweated profusely under the weight of the kit we carried. The Osprey body armour we had been issued with had huge ballistic plates that cut painfully into the shoulders and neck sending tingling sensations up and down the arms and neck, day sacks grated painfully on sunburnt shoulders.

We looked like a rag tag band of mercenaries, with some guys wearing full green disruptive pattern camouflage normally worn in European theatres. Some wore desert pattern or a mixture of both. I opted for a set of tropical DPM combats normally worn in places like Belize and Brunei.

To anyone who thinks that Afghanistan is a purely desert country, they have never seen the fertile land that is Helmand Province's 'Green Zone'. So called because it is broken by the Helmand river running north to south providing water for the crops and compounds we were to be soon patrolling. It was amongst the most beautiful places I had ever visited. I had marvelled at the view on the Chinook ride into FOB Keenan from Bastion at the long green strip. On the way in, we had dropped down into a field to resupply an Afghan National Army unit and their British advisors. I had watched them struggle to wade through the grass as they unloaded the supplies, such was the length and thickness of the crops.

The sentry, whose job it was to open the steel gate to the compound, gave us the nod. It was time. After months of pre-deployment training, it was time to leave the relative safety of our FOB and venture out into the Green Zone. Cigarettes were ground out into the dust and looks exchanged as sweat was wiped clear from eyes. Mine included.

Our issue mark six alpha helmets were lined with leather pads, and this always caused me a major problem. Sweat would run down into my eyes and make me blink, I knew I'd have to solve this. I was always an abnormally committed sweater anyway. Add in full fighting kit, weapon and helmet, taking the weight up to fifty kilograms at least, in the searing heat, it made for a very sticky and uncomfortable combination.

As per orders, the lead section rushed out the gate, using a tactic we had learned from patrolling the Bandit Country of South Armagh in Northern Ireland, called 'Hard Targetting'. After a slight pause, the Boss, Lt Alan Lipowski, headed out followed by 2 Section. Then it was 1 Section, myself and the Reserve Section.

As I passed through the gate, I took in my surroundings. We had exited the rear gate of FOB Keenan and were in a small courtyard surrounded by compounds. Trees and rubble were scattered around the area and disinterested locals looked on as the latest group of Westerners descended upon them.

The eyes of men in coloured turbans followed us as they squatted around the compound perimeters, running prayer beads through their fingers, their tanned, lined and weather-beaten faces alive with hatred, I could see that feeling as I looked into their dark eyes, eyes that blazed. But I doubted they knew or cared who we were. As we passed them, we waved. Careful not to use the left hand. A big no-no. Some waved back, some completely ignored us.

I took the chance to practise some Pashtun I had learned during pre-deployment training. "Tsunga yay?" I said to greet them, or "starey mashe." I was always keen on learning a bit of the language of any country I went to, even if it was just asking for a beer. Something I knew I wouldn't be doing for a while, and the thought depressed me as a nice cold pint of Fosters would have gone down a treat after this patrol.

Although it was still quite early in the morning, the heat had already started to pick up. Heat bars shimmered on the hot, dusty ground. I felt the familiar slimy feeling on the leather pad of my helmet as a river of sweat ran down through my shoulder blades all the way to my arse crack.

Information was passed back and forward between the section NCOs; the lads were reminded to watch their assigned arcs of fire and be mindful of possible enemy firing points. Of which there were many.

The Taliban were out there, and we knew it, in fact they knew exactly where we were and probably had done since we left FOB Keenan. This was where any effective insurgent army gained their strength, where they couldn't beat us with numbers or firepower, they could at least pin us in place with their spy network. And we being somewhat more over-encumbered than our enemy, would present a better slow moving target. The enemy had dickers out on the ground and they were very effective. As if to confirm my suspicions, the small handheld ICOM radio carried by our interpreter crackled into life. I could hear as clear as day the voices of our enemies.

"What are they saying Abdul?" I asked the Platoon interpreter in between the garbled transmissions.

"They say, watch out, the Russians have left their base!" I let out a small chuckle and shook my head. There hadn't been any Russians in Helmand since the 80s. But I guessed all white faces were simply considered to be Russian.

The patrol continued through clusters of compounds that the locals called home, I was struck by the basic yet rugged build of some of the structures. In Afghanistan, and particularly Helmand, a man's home must be a fortress in order to protect his family. Like the castle of medieval times they had few windows, high, thick, hard-baked walls with flat roofs; on closer inspection those walls were made of hard-packed mud, reeds and stones, which gave the impression of a formidable protective barrier.

Children clustered around us in curiosity, full of smiles and begging for sweets and pens.

"Kalam mister, kalam." They said in heavily accented English. "You give me sweet." Probably the only English they knew. I grinned and reached into my dump pouch on my body armour for a packet of Army ration boiled sweets. I distributed them evenly amongst the grabbing hands. My good deed for the day was interrupted by the ICOM blaring again. Before I could ask the interpreter, what was going on, he pre-empted me.

"The Taliban say that they can see you and are ready to attack!" The look on his face told me all I needed to know and I reached for the pressel switch on my personal role radio.

"All three-zero callsigns, this is three-zero Bravo." I paused for breath realising what I was about to transmit. "Fix bayonets!" Shortly after I was rewarded with the clicking sound of bayonets being fixed to the muzzles of SA80s.

"Three-zero Bravo, from three-zero Alpha." My radio came to life through my earpiece. "Do you think that's necessary, over?" Lt Lipowski asked.

"Three-zero Alpha," I responded. "Absolutely Boss. If the enemy are watching, and we know they are. They'll know we mean fucking business."

Little did I know, this would catch on throughout our time in Afghanistan. As soon as the ICOM indicated an attack was imminent, everyone in the Company would fix bayonets. This became an unofficial Standard Operating Procedure (SOP). One which would save the lives of at least two of our guys in the Company.

As it happened, the ICOM chatter was either false or the Taliban had been scared off by the fact we were ready and prepared to take them on in close quarter combat. We were aware that they knew we could hear them and they could, if they thought about it, use that to their advantage. Luckily the rest of our first patrol passed off without incident.

We patrolled through a flowering poppy field, the pink and white flowers blazing against the brown mud of the field. I could not believe that something so pretty could cause so much suffering around the UK and elsewhere. Opium produced in Afghanistan was responsible for eighty per cent of the heroin on Britain's streets. So, in addition to the terrorist element, destroying the drug trade was also very important, or at least that's how I was justifying it to myself.

The poppy fields seemed to stretch on forever and groups of fighting age males were working furiously amongst the blossoming crops. As I got closer to the poppy plants, I was able to see long brown scores along the poppy bulbs and brown sap hardening on the bulbs. I was at first confused about these markings until I saw that all the males working the crops had either razor blades or small sharp knives, which they were using quickly and efficiently to cut three to four scores along the poppy bulbs. I was informed that the sap would then be collected and bagged as raw opium, which would then be sold on to be made into the final product. Heroin.

We returned to FOB Keenan via the main entrance, so as not to be seen setting patterns. Always under the watchful eye of the boys on guard covering us with 7.62mm GPMG cover, as we were extremely vulnerable upon exit and entry from the patrol base. I was the last to enter the base and did a head count of my guys to make sure we were all accounted for.

"Section Commanders," I said. "Make your guys safe and we'll have a kit check in thirty minutes." Quickly the sections all lined up against the HESCO Bastion wall and began to make their weapons safe, the sounds of cocking handles racking back and clearing rifles and machine guns.

I felt relief that we had not been engaged by the enemy, but I knew that we had a long way to go before the end of our tour. There would be no way we would be able to get through the next six months without having to fire our weapons.

As I watched the lads making safe and heading back to the accommodation, I couldn't help but remember what got me here in the first place.

Day Minus 141

Wednesday 21st November 2007:
RAF Chicksands, Bedfordshire, UK

I was three days into the Theatre Intelligence Course (TIC) when I took a call from the Regimental Career Management Officer. He was responsible for every soldier's career progression and posting plots.

"Sergeant McCafferty," he began in a friendly manner. "This is a good news, bad news call I'm afraid."

"Go on then Sir." I replied after a short pause trying to guess what was about to be said.

"Well," he began tentatively. "We've got you a Platoon Sergeant slot within D Company, it was felt unfair to have a Sergeant from the reserves running a Platoon and you in the Intelligence Cell."

My mind started racing, this was both exciting news but tinged with apprehension. This was actually happening; I was deploying with a fighting company into Helmand as a Platoon Sergeant.

"Awesome Sir, so what's the bad news?" I asked warily, acutely aware of the Army's 'shit sandwich' approach to delivering bad news.

"Well Sarn't Mac, you have to stay on the TIC course as there aren't enough bods on it to keep it running." He replied honestly. I was keen on getting back to Howe Barracks in Canterbury and starting to run with my Platoon. Training, pre-deployment admin and just getting to know the lads I'd be fighting alongside.

"Nay dramas Sir," I said. "It's not a bad course anyway." I felt the knowledge gained from the TIC course would only help with intelligence gathering on the ground. So I remained on the course, and did well even though I knew I would not deploy in the role.

As soon as the course finished, I hurried back to Howe Barracks full of the enthusiasm of a new Platoon Sergeant. I was ready to throw myself into my new job; I needn't have rushed.

"Sergeant McCafferty Sir," I said as I came to attention outside Company Sergeant Major WO2 Derek Park's office. "I'm taking over one of the Platoons in the Company for Afghan." The short, stocky, blond-haired Sergeant Major rose up from his desk and thrust out his hand.

"Junior, pleased to meet ye." He said in a heavy Glasgow accent. "But, ye've no goat a Platoon at the moment. Jist you and yer Boss. There's mair boys turning up though and by the time we deploy ye should huv a Platoon." I shook Junior's hand and at the same time let the news wash over me.

No Platoon, no chance as of yet to get to know my troops. For now, it was just me and my Boss, a Lieutenant, my Platoon Commander.

"For noo, jist git yersell sorted oot admin wise. Touch base wi yer Boss and standby for mair troops to turn up." I fell out sharply and made myself familiar with the Company HQ.

The Officer Commanding was Major Nick Calder, who came from a distinguished military background with two brothers also officers in the army, one with 5 SCOTS and the other a Battalion commander with the Royal Regiment of Fusiliers. Nick was from good soldiering pedigree. Just how good he was, I would witness time and time again in Helmand.

The Company was hustling and bustling with soldiers and NCOs coming and going, visiting the Company clerks from the Adjutant Generals Corps. Those whose job it was to administrate the Neanderthals that comprise an infantry Battalion. They handled the pay, bonuses and all other facets of paperwork that are required to keep a unit going.

Being relatively new to Howe Barracks, I decided to have a wander round and get the lay of the land. As I went around from place to place introducing myself, I spotted a bespectacled young officer in a Glengarry. He was juggling what seemed to be a mountain of paperwork. As our eyes met, I saluted him and nodded as we passed.

After tea and toast in the Warrant Officers and Sergeant's mess, I returned to Company HQ to see if there were any developments. As I trudged along the corridors of the HQ building, Junior stuck his head out of his office.

"Ah George," he said. "Yer Boss is aboot here somewhere." He craned his neck around and yelled in the best CSM fashion, "Mister Lipowski!"

From the clerk's office the young officer with the ton of paperwork appeared and in a strong Glaswegian accent introduced himself.

"Lt Al Lipowski," he said. "2 SCOTS." He thrust his hand forward, I grasped it and shook it warmly. Here was my Platoon Commander. For the next year or so, we would be getting to know each other better than our own families.

Over time, as Junior predicted, more troops did turn up to fill our ranks. Most had transferred from within the Company or Battalion, but there was a swelling group of lads that had come from the army's reserve units. There was also a small handful of lads from the Army Air Corps. These guys were drivers and helicopter re-fuellers.

I remember a LCpl by the name of Geordie Morgan introducing himself as one of the guys who'd be driving our trucks for us. I simply smiled back and informed him he was now in an infantry unit. And whilst pointing to his boots, that we had no trucks and he was wearing his own transport.

My introduction to the rest of the command team proper was in the form of a daily 'O' group (Orders Group), which would set the picture for the week and outline what was upcoming. It was a chance to chat informally amongst the Company leadership and iron out any issues and put dates in the diary.

As I walked into the OC's office, I looked around at the senior ranks I'd be working with for the foreseeable future. The presence of the tall gaunt figure of Major Nick Calder, with his easy-going manner, filled the room. The moment he shook my hand and welcomed me to Delta Company, I had that warm fuzzy feeling that I had landed in my feet massively.

Captain Simon Dinsmore, our Royal Marine Company second in command was there too. He was also very easy-going and had a friendly smile to match, and a handshake like a vice. In place of a Scots Tam o'shanter was the rifle green beret of his elite unit, he was short and built like a brick shite house.

The Argylls always had a Royal Marine Captain attached to its Delta Company. Ever since World War Two, when the surviving Marines from the ships HMS *Prince of Wales* and the *Repulse* joined the men of 2nd Battalion Argyll and Sutherland Highlanders in Singapore. They re-named themselves 'The Plymouth Argylls' The affiliation between the two proud units continued post-war.

I remember my father telling me back in the eighties that they had a Marine officer attached to the Battalion and when I expressed an interest in the Marines as a future career, I was given a number of recruiting posters and items which took pride of place in my bedroom.

The Company Sergeant Major (CSM) I had met when I first arrived at the unit, Derek 'Junior' Park, who was a no-nonsense professional soldier. He was a short man with blonde hair and occasionally wore dark framed glasses, a very athletic man who could outrun most, if not every, man in the Company. Again, Junior had a firm handshake and I got the impression that I would like this man very much.

Our Company Quarter Master Sergeant (CQMS) was a tall, skinny Colour Sergeant who had a permanent case of Tourette's. His name was Alan 'Goody' Goodall, and he smoked like a chimney. Goody had a wicked sense of humour, very dark and insisted on calling everyone retards.

Looking around the room I saw the other Platoon leadership team sat together, 10 Platoon was led by a tall and skinny youthful looking lad with bright blonde hair.

"Jim Adamson!" he announced thrusting his hand out to meet mine. This raised eyebrows from the OC and CSM, but I thought nothing of it.

"George Boss," I said. "George McCafferty, here to take over 12 Platoon. Well, 12 section at the moment looking at the massive group of lads I've got out there." I grinned, this raised a small smile from him. His Platoon Sergeant was a man I knew very well, equally as tall and equally blonde as his Boss.

"Scotty mucker," I said greeting an old friend. "How are you?"

"Aye good mucker," he said. "Nice tae see yeh." To say Scotty McPhail and I had known each other our whole lives was probably not far from the truth. Scotty's father and mine had both served together in the Argylls and Scotty and I had gone to school together pretty much from an early age and the beauty of an infantry Battalion is that when you get posted, you get posted together and you don't lose touch with your school friends.

As our ranks swelled the training for the tour became fast-paced. We were training hard now that we had the manpower. 12 Platoon, D Company was taking shape now as a good rifle Platoon. We were, however, a mixed bag. Some veterans, some who were not even infantry. Some part-timers and soldiers straight out of basic training, we were going to hit the ground running!

It was the job of myself, the Boss and the unit's other NCOs to mould this rag tag band into something that resembled a fit for purpose combat unit. One that was ready for a six-month fighting tour to one of the world's most dangerous places. A place that had claimed the lives of many a British and American soldier.

The weeks and month went by in a blur of exercises, which varied from very basic Platoon and Company level training all the way up to Combined Arms Live Fire Exercises. These involved live artillery, mortars and air support from Apache Gunships. They got the blood pumping and gave us an idea of what we might be facing.

My lads were doing me proud so far, enduring the tiring regime and always giving one hundred per cent. I explained that this was the place to make mistakes, here at home in the UK. As long as we could learn from them and not make the same mistakes in Helmand. Where a small hiccup could cost the lives of some of us.

OPTAG tried as much as they could to replicate Helmand. Thetford training area became Sangin, Otterburn became Garmsir and all the other places we would be fighting. One thing we could not replicate was the heat and other conditions, but we would damn well try.

The Afghan community in London were hired to play villagers, Afghan forces and interpreters. This really added to the realism. A company called Amputees in Action provided us with realistic casualties. Simulated Improvised Explosive Devices (IED) blasts would leave casualties who were actually missing limbs.

Nothing quite prepares a young soldier for the sights of people screaming with shredded stumps where their arms and legs had once been. We always said, what will keep us alive are the three Fs. Fitness, firearms and first aid. The three Fs were the things that would save our lives and it was a mantra that would pay dividends in Helmand.

"You have to help these people!" I would shout shaking young soldiers out of their shock. "Get a fucking tourniquet on these stumps now! Don't let them bleed out!"

Shuras, meetings with the village elders, would be interrupted with mock rocket-propelled grenade attacks and small arms fire. Simulated Taliban fighters would conduct hit and run attacks on our patrol base and foot patrols would be met with ambushes everywhere. Normally, our ambushers would be men who had recently returned from Afghan and knew how the enemy operated.

They pulled no punches and showed no mercy as our enemies would undoubtedly not. We ran and tabbed in our full fighting patrol gear, but in the British winter we could not acclimatise for the furnace hell that the heat of an Afghanistan summer would bring.

I worked through my casualty evacuation plans, if any of my lads were killed or injured how would I treat them and get them back to safety? I became obsessed with MIST reports, 9 liners and other ways of communicating what type of casualties we had and how to evac them, it was drummed into us while on Platoon Sergeant's Battle Course, CASEVAC plan, CASEVAC plan, CASEVAC plan.

I bought extra medical supplies off the internet, I got hold of a lightweight stretcher and used heavy-duty rock-climbing carabiners to allow whoever my CASEVAC party were to use their weapons while still carrying their casualty. I also relentlessly drilled my section 2i/c's on CASEVAC drills as I wanted us to be slick and all singing from the same song sheet.

As a Company, we had Standard Operating Procedures as to where we all carried our individual first aid kit. Every soldier would have his in the same place as all the others. Each man carried as a minimum two Israeli bandages, two Asherman chest seals, two tourniquets and upon arrival in Helmand each soldier was issued with two Morphine auto injectors, these were signed out to the individuals, but as Platoon Sergeant, I would account for them.

Also to assist us, we were given slates made of plastic that were held together with a ring in the top left corner. On these slates were important reports such as the MIST report, 9 liner, ECAS (Emergency Close Air Support) and CCA (Close Combat Attack) should we require to speak to aircraft in the event of there being no JTAC.

I checked and re-checked my guy's kit, we found through trial and error what worked for us and what didn't work for us. Every soldier's kit is an individual expression of that soldier's personality and how he feels it best to carry his load.

I started designating gunners, both 5.56mm Minimi light machine guns and 7.62mm General Purpose Machine Gun (GPMG). I worked this out on a process of who was hardy enough to carry the gun and also the weight of the ammo that went with it. But mostly who could hit the fucking target with it! Our machine guns were the weapons that would keep the enemy's heads down while we moved in for the assault. They would provide us with fire superiority, but that was only if the operator knew his arse from his elbow.

My section 2i/c's would have an underslung 40mm grenade launcher attached to their standard SA80 A2 rifle, capable of giving us a better range than hand grenades could. I carried or had a soldier who would use the 51mm mortar, which could lob High Explosive (HE), smoke and illumination rounds at the enemy should we have to wait for 81mm mortar support or artillery.

Throughout training a new lad called Pte Nigel Campbell had been proving a frustration to his section commander, who asked me to have a word with him. Pte Campbell, it seemed, could not do anything right. He was always fucking up and earning the wrath of his section commander, Cpl Andy Johnston. I was concerned about Campbell, if he kept screwing up, he would get people killed! That did not factor into my plan at all. I wanted to bring everyone home alive. I knew however, if I did, I would be beating the odds.

I paused before I spoke to Campbell and remembered back to when I was a young NCO in the Royal Scots. Initially I was a terrible Lance Corporal, but nobody took the time to mentor me or show me how to do things the right way. They simply watched as I floundered and failed, allowing it to happen and even in some cases relishing it happen.

I would not let this happen with my men and it was an ethos I carried with me wherever I went. I would not let this young man down; I would mentor him and help him as much I could. Sitting him down over a brew I let him know that in no uncertain terms he was 'my pet project' whether he liked it or not! Nige Campbell was only a young lad, not long out of basic training so coming to us for OP Herrick 8 must have been a culture shock, he was being dropped right in the deep end. Nige is very much part of this story.

I have always considered myself as a military history buff and loved anything to do with war and conflicts past, present and future. So, when that fateful day in September 2001, when those two planes struck the World Trade Center in New York, I knew my life and military career would never be the same again.

Things were changing, war was taking on a new dynamic. I already had an understanding of the Russian war in Afghanistan, and I began looking at the way the Mujahideen had fought against the Soviet invaders. I guessed that they would, more than likely, use the same tactics against us that the Mujahideen had against the Russians. If it ain't broke, don't fix it. Certainly, the guerrilla warfare style of the mujahideen had worked well against poorly trained and badly led Soviet conscripts. But what the Taliban hadn't allowed for was the fact that we were neither conscripts nor badly led, quite the opposite.

The last time they had fought Highlanders was the during the second Afghan war 1878-1880. Then they knew us to be tough, unyielding fighters. The great-great-grandsons of those Pathan tribesman were about to meet those of Queen Victoria's shock troops, but this time we were bringing with us the fiery death that comes with 21st-century technology.

Day 24

Saturday 3rd May: FOB Keenan, Upper Gereshk Valley

The rest of April passed by with little to report, characterised by a lot of boredom, which led to a more worrying trend of NDs (Negligent Discharges). Not just in Delta Company but the entire Brigade. I had two in my Platoon, luckily these were only with SA80s and nobody was injured.

We kept receiving reports that other units in the brigade had been ND'ing with 66mm LAWs and in one instance a soldier had lost his arm to the back blast of the weapon. This would be the very height of irony, to come to the deadliest place on earth and be killed by one of your own and by accident instead of the enemy.

It was not uncommon for this to happen at all, I guarantee that throughout history there have been plenty of instances of soldiers getting bored waiting to fight and being killed accidently in some silly, unnecessary fuckup. Somewhere in distant antiquity, I could imagine a bored Roman legionnaire pacing along Hadrian's wall, freezing his bollocks off and pissing about with a pilum, waiting for angry Picts to attack and accidently stabbing his mate in the eye.

Boredom and soldiers are not a great combination. The stagnation was terrible and I began to notice a dip in overall attitudes, everything from personal hygiene to kit husbandry. It was my job as Platoon Sergeant to ensure that this did not happen, and we kept an eye on everything we had been issued. We would need it when fighting season kicked off.

It was while I was sat cleaning my rifle alongside my best mate and our JTAC, SGT Bruce Ewart, that I noticed a strange sound coming from the HESCO wall near his bed. We both looked at each other in confusion and put our weapons down. We kept quiet until we located the source of the noise, it was coming from under Bruce's bed.

Quickly we turned his cot bed over and moved his kit thinking that we should be careful just in case we had pissed off a family of camel spiders. We were greeted by the sight of four cute ginger kittens. But where the hell was mummy? I could only imagine the scene as a pissed off stray Afghan cat found us playing with her babies! I think liberal amounts of swearing combined with lots of spitting, hissing and scratching would be the order of the day. But the soppy animal lover in me wanted to care for them until they could care for themselves, so I set about getting milk for them and little bits of solid food. After a while the little guys just disappeared, hopefully happy, healthy and ready to fend for themselves.

Our days were filled with rotations of Patrols Platoon, QRF (Quick Reaction Force), Guard Platoon and rest. It seemed like Groundhog Day, but all around us we could feel the storm building up to something big. ICOM chatter was gathering pace, sightings of Taliban fighters throughout Helmand started to emerge. It would appear to everyone that the enemy were returning from their winter hibernation in Pakistan freshly rested. Only now they were better equipped and reinforced by a raft of foreign fighters hailing largely from Pakistan, Chechnya and sad to say, the UK as well. There were always smatterings of other faithful Muslims from around the world looking to answer the call to Jihad.

The Afghan locals held these foreigners in complete contempt and were not shy in telling us so. In fact, they hated them more than us.

"ISAF does not deliberately use our homes as fighting positions and we know you will not deliberately kill us. The Arabs and Russians (their name for foreign fighters) will use our homes to attack you. Even though they know you must retaliate and will likely cause the destruction of our homes and the deaths of our families ... we hate them."

This was sobering as we knew these poor people were caught, as are all civilians, in a war zone. Stuck between a rock and a hard place. On the other hand, they had no love for us, we did not speak their language and did not believe in the same God. We never stayed long enough to make a difference, at the end of a six-month tour of duty you are only then fully getting to grips with your area of operations, building a rapport with the locals and your Afghan security forces, just in time to leave and hand it over to another unit; and when we leave an area, the Taliban simply take it back, you only own the ground while you are standing on it. If the locals had helped us, they stood a good chance of being killed by the Taliban. If they helped the Taliban and gave them shelter, there was a good chance that out of the blue sky a 1000lb bomb would land on their home. All they wanted was to be left alone by everyone. To farm their piece of land. To raise a family and show devotion to their God. But in a time of war, where the frontlines are not clear, and the enemy dress the same as the locals, it was a miserable existence.

I often found myself trying to put myself in their position, while I sat with little to do but let my mind drift. If a foreign army came to my country who didn't like me, speak the same language as me and didn't believe in the same things I did, would I fight against them? The answer would have been a definite yes!

I justified the situation to myself by arguing I was here to make a difference to these people's lives, or so I hoped. We did not go around indiscriminately killing people. We would only attack property if it was being used by the enemy and we would be careful about proportionality. But again, with the brutal counter-insurgency war going on in Afghanistan, not everything was clear.

We had been at war in Afghanistan since 2001 and this was now 2008. NATO had lost lots of its young men and women to the war on terror. And even more so, the Afghan people, be it civilians, Afghan security forces or the Taliban themselves. I fervently hoped that we would stay to see the job done and Vietnam syndrome would not take hold.

I had once heard counter-insurgency warfare described as 'eating soup with a fork'. It is possible to do but will take a long time and perseverance. But as the casualties kept mounting, would our countries stay the course? Especially now that our countries were engaged in Iraq, too, since 2003.

Day 31

Saturday 10th May: FOB Keenan, Upper Gereshk Valley

We heard the dull booms in the distance interspersed with sporadic bursts of fire. As I looked west in the direction of the sound of battle, I witnessed the arcs of ruby red and green tracers climbing into the sky. In the distance I could hear the chunky thumping noise of .50cal machine guns.

SA80 rifles rattled alongside the heavier weapons, albeit much quieter. I could also make out the distinctive sound of AK-47s firing the larger

7.62 round that our enemies carried. Our Danish comrades in FOB Armadillo, just across the river, were being attacked by probing elements of the Taliban. Most likely just testing their reactions, skills and drills.

Occasionally I could hear the boom of heavier ordnance, I knew the Danes in Armadillo had leopard 2 tanks and 105mm artillery as well as mortar pits and Javelin missiles. I decided to put my helmet and body armour on and head up to a sangar to see what was going on.

In the distance I could see puffs of black smoke on the ground approximately two thousand metres away. Then the sound would reach us and we could hear the explosion. Muzzle flashes would announce small arms being fired. Tracers would emphasise the serious amount of ammunition being discharged.

Suddenly, from out of nowhere, there was an ear-piercing sonic boom of jets coming in low. Two Harrier jump jets coming in from the direction of Kandahar screamed in, burning fast towards the battle now being waged. As I watched in awe, the jets pulled up sharply and then a loud boom let us know that they had dropped ordnance on the Taliban.

I watched the dark pall of smoke rise slowly into the air, staining the clear blue sky a dirty grey. Even at the distance I was observing, the effect was instant and ominous. Somebody, somewhere just had a really bad day.

I peered across the expanse of land between us and FOB Armadillo, I hoped they hadn't taken any casualties. Some of their guys had been visiting us at Keenan only yesterday. It had been Op Peat, the Combat Logistic Patrol (CLP) to resupply our FOB. As we came under Danish command we were resupplied by the Danish Logistic Core.

They used Danish cavalry Light Armoured Vehicles (LAVs). As usual there was chaos trying to get all the Danish vehicles into our FOB. Normally we would have a few more dents in our gates after they had left, but today they managed to take a chunk out of the building where I slept. Needless to say, I adjusted my sleeping arrangements slightly.

Being a bit of a kit fetishist, I stood looking at the nearest LAV. It was almost similar in size to the US Marine Corps LAV. As I sized it up, the top hatch on the turret opened and a head sporting an armoured crewman's helmet popped out.

Almost surreally and in slow motion, the helmet came off to reveal long flowing blonde hair belonging to one of the most beautiful soldiers I had ever seen. As the jungle drums started to beat, a crowd gathered. The statuesque Danish soldier dismounted from the vehicle, grabbed a cot bed and began unfolding it in front of her vehicle.

We all stared open-mouthed as the Dane removed her body armour and combat jacket, revealing a sports bra which was failing to support her considerable assets. Smudger, one of our senior Jocks, got a funny look on his face.

"Ah ken that lassie!" he announced. "Dinnae ask me where frae, but her face is awfy familiar!" He disappeared and about five minutes later returned with a copy of *Private* porno mag tucked under his armpit.

"Ah fuckin' knew it!" he said triumphantly opening the pages of the magazine. There before us, in lurid glossy detail, was the same Danish soldier enjoying the company of a number of male friends. Meanwhile the Dane had adopted the prone position and was encouraging two muscled, bearded, topless behemoths to rub suntan lotion onto her back.

At that point, there was a massive scramble and a flurry of dust and sand. I had never seen Jocks move that fast, even under fire. Suddenly the bunker positions ringing the helipad were given extra manning support. But unfortunately, all eyes were looking inside the perimeter at the Dane. For the only time during Herrick 8 I felt my base was not fully protected.

Looking around it occurred to me that the Viking beauty before us would indeed be slumming it had she even looked at any of us. Given her current male company and the skill in which she normally handled men, we would have been a disappointment.

Delta Company, almost to a man, where short and skinny and given our relative brief time in-country had not adapted to the sun well. As a consequence, each one of us topless looked like we were wearing a white t-shirt. All of us were sunburned and had noses and foreheads that were peeling like a leper in the shower.

Where these tall, blonde bearded sons of Odin were covered with quite well tattooed Norse runes, we were covered in body art of questionable standards. From black panthers with bloody claws, to really badly drawn saltires. But what we lacked in good looks, we would surely make up for with vigour and enthusiasm.

As predicted, the probing attacks did not stop with the Danes. To our north, our colleagues from 2 PARA were experiencing similar probes. Normally RPG fire followed by AK and PKM (Russian general-purpose machine gun) fire. The boys gave back as good as they got and the Taliban fell back in disarray carrying their dead and wounded with them. They were learning a valuable lesson on what happens when you fuck with experienced, highly trained soldiers whose only desire in life is to fuck shit up royally. We, however, did not get the same close attention that our comrades did. This left us feeling very left out, quite clearly the Taliban were racist and hated us Jocks!

'Always the bridesmaid never the bride.' It seemed that all around us, the fighting had developed. FOB Gibraltar had been probed by Taliban fighters and the attacks had been seen off by 2 PARA. In our area of operations, still nothing. I was beginning to wonder if the Guardsman we had relieved had been right. Were the Taliban ghosts, who fired at you then simply disappeared back into the civilian population? We were talking about this around dinner one night, when out of the blue one of the lads suggested: "Here Smudger, maybe they heard aboot the size eh yoor dobber and are too feared tae come anywhere near this place." Smudger stood up and dropped his combat trousers to reveal his huge penis. Smudger, or Private Smith, was one of my senior soldiers, he was tall, fair haired, and built. If there were any problems with discipline, Smudger knew exactly how to stamp it out accompanied by "Ah dinnae gee a fuck, Ahm no an NCO, they cannae bust me!" We all jeered and started throwing food at him until he put it away.

Secretly, the Platoon was relieved that we had been given the time to acclimate (as the Yanks call it) and perfect our patrolling and ground knowledge. Steadily, we were getting to know the area, the names of the little hamlets and the places where we knew we might be vulnerable to attack. And we all knew it wouldn't be long before it was going to be our turn.

Day 49

Wednesday 28th May: North of Zumbelay Village, Upper Gereshk Valley

The pattern began to repeat itself; we would walk and walk trying to acclimatise ourselves to the increasing Afghan summer heat. Our breathing became less laboured, but we still struggled under the weight of our combat equipment. Sometimes the heat became so bad it was a struggle to put one foot in front of the other. But we had to push on. And the boys did. Any chance however, we would stop and flop into a tactical sit and observe our arcs of fire.

To lie down in the prone would mean a good chance of falling asleep on your weapon and a struggle to get back to your feet. To adopt a kneeling position, you would run the risk of your knees locking and you would have to be hauled to your feet. Without help, your kit would over-balance you and send you straight on your arse.

In the British Army L85 Rifle pamphlet, the sitting position is a recognised fire position and the lads were quite happy to point this out to any eager beaver with notions of picking the lads up on their tactical positions. It was nigh on impossible to adopt the prone or kneeling position due to the heavy gear every man carried, to stand up was just to make yourself an easy target.

We were in the scenic little village of Zumbelay in what was known as the witch's hat (due to the shape of the area on the map, a prominent triangular area within the Green Zone). It had been briefed to us as a hotbed of Taliban activity with many IED layers and fighters using it as a base of operations.

As I looked around, I couldn't help but see how peaceful it was. As you passed people by and greeted them with the generic 'Salam alaikum,' you were met with indifference or a slight nod of the head. Sometimes I wondered if they even cared that we were here at all. In the middle of the village, a typical graveyard dominated. A stone wall formed the perimeter of the dirty, dusty cemetery. The graves were all mounds of rock. Between the rocks fluttered sad, tattered little flags and pieces of material in the colours of Islam. The little pieces of cloth offered a bizarre riot of colour in an otherwise drab, dirty vista. The colours I would later learn meant the following. Green (devotion to God). White (purity). Red (sacrifice). And finally, black (martyrdom).

Rubbish blew around the stone monuments and came to rest among the dead. Here and there scruffy looking feral dogs padded around our patrol baring their teeth and snarling. The dogs all looked absolutely fucking massive and would no doubt tear us apart given the chance. I had never before seen the type of breed they were and figured that they must be some kind of mongrel mix. But I found out they were called Kuchi dogs. The Afghans kept them as guard dogs and also as fighting dogs. It's revealing that the two variants of Kuchi dog are known as 'lion-type' and 'tiger-type'! As a dog person, I always found it sad when I saw the dogs chained to a metal pole outside a compound. The chain was so tight that it would cut into the dog's neck causing infected sores to develop. The ears and tail had been brutally cut off. I was told by an interpreter that the reason for this was that during dog fights the opposing dog would have very less to grab onto. It was tragic to see those loyal animals lying in the baking heat with no food or water. Occasionally, a brave soul would venture up to these dogs with a plastic bottle of water and give the dog a drink or throw some spare rations to it.

I was brought back to the here and now by a dust cloud approaching at the head end of the Platoon. The point section suddenly took cover and somebody yelled "Vehicle, take cover!" I called to the guys that were with me to take whatever cover they could and observe their arcs.

Up ahead the vehicle materialised and did not appear to be slowing down. An attempt was made to get the driver to stop, to no avail. A shot rang out and the minibus skidded to a halt. The driver fell out of the vehicle onto his knees praying to us and crying; he was one lucky bastard. In the windscreen of the minibus was a spider web in the glass and a single hole in the middle of it. The shot had passed right through between the driver and the passenger.

"What the fuck is he going on aboot?" I asked our interpreter, the little Afghan terp looked at me.

"Please do not kill me," he replied on behalf of the sobbing driver. "I did not see you." The Jocks all looked at each other, eyebrows knotted in confusion.

"How the fuck did he no see us?" said one of our lads. "Yea cannae fucking miss a load eh sunburned arseholes wae guns! Fucking dobber!" The driver was shown the error of his ways and leapt back into the vehicle, no doubt to change his underpants. He headed off in a southerly direction towards the town of Gereshk.

Some might question the action of firing a warning shot at an approaching vehicle, but we had been made more than aware of the dangers posed by suicide vehicle borne IEDs (SVBIED). A van packed with explosives being driven by someone who believes that death is better than living will kill a lot of people.

You only need look at the experiences of the coalition forces in Iraq during Iraqi Freedom and Op Telic to know how devastating a car bomb can be. Our 3rd Battalion, The Black Watch had been on the receiving end of a particularly brutal SVBIED attack on one of their vehicle checkpoints (VCPs) while attached to the Americans up at Camp Dogwood, near Baghdad. Three of their men were killed and eight were wounded with varying degrees of severity when a male drove a car into the checkpoint packed with explosives, detonating it with catastrophic results. I always said I'd rather be tried by twelve than carried by six, another old adage that we adopted as an unofficial motto. This would happen to Delta Company on many occasions during the first part of the tour, unfortunately you could not take the chance that the vehicle bearing down on you was not a suicide bomber.

As we left the village, we became aware of mirrors flashing in the distance and smoke rising from some of the buildings back in the village. As it wasn't lunchtime these were clearly not cooking fires but deliberate signals, sent by spotters to let the enemy know where we were.

As we moved into a denser part of the greenery, one of the dogs that had been tracking our patrol decided that now would be the time to strike. It picked Richie McCafferty (no relation), a skinny little lad who had just re-enlisted in the army prior to the tour, as a potential meal. The dog started its head-on charge and Richie instinctively brought his rifle up to bear and fired two rounds at the dog. They struck it in the body, but the animal kept coming, even more pissed off than before. He fired again; this time two rounds struck the dog in the forehead.

Everyone on the patrol stood silently, holding their breath as the dog slowed down. Rather than lie down and die, the dog shook its head as though it was nothing more than a fly that had caused the nuisance and walked away in the opposite direction, bored. Richie turned to us all, face white as a sheet.

"Fuck me, ah jist aboot shat masell!"

Day 51

Friday 30th May: FOB Keenan

Following a night patrol, the Platoon had a number of injuries. Mostly ankle injuries, which are associated with operating in such undulating terrain as Helmand Province at night. We were severely shorthanded and what should have been a morning Platoon-sized ground defensive area (GDA) patrol, ended up being two under-strength sections.

The patrol started off fairly well, with us covering the ground quickly but tactically. But pretty soon, as the sun started getting higher in the sky, the temperature began to soar. It was at this point that I received a notification from the Boss that we had a heat casualty. I quickly assessed him and realised that he would need to be evacuated back to Keenan to rest and take on fluids. I informed the Op's room of my intention to extract the casualty back to Patrol Base Bridgehead, given that our location was on a narrow track next to a very deep canal. Much to my dismay, my plan was ignored.

I was informed that the QRF from 10 Platoon under Billy Carnegie would come and pick up the casualty. Billy was a very experienced Corporal and a very likeable, easy-going guy, so I was happy that it was him coming to pick up my casualty,

A pick-up point was agreed and we patrolled back towards it where we would meet up with the Vector Light Vehicles to extract my heat casualty. As we approached the pick-up point, we received word over the Company channel that the track under one of the Vectors had given way and the vehicle was tipping precariously towards the deep canal. In the distance I saw a group of shapes I could only imagine were our QRF and a green shape at a very jaunty angle leaning in towards the dark brown water of the canal.

I approached the QRF team and walked up to Billy. He was visibly shaken.

"Fuck me mate, you boys were lucky." I said. "You must have a horseshoe up yer arse?" Billy mustered a grin from somewhere and pointed at the vehicle.

"Mucker," he said. "We were a baw hair fae gone in that watter. Fucking hing nearly tipped ower, we were lucky tae get oot wae oor kit and gats!" It was every soldier's worst nightmare when travelling in vehicles, aside from IEDs, nobody wanted to be in a vehicle when it tipped into one of the many waterways that crisscrossed Helmand's Green Zone. It had happened, we had heard horror stories of crews ending up drowning due to the weight of their personal equipment. With no way to escape from under the water, we could think of no more horrible way to die. We could all imagine those last minutes of panic as the water started to flood the vehicle, certain in the knowledge that the end was near.

Given there was still equipment inside the vehicle, some of it quite sensitive, it was decided that we would put a cordon in place to allow recovery mechanics from the Royal Electrical and Mechanical Engineers (REME) to recover the vehicle. Surprisingly, as they had to come from Bastion, they arrived before last light.

By first light, after a sleepless night, they were able to fix the vehicle in place and prevent it completely tipping into the water using a number of towing strops, ratchets straps and ropes. This allowed us to remove all the sensitive kit and daysacks from the vehicle in the event that the track did give way and we lost the Vector.

Miraculously, not only did the REME lads get the vehicle recovered, but they also managed to get it going again. Albeit with a huge fuel leak. Feeling relieved and a little bit pleased with ourselves that nothing and no one was lost, we headed back to FOB Keenan for post patrol admin and hopefully a little sleep before our next patrol.

Our good mood, however, was short-lived as we entered the front gate to the FOB. We were met by the CSM who proceeded to blame my Boss for everything that had happened in the past twenty-four hours, the heat injuries and the vehicle problems. Our patrol was made to feel like shit.

It fell to me as the Platoon's Sergeant to lift the mood. I told the lads shit happens and actually nobody died and we lost no kit. The boys should be pleased with that. Also, CSMs tended to try to shift the blame, they didn't want to be the one to have to explain the problems that hounded operations. Shit, as they say, rolls downhill. Just when I didn't think things could get any worse, Big Smudger approached me ashen-faced.

"George, ah cannae find mah binos (binoculars), night sight and NVGs." I scratched my chin thoughtfully, trying to give of an air of calm and took him to one side.

"When did you last see them mate?" I said, hoping he might have a slight clue what happened to them. He shrugged his shoulders.

"That's the weird hing mucker, ah didnae even take em oot on the ground wae me! They were at the end eh mah bed."

Together we walked over to Smudger's bunk and tried to figure out where the kit had gone. He hadn't taken them out on the ground, so they hadn't left FOB Keenan. So therefore, they were still here in the FOB somewhere. I grabbed the Platoon together and laid it out.

"Boys, check all your kit and check the accommodation. This shit couldn't have gone far." I said. "It hasn't left the fucking base." There was a flurry of activity as the entire Platoon began to tear 12 Platoon lines apart. All I could think of was that nobody would be stupid enough to steal from Big Smudger, one punch and you'd never wake up again.

I had the dubious task of reporting the missing kit to the CSM, who was fresh from giving us that post-patrol bollocking. We were already well in his bad books and this was just going to add petrol to an already out of control fire. But the CSM actually seemed calm when I informed him of the missing kit.

This actually unnerved me. I said that the kit couldn't have possibly left camp and he asked if we had searched the FOB. I told him that we had checked everywhere but the burns pit at the rear of the camp. Then the CSM told me that the Company was soon to move further up north in Helmand, we were being shifted north to a place called Musa Qa'leh where a fighting company was needed.

With that info and the fact that Smudger had told me he had kept the kit in a sandbag at the foot of his bed, and therefore could have been mistaken as rubbish. I, Smudger and the rest of 12 Platoon spent one of our last days at Keenan up to our balls in the camp burn pit. We kept looking until it became too dark to see, we would resume the search in the morning.

This was just before I was due to head out on my R&R, I didn't need to be wading in the Company's waste! But, after breakfast we waded out once more and began throwing rubbish out of the burns pit. Until when I noticed a significant shape in the dirt and ash, relief began to wash over me as it was a mounting bracket for a CWS (Common Weapon Sight). I dug a little deeper and found more bits of metal and glass that had not been consumed by the fire.

It transpired that Faisal, one of our LECs (Locally employed civilians). Had been diligently doing his job for which he was paid, generally tidying up the FOB and he had done such a good job that he had grabbed Smudger's sandbag and believing it was full of rubbish had winged it into our foul-smelling burns pit.

As luck would have it, the Chinook coming to take me away for R&R was delayed, so I had just enough time to take a quick solar shower, change my kit and hand the mantle of Platoon Sergeant over to Corporal Andy Johnston. And judging by his face, he wasn't over-fucking-joyed.

Day 54

Monday 2nd June: Camp Bastion

And so it was that I arrived back in Camp Bastion, carrying all my worldly possessions as I would not be going back to FOB Keenan on my return to Afghanistan. All my operational kit would be removed from me and stored in a secure shipping container to await my return. I was however, carrying a clear plastic bag full of burned-out night vision gear and other smashed up bits and bobs. I stepped off the Chinook and straight into the rotor downdraft which nearly threw me to my knees.

As the brownout cleared, I marvelled at just how busy the Airhead at Camp Bastion was, it could almost be a bustling airport anywhere in the world, but here it was an airport designed with one purpose, the support to combat operations in Helmand. The food we ate flew in and out, or was driven out of there, as was our ammunition, our dead and wounded flew into the hospital there and all the combat supplies we required were stored and transported through that airport.

Helicopters of varying sizes and shapes flittered around like angry wasps. An AH64 Apache Gunship hovered menacingly awaiting the troop-carrying helicopters it would be responsible for protecting. US Marine Hueys and Sea Knights in their distinctive grey colour rushed off in all directions. Black Hawk helicopters working in pairs with their ominous red crosses, callsign PEDRO, flew overhead with their Special Forces Pararescue crewmen leaning out the open cargo doors. Some sat dangling their legs out the side like holidaymakers dipping their feet into the sea. On the front of each Black Hawk was a painted moustache on the nose, specifically chosen by the crew of that airframe, some had gringo Mexican style moustaches and others had droopy handlebar moustaches, which personalised each chopper.

Here and there, dotted around, were groups of soldiers from various nations sat huddled into chalks awaiting an RAF groundcrew member to let them know which helicopter was theirs. Bearded Danes in their distinctive Flectarn camouflage, Special Forces operators in multicam and US Marines in their desert digital MARPAT (Marine Pattern), camouflage.

This was truly a departure lounge of badassery. All the troops awaiting their rides were festooned with all manner of killing implements and firearms. The SF guys had suppressors on their weapons and bags to collect empty cases fixed to their carbines. Belts of bullets criss-crossed some of the men who were carrying machine guns. But it was all done with an air of perpetual boredom, like a dangerous group of tourists who had gotten tired of waiting for their planes and just sat down where they were. Some men had given in and were fast asleep, their chins resting on the hard-ballistic plates of their body armour. Some were engaged in conversation, and a few were taking pictures of the machinery of warfare collected around them.

I looked around me for the familiar sight of RAF personnel in their desert coveralls with high visibility jackets and clip boards, scuttling between groups of soldiers like crabs on a beach. Some were pointing and gesticulating at a group of soldiers, some were scratching their heads looking confused. Others led groups of men towards the yawning tailgate of a Chinook.

Rotor blades turned rapidly and the deep thump that they produced blanked out any attempt at conversation. Heat shimmer around the engines distorted the air around the back of the huge cargo helicopters. Always present was the smell of aviation fuel. Nothing smells like it, not even napalm in the morning.

I watched as troops disappeared into the backs of Chinooks as if being swallowed by a giant green beast. The ramp would close slowly until all that was visible was a door gunner sat on the back ramp in coyote brown coveralls. Their heads were protected by green flight helmets, a dark visor covered their eyes. Occasionally I could see their lips move or a head nod. The gunner would then settle behind the antiquated American M60 machine gun. I always felt that the ramp gunner drew the short straw, for sticking out the side doors of the chopper just behind the cockpit were the dark barrels of miniguns. Now that was the weapon you wanted when someone was trying to knock you out of the sky.

I felt a hand on my shoulder, our storeman from the Company CQ store. He beckoned me to follow him as the noise was too loud to talk. I picked up my gear and as I turned to walk away from the helipad, the pitch in the Chinook engines changed. I watched as the huge helicopter lifted gracefully, too gracefully for a helicopter of that size, off the ground and tip its nose forward. It raced off in the direction of Sangin, two AH64s rushed to catch it up. I couldn't help but wonder what its next job after transporting me was.

As we got further away from the helipad we could talk. Andy, our CQ storeman, led us to Delta Company transit accommodation so that I could get myself sorted. I was struck by just how busy Bastion was, as it was not just Camp Bastion anymore, it had expanded to encompass

Camp Leatherneck. Leatherneck belonged to the US Marine Corps and Camp Shorabak, which was Afghan National Army HQ in Helmand Province, was also part of the setup.

The dirt roads were packed with all manner of vehicles, from the humble, ageing Snatch armoured Land Rover all the way up to USMC LAVs and the Warrior MICVs. Everything was covered in a cloying cloud of dust which seemed to stick to the nose and throat making everything a dirty tinge of beige. As luck would have it, our accommodation was not far from the Airhead, so it was only a short hop.

Our temporary home was an air-conditioned tent of a decent standard, there were ten cot beds with mosquito nets awaiting visitors. I found a bed and dropped my kit next to it. As I headed outside to work out my next move, I was intercepted by our Company Quartermaster.

"Ye need tae head up to the RQ wi aw that shite!" he said pointing to the bag of broken glass and scorched metal that I was clutching in my hand.

In the past this would have made me extremely nervous, as to lose or damage kit in the army was a big deal. It could even be career-ending stuff. But out here in Afghanistan I couldn't bring myself to get overly concerned about it. After all, it was only equipment. Equipment can be replaced. I walked the short distance to the battle group quartermaster department and found the office marked RQMS(T). (Regimental Quartermaster Sergeant Technical). With a slight lump in my throat, nervous about what was about to happen, I entered the office and found the RQ sat at his desk.

"Sir," I said confidently. "Sergeant McCafferty, Delta Company reporting with damaged kit from Keenan." I stood rigidly at attention with my rifle slung on my back and the bag of kit in my right hand.

Slowly, the RQ raised his head from a pile of paperwork that he was buried in and looked at me, then the bag of broken equipment. I stood ready for an absolute bollocking, even though the equipment wasn't mine, as I had heard that he had an unforgiving reputation.

"Nae dramas wee man," he said, almost in a comradely tone. "Geez it here." He reached out to take the bag from me, inside was a list of the serial numbers for the items that had been destroyed by the fire. "Whit the fuck happened tae it?" he asked me.

I spent the next five minutes recounting the story of an overzealous Afghan LEC, at the end of my story he chuckled. "At least ye brought back whit wiz left, if there wiz nae bits he'd a bin mair worried." With that he dismissed me. I about turned and exited the building, released a breath that I had been holding and all I could think was 'thank fuck for that!'

We began prepping ourselves for our R&R, but even though we were on an operational deployment, UK admin procedures still applied, even here in Afghanistan. The Battalion was scheduled to have an Equipment Care Inspection (ECI). This would involve an external team coming into theatre, or drawn from units already here, to check all the technical equipment that the Battalion held. Normally, back in the UK, this was a big undertaking. I could only imagine the carnage that was about to unfold. Paperwork, procedures and the serviceability of all our equipment would be checked. In addition to our normal Battalion table of organisation and equipment, we had operationally required kit. We had more weapons, comms kit and all the other technical stuff we needed to wage war. It all added up to millions of pounds. So, for our small part in this inspection, we had to ensure that all our weaponry and equipment we brought back from Keenan was cleaned and any damage noted. Any missing parts such as SUSAT (Sight Unit Small Arms Trilux) washers and locking nuts were replaced. Apart from Big Smudger's barbecued night vision goggles, sight and binos obviously.

When we were not cleaning weapons or assisting the Quartermaster's department, we were allowed to head off to the EFI (Expeditionary Forces Institute). The EFI was a pimped-up version of the British version, the NAAFI. On arrival at the EFI, we were always amazed at the different world the US military lived in. Standing in the queue for a brew, we were assailed by the smells of perfume wafting from not only our female soldiers, but a group of very cute US Marine female helicopter crew. They had their M16 rifles slung over their shoulders, US style.

Soldiers who were not frontline troops were cutting around like it was a UK-based unit. RP (Regimental Police) staff from various units were picking up other soldiers for standard of dress and conduct around camp. The RMP (Royal Military Police) were even conducting speed traps around camp.

Those of us who were from frontline units and were back at Bastion for whatever reason, nodded to one another in understanding. Maroon berets, Caubeens and tam o'shanters all showing where we stood in the combat pecking order compared to our rear echelon brothers and sisters. Any attempt to dress us down was met with growls, glares or stony silence normally followed by a few choice words. We could not believe what we were seeing. It was very clear that everyone's Afghan experience was different. We saw couples kissing and holding hands, even people in civilian clothing. However, I had a huge respect for guys and girls who manned the Role 3 hospital which was located next to the EFI. They saw the same horrible shit that the troops out at the FOBs saw, sometimes worse.

When you heard the tannoy system cackle into life, ears pricked up on the dreaded announcement of "OP MINIMISE, OP MINIMISE, OP MINIMISE." This was followed by a message for all hospital personnel to head back to their duty stations if they were on duty or render assistance if they weren't. This would generally be followed by the dull beat of rotor blades approaching from the distance and blue lights racing to the CASEVAC helipad in a cloud of dust.

Our first night back in Camp Bastion, the lads and I managed to blag our way into a CSE (Combined Service Entertainment) show. These were normally only for personnel based at Bastion. Celebrities would show up and 'raise the morale' of the troops. No one ever came to where the troops needed cheering up the most, right out in the isolated bases and check points surrounded by the Taliban.

As I thought about it more, I realised that I couldn't feel bad towards those who had chosen a different path to mine in the military. We all had our parts to play and were all cogs in a huge machine of war. Without units like the RLC, we wouldn't have our resupply convoys and therefore would have to rely on Chinook flights to bring in fresh supplies of food, ammunition and equipment. Despite the fact that a Chinook resupply would be faster, they could never carry near enough the amount of tonnage to resupply a rifle company that a land-based vehicle resupply column could. Also, as I would find out, risk assessments and vulnerability to ground fire would see a few of us go days without seeing a helicopter.

Without medics, we would almost certainly have difficulty keeping our mates alive long enough to get back to hospitals in the UK. Without the AGC, our pay and allowances would not be processed and essential clerical admin would not be possible.

I had chosen my path and wore it like a badge of honour as I suspected most infantry soldiers did. We carried ourselves with a sense of arrogance and pride, for not many at Bastion could say they had seen or would see active combat during their time in Afghanistan.

That time in Bastion went by in a blur, and before I knew it, I was landing back on British soil for my mandatory two weeks R&R. It was nice to get back and see my girlfriend and also have a nice cold beer back in my local pub. But I could not relax. I still had mates in Afghanistan who had relocated to the focal flashpoint of Musa Qa'leh in Northern Helmand.

Fighting season was in full swing by then and the TV was always switched on to the news. My heart would stop when I heard there had been soldiers killed in Afghan. Almost callously, I breathed a sigh of relief when it was not someone I knew.

I had no war stories to tell when people asked at the bar how Afghanistan was. I had only one response. "Quiet!" I would say. I didn't buy a pint the whole time I was back in the UK and I felt a bit like a fraud. Yes I was home from Afghanistan, no I hadn't killed anyone, I hadn't even fired a shot in anger. These revelations stunned people who had expected me to return on leave with stories of derring-do. But I could offer them none.

That would soon change on my return to theatre.

A number of things happened whilst I was on R&R. The most significant was Delta Company's war had come alive since the move to Musa Qa'leh. The enemy were emboldened by the fact that, until June, the only units operating in the area were ANA (Afghan National Army) with their Royal Irish Regiment mentoring team and the ANP (Afghan National Police).

At the end of Op Herrick 7, ISAF had taken Musa Qa'leh from the Taliban, driving them out in an operation called Op Snakepit. Unfortunately, the ANA's apparent dominance didn't last. The Taliban promptly returned in smaller groups to attack the outlying security bases of Musa Qa'leh. It got to the point where groups of armed Taliban would patrol in eight-man units actually into the district centre with impunity.

This was the catalyst for Delta's move north to Musa Qa'leh. They needed someone who would go into the enemy-dominated areas, hold the ground and take the fight to him. The motto of the Royal Regiment of Scotland is 'Nemo me impune laccessit.' No one provokes me with impunity, in other words, 'take the piss and you'll get a slap.' And there were plenty of Jocks in Musa Qa'leh able to facilitate this.

All in all, there was a Warrior armoured Company from 4 SCOTS, a mechanised infantry Company from 2 SCOTS, our good selves Delta Company 5 SCOTS, and an additional group of US Marines from Fox Company 2nd Battalion 7th Marines.

To the Taliban, this was like a red rag to a bull and most of their focus became Musa Qa'leh, which was symbolic to them. By the end of our tour it would feel like every Taliban fighter, foreign-trained or Jihadist nut job would turn up to our AO (Area of Operations) spoiling for a fight.

On the 12th of June 2008, we lost our Commanding Officer. Lt Col David Richmond was leading a surge north of Musa Qa'leh into an area which would become notorious to us during the tour. Known as Kats, it was a combination of two villages which would be named Big Kats and Small Kats: Qaryeh-Ye-Kats Sharbat (Big Kats), the most northerly of the two villages and Qaryeh-Ye-Kats Shardar (Small Kats). The task force surged north to the two villages with a view of clearing them both out of all enemy resistance. This area was deemed by G2 (Intelligence) as a C2 (Command and Control Node) for the Taliban and their foreign allies, as a place to rest, rearm, and conduct their operations from.

This operation would see the heaviest fighting of the tour so far, with ANA and Royal Irish advisors fighting alongside 5 SCOTS and the US Marines. My best friend Bruce, a JTAC (Joint Terminal Attack Controller), would later tell me that it was the most and biggest bombs he had dropped in a single sitting.

Colonel Richmond was directing the operation from a small hillock when his position was engaged by heavy enemy fire and would be struck in the leg by a bullet which shattered his femur. Colonel Richmond's war was over, but his battle to rehabilitate was only just beginning.

After his treatment in Bastion Role 3 hospital and his evacuation to Selly Oak hospital in Birmingham, his leg would not mend. He was having difficulties with the femur bone trying to heal and knit together. I remember never seeing him after Herrick 8 without a cage around his upper thigh and an eye-watering limp.

Upon my return to Afghanistan we would be led by the cool, charismatic figure of Lt Col Nick Borton, Commanding officer of 2 SCOTS.

Day 74

Sunday 22nd June: Camp Bastion

I was filled with a mix of excitement and trepidation; I was also unsurprisingly struck by the rise in temperature! Summer in Kent is warm, but it was no comparison with the furnace heat of an Afghan summer, pretty much as soon as I landed back in Afghanistan I began to sweat and I don't think I stopped sweating until December. I was excited to be going back to Afghan but also nervous that actually our war was now real and the wounding of the CO ten days ago had brought it all into perspective.

Musa Qa'leh was not Crossmaglen or Banja Luka, it was a war zone where men and women were dying. This was tragically and painfully reinforced by an event that took place almost daily around Camp Bastion.

On 17th June 2008 a snatch patrol vehicle containing three soldiers from the SAS(R), and a female Intelligence Corps Corporal by the name of Sarah Bryant, struck an IED, completely destroying their vehicle and obliterating its occupants.

This would be a watershed moment for the British Army for two reasons. Sarah would be the first female British soldier killed in Afghanistan and the military would finally realise that the Snatch Land Rover was not fit for purpose in a hostile environment such as Afghanistan.[2] The situation demanded that nothing smaller than a Mastiff could operate at this point.

The ramp ceremony for our fallen comrades is always a solemn affair, as the majority of repatriations were largely attended by soldiers from the fallen soldier's unit, it was a chance for them to honour the dead and say goodbye. Anyone not on essential duty was also requested to attend out of respect, although the request was never necessary.

Those who could always did attend and not only British soldiers. That warm evening I noticed among the crowd camouflage and badges from Denmark, Lithuania, Estonia and America. The bodies of Sarah and the men she died with would not leave Bastion until darkness fell, as there was still a major threat from ground fire.

As I stood in solemn silence with the pink-orange sun sinking slowly into the horizon, I couldn't help reflecting personally. We as a Company had been extremely fortunate. So far, no Argylls had received ramp ceremonies and I hoped that it would stay that way.

We were told prior to deployment that statistically five men from our Company would be killed in action in Helmand and possibly three times

---

2 For a review of why savings at the expense of safety have killed too many British servicemen and women, including the Snatch Land Rover being not fit for purpose, see David Hill's *Breaking the Military Covenant*.

that number would be wounded with life-changing injuries. I couldn't help but think of men I'd served with throughout my time in the Army who had made the ultimate sacrifice for our country.

The first was Pte Andrew Barrie Cutts RLC, a keen young soldier who had been a recruit in one of my training Platoons at ATR Bassingbourn in 2003. Andrew was a thoroughly likeable young lad with a shock of red hair, Andrew was a twin and when he died his brother had enlisted. Pte Cutts had been killed in Musa Qa'leh on Sunday 6th August 2006.

Next would be Corporal Damian 'Damo' Lawrence, 2nd Battalion The Yorkshire Regiment. I had gone across to Kosovo in 2006 to operate as a team commander with ISRTF (Intelligence Surveillance & Reconnaissance Task Force) in Pristina, Kosovo. Damo was one of the first men I met from the Company and I liked him straightaway, a lad with a wicked sense of humour.

When I learned of his death, I found it heart-breaking, and I knew that his loss would have hit the Battalion very hard. He was killed by an IED near Kajaki on Sunday 17th February 2008. When I spoke to Matty Cockburn in Bastion on the RiP, we both lamented his death and how it was the good lads that seemed to be dying.

I was brought out of my reverie by the sad tones of the last post being played by a bugler. Even now as I did then, I have a lump in my throat whenever the last post is played. Even more so the piper's lament 'The Flowers of the Forest' played by a lone bagpiper. I felt my body stiffen into the position of attention, the attending officers saluted and collectively a large gathering of soldiers seemed to hold its breath. The only sound was the notes of the bugle disappearing across the dusty patch of Helmand that was Camp Bastion.

As the senior Padre closed the ceremony, people went their separate ways, with those who had known the dead soldiers hugging one another, clearly grief-stricken. I turned and walked away with a group of other Argylls back towards our transit accommodation.

Two days later I began my journey north to join my Company in Musa Qa'leh. Given the threat to helicopters in and around the District Centre, it was decided that rather than travel by Chinook we would be put into the Warriors of 4 SCOTS and driven north. This was going to take two days; the idea of being stuck in an armoured microwave for that long did not fill me with joy.

I had been reissued with my operation kit and weapons. In addition to this I had my own personal gear, which included a gorilla box (a storage trunk) I had purchased from the EFI (Expeditionary Forces Institute) in Bastion, which sold everything from Mars Bars to televisions. I was briefed on the SOPs by the vehicle commander, then told who I would be crewed with. I looked at the motley group and quickly identified Sgt Eric Bader-Hall who was our REME (Royal Electrical and Mechanical Engineer) Sergeant at FOB Keenan. I grinned at him and thrust out my hand.

"This is going to be a right barrel of fucking laughs!" I said nodding my head towards our taxi.

"Yep and just to lighten your mood mate, there's no air con in here, I'm reliably informed that it's… What's the technical term? Fucked!" he grinned.

I groaned and shook my head.

"This could not get any fucking worse!" I said. Then it did. In addition to me and Eric, we were joined by Pte Dobinson from our AGC (Adjutant Generals Corps) Detachment, Pte Dobinson was a large chap to say the least. Eric and I glanced at one another and seemed to read each other's thoughts. "This is going to be fucking snug!" I chimed.

For anyone who has ever been inside a Warrior armoured fighting vehicle. It is designed to carry a full eight-man infantry section, but that includes the crew, so four to five soldiers in the fighting compartment. Then you add in ammo, personal kit, the actual gunner's turret and cage and that leaves not a lot of room. Immediately behind Dobinson were two LECs, Afghan locals who had been 'vetted' and cleared supposedly to work at ISAF locations around Helmand, I for one was not so trusting but decided to make friends.

"Salam Alaikum." I tapped my heart with my right hand then offered it in friendship. The two Afghan men nodded and bowed profusely before shaking hands with me very enthusiastically.

"Thank fuck it's not Thursday mate!" Eric smirked.

At the allotted time, and with all our details on the flap sheet, we mounted up in our allocated Warriors and as predicted it was a tight squeeze. My worries of IED strikes or small arms fire onto our vehicle were rapidly replaced by worrying about cramp. What happens if I need a piss or a shit? What happens if Dobbo falls asleep on me? Fun and games, but hey, we were on our way and I was one step closer to getting back to my Company.

With a jerk that almost gave me whiplash, the Warrior began to move off. I felt elated as we were now beginning the magical mystery tour of central and Northern Helmand.

My elation was short-lived as eight hundred metres out the gates we stopped dead and the Warrior switched off, Eric and I exchanged confused glances.

"What's goin on mucker?" I called up to the commander in the turret. The commander stooped down as much as he could and lifted the right earpiece on his crew headset.

"Ah fuckin piece eh shite min … fuckin oil leak on yin eh the wagons aye!" the commander yelled in an accent that sounded like it was from Inverness. That was it, we were stopped before we even left the security of Camp Bastion. Everyone dismounted their vehicles and hung around, I took the chance to piss as I didn't know when I would next be able to.

The sun was starting to get higher in the sky and with it the temperature began to soar, awesome, now the Warrior really would be like a microwave. I looked around at the inactivity, there were clouds of cigarette smoke around the backs of every vehicle and the Warrior crews all lay out on the front sloping armour of their vehicles.

I learned in Canada that when a vehicle goes down, the crew really can't do anything about it, they just assist the REME as much as their skills allow, even less so the Infantry dismounts in the rear. So, I did what every good soldier does in that situation. I lay down with my back pack as a pillow and closed my eyes, I had done a piss and I didn't smoke so some shut eye seemed the next logical step. Two hours later I was awakened by a commotion as our vehicle crew scuttled over the armour and into their positions.

"Get in min, we're aff!" Yelled the commander. Reluctantly I jumped into the rear of the vehicle and closed the heavy rear armoured door of the vehicle. After an hour I was praying for ground fire!

Travelling in the back of a Warrior is an experience that should not be attempted by those who suffer from seasickness. Imagine you are in a dark metal box with the only light coming from the gunner's hatch or any of the cupola hatches, if they are even open. Inside that box are lots of sharp edges that if struck will open you up, then squeeze another four or five people in there with you and shake the whole thing from side to side, up and down. Then as it's Afghanistan get someone to light a really hot fire under it so that the box becomes hot to the touch. That goes some way to describing out journey from Bastion to Musa Qa'leh.

The hours seemed to tick by interminably slowly. Every time the vehicle stopped, we had to open the back doors, despite warnings from the commander that it wasn't safe. I took the chance while we were stopped to grab a bottle of water from the top of the vehicle. The crew in order to save space inside the vehicle had stored all non-essential items (such as the bottled water) out on the top deck or stuck into the bar armour.

Like a desert camouflaged gopher, I popped up and grabbed a few for the guys in my vehicle, the bottles were caked in a thin layer of dust and were beat to shit, but the MOD crest was still visible on the white label with the words 'Bottled in Camp Bastion' printed on it. I ducked back into the vehicle but left the door slightly ajar.

"Gentlemen I bring you a bottle of the finest Helmand spring," I announced, dishing out the water. By the confused looks on the two LEC's faces I knew my humour was lost on them. Dobinson did not look good at all, the heat inside the vehicle clearly taking its toll.

I unscrewed the lid from my bottle and took a big gulp of water, which I promptly spat out again. The Afghan summer heat had essentially turned the water into a brew, but without the tea, coffee, milk or sugar. It tasted fucking awful. But I knew that if I didn't drink it, I would undoubtedly be in the same state as poor Dobinson, which was not a pretty sight. I decided to make the best of a bad situation and grabbed a pack of hot chocolate powder, sugar, coffee and milk powder.

"Mocha anyone?" I asked, shaking my water bottle. No takers at all, the Afghans looked at me as if I was insane. I shrugged and set about making my concoction. It actually tasted better than it looked and it was almost as though it had come straight out the kettle. The downside was I had a massive sugar rush.

It felt like a short hop before we stopped again, for a lot longer this time. I craned my neck and called up.

"What's happening mate?" The commander leaned down into the darkness revealing a halo of light through the turret, I watched the specks of dust dancing in the sunlight around him. Afghan dust coated everything and stuck in the nose, mouth and eyes dusting everything in a shade of tan.

"Aye fuck me min, twae eh the wagons are fucked aye!" he let me know. The strain of the driving had caused a number of failures in some of the Warriors and the attempt to tow one had made the engine on the REME Warrior armoured recovery vehicle literally blow up.

I sagged, this was going to be a long one I thought and looking across at Dobinson. But I left the door to the Warrior open again as per usual.

"Dobbo!" I called out. "Give me that Vallon (mine detector) mate!" He looked around and found the long green stick with a handle and a leaf like sensor. I extended the arm on it, switched it on and set the sensitivity to covert mode. That way the only indication that there was something was the line of red dots on the display would increase in number. I then swiped it across the metallic door of the Warrior to check it was working properly.

"What are you up to?" Eric asked narrowing his eyes.

"I can't sit in this fucking oven!" I exclaimed. I leant out the back door and began to swipe the detector from left to right exactly where I would put my feet, when I was satisfied the ground was safe, I opened the door slightly wider and put my foot down on the hard, packed Afghan soil. Before anyone could say anything, I had unzipped my combat trousers and was taking the opportunity to have a giant piss on Helmand.

After four hours of sitting around, we got the okay to move off and at last light we moved into a desert leaguer for the night. The Warriors formed a triangular defensive position, with their superior thermal image and night vision kit it would be difficult for anyone to sneak up on our position. If they did, and were stupid enough to attack, a 30mm Rarden cannon and 7.62mm chain gun would quickly show them the error of their ways. Each Platoon apex vehicle would be manned and the radio staged on to pass on info.

I took the chance as the sun was going down to have a poo. Using an upturned ammunition box to sit on over a dug hole, I sat and emptied myself before covering the hole over and returning the 4 SCOTS shit box back to its rightful place.

We were not required for sentry duty as none of us were Warrior-trained, I took a patch of ground next to the right track of my Warrior and using my body armour and helmet as a pillow, I closed my eyes. My SA80 cuddled up in my arms like a cherished lover or a really aggressive teddy.

Pte Dobinson's condition deteriorated through the night and I expressed concern that he may be suffering from heat exhaustion. So, the next day the decision was made to put him in Warrior 33A, the CSM's Warrior, so that the Company medic from the RAMC could keep an eye on him and put fluid in him if need be, and it had air conditioning too.

With Dobinson gone it freed up a good bit of space in the back of our Warrior, which was very welcome. The onward journey followed the same string as the day before and it was just as hot in the back of our vehicle. It was so hot that I had stripped my combat shirt and was topless under my Osprey. It was a relief then when the vehicle commander asked me if I wouldn't mind assisting the dismounts from the other vehicles to conduct a sweep for IED across a vulnerable point we needed to clear. I quickly grabbed the Vallon and my rifle. As I dismounted the rear of the Warrior, I quickly checked where I was about to put my feet down and did a visual check of my surrounding area. The classic five and twenty metre check.

I placed both feet on the hard-packed gravelly track that we were currently travelling along and scanned the distance for any threats. The problem with travelling in a convoy is that it is visible for miles. The dust cloud spewed out as each vehicle churns the ground under it, gives any hostiles advanced warning of our movements and given enough time an attack could be mounted with everything at the Taliban's disposal. I felt better knowing that, should the shit hit the fan, I would be covered by 30mm cannon and 7.62mm chain guns.

I couldn't believe the difference from the inside to the outside of the vehicle. It felt cooler outside the wagon, even if it was above 40. Less cloying and claustrophobic. I thought of pictures I had seen from the Russians in Afghanistan and it made sense to me why their soldiers always rode on the tops of the vehicles. Firstly, inside an armoured vehicle in 50-degree heat is horrendous, so at least they were more comfortable on the outside. Second, if an APC struck a mine or IED, the vehicle's occupants would not burn to death.

Luckily our Warriors were more armoured than a Soviet BTR-60 and Soviet BMP 1 and 2s had fuel stored on panels on the back doors so you wouldn't want to be inside that if it was struck by an RPG or mine, but still it might be possible to blow up a Warrior. Third, the soldiers on the top could maintain better all-round defence that one man in a turret could, and if they came under fire, it was quicker to jump off the side and take cover.

As I hugged the left side of the Warrior and headed for the front of it, I was conscious of trying to stay in the tracks the vehicle had already made. If this beast hadn't set off any IEDs, there was a good chance I wouldn't. Up ahead I could see the ground sloping steeply away from us and I linked up with some of the 4 SCOTS dismounts and we started our sweep.

All the time I swung the detector in front of me. I dreaded the double beep or the lights on my detector going haywire, which would mean I had found something. I was also keenly aware that as my focus was on the dirt in front of me, any small arms attack would come as a complete shock.

We cleared the vulnerable point as a team and the Warriors were able to cross through. It was only then I let out the breath I had been subconsciously holding, and considering I had no shirt on under my body armour I was sweating profusely. Wiping the sweat from my face, I dropped to one knee and waited for my Warrior. As it pulled up to me, I was showered in a cloud of dust and grit which stuck to my sweat like flypaper.

"Cheers ya dobber!" I shouted up at the cupola. Like a jack in the box the commanders head poked through his hatch.

"Aye nay dramas min, get in the fucking wagon!" he grinned. I shrugged and jumped in through the back door of my Warrior and off we went again with a lurch.

The rest of our trip north passed without any difficulty and the Taliban obviously felt discretion was the better part of valour as we received no incoming fire. I occasionally helped with mine sweeping when it was necessary, but mostly I topped up my fluid level and made myself a hot drink from the water on the bar armour outside.

As the sun was beginning to set, the vehicle commander told me that we were ten minutes away from FOB Edinburgh. Quickly I put on my shirt and replaced my body armour before strapping my helmet back into place. After what seemed like an hour our vehicle came to a halt. As there were no windows, I had no idea whether this was Edinburgh or we had broken down again.

"We're here Min," came the commander's voice from up in the turret. I breathed a sigh of relief and opened the back door to the Warrior. I was immediately struck by how dusty FOB Edinburgh was, it was almost like a classic desert. As soon I stepped out of the vehicle my boots sank into the lunar sand of the base. Everywhere people walked great clouds of it were kicked up.

"Scoffs on min," shouted the vehicle commander as he dismounted from the vehicle. We headed for the structure that looked very much like a fighting bunker, covered in Hesco and sandbags. A long line of soldiers was forming outside it, this had to be the cookhouse.

A soldier in the queue waved at me and I saw the diminutive figure of Linda, Delta Company's clerk. Linda hadn't joined us in FOB Keenan as she was the only female soldier in the Company so it was probably felt that she should stay in Bastion, or as I now knew, FOB Edinburgh.

She approached me with a wide smile, I gave her a hug and told it was good to see a familiar face. She agreed as she hadn't seen any of us at all in-country. We sat together for a while, talked and had a brew. I was preparing for a night at FOB Edinburgh as we were told nothing was going to Musa Qa'leh DC until the morning.

After two full days on the road, I stank. And my kit stank, but I was informed there were no solar showers to be had so I found a place near my Warrior and used my camelback water bladder as a shower. It was not the same but at least I was cleaner than I had been. I brushed my teeth and felt a million times better. I was all set to plonk myself down on my kit and sleep when the Platoon Sergeant from the 4 SCOTS Warrior Platoon informed me that we were leaving for Musa Qa'leh within the hour. I felt grateful that I would not be spending the night in FOB Edinburgh and would be re-joining my Company.

We mounted up in the Warriors and began the short hop east to Musa Qa'leh district centre. Again, I could not see where we were going and in the diminishing light it would have made no difference anyway.

Upon arrival into Musa Qa'leh, I stepped down from the Warrior and tried to take in my new home. The base itself was built around a solid stone structure on about two or three levels, it bristled with antennae and all manner of dishes and aerials. Light peeked out from hessian sacking that covered them in the hope of denying enemy rocket or mortar teams an easy target. Against the north wall were individual wooden booths housing telephones, each one had a soldier in it and I could just hear the murmured conversations of lads phoning home. I found the watchkeeper and notified him of my arrival, as soon as he had logged my details on the system and unit flap sheet, he told me where Delta Company were.

As soon as I stepped back out into the humid darkness, I met a few of my guys who had been calling home and they offered to help me with all my kit down to where Delta were bunked.

Day 79

Friday 27th June: Musa Qa'leh DC

I was not given the luxury of relaxation for too long before jumping straight back into the operational tempo, which had been given a nudge into fifth gear. My first patrol was a good way for me to get the lay of the land and deal with the two other new changes.

We were going to have members of the Afghan National Police (ANP) with us. We had never patrolled with them before but, if the stories we had heard were true, it was going to be a very interesting stint.

The difference between the ANP and the Afghan National Army (ANA) was that the ANP were local to their area of operations. The ANA, based out of Helmand, would generally be from other parts of the country. We were told that when an Afghan soldier completes his basic training, he is not told where he is going, until he is on the bus to the flight line, because for those soldiers whose final destination is Helmand, it's seen as a death sentence and many would take the chance to desert if they could.

With the ANP being locals this had a number of added complications, the best analogy I could use is kids running around with gangs back in the UK, or indeed any gang. Everyone knows everyone else in the neighbourhood. Brothers, cousins and best friends run with the same gang or sometimes different gangs, but they still all know each other. They know families, they know where people live, they know who the good guys are, but they also know who the bad guys are. In some cases, our ANP allies had friends or family members who were Taliban fighters. Afghanistan truly was the definition of a civil war, brother against brother.

To us this was a problem as we did not speak their language and they also had mobile phones on them. I had always suspected that the ANP were letting their buddies in the Taliban know we were coming. So, where possible, we tried to avoid patrolling with them.

The ANP were very loose with their discipline, not only personal discipline but also weapon discipline. We had Police Officers carrying loaded RPGs and PKM machine guns. When we questioned them as to why policemen were carrying support weapons, they would get the hump and tell us they weren't Police Officers; they were soldiers! When we tried to point out to them that they had Police written on their uniforms and that their uniforms were sky blue and not camouflage, they weren't having any of it. In addition to their cavalier attitude with firearms, many ANP Officers were habitual drug users. Everything from weed up to opium and, in some cases, joints laced with opium for a better hit. Drugs and firearms were never a good combination.

I found it very hard to trust the ANP and nothing they did during my time in Musa Qa'leh ever changed my opinion. They were corrupt and open to bribery. The only saving grace of the ANP in Musa Qa'leh was their leader, the legendary Commander Koka, a no-nonsense warrior who hated the Taliban with a passion. He was once witnessed while out on foot patrol in Musa Qa'leh drawing his pistol and shooting a man dead out from the saddle of his motorbike. When asked why he had done this? Koko responded deadpan. "Because he is Taliban!" This was proof that by being local, you knew who was bad and who was good.

The other noticeable change between Gereshk and Musa Qa'leh was the heat, it had become far hotter since my R&R which made any movement, let alone patrolling and fighting, very uncomfortable. As soon as you put your body armour on you would begin to sweat. I had brought back a multicam armour carrier from R&R and put the soft armour and ballistic plates from my Osprey into it. It was amazing and made patrolling much more comfortable. It also made me more camouflaged, never a bad thing.

Our Regimental Sergeant Major (RSM) had decreed that all members of the Battalion would wear full desert uniform, there was to be no mix of combats like we had before. So, no one was to wear temperate combats or, in my case, jungle combats. This was great as everyone in the Battalion was now uniform and looked the same. However, what it also did was make us stick out like a sore thumb.

The term 'Green Zone' pretty much spoke for itself. It was lush and green, very much like the jungle. To describe the Green Zone is difficult. It was the most dangerous place in the world at that point in time, a place of strange parallels. Everywhere in Helmand is vast and dusty, a barren desert except a long strip of lush green vegetation that straddles the Helmand River and various other waterways. It is so beautiful and fertile that it was hard to imagine it as a place of death and destruction, it was so difficult not to get sucked in and distracted by the beauty of it.

The day's patrol was another local security patrol, which meant we would not stray too far away from the DC. We were out for what seemed like only a short amount of time when we received a message from the operations room informing us that we had to return to the DC for 19:45 hours.

I was slightly confused as the Op's room generally didn't cut patrols short unless there were specific circumstances. I thought, maybe bad weather was closing in, meaning we would lose our close air support, rendering CASEVAC missions virtually impossible. Or, perhaps, there was specific intel we had been targeted for a spectacular attack by the enemy.

All these options made patrolling very risky and made me nervous. I was anxious to find out what was going on. So, after an uneventful patrol, we returned to the DC. As we came through the gate, Goody approached us and spoke quietly to me.

"Dae yer patrol checks mucker then git yer boys formed up," Goody spoke uncharacteristically softly. "The Boss needs tae talk tae everybody!"

I did the equipment check on the Platoon to make sure we weren't missing anything, this I reported back to Goody.

"Section Commanders," I called out. "Get the guys to de-kit and fall in by the OC's tent." I was met with a chorus of acknowledgments and the lads trudged off to their bedspaces to drop their kit. We formed up as a Company under the canopy of the Company HQ, where the OC, CSM and other members of the Company staff slept. We stood in silence and confusion as to why we had been withdrawn from our patrol. Why indeed did the OC need to talk to all of us?

Major Calder approached from the direction of the vehicle park, his face set and grim. The reason for our early extraction soon became apparent and was far more tragic than we had all thought.

"Men," started Major Calder. "Today the Battalion suffered a fatality." He paused to let the news sink in. We all had friends in other companies and indeed other Jock Battalions in Task Force Helmand. This news was a bitter blow.

"B Company were conducting a patrol near a checkpoint in the Lashkar Gah area when they came under fire, L/Cpl Jimmy Johnston was tragically killed when he debussed his vehicle and hit what is believed at this time to be an old Soviet legacy mine." I personally had not known Jimmy, but the loss of a fellow Jock was still an event of great sadness.

As I looked around me, I could see some of the lads that did know him, their heads bowed and the suggestion of tears on the faces of a few of the boys. I could see others swallowing hard, holding back their tears.

"Let us all bow our heads and take a minute to remember L/Cpl Johnston," Major Calder called out. We all lowered our heads in silence.

I knew what it meant to feel the loss of men you have known or served with, you remember the way they laughed or funny anecdotes from nights out on the piss. You remember them the way they were, the way they will always remain. A kind of immortality. The passage of time assigns them to the past but, for those who knew and loved them, they are never forgotten.

Day 81

Sunday 29th June: Musa Qa'leh

We were still reeling from the news of Jimmy's death and I could tell it was hurting some of the boys really badly. I knew I would have to keep an eye on them and offer my support where it was needed. Sadly, the war was not over and we knew it, it didn't stop when a fellow soldier died. If that was the case it would have ended in 2001. We had to put it out of our thoughts as we continued our cycle of patrols to dominate the area and reassert the authority of ISAF and the Afghan Government. Our task today would see us patrolling north of the DC and trying to draw the enemy into a fight.

As of yet, I had not seen any fighting and the enemy seemed loath to come anywhere near the DC now that there was a British Infantry Company and a US Marine Corps rifle Company there.

As soon as I had put on my kit I began to sweat profusely, the fact that I had a UBAC shirt on underneath my armour was of no consequence. I was still redders, and I was still sweating my tits off. All the boys were exactly the same. I looked at Scotty McGregor, my little Gimpy gunner. He was five foot nothing and if he rested the butt of the 7.62mm machine gun on the floor, the gun was nearly as tall as he was. In his patrol pack he carried eight hundred rounds of 7.62mm machine gun ammo and a spare barrel. In addition to this, I insisted that he carry a tin of gun oil and some cleaning rods in case of stoppages.

He nodded as he passed me by and I winked at him in encouragement. He had a strength at odds with his size and I had chosen him as a Gimpy gunner as he was the best man for the job. He didn't go crazy with his bursts and was always aware of his fall of shot, so he never came close to running out of ammo as far as I recall anytime on tour.

I made the same nod of respect to my Minimi gunners as they went past, too; every LMG gunner carried a thousand rounds of 5.56mm, spare barrels and a tin of gun oil. I found that the Minimi was more prone to stoppages with prolonged firing and therefore it took disciplined gunners to use that weapon also.

This was why I and the section commanders chose carefully when allocating our most important firepower around the sections. Due to the fact that the gunners could only carry ammo, food and water, any luxury items (if there were such a thing) were carried by the rest of that gunner's section.

As we left the DC, I took up my position in the patrol just in front of my reserve section and we headed out. Leaving the DC felt like another world, you looked out over the Musa Qa'leh Wadi and through the heat shimmer you could make out the shapes of Afghan civilians trudging wearily towards the market, small Honda motorbikes racing through the wadi left a cloud of thick dust in their wake. Turning right you could see all the way up the wadi and to the mobile phone mast at Roshan Tower off to the north-west on a high cliff face. The lush greenery was interspersed with the mud-walled compounds that made rural Afghanistan unique. We all scanned our arcs of fire and called out over the radio anything we saw that was suspicious.

The patrolling and the heat always seemed to sap the strength from your legs and the heat combined with fatigue made a soldier's mind start to wander. All the pains and niggles seemed to magnify. Your daysack seemed to feel as though it had doubled in weight and the straps cut into your shoulders.

Every so often we would stop and take on water and giver the lads a chance at a breather, it was almost too dangerous to take your helmet off as the enemy could attack with sudden ferocity at any moment. Nobody wanted to be caught short by a stray bullet. Another effect of the heat and amount of weight carried by soldiers in Afghanistan is that it was impossible to adopt anything close to a textbook fire position as dictated by the Army's tactics pamphlet. Most soldiers adopted a kneeling position generally leaning on something, or a seating position. I had no issue with this as long as the troops were covering their arcs herringbone style. I knew that if a man was down in the prone position there was a good chance he would not get back up and could not react in the event of a contact, plus your field of view was massively reduced. I would rather have my guys comfortable and in a better position to respond should the shit hit the fan.

I adopted a kneeling position and began to scan around my Platoon, here and there I could see little puffs of blue-grey smoke and detected the distinctive smell of Afghan cigarettes, Pine lights or Seven Stars were the preferred brands. The lads didn't have access to any of the brands from back home, so they made do. Plus, at about five dollars for two hundred it was a no brainer.

I personally did not smoke and I never had, which is bizarre considering I come from a family of heavy smokers. I made sure the boys were also taking on water. I had started wearing a desert-coloured sweat rag under my helmet to stop the sweat from running into my eyes. As soon as I started to heat up, I would sweat buckets which would sting my eyes and blind me, so the sweat rag was effective.

"Prepare to move!" the Boss called on our Platoon radio channel. The boys all moved up to the kneeling position, cigarettes ground into the dirt and caps placed back over the mouthpieces of Camelbak water carriers. As we walked through the lush, green bushes and little copses of the Green Zone, we met locals going about their business. Some waved but most seemed indifferent or outright hostile in their stares. The children, however, were more friendly as they knew British and American soldiers carried treasures like sweets and pens and pencils. As soon as they saw us, they would mob us asking for these items in their excited little voices. They learned the English for sweet and pen very quickly and I for one had no problem letting them think I was a walking pick 'n mix or stationery store.

I recalled speaking to my dad many years ago about his service in Northern Ireland and how the patrols in Belfast would encourage the kids as they kind of knew that PIRA would not be so callous as to kill a load of kids just to get one or two British soldiers. I did not have the same faith that 'my' enemy would show such restraint and humanity.

The rest of the patrol passed without incident, but we noticed a shift in atmosphere the further north we got. We kind of knew where the line was and when we were firmly in enemy territory. People talked to us, but out of view of others. They complained about the Afghan police who they said were highly corrupt. Robbing and stealing from the locals, arresting people without evidence and people not even guilty of any crimes, let alone being suspected of Taliban support or activity.

We extended our patrol into the night, snapping our night vision goggles into place, which bathed the world in an eerie green glow. Given the conditions – no pollution, no light pollution, no clouds – it was like broad daylight through the NVGs.

Day 84

Wednesday 2nd July: Musa Qa'leh

We had received orders from Major Calder that we were going to conduct an advance to contact north of Musa Qa'leh for three days. For anyone unfamiliar with the concept of an advance to contact, it is quite simple, you all walk in a given direction until someone shoots at you. You deal with it and then do the same again. To the sane mind, this is not a normal thing to do for one day, let alone three. But here we were, battle prepping for the operation which would likely take us purposely into enemy fire.

As part of the orders process, I, as the Platoon Sergeant, was required to give the CSS (Combat Service Support) paragraph of the orders. This had to be comprehensive and rehearsed, with a good CSS paragraph taking an hour, almost as long as the orders themselves initially. But with time and familiarity, it could be cut down, as most things became standard operating procedure.

The CSS paragraph would normally highlight all admin functions the Platoon would be required to undertake as part of their battle preparation. The most important part of the CSS plan is the CASEVAC (Casualty Evacuation procedure). In other words, if you are killed or wounded, how do we intend to deal with you and get you to hospital in Camp Bastion?

So, reaction times of the choppers were noted. Also, where every soldier was to carry their IFAK (Individual First Aid Kit) and morphine. The rule was that you never use your own kit on another soldier, their kit is to be used on them and if it is carried in the same location on your person it would be easy to find in a high stress situation.

Our SOP as a Company for IFAK carriage was the left arm pouch on your UBAC shirt or, if you were wearing a standard desert shirt, in your left leg map pocket. I had almost finished my CSS paragraph when Scotty McGregor suddenly turned very pale and darted out the tent, I could hear him retching outside. I carried on with my brief and thought nothing more of the incident other than asking Scotty if he was okay.

"Aye no bad," he burped before rushing away to the toilet stalls to throw up again. As it was, I continued with my pre-operation checks on all the lads' kit. I updated my ammo/casualty card and made sure that the Platoon flap sheet was ready to hand in to Goody. The flap sheet contains the details of every soldier in the Platoon who is taking part in the operation, the weapons they are carrying complete with serial numbers, the soldier's blood group and ZAP number.

Once I was satisfied that we were ready for the next day, I went for a shower and settled in for the night so I could catch what would probably be the last decent sleep I would see for three days. How accurate that thought was would not hit me until 03:00hrs in the morning.

I awoke with a severe burning in my guts and the desire to throw up. I rolled out of bed in order to get to the toilets to be sick. I was doubled over in severe agony, initially thinking I had a bout of appendicitis. I got a third of the way across the dusty vehicle park that we shared with the US Marines, before a fart told me it was not appendicitis! It was something much worse. One fart followed another and then I became a one-man science lesson, showing how the body can produce solids, liquids and gasses at the same time.

I had successfully shit myself and puked twice before I made it the thirty or so metres to the wooden toilet stalls that we used to relieve ourselves. I swung the hastily constructed wooden door open and parked myself over the hole cut into the wooden bench. Beneath me was an oil drum that had been cut in half and was now the receptacle for catching the shit of some two hundred or so soldiers. Once they were full, they were taken out the back of the toilet stalls, mixed with diesel and other flammable materials and set fire to.

Nothing quite prepares you for the odour that accompanies such a faecal barbecue. Not only has it been baking away nicely in fifty-degree heat all day, somebody then sets fire to it. Even when all the shit, toilet paper, and baby wipes and are burned away, you are still left with the lingering aroma of burned crap and diesel fuel. There was no way even the cunning culinary science of Heston Blumenthal could make this barbecue sound appetising.

Mine was almost full to capacity again. When I wasn't shitting myself, I had to puke. Which meant placing my face over the hole which was now releasing methane at an alarming rate. I sat on that bench for thirty minutes before I felt it was safe to go and wash myself off and go to bed; unfortunately for me, it was an ambush. I had gone ten steps if that, before I shat again and had to about turn. It suddenly occurred to me in between all the shit and puke, that wee Scotty had puked just at the head of my bed during the O Group and I had not realised the fallout of this until it was actually falling out of me!

"Wee bastard!" I yelled into the approaching dusk, which was quickly followed by a large stinking 'phooooooooot, splash'. When I was absolutely certain there was no fluid left in my body, I wobbled back across to my Platoon tent where everyone was still snoring away. I grabbed my solar shower, wash kit, towel and fresh underpants. The soiled ones I had been wearing had been abandoned in the hole in the bench, hopefully to being cremated. After cleaning myself off, I headed back towards my bed. I must have lay down for all of five minutes before

I had the burning in my guts again, luckily enough I made it to the toilet before my bowels decided to ambush me again.

At this rate I thought I would be out of pants by the end of the day. After another long stint on the crapper, so long that I lost the circulation in my legs, I staggered back to the tent. As I approached, I could see signs of life starting to appear from most of the mosquito nets. I had to pass Company HQ to get back to my bedspace and I as I did, Andy Pettiford our CMT (Combat Medical Technician) caught sight of me.

"Fucking hell mate, you look like you've just been dragged out the canal!" I let out a large belch and managed to hold in the puke.

"Mate, I've shat myself about ten times since 3 o'clock this morning and I 've gone through two pairs of pants and nearly a full pack of baby wipes." Andy grabbed me and began to look me over; he raised an eyebrow and began to bombard me with questions.

"You need to see the doc mate! Don't go back to your Platoon or you'll infect everyone else." I grimaced and once again cursed Scotty McGregor, hoping that he was feeling as bad as I was.

"Viral D&V," the medical officer announced and pointed me in the direction of a quarantine tent. It was a twelve- by twelve-foot green army tent with the door panels removed, ominously surrounded by razor wire. Yellow biohazard bags were hung from every possible place and warning signs were attached on the razor wire about cross-contamination.

Andy Pettiford kindly got some of the boys from my Platoon to drop my bed, mozzy net and other bits and bobs at a safe distance outside the razor wire. I became one of four occupants in the tent and we were all in the same shit- and puke-filled boat.

As I lay on my camp cot reflecting on my predicament, I looked around. How the hell could we catch D&V in this place? But it soon became apparent as a Chinook helicopter on a standard milk run came in to drop off supplies and ammunition. It had to fly over the kitchen, the quarantine tent and another set of toilets before it got to the helipad. I watched in dismay as it made a low pass over the DC chucking up a huge cloud of dust and fuck knows what else in its downdraft! Our chefs had basically given up on life anyway judging by the standard of the meals they were producing, so it occurred to me that they were unlikely to give a rat's ass about the hygiene associated with Chinook downdrafts.

They probably hadn't even made the connection between the huge helicopter flying over the shitter and blowing shit particles everywhere and their proximity to said shitter. Even more humiliating than the D&V

was the fact that my Company were about to deploy out on an advance to contact and were very likely to be in a firefight within a few hours.

Before the Company formed up to leave, Goody and Al Lipowski came across to see me. If I was expecting any sympathy from Goody, the smirk on his face quickly cut that idea straight out my head.

"Yah big fanny! This is one way eh gitting oot eh the Op!" I couldn't even bring myself to laugh, my sense of humour was being burned in an oil drum along with litres of my liquid evacuations.

"Get better soon Sergeant Mac!" Al said as he turned away in the direction of the DC's exit.

As predicted, within hours the Company were fighting and I wasn't with them. I was filled with a mix of rage and self-loathing. I could hear the battles raging on to the north but could do nothing about it. I decided to break my quarantine and go get my radio. If I couldn't join the lads, I could at least listen to what the hell was going on as it was agonising listening to the fierce firefights raging in the distance.

For three straight days the battle ebbed and flowed between peaceful silence and unadulterated violence. I could only listen as contact reports were sent in and SITREPs reported to battlegroup HQ, but mercifully no ATMIST or 9 liners were reported. Satisfyingly though, reports of enemy dead flowed in after each engagement.

The Company returned weary and tired from their operation, I watched from the death tent as the boys flowed in grabbing bottles of cool, refreshing water, able to relax after being in enemy territory. It was during the post Op admin that the reality of how close death hit home.

Dave Poderis removed his helmet to allow his head to cool down when he noticed a huge gouge on the inside; turning it around in his hands he noticed a small tear in the front of his helmet cover near the top and a larger one out the back. With a confused look on his face he removed the cover and his eyes widened.

"Jeezis fuck man!" he yelled excitedly, holding his Mark 6 Alpha helmet up. The sunlight caught his helmet and a ray of light passed front to back, showing the passage of a bullet. "Ah jist thought mah NVG bracket had fell off coz it wisnae that well fitted on!" he said, paling visibly.

He recounted how as an LMG gunner he was on the roof of a compound providing fire support against nearby Taliban positions. He felt a knock to his head and his NVG bracket fell across his vision. Thinking nothing of it, he pushed the bracket out the way as there was no time to sort it and continued engaging the enemy with bursts of fire.

We came the conclusion that the enemy had pinged his position on top of the compound expecting that he would not move positions between bursts: they were right! Dave was one lucky bastard, if the bullet had struck a few millimetres lower, it would have hit him in the forehead. That was the reality of it, trigger snatching or even not gripping the weapon properly was the difference between a great war story and a metal box back to the UK.

As it turned out, my recovery from viral D&V went really slowly and given the hot temperatures we were experiencing, they were an extremely uncomfortable few days. I tried to sleep and eat, but when I did, it all came back up. Occasionally a medic would come by to check on us and give medication. But I found that just drinking as much water as I could, along with a lot of dioralite powder in it, began to help. My body was starting to fight the illness, and I soon became strong enough to shower without shitting myself.

I was extremely thankful to the lads from my Platoon, particularly Scotty McGregor and Davey McGhee, who stopped by once a day to bring me water and in one instance a can of Miranda orange. Even though it was slightly warm, it was more than welcome as the sugar in it gave me an energy boost.

The lads also let me know that we were being pencilled in for another patrol. Two days this time and down to Yatimchay, north of the AO. I began to run the battle procedure through my head again, as there was no fucking way I was missing this operation. A day later, on 6th July, I was cleared to return back to the Company and began lugging all my stuff back to my Platoon tent. I was met by Goody who had his lopsided grin plastered all over his face.

"Good tae huv yea back shitey, but ah'll no shake yer hand... Ya diseased fuck!" His way of welcoming me back.

It was good to see the boys were all well and ready for the next Op, Davey Poderis showed me his helmet and I let out a long breath.

"You are one lucky bastard mate; I'd put the lottery on if I was you." He grinned at me with his gap- toothed smile.

"Ah ken George," he said. "Fuckin' hell ah didnae even know ah'd been hit!" I started to think of soldiers I had read about that had similar experiences in other wars and had refused to get their helmet exchanged, through superstition or whatever, they finished their war with the same bullet-holed helmet.

As it happened, Davey Poderis did not have a choice. His helmet had been shot through and it would have to go away to a lab somewhere to be tested by the boffins. His story made it into the newspapers back home and the helmet would eventually end up in the Argyll and Sutherland Highlanders Museum in Stirling Castle.

I told him it wasn't the helmet that had saved his life, it was his weird, flat, inbred-shaped head that had done it for him.

Day 89

Monday 7th July: Hotel India Grid Quadrant, 3 km South of Musa Qa'leh DC

We had the relative luxury of being dropped off by the Army's new Mastiff armoured vehicles, which were crewed by the lads from 2 SCOTS. It was nice to know that if the shit hit the fan, it would be brother Jocks coming to our rescue.

What I liked about the Mastiff most wasn't the nice thick armour or the suspension giving us a slightly more comfortable ride, but the fact that they had air conditioning that actually worked! The interior of a Mastiff was a lot less cramped and claustrophobic than a Warrior.

I gazed out of the front window and checked my map so that I would know where we were in relation to our drop-off point. I need not have worried, we were dropped exactly where we were supposed to be – and rapidly, which was ideal as we were only in a vulnerable position for minutes and then we went our separate ways.

As the din from the vehicles disappeared into ambient background noise, I watched the guys in all-round defence observing their arcs. Machine gunners had naturally taken up positions to cover likely approaches and killing zones. The lads worked in pairs to take a drink of water and then prepared to move.

The plan was to push south and entice the Taliban into revealing their positions, bring them out of hiding with a tempting target and then paste the shit out of them with everything we had. Almost immediately, the excited chatter started up on the ICOM and we began to feel that a fight was in the planning.

"What are they saying John?" (a pseudonym obviously) I asked my interpreter. John, who was a very tall, skinny Afghan gentleman from

Kabul. He turned the volume up slightly and knotted his eyebrows as he listened in.

"He says Sir, that they can see ISAF and are moving their fighters into position to attack." He wiped a bead of sweat from his forehead. As if to confirm what was being said on the ICOM scanner, I began to see groups of civilians in the distance leaving their homes and heading west towards Musa Qa'leh Wadi and potential safety.

"That's not a good sign," I said, pointing through the heat shimmer. The dark blurry shapes that were enveloped in a cloud of light brown dust looked like a weary band of refugees heading away from danger. 'This is it,' I thought, part of me was nervous and part of me was excited, the enemy was about to reveal himself and actually I might get to use my weapon before the tour was out.

The Company bounded by Platoons through lush greenery and groups of dirty mud compounds, every pair of eyes was checking potential threat locations for any sign of ambush or the IEDs which were rapidly becoming a new threat to ISAF forces in Afghanistan. We were aware of IEDs and those of us who had served in Northern Ireland were familiar with the tactics of booby-trapping things and vulnerable point recognition. Those who didn't have that knowledge would have to rely on us; the whole concept of IEDs and booby traps is that those who plant them are hoping you will take the easy path and they rely on man's laziness in order to achieve their effect.

It turned out to be anti-climactic as the enemy did not do anything. But, as we were finding out, you can never take it for granted when you hear ICOM. Sometimes it's an attempt at misdirection or to confuse. But other times it's accurate and the Taliban were getting ready to hit you.

As we were discovering, even though we did not speak Pashtun, a sudden change in pitch or speech pattern would indicate that you were under observation and were about to be attacked. All semblance of security went out of the window, the enemy commanders became excited and began using plain speech instead of their usual codes for things.

We continued to patrol near Yatimchay until it became time to occupy night defensive positions. These normally took the form of civilian compounds that we would take over and turn into Platoon forts. We would give the occupants the option to remain in the compound with us or relocate. Most chose to relocate as it was safer than being near us. We would pay the families compensation in the form of US dollars to thank them for the use of their homes, but sometimes we had to be quite sensitive, and tonight was one of those nights.

Our intended defensive position was to be compound number Hotel India 8-5, which would give us overlapping arcs of fire and cover with 10 and 11 Platoons, giving the Company all-round defence.

As we approached the compound, I informed John of our plan. He nodded that he understood and I trusted him to make our intentions clear to the compound owners. As he rapped on the rusting blue iron door, he called out to the owners in Pashtun. After what seemed like forever an old man pulled open the door with a grinding of rusting metal on metal. He was a short, hunched, elderly man, with the light-coloured baggy shirt and trousers we now came to associate with Afghan men. Over the top he wore a dark brown waistcoat and on his head he wore a little sparkly hat that sat on the back of his crown.

The conversation with John went back and forth, but I could tell the old gentleman was not happy with the intrusion of foreigners in his home. To get my guys into cover, I advised Al that we should discuss business inside the compound. He agreed and the Platoon filed in past the old man and, without prompting, the sections all moved to cover arcs on the walls of the compound.

"What's the problem John?" I asked as the conversation progressed and became more animated.

"He say his wife is very sick and having soldiers in the house will make her worse!" I would normally smell bullshit in what the locals told me, so I decided to check for myself. The old man led us to a door in a building against the northern wall. I had an LMG and three riflemen on the roof who were observing the area as the sun began to set. I pulled out my head torch as we entered the darkened room, I was careful to let the old man lead us because if he was lying to us and there were enemies inside the compound, he would get it first.

I shone the beam across the room and the light fell onto rows of wooden shelves with tin kettles, small glasses and folded up blankets. In one corner of the room was a mattress with an obvious lump that could only be a human shape covered by blankets. As my light caught the shape, it moved gently and I saw a shock of grey hair. I turned to John and whispered in his ear.

"Tell him we're sorry to disturb him," and we decided that we really did not need to take over this compound.

Al, Goody and I looked over the map and decided to try compound number Hotel India 8-2. As it turned out this was a better option, it had a water well inside it and electricity. As soon as defensive positions were set up, I got the section 2i/c's to meet in the centre and gave them a brief. We confirmed the sentries knew where 10 and 11 Platoons were, to prevent friendly fire, direction of enemy threat, passwords and reveille times for the morning. Then Al got the section commanders together to outline the next day's activities.

The night passed quietly with Al, Goody and I maintaining a radio stag. We conducted radio checks to the OC's group every thirty minutes and I would walk round the compound before resting, just to make sure the gun positions were okay.

I was never worried about the lads falling asleep on duty as the potential outcome in combat was not lost on anyone. I lay back in the darkness and wrapped myself up in my US Army poncho liner. I was struck by how humid it still was. I found the nocturnal noises of the insects around the Green Zone reassuring. Because if it went quiet, it meant the wildlife had been scared off by something, more than likely the Taliban. I was also struck by the beauty of up above, a blanket of stars seemed to paint the dark blue sky with dots and swathes of light. Only the Northern Lights in Canada were more beautiful than the Afghan night sky.

Prior to first light, the Company stood to. This was an SOP that the British Army had adopted since it had a formed standing fighting formation, and it took me back to when I trained my recruits. On the first week of basic training, I gave every recruit a copy of Roger's Rangers standing orders and No.15 always came back to me. 'No.15: Don't sleep past dawn, it's when the French and Indians attack.' I could still see that validity of that standing order.

After first light stand to, we conducted admin, which was a quick oil of the weapons if they hadn't been fired and being pulled through if they had. This was known as battle cleaning your weapon, a deeper clean would normally happen on return to a safe haven or if the weapons were really fired. Change socks if need be and eat a hot meal and a brew. Once we were happy that everyone was sorted, we began pre-patrol checks to ensure nothing had been left behind to be of use to the enemy.

We took the chance to fill our camelbaks with cold water from the well we had located inside the compound. I looked around at the tanned faces with tired, red eyes as they took a sip of water and helped one another fill bottles and camelbaks for the day ahead. Those who did light up disappeared in a cloud of blue-white smoke and the aroma of Pine lights and Seven Stars began to tickle my nostrils. We helped one another heft our packs on and lifted one another up to our feet and began to leave the compound ready for the day's patrolling.

As we moved between compounds, I noticed the temperature start to rise and already I was sweating like crazy. Like me, a number of my Platoon had also begun wearing a bandanna over their hair under the helmet in order to keep the sweat out their eyes.

I became aware of the smell of ammonia rising from my UBAC shirt. Patches of white salt appeared in places where I would sweat more than normal, armpits, the inside of my elbows, my shoulders.

We were heading towards the village of Dagyan to our west to support an Afghan Army clearance operation. They were also supported by their advisors from the Royal Irish Regiment. We had planned to adopt blocking positions for the ANA to prevent both the infiltration of Taliban fighters and the escape of fighters from the area. It was decided that we would take over compounds near the village and use them to dominate the locale.

We patrolled around, interacting with the locals, who, for the most part seemed indifferent to us, apart from the kids (mostly little boys), as usual. We were mobbed almost immediately by groups of youngsters who would yell at us "Sweet mister!" or "Kalam (Pen) Mister!" while tapping the palm of their hand, mimicking a writing motion or pointing to their mouths. For the most part we were happy with this form of human body armour, but it had a tendency to get fucking irritating fucking quick! I made the error on my first patrol of leaving all my pens on display in my commander's pouch, but after my first 'mugging' they remained hidden. But I was always happy to dish out G10 boiled sweets and small bars of Duncan's chocolate which had melted in transit, cooled and then melted again, so that when you opened it the chocolate was always white and stuck to the inside of the wrapper.

Major Calder decided that it would be a good idea to have a Shura (town meeting) with some of the local elders. I was not party to the meeting; however, Al Lipowski told me as the meeting dispersed that they were happy to see us, hadn't seen the Taliban in months and were not happy for us to use their compounds as patrol bases.

"So, the standard party line then Boss? We didn't receive any messages and Captain Blackadder did not shoot this delicious plump-breasted pigeon." I answered. Al didn't need to say anything else, he simply nodded.

In light of this, Nick decided to patrol the Company north at the end of the ANA clearance, back to the US PB, which was an ANA checkpoint south of Musa Qa'leh, to get the Company out of the heat of the day. As we entered the PB we flopped down where we could, removed our armour and piled our kit neatly but never left it out of our sight. In the Army if it is not nailed down it's fair game, but then even if it's nailed down, you still have the option to bring a claw hammer. Once it had cooled down enough, we all began to wake up and get ready to move back to the DC, seeing the end of our patrol.

Day 96

Monday 14th July: Musa Qa'leh DC

We had been geared up for a clearance/advance to contact operation back down into Yatimchay, as it was believed the Taliban were using the area around the village as a patrol base from which to mount operations against the DC.

We were going down to kick them out and hopefully kill a few, restoring some sort of order to the area. But something happened that would change our Op focus; as we knew, flexibility is a principle of war and plans can change at any moment.

This morning an ANA clearance patrol operating north of the DC was contacted and, in the process of following the Taliban up, a young Ranger stepped on a pressure plate IED. It was assessed that actually it had been part of a ten-IED daisy chain. The lad had lost one leg at the hip and the other at the knee, also suffering horrific facial injuries in the explosion.

This sent a shock wave throughout the battlegroup as IEDs of this nature were something new in Afghanistan. The tactic had been used to devastating effect in Iraq, but not yet in our theatre of war. The daisy chain was something altogether new and the Counter IED task force wanted to exploit the site to see what intel they could glean from it. Were Iraqi insurgents or other state-sponsored players migrating the tactics out to the Taliban? This was an all-new phase of the war in Afghanistan. The young Ranger had been on his last patrol before heading home for his two well-earned weeks of R&R.

We mounted up into Mastiff APCs in order to get us into the area quicker. Before last light we were able to occupy a compound that had been hit, one wall was missing. This did little to give us security, but as things stood this was the best we could hope for. To our north, a Company of Warriors from 4 SCOTS formed an armoured block between us and the Taliban's main line of resistance. As it was getting dark, they struck.

Tracer fire strobed lazily over the top of our compound and we could hear the sounds of 7.62mm chain guns from the Warriors kicking out a furious fusillade at the oncoming enemy. This rapid chatter was punctuated by the deeper thumps of the 30mm Rarden cannons. Three-round bursts, 'thump-thump-thump', went out to meet the enemy, who thought they were safe under the cover of darkness and had not yet realised that they were facing armour. This, however, did not dissuade them from attacking. They brought up RPGs and as we stood to in our compound, I heard a sound that would become familiar to me.

'Fwoosh'. An RPG arced out over the top of our compound and detonated in the air, I could hear shrapnel slicing through the foliage and hitting the mud walls of our compound. This was followed by two more. Our Fire Support team commander, Captain John Axcell, was on the radio calling in the guns from FOB Edinburgh. The gun line was so close we could hear the guns being fired and follow the trajectory of the 105mm rounds as they struck targets to our north.

For three hours the fight raged on with the Taliban attempting to assault the Warrior positions, being forced back and their retreat being cut off by our artillery. As silence reclaimed the night, we keep a watch up and spent a sleepless night under the stars awaiting the return of the Taliban. We were a flame to a moth. Any fighter who had aspirations of reaching paradise would no doubt be arming up for the coming dawn, ready to continue the assault.

At 0430hrs, we began to push north. From our night defensive position, we crossed an open field. In the coming light, I could see the churned-up mud and tank tracks made by the Warriors. Out of the morning mist I could make out the blocky, menacing shapes of the armoured personnel carriers; their turrets turned occasionally to show that they were very much ready for what the Taliban had to throw at them.

As we got closer, I could see piles of spent cases around every Warrior. In places their armour was scorched or chipped, especially on the bar armour where enemy gunners had scored hits. Foliage was stripped from trees and there were RPG impacts on compound walls near where the Warriors currently sat immobile, ready to reach out and strike the enemy again.

We pushed forward to a compound that we knew the enemy had used as a firing position. We had all fixed bayonets as there was a strong likelihood we would meet the enemy in and around these compounds, and in the greenery the fighting would be very close.

As we approached, we prepared to make entry stacking up on the metal doorway. As soon as the door went in, we pushed inside and began to clear the compound. We were acutely aware that there may be civilians in here that had no way to escape. Sure enough, we were met with the terrified stares of women and children as we checked each of the buildings inside the compound. All around the compound was evidence of the Taliban, empty AK ammo boxes and the bullet cases associated with 7.62mm short rounds, those fired by the AK family of weapons.

"John!" I called, "Get the man of the house and tell him to get his family the fuck out of here." John went away and spoke to the man, who did not need to be told twice and pretty soon a sorry trail of women and kids began to leave the compound, heading south to safety.

As soon as I was happy that the place was empty, I started placing the Platoon into defensive positions. The ICOM came alive with chatter as the enemy began congratulating themselves on a job well done.

"John what are they saying?" I asked. John scratched his unshaven chin and strained to listen as though he couldn't believe what he was hearing.

"The commander say to his men, 'well done mujahid you killed many Russians last night.' He also say, prepare the big things (Chinese 107mm rockets) to kill the rest of the Russians."

"Russians John?" I chuckled. "They know the Russians haven't been here since the 80s right?" John smirked and continued listening.

Again, it turned out anti-climactic, the rocket attack did not materialise and neither did the enemy. The Warriors must have taken quite a toll on the enemy the previous night if their commander was having to give them a pep talk. The Warrior Company had quite clearly caused them more casualties than they cared to admit.

We were joined by members of the ANP who just sat around getting stoned, the sweet aroma of cannabis wafted over the entire compound; and not for the first time I began to wonder at the safety implications of drugs and heavy weapons.

Our interpreters found some scruffy looking chickens and killed them and cooked them for breakfast, the ANP joined them and began looting the compound for bread and anything valuable. I could do nothing but shake my head and worry at the future we were fighting for when the men who are supposed to enforce the law were often criminals themselves. Once the Counter IED team had exploited the area of the explosion, we were withdrawn back to the DC and driven home by Mastiff.

Day 100

Friday 18th July: Musa Qa'leh DC

Up until now the focus of Delta Company operations had been to the north and south of the DC, with elements of the ANA, USMC and other units in the battlegroup patrolling east and west.

It had been decided that Delta would push south-west of the DC, moving before last light and spending the night at a mentored ANA checkpoint, known by its geographic location Patrol Base South West (PBSW). There would be members of the Royal Irish Regiment there in support of the ANA and we could at least get a decent ground brief from the lads who worked there and knew the ground better than we did.

At 17:30hrs we left the DC and patrolled west across Musa Qa'leh Wadi, which was a dry riverbed. At some point it must have been deep and fast flowing, but then it was dry. I could imagine that during the winter months in Afghanistan, it may have been a slightly wetter crossing point. Being dry it served as a perfect highway for people travelling north from Sangin and south from Baghran. So, strategically, it was key terrain to both ISAF and the Taliban.

All manner of traffic could be seen travelling up and down the wadi, minibuses full of families with bags of produce on the roof and the odd goat. There was a great number of small Yamaha motorbikes with everything from a single rider to, in one instance, a male Afghan with his wife and two kids behind him and a lamb on the handlebars. All bouncing along the rocky ground, kicking up a big cloud of grey-brown dust.

It was hard to tell who was who in the wadi. The enemy mingled seamlessly with the locals and they buzzed in and out of and between military convoys. From time to time, you would see a blue-grey Ford Ranger ANP pickup truck racing down the wadi with blue lights flashing for no other reason than that the vehicle had them, it was more for show than anything to do with an emergency.

As the convoys got closer you could see the rear flatbed filled to capacity with grubby, scruffy looking ANP officers all hanging on for dear life, their weapons looking like the spines of a weird porcupine. I often looked at those guys and wondered how many would be killed when one man carrying an RPG had an ND in the back of the vehicle. It would kill every single one of them and anyone unfortunate enough to be in the nearby vicinity.

Afghan Army convoys were very similar in that they relied on the Ford Ranger as their primary mode of transport. However, their vehicles were a coyote, dirt brown colour and the windscreens were normally packed with plastic flowers and had photographs taped to the glass. I could never figure out how the drivers managed to see through all the crap in their windscreens, but they did. I got the impression that Ford had made an absolute fortune off the back of the Afghan war, but I realised with a shrug that any company winning a military contract during wartime was bound to make a killing.

Our passage across Musa Qa'leh Wadi went off without a hitch, but we had the benefit of being covered in the wadi by the Mastiff Company of 2 SCOTS, their callsign a strong-sounding Titanium two-zero.

As I got across the wadi and touched the western bank, I nearly stepped on something which on closer inspection was the cutest little puppy I had ever seen, it looked almost newborn. An Afghan Kuchi mountain dog, it could have easily fit into the dump pouch I carried on my armoured vest. I stooped down and picked the little creature up and was tempted to do just that and take the puppy away. I had seen the life that these dogs faced as they got bigger. It was a hard decision I made to put the little girl down and walk away. I knew in my heart it was impractical to take the pup with me, and plus it probably belonged to a family who would use it as protection and firstly as a pet for the children, I could not take it with me.

We came upon the PB and were shown by the Royal Irish where we could sack out for the night prior to our patrol in the morning. The ANA guys were friendly lads and we bought loaves of Afghan flat bread from them and provided tins of Pepsi and Miranda orange to supplement their rations.

I got the guys settled for the night and we had an O group with Nick and the PB commander, who gave us the situation as it stood. I took notes and pored over the map looking at the route we would take the next day; this was new territory for us and would be quite interesting I thought. As I left the main bunker and headed back to my Platoon, I stripped off my UBAC shirt and began to brush my teeth and give myself a quick wash. Suddenly, John's ICOM scanner came alive and to the east in the distance we could hear an explosion. A US Marine MRAV had hit a mine, fortunately no one was killed or injured. Then the Taliban launched a small arms attack on PB South using rifle and RPG fire, but again, there were no ANA killed or injured. John was listening intently to the ICOM scanner and looked up at me.

"Sir," he announced. "These men do not sound Afghan. They sound Pakistani, maybe from Waziristan?" We had always known there were foreign fighters operating with the Taliban since the invasion in 2001, but here was evidence that they were operating at will within our AO. A small team of dedicated Jihadis who had answered the call to come and help their brothers in Afghanistan. Everyone knew from the pre deployment briefs that Waziri fighters were loyal only to Osama Bin Laden and the Al Qaeda network, so this news added a whole new dynamic to the war.

We stood to and helped man the walls. As I gazed out to the east, I could make out the faint lights of Musa Qa'leh town. I could also hear fighting from that direction. I could see lines of ruby tear drops travelling in a horizontal arc, heading in a southerly direction. They were answered by pale green tear drops heading back, occasionally one of the lines of tracer would strike something and ricochet up into the night sky. Rocket flares and mortar illumination rounds lit the sky in the distance, the flares dangling under their parachutes, bathing the surrounding areas in a pale, yellow light that would make target identification so much easier.

It was almost hypnotic watching the flares as they pulsed then faded into darkness, replaced with a sudden bright glow as another flare burst into life ensuring constant illumination across the contact point. I flipped down my night vision monocular and marvelled once more at how, with the right light conditions, the army's NVGs were almost perfect, with everything rendered in hues of green. I could see the tracer fire clearer through the monocular, but it looked like orbs of light green light. Closing one eye made everything green and opening it again gave the confusing melding of both natural views and night vision. The trick was to do both and operate at night with both eyes open.

As the sounds of battle faded away and the insect noise returned, we stood down ready for the next day's task. As we did not have to stag on, the lads all passed an undisturbed and restful night.

Day 101

Saturday 19th July: PB South-West Musa Qa'leh

The Company went through its usual stand to drills. Everyone woke, yawned and rubbed their eyes. Pretty soon the area smelled of farts and cigarette smoke as each man went through his ritual. I ripped the top off a bag of sausage and beans and began to tuck in, washing it down with a bottle of tepid water. I normally had a full Camelbak and a few bottles of water in my kit. However, the luxury of overnighting in a friendly checkpoint meant they had shipping containers full of Camp Bastion bottled water.

Some FOBs and PBs had a refrigerated shipping container for their water. Others had to make do with the tepid stuff, but even then we had learned a life hack from previous tours of duty in the summer months. If you take a black Army sock and soak it in water, then wrap the sock around your water bottle, it keeps it nice and cool.

Once we had had sorted our admin out, I did a kit check and pre-patrols checks including radio checks back to the Company signaller. Another bonus of being in a friendly location meant we could turn our radios off at night to save battery power and we could swap our used ones for fresh from the PB Op's room. Just as we were getting ready to head out on patrol, Goody came out of the PB Op's room and made a slashing motion across his throat.

"Dinne git too excited," he called removing his helmet. "Some c**t's fucked up!" We all looked at one another in confusion and I told the boys to chill out and wait for further instructions. I grabbed my helmet and walked up to Goody.

"What's going on Goody?" I asked. "Our fuck up or their fuck up?" I continued jerking my thumb back in the direction of the DC.

"Dinne ken mucker, Boss is on the dog to the DC noo." After what seemed like an age, Major Calder called all the Platoon HQ staff together and sat us down in the Royal Irish rest area.

"Okay!" he said impassively. "Some dodgy fucker from the ANA has been arrested for selling information to the Taliban." He paused to let it sink in before continuing. "The DC seem to think that part of that information was our fucking patrol trace!"

It always made me smile when Nick Calder cursed as he was extremely well spoken and a very mild-mannered man, which made it all the more funny.

"Upshot guys is no one is going anywhere until we find out what the bloody hell is going on." As soon as we were dismissed Al Lipowski and I went back to 12 Platoon to deliver the news.

To the guys it was great news, as we could sit and relax as you never knew when these situations would resolve themselves, it gave the lads a chance to catch up on more sleep or just to simply marvel at a few more hours where nobody was trying to kill them.

At around 17:00hrs we found out that the patrol was back on, so we kitted up, said our goodbyes to our Royal Irish hosts and left to go out on patrol. It would later transpire that the ANA soldier had been wrongly arrested. The problem was communication security as the Taliban had been able to listen in on ANA radio frequencies to glean information, but it hadn't compromised our operation.

That night we took over an Afghan compound to use as a temporary PB. No one had answered our calls or those of John, so we kicked the door in and conducted a sweep of the compound to ensure there were no surprises waiting for us. During the sweep we found Taliban posters, tapes, potential IED parts including a dual tone multi frequency cordless phone. All were placed in clear plastic bags so we could exploit the forensic value of our finds, something we had done to great effect in Northern Ireland.

As I walked around the compound, I came to a pit in the middle and inside it was a seat from a Vector armoured Pinzgauer, British 7.62mm ammo tins and other assorted bits and pieces. The significance of the location was not lost on me. When the British had been retaking Musa Qa'leh on Operation Herrick 7 part of the forces involved were members of the 2nd Battalion The Yorkshire Regiment (Green Howards), with whom I had served in Kosovo as a surveillance team commander. I was acutely aware that Sgt Lee Johnson, nicknamed Judo, was killed near here in a suspected mine strike and that his vehicle had been a Pinzgauer; the thought was quite a sobering one.

The owner of the compound we suspect had fled when he knew ISAF troops were coming, otherwise he would have had to answer some awkward questions about the items in his home and no doubt the Afghan NDS (National Directorate for Security) would have whisked him off to a bijou little hostelry in Kandahar where he would have been 'persuaded' to help them with their enquiries. We made the gate to the compound secure and posted sentries, but after all the excitement of the day, nothing materialised and the Taliban remained elusive.

The next morning, we geared up ready to continue our sweep. We would be heading back north towards Musa Qa'leh, dominating the ground and trying to engage with the Taliban.

After taking pictures of the compound and sending a ten-figure grid to the Op's room at the DC, we headed out into the cool morning air. The sun was rising, bathing the whole area in a yellow, orange, pink glow. We could also feel the temperature start to rise and knew it was going to be a hot one.

The ground we were traversing was rough under foot and required stamina in order to keep going, but Afghan heat can sap that stamina right out of you. As usual, water and electrolytes were the order of the day, along with boiled sweets.

We had not gone far when a loud explosion reverberated through the Green Zone. Fearing the worst, everyone automatically dropped into protective postures and began to cover their arcs of view and fire until we had figured where the blast came from. It came across the radio that one of the 2 SCOTS Mastiffs had hit a mine as it had moved into a position of cover. This was another indication that the enemy were looking at likely overwatch positions and anywhere they knew we would take cover in the event of a contact.

As we patrolled past the stricken vehicle, I marvelled at not only how lucky the crew were, but also how well protected the Mastiff was. The Mastiff was on a small rocky outcrop surrounded by trees and I could see that the whole front left corner of the vehicle had taken the blast. In amongst the light coyote tan paint job was jagged, scorched metal and I could clearly see the suspension spring and shock absorber. The wheel was completely destroyed, this Mastiff was going nowhere. The vehicle had struck an anti-tank mine.

The heat began to build up as we moved through the village of Deh Zohr-e Sofla and once again we were met with indifference or hostility.

"Have you seen any Taliban activity?" we would ask.

"No, we have not seen the Taliban for months," they would answer. Of course, we knew there were lying. But you can't detain someone for lying to you and besides, I felt kind of sorry for the locals. As with any civilians caught up in a counter insurgency war like Afghanistan, they were caught in the middle. Side with ISAF, the Taliban will kill you, side with the Taliban and allow them to use your homes, you risk being killed by ISAF. The average Afghan wanted exactly what we wanted, to get on with their lives and raise a family in safety and security without fear of being killed.

We left the village not long after and continued our way north, but not before stopping at the village well, ironically built with American money by an NGO, and refilling our water. By now the heat had become unbearable, almost fifty degrees. It was taking its toll on everyone and before long I started to notice Nige Campbell starting to struggle. I called up on the radio to the forward elements to ask for a halt so that I could check his status, I also noticed that one of our attachments was flagging, too.

"Whit the fuck is goan oan?" said Goody as he strolled up with a face like thunder. I pointed to the two lads struggling with the heat and told him as there was quite a way to go to get back to the DC. I doubted both lads would make it back. Andy Pettiford came up level with Goody and he nodded.

"George is right!" he said. "We need the Mastiffs to evacuate them." After a brief chat to the CSM of the Mastiff Company, we made the lads comfortable and got them loaded onto a vehicle. They both looked utterly crestfallen as though they had let us down.

"Nige, don't worry mate I'd rather we got you evacuated than have you drop on me later and have to be flown out!" This seemed to make him feel a bit better, but he still looked miserable as the back doors of the Mastiff swung closed on him.

Without further incident the Company moved north towards Musa Qa'leh and in the falling sunlight we caught the distinctive shape of the DC standing proud on the east bank of the wadi. I could make out sangar positions and large Afghan flags flapping slightly in the breeze.

We got into Musa Qa'leh as the sun set and, as we got into the DC, we all breathed a sigh of relief. Another day that we had come off the ground alive and with no casualties other than from the heat. As we finished our kit check under torchlight, Goody yelled "The chefs huv pit scoff oan fer us as soon we've dumped oor kit!" This was met with a sarcastic cheer, then boos. Everyone had come to the conclusion that our RLC (Royal Logistic Corps) chefs had basically given up the fight. Every meal we had was bland, tasteless and pretty much inedible. Many of us had survived thus far by eating what we had received in care packages from home or by buying Afghan toenail bread from the ANA. As we queued up in the dark, we could see the chefs working away at the hot plate. Steam rose from cauldrons of fuck knows what. As we got closer to the hotplate, the smells normally associated with a decent meal were not there. As we chatted over the last few days, we could see what awaited us. Some dry strips of beef and noodles, no sauce or anything to make it more palatable. From the cluster of tables one of the Jocks shouted, "Here you! How the fuck can ye fuck up noodles fer fuck sake?" The head chef went visibly scarlet.

"If you don't like it mate? Eat somewhere else!" Anger in his voice. To which the Jock replied, "Aye nay danger ya dobber, maybe the Taliban are recruiting? The canny be eating any worse shite than this!" The dining area erupted with laughter and the head chef retreated to the back of the cook tent leaving the rest of his staff to face the barrage of insults levelled at the food; and there were a lot of comments as to the head chef's parentage.

Day 104

Tuesday 22nd July: Musa Qa'leh DC

We were recovering from the Operation to Deh Zohr-e Sofla when word came down that we were heading back to Yatimchay. We were to stir up some trouble with the Taliban who had now taken up residence down there.

All the battle procedure had been done and kit checks were completed, my section 2i/c's by now knew what was expected of them. Ironically given the weak strength of my Platoon, and the Company as a whole, men were stepping up. I had Lance Corporals commanding sections and Private soldiers as my section 2i/c's, which was quite stressful for them as it was a great responsibility placed on their young shoulders. I knew who I could trust in positions of leadership as I had trained a few of the lads as recruits when they were mere boys.

One of, if not the best of, my NCOs was Pete Breen. He had accepted the responsibility of Section Commander of 3 section without question, and his performance thus far had been exemplary. Pete had been a recruit at ATR Bassingbourn when I was an instructor there between 2002 and 2004. I had seen in him great potential and he had not let me down; I was extremely proud of how he had matured from a fresh-faced, teenage recruit (soldiers at the ATR join when they are sixteen or seventeen years old). To a … well, he was still fresh-faced but no longer a teenager. He was a father and a husband, and I'm proud to say one of my Platoon.

A rifle section in the British Army is supposed to be eight men. But on average due to sickness, injuries and R&R, I was generally working on five or six men per section. Given the interesting and eclectic mixes of cap badges within the Platoon, there were those lads who were not even infantry who stepped up to the plate. My Army Air Corps attachments who naively thought they were coming to 12 Platoon to drive vehicles for me, soon found they took to combat soldiering like a duck to water.

Geordie Morgan and 'Ammo' Armstrong were two strong characters. I didn't know it then but very soon, when the real fighting started, whenever I turned around during a firefight, those guys would be right there with me. A look of determination on their faces said 'Right! Who needs killing?' I was so proud of my misfit Platoon. Even thinking about it now, so many years after the tour, it still swells my heart with pride.

Our operation was given a delay of twenty-four hours or so due to lack of air support. We found out that the Taliban were mounting a surge somewhere nearby and the rumour mill said Now Zad's AO. But all I knew was that the constant artillery fire coming out of FOB Edinburgh could only mean one thing, someone somewhere was in trouble.

In Afghanistan at the time, if air cover was not guaranteed no one patrolled because it normally meant that CASEVAC missions could not be deployed. This would happen for a number of reasons: the weather, if it was misty or there was a chance of a sandstorm, aircraft were grounded, also if the threat level went up, especially from MANPADs (Man Portable Air defence weapons), such as Stinger or the Russian equivalent, the SA-7 Grail. If you couldn't be evacuated should you be injured, you didn't patrol. Simple, but it handed the initiative to the enemy and allowed them freedom of movement and the Taliban were smart enough to realise this.

Finally, the go-ahead was given for the Company to surge south and conduct a clearance of Yatimchay again. We would patrol to PB South, where we would overnight, then patrol south at first light before morning prayers. Our intelligence had suggested that the area of Yatimchay was full of Taliban fighters and Foreign jihadis hell-bent on pushing north to secure Musa Qa'leh.

As we left the DC we turned left and patrolled south towards a crossing in the wadi. We had to pass through a massive field of cannabis and, being quite naïve in the way of drugs, I could not believe how big some of the cannabis plants were! Some were like trees, at least seven feet tall. As soon as you walked through them, the smell of cannabis pervaded your uniform. As we cleared through the field, I saw the large expanse of the wadi running west to east and a large ANP checkpoint six hundred metres to our east covering a crossing point. A large volume of traffic was heading north-south between Yatimchay and Musa Qa'leh. As soon as we got to the wadi it was decided that my Platoon would provide overwatch while the rest of the Company crossed. Once they had crossed, another Platoon would cover us across. I turned around and shouted to Pete Breen, "Pete, bring the L96 up mucker!" Pete Breen sauntered up with the green sniper rifle cradled in his arms. "Mate, I need you to cover the wadi while 10 and 11 get across!" I informed him. He grinned his big boyish grin and gave his section the signal to come forward.

As soon as they were on the north bank of the wadi, extended out left to right, he flicked out the bipod on the sniper rifle and dropped to the prone position. I watched as he limbered up and got into a comfortable position before putting his eye to the Schmidt and Bender scope on top of the rifle.

I stayed at the rear of the Platoon with my reserve section and watched as the remainder of the Company began to file through us before making the approximately two-hundred-metre crossing to the southern bank. We needed to have our edge sharp and awareness shit hot because if the Company got contacted crossing the wadi, we would be there to provide fire support for their extraction from the killing area.

I had an SOP within my Platoon for crossing such open ground: if you were closer to the bank you had just left, go back there; if you were over halfway across the open ground, head for the far bank in fire and movement.

As luck would have it, we crossed without incident and began to patrol south and east towards PB South, the mentored ANA checkpoint. When we arrived, we realised just how nice it was. A pretty modern building surrounded by a high compound wall. The building was three to four storeys high and had a commanding view of the surrounding area.

Once the guys were settled in for the night, I decided to explore the PB but I didn't go without advising the lads to not leave their kit unattended and always have their weapons on them. I did not trust the ANA as far as I could throw them and knew that given half the chance, they would steal our kit.

I began climbing the marble stairs inside the building until I got onto the roof. The architecture looked almost Chinese and I was struck by how agreeable the compound was. No doubt the gentlemen who owned this place was either very rich and had rented the place out to the Afghan government or was extremely pissed that the ANA had had taken over his house for the cause.

I walked up to the parapet, which was sandbagged up. In one corner of the roof was a sandbag position with a 12.7mm Russian Dushka (DShK) heavy machine gun. Sat around it were three bored-looking ANA soldiers who were smoking and giggling like children. Attached to the machine gun was a large belt of huge bullets. If one hit you, you would probably never know about it.

In the other corner was a Russian recoilless rifle, I looked over at it and thought how brilliant this weapon would be at destroying Taliban positions. I looked over at the ANA guys and pointed to the recoilless rifle mimicking firing it, the ANA guys seemed to understand what I was trying to get at and shook their heads.

"No bang!" their Sergeant said in broken English. "No bullet." I thought it was a shame as this weapon could really make a difference. After taking in the sights and looking at my patrol route for the next day, I headed back downstairs. As I got down, I noticed the ANA were lining up for dinner. A little Hazara Sergeant was ladling rice out of a huge cauldron into the bowls of his soldiers as they approached the hole in the wall that was the serving hatch. I couldn't help but notice that the serving hatch had a huge smoke streak all up the wall, as though there had been a huge fire in it, or it had been blown up at some point.

We soon saw the nicer, human side of the Pashtunwali code that Afghanistan was so famous for. Once his troops had been fed, he offered rice to the Company, which the lads gratefully accepted. It was known that Afghans always share what little they have with their guests as part of their code, even if it meant they would go without.

We returned the ANA Sergeant's kindness with gifts of our own, the Platoon chipped in any spare rations, sweets and cigarettes as a thank you to the Afghans for sharing their meal. I caught the little Sergeant's eye and bowed to him with my right hand over my heart. The gesture and the meaning he understood perfectly and his face broke into a wide grin.

As the lads were setting out their sleeping area, Goody came and grabbed me and the other senior NCOs.

"The Ops been postponed again," he said frowning. "SF have put in an Ops box in oor AO that were goan tae the morra. So hang tight, fuck all happenin' fer at least 24 hoors!"

The news was received by my Platoon with mixed reviews, most of us wanted to just get the patrol done and get back to Musa Qa'leh. But a day we were not out on the ground was another day we were not under fire.

A Special Forces Ops box was an area designated by a joint coalition special forces task force (in our case TF-44) that was no-go to green (Non-SF) troops. It could only mean a raid or high-value target hit. We were ordered to stay out the area so that we would not compromise the SF activity in our patrol area, but what it did do having us at PB South was to draw the Taliban's attention away from the Ops box. We were not stupid or naïve enough to believe that the enemy did not know we were in the area.

Their dicking screen would have passed us from Musa Qa'leh all the way to PB South, and you could bet the Taliban knew how many of us there were and also a potential destination for us. But stopping and overnighting at the ANA checkpoint had thrown a spanner in their works that could only have left the Taliban commander asking "Why have they stopped? Where are they going and what the hell are they planning?" But a big part of war is deception and misdirection, something we were good at in Northern Ireland. If you can confuse the enemy spotters, you take the initiative away from them.

I passed an uncomfortable night's sleep on the cold hardpacked ground using my helmet for a pillow and my knee pads as a mattress. It was totally unfeasible to carry sleeping bags and roll mats; these were unnecessary luxuries when you consider how much kit each soldier was carrying already.

The only bonus of a summer tour is that it is still warm at night, so you won't freeze to death under the stars. The temperature at night was actually bearable. I lay on my back listening to lads snore and talk in their sleep.

Day 106

Thursday 24th July: PB South, Musa Qa'leh AO

I awoke with the sun coming up over the PB compound walls. Somewhere in the distance a cockerel began to gob off and was soon joined by others. Wild birds began to chirp loudly and from various little Mosques around the area, the faithful were being called to prayer. I sat up and rubbed the sleep from my eyes and caught sight of the ANA guys all lined up in rows with their prayer mats facing towards Mecca.

I was not a religious man but the sight of all those soldiers practising their faith was quite humbling and I chose to keep quiet so that I would not disturb them. I picked up my helmet and caught a glimpse of the picture I had put inside it.

Most guys had pictures of their families, wives and kids etc, even their pet dogs inside their helmets. But not me, I had cut a picture of Big Brother star Chanelle Hayes from a copy of *Nuts* magazine and put it inside my helmet so that every time I took my helmet off, I would have something pleasant to look at. I had not seen a western woman since R&R, so I had to make do with what I had, and Chanelle was just fine. As I looked at her, I couldn't help but think of another female who was important to me, but sadly not in my life. My estranged daughter Shannon. It was her birthday that day and all I could think of was, 'Was she happy? Would she be spoiled today?' I hoped so.

"No go again the day mucker!" Goody brought me out my reverie, he stood in his UBAC shirt with a cigarette on the go and the sardonic look he always wore. I frowned back at him.

"Fuck sake! Any idea when mate?" I asked, he shook his head and walked away back to where he had slept for the night. I saw no point in waking the lads up, I would let them get up when they wanted. As long as they oiled their weapons and gave them a dust over and had something to eat, I had no issue with that at all.

I learned very early in my career in the infantry, that you sleep whenever you can as you never know when your next decent rest will come. Once again, another old adage seemed to ring true. 'Why run when you can walk? Why walk when you can stand? Why stand when you can sit down? And why sit down when you can sleep?' I totally subscribed to that idea.

Some of the lads were already up and starting to prepare the breakfast I had encouraged them to have. While we were fairly safe to keep their socks and boots off and allow their feet to air, although the Lowa desert boots we were issued were excellent quality, the feet still tended to get hot and sweaty, adding their own set of complications.

As the day wore on, we started to get to know our ANA brothers in arms a bit better. Along the north side of the building was a marble porch and walkway with stairs either side and a black metal rail running its length. The ANA soldiers were sat in the shade of an awning covering the porch drinking tea and talking. A few of my guys along with John, our interpreter, sat talking to the ANA and the Afghan soldiers offered us tea. For those who have not experienced Afghan tea, it is something else, they leave the tea leaves in the glass mugs and use copious amounts of sugar to flavour it. And when I say copious, you can actually see the thick layer of sugar at the bottom of the glass, but I found it surprisingly refreshing.

As we got talking to the ANA soldiers, we realised that there was not a lot of difference between us other than the language barrier. They talked of home and loved ones, wives, children, mothers and fathers. We showed one another pictures of our families and lamented that we were not with them.

The ANA 205th Corps was not called 'The hero Corps' for nothing. Their Brigades were responsible for Kandahar, Helmand, Zabul, Oruzgan and Nimroz provinces. Some of the deadliest areas of operation in Afghanistan. For we Brits, our war lasted for six months, but for the Afghan soldier his war ended with victory or death and sadly for most of them the latter came to be the norm. Most of them told us how they had not been home for at least six months and more shockingly they had not been paid in nearly a year!

I was therefore not surprised that the ANA had desertions, but through it all these men still faced the same hardships we did but did it with the knowledge that their senior officers were corrupt and generally incompetent. Anyone above Platoon commander rank did not go out on the ground even on Kandak (Battalion) or Toli (Company) level operations.

Young Lieutenants and Non-commissioned officers were left to command the operations. A lot of these men had little or no leadership training and their ability to read maps and coordinate a combined Ops battle was non-existent, forcing them to rely on their ISAF advisors. Which for me, did not bode well, should Afghan troops be left to their own devices.

We all knew that at some point, ISAF would leave, and the Afghans would have to fight their war alone. I couldn't help thinking of a similar approach in the 1970s that Richard Nixon called 'Vietnamisation', I was also beginning to draw a parallel between the two ideals.

For years the ANA had been mentored and advised, by 2008 they were starting to look professional and drug use was coming down among ANA soldiers. They were now trading in their old Soviet small arms for more modern American M16s, M-249s and M-240s. I suspected that one of the main reasons for this was that the average poor ANA soldier who had not been paid for months could earn some cash by selling his ammo to the Taliban, ss their weapons fired exactly the same cartridge as the ANA weapons. Switching to American weapons prevented this. The Afghan National Police however had not received the same love and attention, which showed in their high levels of corruption, drug dependency and illiteracy.

As the sun began to set over PB South, we got word that the Company would be deploying tomorrow at 17:00hrs to hopefully be in position before last light in Yatimchay. Which would confuse and confound the Taliban dicking screen. as we knew that other than a few high-level commanders, none of the fighters had night vision equipment.

As we settled in for the evening, the smell of cooking rice and roast mutton began to fill our nostrils and once again, after the Afghan soldiers had been fed, they offered what was left to us. This time I respectfully declined but did have a few cups of tea. Pretty soon after dinner the lively sounds of Afghan music began to drift around the PB and, ever the chance to take the piss, the Jocks thought it would be a great idea to have a dance off with the ANA soldiers. At first the Afghans were utterly confused by the sight of fifteen Westerners with tanned arms and faces gyrating and doing Cossack style dances and, in some cases, old school raving to the sounds of Afghan music. Soon laughter filled the air and the Afghans began to join in, proving that music and dance were a universal language.

Day 107

Friday 25th July: PB South, Musa Qa'leh

This morning we were shown the error of locating our sleeping area where we did; the Afghans decided to do block jobs before we had awakened. The sound of splashing water was our alarm clock followed by the sound of angry Jocks threatening to remove certain body parts as we tried to retrieve our kit from the encroaching tidal wave of soapy water.

My Fijian attachment from the Rifles decided to do his bit for Anglo-Afghan relations by trying to punch the ANA soldier carrying the now empty bucket with a confused look on his face. After grabbing the Fijian and pulling him away, we managed to calm the situation down and apologies were forthcoming. We sat down to breakfast with the ANA, again enjoying some of their flat bread and tea. The rest of the day was spent cleaning weapons and final kit checks before we deployed south into the enemy FLET.

At around 17:30hrs, the Company left the PB by the eastern metal gate and began our turn south towards Yatimchay. We were the last Platoon to leave and as we headed across the open ground the atmospherics on the ground seemed normal with people going about their business. Children were out playing in the fields so we knew a contact at this point was highly unlikely, but not impossible as we also knew that the jungle drums would already have started beating and the Taliban would know we had left the security of the PB.

I turned back to cast a glance at the PB and hoped whoever was on sentry duty on the roof of the PB was 1/ Awake and 2/ Not high as fuck! A 12.7mm Dushka on fire support would be very nice.

We moved further south without incident until we got to the southern end of the small village of Dagyan. As soon as we hit the last set of compounds all hell broke loose. 10 and 11 Platoons, who were up front, started receiving heavy fire and even my Platoon in reserve were starting to draw attention.

As we charged to the cover of a five-foot mud wall the distinctive 'cack-cack-cack ... thump, thump, thump' hit us. The mud compound walls around us took hits from smalls arms fire, but luckily the Taliban had misjudged the distance and the rounds were over our heads.

I skidded to a halt against the wall in front of me and peered in the direction the fire had come from, as though to confirm my hunch we were rewarded with the three distinctive sounds of an RPG being fired. 'Bang ... Fwoosh ... Boom.' As the enemy knew we were in cover they had tried to airburst RPG us.

The first was followed two more. Then more small arms fire: 'cack-cack-cack ... thump, thump, thump'. I started to laugh out loud and Goody looked at me as if I'd lost it. "Whit the fucks say funny?" he asked raising his eyebrows. From my crouched position I looked at him and put on a mock American accent.

"A hiss means it's close, a snap means .... now they're shooting at us!" I began paraphrasing from the film *Black Hawk Down*. Just at that moment, the Taliban got their range and the wall I was leaning against started taking fire and I could feel the impact on the other side through my arms.

Just in front of me was a jagged 'V' cut into the mud wall. Thinking quickly, I removed my bayonet from the end of my rifle and began making the 'V' bigger so that I would not have to expose myself to engage the enemy. Satisfied that I had made a good enough firing port, I pushed my rifle through it and scanned across a patch of open ground between us and a set of compounds. Suddenly through my SUSAT I spotted movement on the roof of a compound around one hundred and fifty metres to our south. I realised that it couldn't be our guys as they were off to the east and besides, these guys were wearing dark clothing and didn't appear to have any patrol packs with them, armour or helmets. I flicked my safety catch off and yelled at the top of my voice, "Watch my tracer!" and began to engage the figures with rapid fire. Through my sight, I could see my tracer strike the top of the compound wall and one of the figures fall out of sight. He did not get back up.

The rest of the lads with me identified where my fire was going largely due to the fact that the magazine on my rifle was always loaded with thirty tracer rounds. Then I loaded the rest of my mags in the following configuration: five tracer, twenty ball, three tracer, then two ball. That way, I would know when I fired tracer again it would mean my magazine was almost empty and I could change it.

I was joined by Scotty with the GPMG and Davey McGhee with his Minimi and they began to suppress the position with me. Once I was happy the lads had it covered, I drew back slightly and listened into the radio. As I looked behind me, I could see the rest of the Platoon in the cover of an irrigation ditch running parallel to the large compound we had been contacted at.

As I listened, 10 and 11 Platoons confirmed they were going in to assault the enemy positions. So, on my call, I upped the rate of fire to keep the heads down of any fighters who had or were thinking of taking up rooftop positions to hit the other units. Soon I could hear the distinctive 'thump' of hand grenades exploding and in the failing light could see our sister Platoons moving across a small path near where I had engaged the enemy.

"Watch and shoot!" I called to my gunners. "Watch and shoot!" I took the chance to check the magazine I had on my rifle, on looking into it I could see I had fired quite a lot of ammo and I decided to change it for a fresh one.

As suddenly as the fighting had started, silence fell upon the area and I could hear NCOs in the other Platoons shouting out orders to their men. I never found out whether I had killed the fighter on the roof as the enemy took the bodies away where they were able to.

There were reports of blood on the roof of that compound which made me feel relief, I had taken a fighter out the game. Killed or seriously wounded, but I hoped killed. As it got dark, we began to move into night defensive positions within our immediate area.

As per our SOPs we got in and stood to on the compound walls until it got dark, then Al Lipowski and I sited night sentry positions and made sure the guys were in cover for the night. The ICOM was still alive with enemy chatter, their commander telling the surviving fighters to stay where they were and attack at first light.

Throughout the night, rocket flares shot up from our compounds and from the other Platoons an occasional burst of fire would disrupt the peace and quiet. The parachute flares were augmented by mortar illumination rounds from Musa Qa'leh. 'Whump ... whump ... whump' as the mortar round separated and the large flare inside the illumination round bathed the area in bright light. The Taliban were on the move, trying to sneak into ambush points under the cover of darkness but what they forgot was that we had night vision equipment and would spot them moving.

Day 108

Saturday 26th July: Southern End of Dagyan Village, Musa Qa'leh

We stood to in the morning for first light and the planned attack by the enemy did not materialise. We decided he had had enough for one day and had perhaps withdrawn to the south to rest and rearm. The lads all ate a cold breakfast and began to sort out their admin for the patrol that day.

I had fired my weapon, so I stripped it down before I did anything else and pulled it through, gave my gas parts a scrub and heavily oiled the inside of the rifle. Once I was happy, I put it back together, put my mag back on and chambered a round, then I sat the rifle down on my kit.

I took in a deep breath, held it for a short while then exhaled. I wiped the thin layer of sweat that, despite the early morning air, had already started to form on my forehead. It was first light, I looked around the compound we had secured the previous evening. It's low, brown, crumbling walls had given us cover throughout the night.

Still, I hadn't slept much. We never did, especially when we knew we were surrounded. The brain is always occupied, a primitive need to constantly be on guard for danger that never fully allows you to shut down.

We had been out on the ground for three days now and it was time to give the enemy a false sense of security. We were to fake our withdrawal by heading north out of the compound. Our task had been to push the enemy out of the area and we had succeeded, it was time to head back in. Mournfully the Mosques in the local area had begun to call the faithful to morning prayers, at least this would keep the enemy busy while we ran through our first light stand to and pre-patrol administration.

I looked over to my reserve section, gathered near a collapsed, roofless building. I made my way over in the low light, walking carefully over the boulder-strewn ground. My boys looked at me as I approached. They knew I had the latest from the orders group, and I could tell they were waiting to hear what was going to be asked of them that day.

Pete, the section commander, stood up. His combats were dirty after being on patrol for two days. They hung off him. He, like the rest of us, had lost an uncomfortable amount of weight since arriving in country. Despite having normally been a big lad, he was still as strong as an ox and I trusted him with my life.

"George," Pete said in a hushed tone. "Whit's the plan mucker?" I stopped short, keeping all the boys in my field of view.

"SITREP no change mate... Prep your kit boys," I said. "We're moving out." I saw the two Daves grow a few inches as they filled their lungs with the dry, dusty air. "We're continuing with the fake withdrawal. Go to ground for a while as the other Platoons re-org, then head east as a deception before making our way back to base, if Terry has a go at us, he gets it fucking back."

"Cool," said Pete in his unshakable style. "Are we still in reserve? Them fuckers are all round us mate."

"I know mucker," I raised an eyebrow. "We're still reserve. So, Goody and Andy P will be with us."

"How long we got mate?" asked Dave Pods rubbing his three-day old stubble with his gloved hand.

"We're oot of here in twenty mate." As reservist, Dave didn't even have to be there. As a volunteer he had taken the time out from his normal life to fight in Afghanistan. He jumped from operational tour to operational tour, that alone demanded respect. "Get some scoff doon yer neck and take on some water, it's gonnae git fucking hot oot there the day."

"Nay dramas mucker," said Pete. "Get yourselves ready to move." With that, the boys clambered to their feet and started their morning routine. I didn't need to micromanage these boys, they were pros. I moved over to my own equipment. I fumbled in my daysack for my rations. I pulled out the silver foil packet. I sighed quickly as I read the 'sausage and beans' print on the side.

'Fucks sake,' I ripped open the packet. I hated breakfast rations. As we were on hard routine, we couldn't light fires, so all food was to be eaten cold. I folded the packet in half and began squeezing the contents down my throat. I chewed the hard-baked beans and soft, mushy cocktail sized sausages. I tried to swallow without tasting, though admittedly of all the ration pack breakfasts, sausage and beans was the nicest and corned beef hash by far the worst. I washed it all down with water from my issue water bottle. I looked around as covertly as I could to make sure the lads were squaring themselves away. I needn't have bothered; they knew what they needed to do. We'd been together through training and the previous three months on Ops, I watched with pride as the boys sorted their kit out.

I folded the now empty silver foil packet into a small square and slid it into one of the pouches on my body armour. I hoisted the armour over my head and velcro'd it into place. I smelled the moist sweat from the previous days that hadn't managed to dry due to the high humidity. I squirmed in an attempt to make the armour settle into a comfortable position. I searched for the radio earpiece dangling freely from the set. I found it and placed it into my ear. I pressed the pressel to hear the comforting bleeps that meant it was working, far too often comms was a deadly problem. Next, I looked down at my daysack. My shoulders ached so much from its weight, I really didn't want to pick it up. It bulged; its seams almost bursting. Radios, batteries, 51mm mortar rounds, extra ammo, water, red phos and more all added up to nearly fifty kilograms all in. But I would never complain as all the boys carried similar loads. I swung it over my shoulders and took the weight, I stood up as straight as I could. Fuck the discomfort.

I looked over my left shoulder, the boys were at the same state as I was, sets of bright white eyes and teeth greeted me through grimy faces as I looked around the Platoon, I smiled a wry smile in anticipation of the day ahead. A pang of excitement shot through my body, or was it nervousness. Hard to tell. Around the compound I saw the other sections preparing to move.

John walked over to us through the dusty haze. His mixture of military and civilian clothing made him stand out, stony-faced and oozing confidence. I tapped the top of my head with the palm of my hand signalling 'on me'. He sauntered over as cool as ever.

This man I trusted. I had no choice. He would listen to ICOM chatter and give us the heads-up if something was about to happen. He was an interpreter for U.S. special forces and his father was a colonel with the Afghan army. When his father was murdered by the Taliban, he had volunteered to help us, he hated the enemy and that's why we loved him. He was a Godsend.

"John mate!" We shook hands, gripping as if our lives depended on it. "Glad you're with us mate. Ready?" He nodded as if what we were about to undertake was nothing at all. The wry smile from before returned, although this time I couldn't contain it. John, almost, smiled.

I put on my helmet and clipped the leather chinstrap into place. The damp chinstrap, still soaked with sweat, squelched on my chin. I always hated that. But, again, I'd never complain.

"OK boys," I said, for the first time speaking at a normal volume. "let's join the column." Lead Platoon with the Officer Commanding was preparing to leave the compound. We watched as they left the safety of the walls. This was always the most dangerous part of a patrol. The enemy had all night to set an ambush or place IEDs for us. We waited with bated breath.

Soon enough it was our time to move. We left the compound in staggered formation; I waved my hand indicating I wanted more spacing between my lads. Fighting the human urge to bunch up, they gave extra space between each man. That the lead section hadn't come under contact didn't mean we wouldn't. I felt the tension build in my guts.

The locals, who by now had finished morning prayers, were going about their daily routine moving around the small village. I caught the eyes of several men dressed in black wearing turbans, the look in their eyes was one of utter hatred. I knew who they were, everyone did but without weapons and positive identification, there was fuck all I could do about it. As there were women and children around, I figured they would not start anything just yet.

I looked left and right, watching the other sections move to their lying up points as we moved to ours. We cautiously approached our assigned field. A dry poppy field, it was cleared ready to plant the maize that would soon cover the area in eight-foot-tall green stalks. I moved us to an extended line formation as we approached. I took a knee and the lads followed suit. I studied the area, taking in all that was around us.

'There's fuck-all cover' I thought to myself. Ahead of us, across the field at about thirty metres, was another two compounds with a narrow walkway between the two. I didn't like the look of that gap. The only available cover was a shallow irrigation ditch lining the field.

"In the ditch boys," I said. "Bound out, I want plenty of spacing between us." I looked at the field stretched out ahead of me. "Watch your arcs boys."

The field had squared-out bun lines dotted across the cracked, dry mud. I had to get some front cover out, covering the obvious line of attack from between the two compounds.

"Davey," I said. "Get out there, use the bun lines as cover." I pointed with my open hand, towards the gap. Davey McGhee knew what I needed. He moved, keeping low, into position and un-clipped the bi-pod of his Minimi and went prone. I saw him place the section weapon stock into his shoulder and set it into place.

I looked left and right at my boys, each observing their areas of interest over the top of their weapons. I wiped the dust from my lips with the back of my glove. Still, I could feel the grit crunching between my teeth. There was nothing I could do about it. Goody approached our position from behind, keeping low as he moved. He slid into the ditch, stopping next to me.

"Alright George," said Goody. "How're yer boys holding up?" Goody looked tired, but we all did. Following behind, Andy Pettiford, our team medic joined us in the ditch.

"Aye No bad mate," I said looking at the compound we had just left. Locals were starting their daily work whilst children played. "That's a good combat indicator." I motioned towards the civvies with my head.

"Aye they fuckers would nae shoot with weans about," said Goody. The locals knew what's going on around them, if they were hanging around it generally meant nothing was going to go down. "Whit the fuck are they retards daein?"

I looked in the direction Goody was talking about. Two Afghan Police officers had settled themselves down in the middle of the field directly ahead of us. They'd both put their weapons down on the hard-impacted mud and sat on their arses.

"Who knows why those guys do anything they do, they're probably aff their tits," I said. "John," I called out. "Get they two oot eh there." John began a dialogue with the two Police officers, but they looked uninterested.

"You alright Davey?" I was concerned about Davey McGhee out on front cover. He was using whatever cover he found, but he looked too exposed. He didn't look away from his weapon sights, he simply raised one hand and give a thumbs-up.

A young local boy and his father slowly approached us from the compound to our rear. The young boy had a tray with tea and some sort of local sweets on it. They offered us some, but we politely refused. They walked through our position and joined the two Police Officers in the field.

"Fucking mental," said Goody shaking his head. "We're gonnea be moving oot soon, heading east. ICOM thinks there are Taliban moving aroond trying tae work out whit we're dayin. But for noo, jist be ready. OK?"

"Yeah, just let me know and I'll pull Davey back in." Goody acknowledged with a nod.

"Is that yer arse?" Goody said changing the subject, the smell of human shit that the local farmers used for fertiliser was overpowering as the sun started to come fully up.

"Maybe! I have no had a shite for two days." Suddenly my attention was drawn to something off to the east. "Do you hear that?" I squinted trying to work out what I had heard.

"Soonds like bikes," said Goody. "That's they fuckers cuttin aboot."

"And where are they going?" The young boy and his father had left the Police in the field and hurried back towards their compound.

"Aye," said Goody. "Here we fuckin go." I could feel the atmosphere change. Within seconds there were no civilians around. "Get Davey back in, we're getting oot eh here."

"Davey!" I shouted. "On me, and bring they two mutants with yae." I watched as Davey collapsed his position, stood up and headed back towards the ditch. He motioned to the Police to follow him, but they didn't bother. "Alright lads, move!"

I stood up, hauling the weight of my body armour and daysack with me. For some reason I felt the need to look to my right and as I did, I saw a dark shape moving fast but still visible. I heard the pop and whoosh. The dark oblong shape screamed past from right to left, I could feel it. "RPG!" I shouted.

Dust and shrapnel filled the air, a thick brown cloud completely obstructed my vision. I, as well as the other lads, had instinctively dived back into the ditch for cover. My ears rang from the concussion of the blast. My lungs filled with dry dust as I dragged in air in an attempt to gain control of the disorientation in my head.

'Holy fuck,' I thought shaking my head and blinking my eyes. I could feel the grit clogging my eyelids shut. All feelings of fatigue had gone, Adrenaline was coursing through my veins. My heart pounded in my chest, I could feel the blood pumping past my ears. I waited for the ringing to stop, it felt like a lifetime but was only a matter of seconds. As it subsided, the sound of my own heavy breathing was all I heard over the silence. From my crouched position I peeked over the ridge of the ditch towards the two buildings across the field from our position.

"Is everyone OK? Sound off!" I shouted; my throat caked dry. As I spoke the whole world seemed to open up on us. The air around us filled with lead, I could feel it crack overhead and thump into the dirt, that 'cack-cack-cack … thump-thump-thump', a confirmation that the Taliban were zeroing in on us. I could tell it was 7.62 rounds, either AK-47 or PKM. I saw the muzzle flashes through the haze of billowing dust still swirling from the explosion. It was coming from the buildings and passageway only twenty or so metres ahead of us. We were taking accurate enemy fire.

"Is anyone injured?" I shouted over the deafening incoming fire. I needed to know the state of my men if I was to take any action against the enemy. From the ditch I heard a chorus of nos. Then silence. My heart skipped a beat then sank.

"McGhee's hit," I heard from my left. "He's fucked. He's fucking fucked!" I didn't think about what to do next, I felt such a deep-rooted responsibility for the boys. I gripped my SA80 rifle and slid out of the ditch. I kept as low as possible and ran down the dust track towards McGhee's position.

The firing intensified and I got the feeling that all the Taleban in Helmand were trying to hit me and were bracketing me with fire, ahead and behind. I no longer heard the crack of the rounds; they were getting more accurate. Bursts of 7.62 hit the building the young boy had come out of, narrowly missing me. I sprinted past Tam, still in the ditch. He looked up as my boots pounded past his head, his eyes wide with shock and surprise.

"George!" he shouted. "They're shooting at you!" I continued towards the sounds of distress.

"Tell me something I don't fucking know!" I yelled back. I spotted McGhee in the ditch with Pods. I slid back into the cover of the ditch and turned my back towards the enemy. The ditch, at this part, was so shallow I was still on show to the incoming fire. And that meant so were my boys.

Pods was doing his best to help Davey McGhee. He was covered in McGhee's blood and had his torso resting on his thighs as he worked on his friend. Davey McGhee was still conscious; he was drenched in blood but was pale from the shock.

"George," he said looking up at me. "You've gotta get me oot eh here." The look of fear and pain evident in his stare.

"Don't worry wee man," I said. "Ahv got ye." He had been peppered with shrapnel and had obviously taken the brunt of the blast. The sleeves of his shirt were soaked with blood, I ripped them open. I needed to see what I had in front of me.

"Am I all right?" asked Davey as he coughed through the pain he was feeling. "Is it bad?"

"Fuck!" I said when I saw the state of his arms. They were so sliced open I could see the muscles. I worried about the extent of his other injuries. I looked past Pods and saw a doorway, the doorway the young boy and his father had used. At the metal door, blasted open by the RPG strike, I saw Goody and Andy Pettiford. I knew they would provide cover if I needed it. A stray round impacted on the mound behind me, showering me in dirt and making me instinctively duck. We couldn't work on Davey where we were, we had to move him.

"There!" I shouted and pointed. "That doorway, let's move him. Now!" Pods and I grabbed an arm each and hauled McGhee from the ditch and dragged him over the gravel towards the blasted open compound. Davey groaned the whole way as his wounded body was dragged to the safest area I could see.

We bounded into the compound and, in a controlled manner, fell to the ground with Davey. We laid him on his back and I checked his level of consciousness. I could see he was still breathing, I wiped blood away from his eyes with my thumb and his eyes opened, they flicked straight to me. We made eye contact.

"Andy's here mate," I said as Pettiford took over the care of the casualty. I patted the medic on the shoulder and pulled myself to my feet and headed over to where Goody held the compound entrance. I still had men out on the ground, they were still under contact. I left the safety of the smashed compound and sprinted back over to the irrigation ditch.

I took up a standing firing position on the edge of the ditch, pulled the rifle into my shoulder and leaned forward in the direction of threat. I pulled the trigger and let loose a volley of shots, single fire but so rapid it could have been set to automatic.

"Lads peel left!" I shouted. "Peel left." Under the cover of fire, the boys began to withdraw along the cover of the ditch and into the compound where McGhee was receiving first aid. One after another they leapfrogged to the compound entrance. I knew I was about to run dry. When I did, I began a magazine change. I dropped the used mag into my drop pouch and inserted a fresh one into the housing of my rifle. I reached over the rifle and knocked back the cocking handle, allowing the working parts to slide forward. I looked up at the two buildings, where the fire was coming from. I saw a muzzle flash from the passageway between the two. I tapped the cocking handle forward to ensure the first round was in the breech correctly and opened fire again.

I heard the most God-awful shriek come from the direction of the muzzle flash. It immediately occurred to me I may have taken my second life in twenty-four hours. I dismissed the thought almost as quickly as it came to me and carried on firing until the last of the lads was on the move. I joined onto the tail of the extraction and ran towards the compound. Goody was still in the entrance providing cover.

Pete Breen stopped short in the ditch and began to prep a 66. As opposed to the old, green Vietnam-era weapons, these newer grey tubes were known as Light Anti Structure Munition. They had a little more punch to them.

"I'm gonna hit 'em with a 66!" he said as I dropped to a crouch, still eyeing up the enemy position. He pulled out the safety pin and popped open the tube. The weapon's sights flicked up and he placed the elongated tube over his shoulder and peered through the sights. He let it go and it thudded into the ground just before the compound. Despite the situation I let out a loud laugh, "Fuck me Pete, that wiz a waste u a 66! Saves them digging this field up noo dunt it?" Sheepishly Pete ran along the ditch towards me, his face flushed with exertion – or embarrassment.

I peeled into the crumbling building followed by Pete, Davey was being worked on by Andy Pettiford and Pods. It looked like they had used everything they had, tourniquets, blast bandages and Israeli emergency bandages. Due to the nature of his injuries, Davey had to have all his clothes removed and be made what is termed 'trauma naked'.

He was wrapped up like an Egyptian mummy with Israeli pressure dressing on every major bleed, and there were many. I was concerned that we were going to have to dip into our own personal IFAKs for more dressings, but Andy Pettiford had this in the bag and was doing what he could to ease Davey's pain and blood loss, poor Davey looked completely out of it. I reckoned that Andy had given him a decent shot of morphine.

The old man from earlier was running around trying to help, offering us water. Some accepted the help, others batted him away like an annoying fly. I was suddenly struck by how the compound was lush and green, a stark contrast to the surrounding countryside. The old man must have worked hard on his land to have it like that. I didn't see his little boy.

"We've still got troops oot there," shouted Goody from his position in the doorway. "11 Platoon are pinned doon, still in contact."

I could hear the firing coming from a location slightly further south where I knew 10 and 11 Platoon had advanced.

"We're gonnae get some fuckin fire doon on they c**ts." Just as Goody finished speaking, a message came across the radio.

"Stand by, stand by." The signal vibrated through my earpiece. "105 light guns incoming from FOB Edinburgh," courtesy of Captain John Axel and his Fire Support Team (FST). I moved over to Goody's side and peered out into the contact area. A low rumble could be heard overhead as the first rounds came in.

"That sounds really fucking close mate," I said, my eyebrows knotting slightly in confusion. The rounds sounded really low and I could tell that there was something not quite right. I waited in silence with Goody for the impact. We saw and heard the explosions, a dark pall of smoke rising up in the near distance. "Christ, that's way too fucking close."

"Check fire, check fire." The radio burst into life. This time it was our boys, not the artillery at FOB Edinburgh. "Blue on blue. Blue on blue. Men down."

"George," said Goody over his shoulder. "Take three guys, clear an emergency landing site." I acknowledged by bursting into action. My heart dropped, we had gone from having a single casualty to four casualties, three of which from our own artillery. My concern for the safety of the boys in the other Platoon was mounting, you generally don't take a direct hit from a 105mm round and live to tell the tale.

"You, you and you." I said indicating to three random men. "On me." I moved through the crisp, green compound for the area directly behind it. I was hoping there would be at least some cover from fire for the evac chopper.

I scanned quickly to see if there was a better evac point, there wasn't. Directly behind the compound we were occupying was an empty poppy field, its crop having been harvested it was wide and open. The square scooped-out fields provided a small lip of dirt we could use as cover to protect the incoming choppers from any flanking move by the enemy. My Platoon were already in a good enough position to cover an arc, south, west and east, I could leave a fireteam on the ground to hold it and cover north, north-west and north-east; luckily the western side of the LZ I had chosen was screened by thick green trees, which would give a good bit of cover from view.

As I moved, I could hear guys sending messages across the radio net. MIST reports and 9 liners being sent back to HQ. I knew MERT would be lifting off if it hadn't already.

"There," I indicate towards an area of flat ground. "Clear that area, sweep it for IEDs lads." The boys started on my orders immediately.

"Casualties coming in." Someone shouted from the edge of the compound. I held up my hand to tell them to stop at the edge whilst the boys swept with mine detectors. I saw Davey McGhee laid on a makeshift stretcher with Goody and Andy by his side. Also there, I saw the 11 Platoon casualties. The Platoon commander, Sergeant and a 51mm mortar man were down with blast injuries.

I could hear a chopper, I looked skywards but couldn't see it, but the deep thud of its rotor blades beating the air was obvious. It would have been way too low to be seen and the sound of its rotors were deceptive, you could gauge what compass point the chopper was coming from, but it was hard to pinpoint, which was paramount to avoid incoming ground fire.

"George," shouted one of the three guys I had chosen to clear the HLS. "It's done, it's clear."

"OK," I said waving them over. "Get to the casualties. Get ready to get them on the chopper." I popped smoke as I knew the chopper was close and would see the contents of the canister, I lobbed it near to the cleared site. Slowly the purple cloud began to whisp up into the air, showing our position.

At tree top level. The Chinook evac helicopter flew overhead clearing the smoke with its downwash. It spun in the air and lowered its tail ramp. It would want to be on the ground as little time as possible. It landed quickly and hard, its suspension absorbing the impact.

The rotors were throwing up a cloud of dust mixed with purple smoke, forcing everyone in the CASEVAC party to drop their eyes to the floor, the dust and dirt being thrown up by the downdraft was like millions of tiny bullets striking the exposed areas of skin. I ran back over to where the casualties were. Davey was on a poncho; I was shocked to see him grinning away. As I grabbed a corner of the poncho, I jammed Daveys' helmet on his head and it was then I noticed just how much of the blast he had taken, the front of his helmet looked as though someone had taken a cheese grater to the front of it, scoring the Kevlar and scorching the desert camouflaged cover. I wrapped my hand into the material of it, I didn't want to let it go as we moved.

"We need to spin him round," said Andy Pettiford above the noise. "He needs to go in feet first." We lifted and slowly rotated him round, then headed towards the chopper. The Chinook's security team had disembarked and was forming a semi-circle around the tail of the chopper.

We carried him up the tail ramp and into the belly of the airframe, the smell of different types of oils and lubricants assailing my nostrils over the overpowering smell of aviation fuel. We lowered him down slowly and Andy began a quick handover to the on-board medic, I could see him yelling into the ear of the doctor on board, who was wearing a flight crew helmet; occasionally I would see the doctor nodding in acknowledgement. I looked down at Davey, still gurning. He raised a thumb and smiled at me.

"Hiya mucker," he slurred. "We'll git a brew back at Bastion." Confused, I smiled back, patted him on the shoulder and left him lying on the floor of the helicopter. We all left the chopper and watched the security team file back in before the chopper took off leaving us in an other-worldly silence. I found myself stood next to Goody and Andy, who had also helped to carry Davey McGhee onto the chopper.

"Git a brew," I said looking over at Andy. "He'll be back in the UK within the next day or so."

"He was so off his tits on morphine," said Andy shrugging. "He didn't know what he was saying."

"Fucking hell mate," I said noticing Goody holding his upper left arm and wincing in pain. "Are you alright?"

"Aye nay dramas mucker," he said as Andy took control of the arm and ripped open the sleeve. "I took a wee bit eh shrapnel back there. It's hee haw."

"That ain't nothing," said Andy un-rolling a bandage. "You should be on that chopper with the rest of the casualties."

"What? And leave you fuckin retards here by yersells? Nay danger."

"Come with me," said Andy leading Goody back into the old man's compound. "I need to clean this up."

I looked back towards the chopper and watched it disappear into the distant haze. I took a deep breath of dry, dusty air, held it then exhaled quickly. I looked down at my hands, my gloves were covered in blood that had rapidly dried in the heat, Davey's blood I guessed. I noticed them shaking slightly as the adrenaline began to wear off and fatigue started to set in again. My heart pounded in my chest and my head throbbed. I thought back to what had just happened, what I had just witnessed. My thoughts shifted to Davey on that chopper, how we had nearly lost him. I wished him all the best. Then I thought, that could have been me.

As I watched the Chinook disappear into the distance, I could still hear the pop of small arms fire from the south-east. 10 Platoon were still fighting and now we had been joined by the ANA from PB South and their Royal Irish advisors. Given the volume of fire they could hear, the ANA seemed reluctant to push any further south, but the Royal Irish lads made it clear that staying where they were or falling back was not an option. So, they pushed forward again.

From my vantage point on the compound wall I could see the ANA fanning out into their Platoon and section groups ready to assault the Taliban, and now the artillery had been corrected I could hear the displacement of air overhead that followed the passage of a 105mm artillery round. This time the sound was different showing that the trajectory was different, and as I followed the sound with my head all the way to its intended target, I saw the flashes and smoke billow up from where the artillery had struck.

My thoughts were with our wounded now and the guys of 11 Platoon, the MFC (Mortar Fire Controller) Cpl Jeffries, nicknamed 'Fish', had gone from a fire support role to Platoon Commander in the space of seconds. It was something we always trained for and practised on leadership courses, our instructors in Brecon on Section commander's and Platoon Sergeant's battle courses always said "You are always only a bullet away from command!" Fish had now learned this first-hand, the look of shock on his face still lives with me now.

The ANA took over the fight for Yatimchay and Dagyan from us and it was a very sombre D Company that headed back north towards Musa Qa'leh at the end of that patrol.

There was a good chance that young Davey McGhee would not be coming back due to the severity of his injuries and indeed, it was a long time before I saw him again. Sadly, he is still suffering now fifteen years after the tour.

Danny Carter was extremely lucky, a piece of shrapnel that would have ripped into his thigh was instead absorbed by a red army issue plastic notebook he kept in the thigh pocket of his combat trousers. Cass Cassidy, a mere boy whose mother had hidden his passport from him so that he could not go to Afghanistan, only relenting after he told her she would land him in severe trouble, lost the use of his hand when shrapnel from the 105mm round severed the tendons in his wrist.

Jim Trickey had taken a large piece of shrapnel to the inner thigh and it was only on closer inspection of the wound that we realised how close he come to bleeding out. The shrapnel had almost cut the femoral artery. Jim we would not see again, he would be replaced by Charlie Grant and Jim would eventually leave the Army.

There were a lot of questions asked about how a blue on blue like this could occur. This mistake had decapitated a Platoon nearly killing its commanders and the Fire Support Team. The explanation was very simple and maddening. In Afghanistan, for accuracy with our fire support, we would give the ten-figure grid reference of our location and then give the corrections to the enemy position e.g. "Zero this is three zero Alpha, Fire mission *my grid* 59467 90012, direction two-zero Mils magnetic, distance to enemy four hundred metres, enemy in compound, destroy in one minute for five minutes."

Unfortunately, the crew in the Op's room decided to ignore the fact that there were troops in contact and were conducting a shift relief, so the only information received by the gun line at FOB Edinburgh was the ten-figure grid reference of Capt Axcell's GPS reading. Consequently, the first 105mm round fired hit the compound wall above 11 Platoon's command team as they were giving quick battle orders (QBOs).

Capt Axcell went into a sullen, dark mood blaming himself for what had happened and took all the guilt for 11 Platoon's casualties on his own shoulders. No one in the Company ever blamed John Axcell for what had happened, he was an exceptional FOO and would go on to prove it as the tour only got deadlier.

Goody, even though wounded by shrapnel and having every right to be evacuated with the other four casualties, refused to be moved out and continued as he had begun the operation, shouting, swearing and smoking his way round Dagyan.

I believe he should have been mentioned in despatches for that.

Day 110

Monday 28th July: Musa Qa'leh DC

It was still a very subdued Company that prepared for our next operation. We missed Wee Davey a lot and it was with a heavy heart that we had sanitised his bedspace and packed all his kit for back loading to Bastion, and eventually to Canterbury. Every time we passed by the empty cot bed and mozzie net that belonged to him, it brought it all back to us. Our only consolation being that at least he was still alive and would no doubt be on his way back to Selly Oak Hospital in Birmingham, where all our wounded went.

We were heading north this time; our objective was an area known to us as Hajji Rashid Gardens, or simply the Gardens. This was the Taliban front line to the north of Musa Qa'leh and as soon as you reached the 83 Northing on the map, you were guaranteed a firefight of epic proportions.

So, as we prepared ourselves, we tried not to think about the Battalion's predictions for our dead and wounded for this tour. Was it starting to come true? We had taken our first severe casualties. Technically only one of those could be attributed to enemy action, but still men were being wounded and the tour was nowhere near over.

We ran through the usual pre patrol checks, making sure our night sights all had batteries and that we had spares to last us at least three days. We made sure we had enough rations and enough water to last until resupply. Those of us who needed to replenish our ammunition from the last patrol, did so. I looked at my armoured vest, on the front I had my magazine pouches and I had bought spares. I now carried ten full magazines on my vest and in my patrol pack I carried two green canvas bandoliers with clips of 5.56mm ammo, each bandolier contained another one-hundred and fifty rounds of 5.56mm totalling six hundred rounds. In addition to this I carried two L109 HE hand grenades, one smoke screening grenade (white smoke to aid movement) on my vest and on my pack I had three smoke signalling, a different coloured smoke to allow us to identify ourselves to air support or one another on the battlefield. Also, one Red Phosphorous grenade which kicked out a large cloud of smoke but also deadly burning phosphorous that burned though most things and had to be submerged in water then removed with a blade or a stick. If you tried to remove it with bare hands, the phosphorous would transfer to you and keep burning.

I checked this against my Platoon Ammo casualty card and then went around checking on my boys to see how their ammunition level fared with what I had written down. Any amendments were made so that when I went to Goody to brief him on what I had, he knew where the Company stood in its ability to sustain a firefight.

Satisfied that all the pre-op admin was in place, we received a full set of orders from Nick about the upcoming patrol. It would be a combined Op with us the ANA and 2 SCOTS Mastiff Company all deploying to designated locations and surging into the enemy's safe areas; or so he thought.

Joining us would be members of the Battlegroup headquarters, the cynical part of me wondered if it was a sightseeing trip or whether they had come to lend us a hand! After the orders were over, we relaxed and readied ourselves mentally for tomorrow and the coming operation.

Day 111

Tuesday 29th July: North of Musa Qa'leh

As soon as we left the DC, the ICOM chatter started. The dicking screen was in place and no doubt they would be counting us out of the DC and letting their commander know direction of travel and numbers of troops going out. The only thing we could do was use the ground to our advantage and stay hidden – as much as one hundred heavily armed Jocks can hide themselves.

The enemy kept describing us and gave each other a running commentary.

"We will take them in the gardens! Bring the pineapples up to give them a warm welcome," the commander would say cryptically, but we all knew it was code for explosives.

I had to admit, listening to the ICOM chatter was worse than actually being under fire. At least when the fighting kicked off, all pretence of security was lifted by the enemy and they started to plain speak on their radios. Letting us know where they were. And the bonus of them firing at us was we had a good indication of where their firing points were and could hit them hard.

The advance north was uneventful until we hit the 83 Northing and as predicted, the shit hit the fan. We were on the enemy FLET but at this point it wasn't D Company being singled out for the love. The Mastiff Company in the wadi to our north-west had hit an IED, which had blown one wheel off and burst the other tyre, rendering it immobile.

The enemy followed up with RPG and small arms fire, which was returned with gusto. I could hear the chunky sounds of the .50 calibre machine guns on the Mastiffs firing their destructive large rounds and the 'bloop ... bloop ... bloop' of grenade machine guns hurling 40mm grenades at the enemy positions; hopefully riddling them with shrapnel and forcing the enemy to flee. Potentially into the waiting arms of D Company, as we pushed up through the Green Zone towards Hajji Rashid.

As we came to a patch of open ground, Nick called a halt to the Company and I pushed my lads into cover and they all adopted fire positions watching their arcs for fleeing or reinforcing enemy fighters. As I took in my surroundings, I realised that we were in a small orange orchard and the fruit looked nice and ripe. I took the chance to sit down and take a sip of water, as I lay on my back propped up on my daysack I looked up at the sky and took a deep breath. John came running around the Platoon with oranges from the trees.

"Sir, would you like an orange?" he asked. I smiled at him and reached up a gloved hand to accept the offered fruit. As I lay back basking in the warm sun and glad that I wasn't being shot at, I began to break my orange in two parts. As I bit into the fruit, it tasted bitter as hell but as it was the first orange I had tasted in a while, I was going to finish it.

Suddenly the branches in the tree above me began to disintegrate and a stream of green tracer flashed through its boughs covering in me in leaves and bark. The distinctive cacks and thumps echoed around the orchard. The lads started to get into better fire positions but still remained covering all arcs in case the enemy tried to flank us. I put on my helmet and hauled myself to my feet. Grabbing my rifle, I walked around my lads.

"Keep your eyes peeled boys! Everybody okay?" I asked, I was met with nodding heads and choruses of "Aye George, all good." I found myself standing over a ditch where the officers of the battlegroup HQ were huddled.

"Sirs," I said, "there are five rifles in this ditch that could be more useful covering an arc!" I paused to await their reaction, suddenly remembering that my tone may have come off as somewhat insubordinate. "Can I suggest you push into some cover where you can best use those rifles? If you haven't been hit in the first five seconds you're not going to be unless you do something stupid."

Sheepishly the officers moved around until they were in amongst our forward platoon, covering an arc of fire. The rounds were still coming into the orchard but now they were being returned by our guys. I came up to a dyke wall covering open ground to the north where the enemy had taken root and were engaging us. I peered out over the open field at a number of compounds to our front in an L-shape, hoping to catch a glimpse of the enemy and help suppress their positions, but nothing was visible, no smoke, no muzzle flashes and no suggestion of any movement by enemy fighters.

As I dropped back behind the dyke I caught sight of a new lad who had only just joined the Company, he was propped up against the dyke covered in mud with a pale look of fear on his face.

"Welcome to Musa Qa'leh wee man!" I said patting him on the shoulder before walking back to my position with my Platoon.

The enemy however, melted away soon after. The heavy weight of return, accurate fire had no doubt blunted the Taliban's enthusiasm for a scrap and they were surely heading back to the north to sanctuaries in the villages of Big Kats and Small Kats. We continued pushing north until we found compounds good enough to occupy for the night.

The next morning, we awoke and stood to in silence. An expected enemy counterattack never happened, as I guessed the enemy had taken quite a beating the day before. There were no reports of enemy dead from either the ANA operations or from the Mastiff Company, but they had engaged the enemy with heavy fire and received heavy fire at the same time.

We figured the Taliban would be ballsy enough to try and infiltrate fighters as close as possible to us, but as we stood to on the building roofs inside our compound the lads were on full alert. Everyone laid flat on the roofs presenting as low a silhouette as possible, tense fingers hovered over triggers waiting for AK fire to burst from the treelines and ditches surrounding our compound.

As the sun started to come up, our noses were assaulted by the smells of Afghanistan, animal and human waste that was used to fertilise the fields, our own sweat, and the sappy smell of carbon and gun oil. The call to prayer echoed out across the area from a number of small Mosques and we could see people start to move around. Little palls of smoke rising up from some of the surrounding compounds told us people were cooking breakfast. The smell of burning wood soon reached us, too, adding to the mix of odours.

We could see men in groups of two and three strolling along in their loose-fitting shirts and trousers, some had scarfs or small blankets thrown around their shoulders and in their hands they carried prayer beads. We never saw any women with them, just men and boys on their way to pray.

As soon as we had completed our morning routine, it was time for the Company to begin patrolling back south to Musa Qa'leh. This happened without incident, apart from when I passed a small boy stood in a compound doorway. I waved to him and as soon as I turned my back, I felt a sharp pain in my arm that sent hot needles of pain all through my arm and neck. The little bastard had hit me with a catapult and done a runner. He was learning fast I thought, it wouldn't be long before the catapult was swapped for an AK and he would be firing at us. Possibly in some show of misguided loyalty or perhaps because his father was Taliban or his friends would tell him it was the right thing to do. Either way, all bets were off with an AK.

On my arrival back in Musa Qa'leh, I was grabbed by a soldier from 4 SCOTS with a grim look on his face.

"You yased tae be Royal Scots didn't you George?" he asked.

"Aye mate, that's right. Why?"

"Jon Mathews is goan hame the day," he said waiting for my response. I took my helmet off and rubbed my eyes. It didn't make sense unless he was posted end of tour or something.

"But you guys aren't finished yet? Are you?" The lad's face dropped.

"You didnae ken mate? He wis kilt a few days ago and he's goan hame the day." My mouth went dry. I shook the soldier's hand and thanked him for letting me know.

I was so shocked that I kept turning it over in my head, somehow it didn't seem real. I had known lads killed in action that I had served with or been on courses with, but this was real, different and personal. I had known Jon very well and had liked and respected him immensely, it wasn't sinking in that he was dead. I felt a heavy weight in my chest and what I can only describe as my heart actually break. As I tried to process it, I realised that I needed to do a post Op kit check on my lads before we could stand down and sleep.

I had all my guys lay their kit out next their beds and I came along with my FLAP sheet and AFB115 and checked off all the serial numbers of their kit. Once I was happy we had everything, I reported back to Goody we had all our kit. But I was like a zombie as I checked off my lists.

I kept thinking of Jon and the last time I had seen him alive. I could remember his goofy smile and his easy-going manner and that made it even sadder, it was definitely the good guys that were taken too soon. Jon was a consummate professional soldier, but he had a heart of gold and would do anything for anyone.

I knew right now there would be a lot of other people feeling the same as I did right then. I kept everything in and put on a brave face as I conducted checks, then began to strip down my rifle to clean it. I change my radio batteries and requested an ammo resupply for my Platoon so that should we get a short notice deployment, we were ready to go.

Once I was all sorted, I stripped down to my boxer shorts, grabbed my towel, wash kit and solar shower and walked alone across to the shower stalls located near our toilets. I hung up the solar shower and let the warm water flow, only then letting the tears roll down my face.

Day 114

Friday 1st August: Musa Qa'leh DC

The Company as a whole had stood down for a few days to rest and refit before any more major surge Ops in the area. However, that didn't mean we stopped patrolling completely and conducted Platoon level patrolling to maintain our dominance of the area.

My first Platoon task was to conduct a reconnaissance for an R&D task (Reconstruction and Development), with a WO2 from the Royal Engineers in tow. He had been given grid references and been told to do a feasibility study of those grids for future building projects. As part of our patrolling strategy in Musa Qa'leh, we would engage with the local elders and discuss R&D projects on behalf of NGOs and ISAF rebuilding teams. Invariably, the subject would always arise of what the village elders would like to see built in their village and the conversation would go something like this.

"Hajji Mahmoud, we have been given money to help make the lives of your villagers better. We would like to build some things for you. We have funding for a well, clinic, school or a marketplace. Is that something you would be interested in for your people?"

We would be met with stony silence and a glare. After much rattling of prayer beads and tea drinking, the lead elder would finally give his answer.

"We would like a Mosque!" This would be met with exasperation, but no surprise.

"But Hajji, you have three Mosques in this village already, wouldn't you like clean running water or perhaps a marketplace to bring more money into the village?"

"No, we want a Mosque!"

"Okay, Mosque it is!" Would be the response.

This patrol was a follow-on patrol from one of those meetings, the Sergeant Major had briefed me on the locations and in concert with my NCOs, we decided which routes to take and which areas to avoid as we knew they would be trouble.

Our first location was west across the wadi, which was crossed with a modicum of security, dodging the motorbikes and Toyota Corollas flying down the dry riverbed. We made it to the other side without being roadkill or having to fire warning shots/flares at people.

The first location we found easily, and it was perfectly suited to the R&D team's requirements. A large piece of churned-up open ground that would soon be home to a shiny new Mosque. The Sergeant Major confirmed the grids and made notes, then took some pictures of the site and we pushed on.

Even though we were on our own, I heard the reassuring buzz of an AH-64 Apache Longbow overhead. I remained in constant coms with the DC sending SITREPS (Situation Reports) back at every stage of our patrol and allowing the Op's room staff to know where we were on the ground should we require support.

Bruce, my best friend and our JTAC, was listening in to the radio and was able to pass messages between us and the Apache. The radio callsign for an Apache gunship was 'Ugly.' But when you need her cannons and rockets to help you, nothing ever looked so beautiful!

After confirmation of grids with the Sergeant Major, we pushed north. Patrolling through a mix of Green Zone and arid desert, the signs were good so far. People paid us no heed, but in the back of our minds was the ever-present thought of enemy activity.

The ICOM was still very active but I believe that because we had the Apache up, they were too afraid to engage us. As the moment anything got fired at us, the crew on board that death machine would spot the source and hit it with 30mm cannon fire.

We reached the location for the next Mosque and the Sapper stopped in his tracks and scratched his head.

"This doesn't look familiar mate, this piece of land should be a bit more ... landy!" He exclaimed. We stood looking at the location given, straight in front of us was a patch of trees with a nice little stream meandering lazily through it.

"Aye, I see what you mean." I said. "It's kind of ... oasisy?" I told the lads to drop into all-round defence, which they did after conducting five-metre checks of the area they were going to take cover in. With the emerging IED threat, you had to check where you were going to sit, kneel or lie down.

"I haven't walked this route," the Sapper continued. "Just seen pictures of the location." I pulled out my map and asked him to check the grid again. Sheepishly, he read out the grid again and as I checked it, the location was six hundred metres to our north. So, I check navigated, set my compass bearing, tapped the grid into my GPS and off we went.

It was a slog as now the temperature was rising. Our uniforms had turned a dark brown with sweat and it streamed down our faces, down the middle of our backs and uncomfortably down the crack of my arse.

After negotiating the ground, we arrived at the next location, which looked more realistic. Once he had taken the pictures and gathered all the relevant information, we pushed back east across the wadi and into the DC. As we passed through the barrier into the DC, we breathed a sigh of relief. The sangar position watching over the barrier had a good view of the wadi and the entrance to the DC.

I had made sure that I told the Op's room of my approach so that the sentries could give us cover as we got closer and I didn't want the

ANA sentries on the roof to get twitchy and open fire on us. It would be insult to injury to be killed by our allies.

Over the next few days we acted as QRF (Quick Reaction Force) for a counter IED operation going on in our area. There had been an alarming number of IEDs located in the wadi and sadly civilians were bearing the brunt of it. The popular IED with the Taliban were now pressure plate IEDs, crudely built but extremely effective. You take two saw blades and put them inside a car tyre inner tube to keep out any water and make sure the blades are kept apart using springs or wooden blocks. Rig it up to a battery and an explosive charge, then bury it in the ground and camouflage it.

The problem with pressure plates is that they do not discriminate amongst those who stand on them, an ISAF soldier or a child walking his family goats to a field. All that is required is that the when the saw blades touch, they close the circuit on the IED. The result is always devastating.

Day 117

Monday 4th August: Musa Qa'leh DC

I was given a warning order for a Platoon level patrol to retrieve a set of remote ground sensors. I was given a set of grid references from the team who put them in from 11 Platoon. I asked the Op's room when the last time there had been an alarm on the sensors. No one could give me a straight answer, just that I had to retrieve the kit from the ground.

In my previous job I had used the ground sensors and knew that there should be an alarm whenever people or vehicles passed them, and a camera could record exactly what was setting the alarms off. My plan was simple, head west across the Musa Qa'leh Wadi and drop off a section at a location called Himal OP. That section would create a diversion while the rest of us would use metal detectors to locate and dig up the sensor equipment. Once we had retrieved the kit, we would reform at the bottom of Himal and then patrol back across the wadi and into the DC.

My deception plan was to conduct a test fire of weapons from Himal OP and for that I needed a lot of ammo. Cpl Wullie Rankin, would be the commander of my deception group and I would lead the team digging up the sensor and camera units.

I spoke to Goody before I left and outlined my plan with regards to my deception plan, he grinned at me like a wolf grins at a flock of sheep.

"Ah'v got jist the hing fer ye mucker!" he said and motioned for me to follow him. There was a stockpile of ammunition that would probably have been destroyed by EOD waiting for me. The ammunition was still usable, but the batch was nearing its use-by date, so to speak, and with the Afghan heat there was always a concern that it would make the ammunition unstable. This way, we killed two birds with one stone. The ammunition would be disposed of, and I would be able to conduct my deception Op for quite some time. We all loaded our patrol packs up with extra ammunition, but we knew that we would not be bringing it back so that made the job easier.

I conducted my pre-patrol checks on the Platoon and then radio checks to the Op's room. As always, I brought John with me in case we had any ICOM chatter or we needed to talk with the locals. Once I was happy, it was a very heavy 12 Platoon that waddled out the main gate of Musa Qa'leh DC.

We crossed the Musa Qa'leh Wadi without incident and pressed on through a small village which was not named on the map. I passed the word on for the guys to keep their eyes peeled as we were on a main route between FOB Edinburgh and Musa Qa'leh, which we knew was frequently travelled by the Taliban.

The risk of suicide bombing was now coming to the fore as another tactic the enemy were deploying. It was at the forefront of my mind. We passed through the village without incident and waved to locals and chatted to people as we went. I was still conscious that the Taliban were watching us and could see every move we made, which John confirmed with the ICOM scanner.

We reached Himal OP quite quickly and made our way up the slope. When we saw Himal OP for the first time it reminded me of pictures I had seen from the Soviet occupation of a small, lightly manned outpost; probably a Platoon-sized base, stuck on a dry, sandy hilltop.

It was perfectly placed, and had I been a betting man, I would wager the Soviets used it for exactly the same purpose we did. It had a commanding view of the ground between FOB Edinburgh and Musa Qa'leh Wadi. The OP itself was a ramshackle collection of HESCO Bastion and tents. Wire and sandbags added an extra layer of defence to the OP.

It was on the western side of the OP that my deception plan would happen, I had the presence of mind to radio the Op's room and inform Himal OP that I was approaching their perimeter. I shook hands with the Captain in charge of the OP and introduced myself.

"Sarge," he said. "I didn't even know you were coming up here!" I rolled my eyes; I had been told when I went to hand in my FLAP sheet to the watchkeeper that Himal were aware of my arrival and would be expecting me.

"No dramas Boss, sorry to impose on you like this." I said apologetically. "I've been given the task of finding and digging up some kit and to divert the attention of the Taliban and locals in the area, I've decided to let my guys test-fire their weapons systems." The Captain smiled.

"No problem at all, let me show you the best place to conduct that." He motioned for me to follow him, which I did, bringing Wullie Rankin with me so he could see for himself. The Captain led us to the perimeter where there was a decent sandbag wall with razor wire coils out in front of it. As the three of us looked out over the area we could see for miles. Ahead of the wire was a lower slope which would be perfect to fire our rounds into. This was about a hundred metres away from the wire.

"Wullie, bring your section up. Collect all the spare ammo and I'll leave it to your discretion to manage the use of the weapons," I informed him. "As soon as you start firing, I'll move the rest of the lads out."

Wullie spoke on the Platoon channel on our PRR (Personal Role Radio) channel and told his section to come up, grabbing all the extra ammunition from my element of the patrol. As he was setting his guys up along the sandbag wall, I briefed my team up. We had extra metal detectors in order to find the sensor kit quicker.

I left the security of Himal OP's perimeter and headed round and to the north of the OP to my first location, which should be the camera position. We had just stepped out the wire and Wullie began to let loose with everything he had, it sounded like the fifth of November and and the fourth of July on steroids.

We moved into the dead ground south-east, then north of the OP and could clearly see where the camera would be watching. I pointed the areas out to the lads with the metal detectors and they began sweeping. Before long they were rewarded with a high pitched 'wheee!' noise that made you wince.

Just to confirm, the lads boxed and four-leaf-clovered around the alarm area and were rewarded with double beeps that meant there was metal in the ground. I set a fire team on overwatch to cover us as we began to dig using collapsible entrenching tools that we had brought with us. We were slightly vulnerable at this moment, but with the fire going on over our heads and the fire team on overwatch I was happy we had cover.

The digging revealed the camera equipment cleverly camouflaged using sandbags that had been weathered and spray glued, which made the sand in the area stick to the hessian sacking. We placed the camera kit in our patrol packs, and I informed the Op's room at the DC that the kit was secure.

Our next task was to patrol into the wadi to the west of the OP and pick up the actual sensors. I once again informed everyone that we were moving and Wullie passed this on to the commander of Himal. The descent into the wadi was steep and rough going underfoot as the sand and dirt was covered with loose stones. We kicked up a small cloud of dust in our wake, but nothing that would get us noticed until we were in the wadi.

I was aware of how very bare-arsed and open the ground was that we were to check, and I didn't want to be in that spot longer than necessary. Once again, I pushed out a fire team to cover the guys doing the detecting and then if we found the kit, to cover us digging it up.

After thirty minutes of scanning the ground, all we found were empty .50 cal bullet cases. I was getting frustrated; we had the right grids which would have given us a long line of sensors covering the open ground at the bottom of Himal OP. John took the earpiece out of his ear with a concerned look on his face.

"Sir, the Taliban can see us, and they are preparing an attack on us!" I wasn't overly concerned as we had intimate support from my own guys. Our deception team on Himal could provide fire support and if necessary, the troops at Himal would also give us support. I was also pretty certain that the minute I sent a contact report TIC (Troops in Contact), Bruce might be able to rustle me up an Apache.

"Hello zero this is three zero Bravo, I have ICOM chatter and no sign of the sensor equipment. Can you tell me the last time anyone had an alarm from these sensors? Over." I called the Op's room. There was a moment's silence and I could imagine the Op's room staff running around to get me answers, shortly after a voice came on the net.

"Three zero Bravo, this is zero. The last time anyone had an alarm or any kind of indication was three weeks ago!" I let out a groan.

"Three zero Bravo roger, can you confirm alarm type?" Again silence.

"Zero yes, it was a tamper alarm so it suggests if you can't find the kit it has been lifted!" I shook my head in frustration as I had already asked the question before I left the DC, now my patrol was out in the open to retrieve kit in broad daylight that had apparently already been taken; at this point, I didn't care whether by ISAF or the Taliban.

"Three zero Bravo roger, requesting permission to collapse task and return to your location, over?" I asked and common sense obviously prevailed as I was given permission to return to the DC. At least I had the camera kit and not a moment too soon, as Wullie informed me that all the deception ammo had now been used. He was leaving all the working parts on the weapons open to prevent overheating due to the sustained fire they had been putting out.

"Okay mate no dramas, see you at the bottom of the hill," I told him over the Platoon channel. As I led the boys out of the wadi, I became aware of the sound of an approaching engine which sounded like a motorbike. I brought my rifle up to the aim and dropped into a low-profile shooting position.

My finger had literally pressed the safety stud on my rifle to fire when a red motorbike with two people on it sped into view. As loud as I could I shouted "Wadarega!" which is Pashtun for stop. The bike kept coming and it was obvious the driver could see me; I began to take up the pressure on my trigger.

At the last minute the bike skidded to a halt, the rider nearly falling off and his pillion being ejected off the back. The pillion was a woman, which became evident as her veil came away. I advanced on them with my weapon still up and through John shouted for them to show me their hands and then the man to lift his shirt to show me he wasn't wearing a suicide belt or vest.

The woman in the meantime was wailing and crying and the man was apologising profusely. I was still angry and asked him why he had stupidly ridden towards an ISAF patrol at high speed, did he realise how lucky he was that I had not killed either of them. Again, the man offered no explanation other than he had not seen us and once again apologised, I told him next time to be more aware as he might not be so lucky.

We reformed the patrol at the bottom of Himal and began moving east towards the DC. As we got to the western bank of Musa Qa'leh Wadi, my radio burst into life.

"Three zero Bravo this is three three Alpha!" What did Goody want? I had fired all the rounds off and brought the camera kit back!

"Three zero Bravo send over," I came back.

"Make yer way back tae the DC best speed mucker, I've got another jobe fer ye!" he called informally. Then there was a pause. "CASEVAC mucker, need ye tae git yer guys on a Mastiff and pick up a casualty fae the Royal Irish."

I looked at all my guys, they'd heard most of the message and they all nodded their assent with a grim resolve now on every bronzed, dirty face. Gone was the lethargy of the heat and the let-down of a wild goose chase, this was something vital, a brother soldier was hurt and needed to be extracted, regardless of unit we were going to get him.

We made our fastest way back to the DC, I arrived to find three Mastiffs waiting for me and I quickly split my team between the vehicles. Me in the front one and Wullie Rankin in the last one, all the guys equally split. I stuck the headset on in the back of the Mastiff and spoke to vehicle commander. "Do you know where we're going mucker?" I asked.

"Aye mate, nay dramas we're heading doon south. Yin eh the Royal Irish boys got hit by an AK round in the shooder, we jist need tae RV wae his Platoon Sergeant and get him in the wagon and oot the area!" I nodded.

"Awesome buddy, as soon as we hit the RV point, I'll debus my guys and we'll grab him!" With that the three-vehicle rescue party sped out of the DC and turned left heading south then east then south again down a 'major' road that we had patrolled many times; we were heading back to Dagyan.

I sat as close to the vehicle commander as I could so that I could see through the front windscreen of the Mastiff. Next to me the legs of the gunner on top cover moved around as he covered his arc of fire. Anyone who had operated in Musa Qa'leh for these past few months knew that where we were going was definitely hostile territory.

I watched as people parted on the road for us as we headed south towards an RV with the Royal Irish CASEVAC party. Before long I could see a line of desert-coloured and American leaf pattern DPM uniforms moving towards us. I told my lads to stay on the vehicles as there were more than enough troops out there to provide security for the CASEVAC. I watched as a soldier with no shirt on and his body armour loosely fitted was assisted by his mates to towards the Mastiff. I quickly threw the handles on the inside of the door up to open the heavy armoured door and there they were waiting for me at the bottom of the metal steps.

I leaned out and thrust my hand out to assist the wounded Ranger up the steps, he grabbed it and I hauled him in, the front of his armour was stained with blood and he looked quite pale. I got him into the vehicle, sat him down and began to assess his injuries.

"He's on mate!" I yelled to the vehicle commander. "We're good to go," the commander who had turned in his seat to observe the goings on, nodded to me and spoke into his vehicle crew headset and before long we were moving. I removed the wounded Ranger's Osprey off him now that he was safely inside the massive armoured vehicle.

"What the fuck happened?" I asked as I looked at the bullet wound on his left shoulder. The tall, dark-haired Ranger took a breath and in his Northern Irish accent began to recount the story.

His team supporting an ANA patrol were moving through an alley between two compounds where fire had erupted to their front, he had immediately been struck by a bullet and went down. When he looked around, he saw that he was alone. As he had gone down his team had initiated a break clean drill from contact and were now putting down fire on the enemy with a view to coming back to get him. He had lain still as fire had been traded between the Royal Irish and the Taliban down the alleyway, he could only cover up and try to roll into cover, which there was not a lot of.

It was at that point the enemy decided to try and advance and take him alive. He watched as the enemy crawled towards him thinking he was unconscious. When he fired at them, they knew that was not the case and he became the focus of a tug of war and at one point the Taliban nearly reached him. His teammates began to push forward firing and manoeuvring in bounds to reach and extract him. The Taliban withdrew under withering fire and his mates had reached him, throwing hand grenades down the alley to disperse and hopefully kill the enemy still lurking in the area.

They had gotten him out the alley and extracted him to a safe area before requesting a CASEVAC. That was where my team came in, provide an infantry dismount to the huge targets that were the Mastiff Platoon.

"You are fucking lucky mate!" I said to him, he grinned through the pain and said "To top it all off, I've only got three units of PAX!" I shook my head and laughed.

"Fuck me mate, you'd have to have lost your arm to make it worth your while, what are you going to get for this? Hundred, two hundred pounds, if that."

PAX was an insurance scheme run by the Military where you basically bought units of insurance and the more you bought, the bigger the pay-out should you be hurt. This covered you on and off duty, which was very handy.

Prior to Afghanistan we had been 'encouraged' to take out the maximum level of cover, which I had anyway as it made sense and the whole Battalion did too. We could only imagine that in other Battalions it was not enforced, soldiers could take out the level of cover they wanted or could afford. PAX had issued leaflets prior to our departure with what can only be described as a shopping list of despair, as we scanned through the list of injuries and compensation we all wondered 'What was the smallest, least painful injury I could get, but still leave me able to work AND get a nice big claim?'

Thumbs and trigger fingers seemed to be that type, but we all liked our thumbs and fingers exactly where they were. Losing a pinkie didn't really get you much of a claim but with the operational bonuses and the fact there was nowhere to spend your money, we would be coming home with a nice bank balance.

As we returned to Musa Qa'leh I wished the young Ranger luck. I doubted he would re-join his unit anytime soon. We pulled into the vehicle park adjacent to the Op's room building and debussed, the wounded Ranger was whisked off to see the doctor and we headed back to our accommodation to kit check and hand in the camera equipment we had managed to retrieve.

"Well done mucker, ye were in the right place at the right time so ye got volunteered!" Goody said as he met us as we arrived back at our lines. I nodded and smiled.

"Aye nay dramas mate, it made sense, we were still kitted up ready to go so were the best option." I recounted to him the story the Ranger had told me, Goody whistled.

"Lucky boy, if the Taliban had goat him, his tea wid huv been right oot!" I nodded in agreement, took my helmet off and went to re-join my Platoon.

After a kit check, the guys settled down to clean weapons, with a load of grumbling from Wullie Rankin's section. They hadn't been out digging for sensors under the watchful eyes of the Taliban, but their weapons were so full of carbon after the test firing that it would take a good hour of cleaning, especially the machine guns, to get them back to an acceptable state for future patrols.

Day 118

Tuesday 5th August: Musa Qa'leh DC

Throughout the tour, members of the Company were still going on R&R and on this rotation Major Calder went on his, as did Al Lipowski. This left Captain Si Dinsmore in charge of the Company and me in charge of 12 Platoon. Just because the head shed had gone, didn't mean the war stopped. We all stepped up and, in my case, I was now Platoon Commander. Wullie Rankin as my senior Corporal took over as Platoon Sergeant. Wullie was a big, gentle giant of a man but not one to cross. He was a devoted family man and all in all, a very good guy to have around you and on your team.

As if to test the new structure, I was given a warning order for a Company operation back south, to Dagyan near where we had lost Davey McGhee and where we had picked up the wounded Ranger.

On the Platoon Sergeant's battle course, I had failed my Platoon Commander command appointment! I was very glad that there was no Infantry Battle school Brecon Colour Sergeant looking over my shoulder. I would gladly face the Taliban in my pants than go through that again.

On receipt of the Company warning order, I quickly put out my Platoon warning order, which set the battle procedure in train. I then started my process and prepared to receive the OC's orders. It was not lost on me that in the area we were to operate, every time we had gone down to Dagyan it resulted in heavy fighting. I had probably killed two people there and we had lost four men from the Company wounded. I suddenly felt the awesome weight of responsibility falling on my shoulders and I resolved that no one would get killed on my watch.

After I had received my orders, I delivered mine to my Platoon and issued tasks. Si Dinsmore's plan called for us to forward mount to PB South again with our old ANA dancing partners, stay overnight and then push south towards Dagyan before first light. Hopefully before the enemy realised, we were there.

I liked it, the plan was sound, and I understood my part in it and the part 12 Platoon was to play. As I looked around at my Platoon, I suddenly felt even more paternal towards them. Even Wullie Rankin who was about the same age as me, all the way down to young Nige Campbell. We looked at one another and it was as though he had read my thoughts.

I was unbelievably proud of this kid, straight out of training he had come to Delta Company and my Platoon. Back then he was an absolute cluster of a man and now before me sat a confident, dependable young soldier who was proof if ever it was needed that war matures people and ages them beyond their years.

As always, I questioned the Platoon to ensure that they had all been listening to the orders and knew their part in Si's plan and mine. Satisfied, I allowed the lads to chill out and got my NCOs together.

"Look lads, this is not our first Op together, but it is my first Op out as Platoon commander." I paused to let it sink in. "Let's keep working the way we have been, we're a fucking good team – even though we 're a band of fucking misfits." The NCOs chuckled and nodded.

Keenly aware that we may have been setting patterns every time we left the DC, Si tasked my Platoon with leaving via the back gate next to the governor's house. Known as the White House as it was huge and – white.

At 17:30hrs I had my Platoon formed up with Loone McCarthy's section taking the lead, the jovial Highlander had a grin plastered on his face. Loone had come to us from The Black Watch (3 SCOTS). He was a short, stocky man with a wicked sense of humour. Never one to panic or flap, he was loved by his section.

"Ready when you are mucks!" he said. Leaving via the back gate meant that we would have to turn right and head south through the bottom end of Musa Qa'leh itself. Even though it was late afternoon it was still going to be busy, so over the Platoon channel I reiterated the need for vigilance.

2 Para had suffered a loss of three of their brothers up at FOB Gibraltar on 8th June, when a suicide bomber had walked into the middle of one of their foot patrols and detonated himself. The rumour had gone around that the bomber was a small boy who had been wheeling a barrow of dried poppy stalks so as not to look out of place. He stopped to talk to the lads then killed three of them outright. We were always mindful walking through villages that the threat of suicide attacks was ever present and we never let people get too close to our personal space. But this potentially new tactic of using children as bombers added a whole new level of underhandedness that fried the civilised mind. As we were always mobbed by children begging for sweets and pens, how long would it be before something similar happened to one of our patrols? The Taliban knew that the Western psyche recoiled at shooting women and children, so they would use that weakness against us.

As we pushed through the gate, we came into an alleyway of tumbledown compound walls and had to squeeze our way through until we were out onto the main road running through Musa Qa'leh from north to south. I gave the had signal for 'Staggered file' by raising both my arms one hand higher than the other and pretty soon my Platoon was covering both sides of the street.

We passed by shops selling everything from meats to cartons of cigarettes and the locals eyed us suspiciously or with outright hostility, but when we waved, they waved back. Our eyes never stopped scanning for threats and I was pleased to see that the lad's hackles were up. No one was looking at his feet, everyone covered their arcs and spun around as they moved to make sure the lads behind them were still there and had not been snatched.

The smell of cooking meat filled our nostrils and made us all drool, it was the best thing most of us had smelled in months and I don't think there was a man in the Platoon who wouldn't risk getting the shits just for a bite of whatever was cooking. After all, it couldn't be any worse by a long shot than what they were feeding us at the DC. We looked forward to patrols as we would be on twenty-four-hour ration packs, which at least had variety and tasted better.

We came to the north bank of the wadi that split off east from the Musa Qa'leh Wadi, this area was dominated by an ANP checkpoint with a huge Afghan flag flying from an improvised flagpole. Dotted along the walls were bored-looking ANP officers in various bits of uniform and civilian clothing, all toting AKs, RPGs or PKM machine guns. They squatted to get a better look at us and stared as we passed beneath them, even though they were our allies we were taking no chances and the guys all covered the police checkpoint as they passed it.

Even though they were in a position to cover us across the wadi, I chose not to rely on them, instead I halted the point section and the wadi and had them cover it and I led the rest of the Platoon across looking left and right as we crossed the massive open ground. On the south bank I halted the Platoon and placed them in positions where they could cover both banks of the wadi and allow Loone and his section to cross.

I let the breath out I'd been holding as Loone crossed over and we were all together again on the southern bank. I let Capt Dinsmore know where we were and that I was heading towards PB South. He acknowledged and told me to proceed. I decided that rather than use the obvious hard standing to take my guys to the patrol base, I would use rat runs and patches of trees to screen the movement. This worked, as the Taliban had seen us on the wadi but could now not see where we had gone and therefore couldn't shoot at us.

We reached PB South as the sun was setting and joined up with the rest of the Company. As I got the lads settled in for the night, Si got all Platoon commanders and Sergeants together, along with Company HQ to outline the next phase of the operation. We all sat in a circle stripped to the waist and had our maps, compasses, GPS and notebooks to hand as we waited what Si had to say. He gave each Platoon its assignment and we each acknowledged our part in his plan.

"Sarn't Mac," he said to me. "I want you on the right flank and be sneaky getting down the AO like you were today, I don't want the enemy to be able to pin us all down, I don't want them to see us all until it's too late." I nodded and looked at my map.

"No dramas Boss, I have an idea where I'm going already." I scratched my chin and eyed the east bank of Musa Qa'leh Wadi, it had cover and it was sparsely populated with very few compounds to signal the enemy of our approach.

Once Si was happy we were sorted with his plan we all dispersed to our Platoons and set in for the night. Normally I slept quite well when I was in compounds but tonight I just couldn't and it wasn't just the humid night or the fact that we were camped out next to PB South's generator. Tomorrow we would definitely get into a fight: how would I cope as the Platoon commander? My failure on PSBC kept nagging at me even though I told myself 'training is training, this is real,' I couldn't shake the feeling of nervousness. I had performed well so far, so hopefully this would continue. I would do my job and trust the boys under me would do their part when the deal went down, and I would do my best not to get them killed. Eventually I got to sleep, but it only felt like ten minutes before I was being shaken awake.

Day 120

Thursday 7th August: PB South, South of Musa Qa'leh DC

Lethargically, I got up from my body armour mattress as I was shaken awake, I rubbed my eyes which were full of sleep and dust. Yawning I looked around me, the sun was not yet up and as I checked my watch the luminous display showed 03:00, I groaned.

The boys were beginning to stir and get up, some quicker than others. I rolled up my US Army poncho liner and strapped it to the side of my Camelbak patrol pack and began to rummage through it for something to eat.

"Corned beef fucking hash!" I hissed as I checked the blue writing on the silver bag. I had well and truly seen myself off, but luckily, I carried a bottle of Tabasco sauce with me. Every army ration pack came with a small bottle of the hot sauce, it was about the size of a fingertip and contained enough hot sauce for two maybe three splashes into a ration bag. But this was not enough, so I had bought a bigger bottle in the UK and kept it in my patrol pack.

As we were friendly with the ANA, they had put a large pot of water over a cooking fire for us and we dumped our ration bags into the mix so that the hot water would boil the food inside the bag and we could have a hot meal. We made a habit of putting our names on the bags, as nobody wanted to be shafted with corned beef hash. So straightaway I had shit out, and nobody wanted to kill someone over a boil in the bag breakfast.

As I sat eating, I once again pored over my map and planned the route in my head, but I was also keenly aware that I needed to be within a good reaction time to assist the other Platoons in the event of contact or casualties. The route I had chosen was still ideal but we would see how it would work on the ground. Stealth and surprise would hopefully work in 12 Platoon's favour. By 04:30 the Platoon was up, our radios were switched on and radio checks completed. We took our last sips of water before heading out, or for some a chance to have a last cigarette before we stopped again later in the day.

We pushed out of PB South and began heading west towards Musa Qa'leh Wadi, turning south again before we came to it. The ground we crossed was typical of the area, little patches of open ground where it looked like there had been a field as they were bordered by little square banks of dirt, I presumed to keep water in the patch for irrigation. Clumps of trees were dotted around and they gave us good cover. Occasionally we would come across a compound, but as it was only just getting light there was little sign of movement.

We crossed ditches of varying depth and it was plain to say that other than irrigation, these ditches were used for other tasks. Large piles of human shit lurked at the bottom like bio landmines, there were also cigarette butts and sweet wrappers. I hoped that if I had to take cover in any of them, it would be one that was not an Afghan shitter. As we came along a craggy outcrop of rock which had hidden us, we crested in the area of compound HJ1-36. It was there we came face to face with the enemy.

Two Taliban fighters, who had clearly not expected to see us, panicked and one fired an RPG at us. It sailed over our heads and was followed by a burst of fire from a PKM machine gun, which again went wide of the mark. It was Nige Campbell who was the first to react and as I said the words into the radio "Contact wait out!" he fired a huge burst of fire at the Taliban fighters, silencing their fire. As we all knelt and observed the area of the firing point, I sent a full contact report to Si, which was acknowledged by the Op's room in Musa Qa'leh. Nige poked his head up over the wall we had taken cover next to and wondered, "Ah hink av jist kilt some c**t?" And despite the seriousness of the situation, the look on his face and the delivery of his kill confirmation had us pissing ourselves with laughter. I informed Si that there were potentially two enemy seriously wounded or dead now in 10 Platoon's path, so we continued south towards our objective.

"Three zero Alpha this is one zero Alpha, good shooting we have one times enemy KIA located." I heard Jim Adamson report, this was reiterated by Si Dinsmore. "Good effort three zero!"

"Nige!" I called down on the Platoon channel. "You did kill some c**t, good effort wee man!" Nige looked back at me and gave me a wide grin. From the location Jim Adamson have given over the radio for the EKIA he had crawled or staggered two hundred metres or so after being riddled with 5.56mm from Nige's Minimi and died propped up next to a tree.

10 Platoon would later show us a picture of the fighter Nige had killed, the guy was over six feet tall and had been carrying an RPG with spare rockets and a PKM machine gun with extra belts. The guy was an Afghan fucking Rambo, the weapons and picture of the fighter were passed to intelligence on our return to see if they could get any forensics off them or ID the fighter through other channels.

As the heat of the day started to set in, we pushed into compounds for a few hours to rest, get something to eat and drink ready for the next phase of the patrol. As we were pushing down an alleyway between a set of compounds, an Apache that had been circling the area suddenly let loose with its cannon at an enemy further south that we clearly couldn't see. The noise was deafening and made me jump.

"Thanks for the fucking warning!" I yelled, shaking my fist up at the gunship now hovering over my Platoon and raining empty cases down on us. We found a compound big enough to take the Company and each Platoon took a sector of the roof to cover and hit the Taliban if they decided to assault our position. But it soon became an unwritten gentlemen's agreement between us and the enemy that during the hottest part of the day, we wouldn't bother them, and they wouldn't bother us. They prayed and we ate and slept.

Si came over and put his hand on my shoulder. "George, I need you and your guys to push forward and assault compounds HJ1-1, 1-2 and 1-3." He let it sink in before continuing. "You'll have Mastiff support in the wadi, and we'll provide fire support from here if you need it."

I looked at my map, my target was a cluster of three compounds just east of the Musa Qa'leh Wadi at the top of a slope. I decided that my best approach to my FUP (Forming up Point) would be to use the wadi as I would have cover and support on both sides. From where we were it would be approximately five or six hundred metres of open ground and I did not like the thought of giving the Taliban the drop on us.

I got my Platoon together around the map and told them my plan. Loone would be my lead section and fire support, Pete Breen would be next with me as the first assault section and that left L/Cpl Tam Meighan as reserve with Wullie Rankin. I told them that they would each have a compound to assault and I was giving them permission to 'Go Red' on them all, which meant they could use hand grenades to clear out the buildings. We knew the enemy were there, ICOM had caught them reinforcing from Yatimchay and would certainly be ready for us. All the lads nodded and told me they understood the plan.

At H-Hour, I left the security of compound HJ1-33 and tabbed my Platoon west. We plunged down the sandy slope into the Musa Qa'leh Wadi. In the distance to the south I could see the Mastiff APCs through the heat shimmer and hear their engines idling as they stood sentinel for me in the wadi.

I had gone approximately three hundred metres down the wadi when I started to receive heavy small arms fire from the west bank. It was not particularly accurate but an unaimed bullet will kill you just as well as an aimed one.

"Zero Alpha, three zero Alpha!" I called to Si. "Contact, contact, contact. I am receiving small arms fire from the west bank of the Musa Qa'leh Wadi, request fire mission over?"

There was a second or two of silence on the net then Si got back to me.

"Three zero roger you have it! Pass me the coordinates, FOO is listening!" By this stage all the lads had taken cover where they could and were covering their arcs of fire. Looking at my Garmin wrist-mounted GPS I gave Si my grid in ten figures and the distance and direction to the enemy. Remembering what happened to 11 Platoon I hoped the Op's room staff had learned their lesson not to change shifts during a TIC.

"Artillery coming in on the far bank, as soon as it hits, we're moving again... Happy with that Loone?" He raised his thumb and gave me his big wide pumpkin grin. "Nay dramas mucks," I heard Si's voice in my ear again. "Shot over!"

"Shot out!" I replied. I heard the artillery rounds rushing through the air and they were spot on target, I watched as the fire position that had been harassing us disappeared in dull flashes and clouds of shrapnel-laden smoke. Loone did not have to wait for my orders, as soon as the rounds struck, he was up and running and I with him.

"Fire for effect!" I called into the radio and the artillery at FOB Edinburgh did just that, the area we had been engaged from was obliterated in seconds. We continued pushing south until we were parallel with our Mastiff support and as if on cue the enemy starting lobbing mortar rounds at the Mastiffs, obviously hoping to hit us, too, as we were on foot.

I could see where the fire was coming from but at that range it would have been impossible for our rifles to hit them. But it occurred to me that the Browning .50 cal machine guns, Jimpies and 40mm GMGs on the Mastiffs could easily hit them. I called up on the radio which I knew the Mastiff crews could hear and gave them a target indication. A hellish amount of firepower was suddenly laid down on the enemy positions and another artillery barrage.

I started to focus on my task at hand and I turned around to my Platoon who had by now taken cover again because of the fire. I held Tam Meighan and his guys with Wullie Rankin in a ditch and a covered area of rock wall where they would be safe from any further fire and began to head to my FUP.

As Loone's section and I moved, we received more small arms fire, this time from the south. Loone and his lads did not hesitate and began to return fire. All the while the rounds from AK and PKM fire snapped over our heads and in a few instances so close that the passage of the bullets deafened me in one ear and left me with temporary tinnitus.

I raised my rifle and began to put rounds into likely enemy positions, realising that this was very much going to be an infantry fight, I turned to John and a Captain from the PSYOPS team who had tagged along and told them to stay in cover. Luckily, near us was an old roller, the type you see attached to tractors for flattening football pitches or the tarmac on roads, it was wide and solid and would give excellent cover from fire.

"Sorry guys this is going to be a battle for grunts only, you need to stay here!" I ordered, I expected the PSYOPS Captain to pull rank on me, but to his credit he didn't, and I think he wholeheartedly agreed with me.

Our FUP was a very larg,e sandy slope with grass in places and little rocky outcrops that could give us cover from fire. The enemy were still engaging us from the south, but the fire was desultory, as though they were doing it just to save face. Their rounds snapped over our heads and we fired in their direction in order to keep their heads down.

Loone had pushed his section just ahead of me and they had shaken out into an assault formation. He turned to me and looked for confirmation. I keyed my pressel on my radio and began to transmit. "Zero Alpha, three zero Alpha FUP secure, pushing forward to assault!" I received nothing but static, that was *not* a good sign. I nodded to Loone who pushed Nige with his Minimi forward. I watched in horror and incredulity as Nige crested the ridge of the FUP. He was suddenly met with a wall of small arms fire and rolled back down the slope, luckily uninjured but possibly in need of new boxers. As he slid down the sandy slope I watched as enemy fire stitched the ground to his left and right before ricocheting past mine and Loone's heads.

Our rifles were in our shoulders and we could see the top of the first compound we were to assault. The windows facing us were hammered by us, hopefully neutralising the shooter who had tried to kill Nige. Loone and Nige pulled a grenade each off their Osprey and pulled the pins.

"Don't fuck this up mucker," I said, "or they are coming right back down into us." Loone and Nige stood together and I watched as their right arms let fly. The small green baseball size devices sailed through the air and I watched as the fly off levers were thrown clear of the body. That's it, the clock was ticking now.

"Grenade!" yelled Loone at the top of his voice, everyone took cover as it was ingrained into every soldier what happens when that call goes out. After what seemed like an eternity, we heard the thuds of both grenades going off, no blinds (grenade failing to explode). A cloud of dark grey smoke sailed lazily into the air where the firing had come from.

"Awesome, let's try again Loone shall we?" I asked, no sooner had I uttered those words I heard someone behind me yell, "George look out!" I turned and my eyes widened as I watched an RPG heading towards me. There was no time, this was going to fucking hurt! I ducked and tried to make myself small, the RPG struck to the right of me, blowing me off my feet and showering me in sand. I got up, dusted myself off and began to engage where the RPG had come from. I watched through my scope as shapes moved into position.

"Motherfuckers!" I let loose with almost a full magazine of rapid shots into the treeline where the Taliban were hiding. Satisfied that I had killed or suppressed them, I turned back to restart the assault on compound HJ1-1. The moment my back was turned I heard the stomach churning 'Bang ... Fwoosh', another RPG, I watched as it came towards us and it was heading for me and Nige Campbell. Without thinking, I dived at Nige knocking him over into the sand and covered him with my body. "Stay down mucker!" I shouted; the resulting explosion again covered me in sand. By this time, I was fucking raging. I stood up again and turned yelling "Watch my tracer." I again let a stream of ruby tracers find their mark and by this time the Mastiffs had joined in too, lending .50 cal and 7.62mm firepower to my cause.

I still hadn't had any contact from Company headquarters, and it occurred to me that someone, if they didn't already, needed to know we were under heavy small arms and rocket fire. I did something that every British unit has done when comms fail, all the way back to the trenches of the Great War.

"Pete, I need a runner!" I called. "Tell the OC what's going on mate and that we have no comms!" Pete nodded, pointed to one of his section and soon the lad was sprinting off like a gazelle back to the Company.

After a while, the firing died down. It soon became apparent why. My runner obviously got through because above us hovered an Apache. But that was all it was doing, hovering. Loone looked up it and yelled to me, "Is this Apache gonnae gae it the malky or whit?" The same question I had been asking myself, why the fuck was it not engaging enemy targets around us? But I figured that as Bruce had no comms with us and I couldn't directly talk to the Apache itself, we were at an impasse.

I heard one of the other lads come to his senses after the RPG explosion and yell at me "What the fuck was that?" As I bounded up the slope I called "RPG!" and almost on cue another RPG slammed into the slope behind me, once again showering me in sand.

I had managed to push Pete Breen and his guys up to my right and they began returning fire to our south and back behind us to the west. This was getting pretty fucking hairy now and I had two choices, I could charge the positions on the crest of the ridge or stay where I was and hope that the Mastiffs who were now returning fire again and the Apache would give me covering fire until I could find another way in.

But the decision was taken away from me by my radio, which decided to start working again and soon I could hear a very concerned Si Dinsmore in my ear. "Three zero Alpha, you need to withdraw. The light is fading. Extract back to my location!" Holy shit, in the chaos of the firefight I had not realised that the sun was going down, what had seemed like a twenty-minute battle turned out to have been a couple of hours. All concept of time had gone in this very small patch of hell.

"Three zero Alpha roger! Extracting now, still receiving small arms fire, will extract in bounds." With that I called to Pete Breen to stay in position and cover Loone as his guys withdrew down the slope. I stayed with Pete's section and then we extracted. As I moved down the slope I could not fail to notice the three smoking RPG tail sections sticking out of the sand and all of them were within a few metres of me. It was not lost on me that I was one lucky fucker, it had not been my time.

Once in the wadi, I grabbed my reserve section and my terp and we moved off. Wullie Rankin grabbed my arm as I passed him, his face was pale and full of concern. "I thought ye were fuckin' deed man! Ah watched they RPGs come in and heard the bangs!" He shook his head and fell in with Tam Meighan's section and we all made our way back to the Company RV back at HJ1-33.

When we returned to the Company, nobody said a word, the looks on our brothers' faces said it all. We slumped down and took on water, our faces blackened with smoke and dirt with little clear streaks where sweat had cleared a patch through the grime. Every face said, 'Why the fuck is 12 Platoon still alive?' I asked myself the same thing. When I looked around at my Platoon, I felt a fierce sense of pride. Geordie Morgan and my Army Air Corps Lance Corporal, big 'Ammo' Armstrong, had been right next to me during the fight and never wavered. Even though this was not their trade they were like professional infantrymen.

All my boys had grown an inch taller; we were fucking invincible and most of them looked at me strangely. Loone slumped down next to me and tapped the small video camera on the side of his helmet.

"Yeh Ken ah got aw that oan video?" he said.

"Mate," I replied. "Nobody would ever believe this story without that video! It's fucking mental."

The sun set on us and as it was getting dark, Si Dinsmore decided to extract us back to PB South for the night. So we tabbed best speed back towards the ANA checkpoint. I for one was looking forward to sleeping, that was for sure. As soon as the action stopped my adrenaline rush had dumped and now I was beginning to feel like I hadn't slept for a week. But we all put one foot in front of another until we saw the patch of open ground and the silhouette of PB South in the gathering twilight. We got into the checkpoint and I kit checked the lads and told them to get to sleep. I felt a presence behind me and turned to See Si Dinsmore appear from the shadows.

"Sergeant Ewart had to be restrained today, as soon as he knew you were in the shit, he wanted to solo it down to you and give you air support!" I couldn't see his face under the shadow of his helmet, but I could tell he was grinning. "Good effort today Mac!" he said. I frowned and nodded. "Not bad for a guy who failed his Platoon commander appointment on seniors!" As he walked away, I could make out the stocky shape of my best friend and our Company JTAC Bruce Ewart.

"So, what's this I hear about you wanting to come to my rescue today?" As he got closer, I could make out his lopsided grin.

"Just didnae want to see you git hurt."

"Mate, even though that Apache didn't fire, I reckon it scared a few of the Taliban away, so thanks buddy I appreciate that." We shook hands and he disappeared back to Company HQ.

That night, I did sleep like the dead. Exhaustion physical and mental took me and I was out like a light. We returned to Musa Qa'leh the next morning and began our post Op admin. It was a time to clean our weapons thoroughly, sort out and repack our kit and replenish our supplies. But also, it was a time to reflect for those of us who had been involved in the firefight in the wadi. It was something none of us would forget until our dying day. As I was cleaning my rifle, Loone approached my bedspace with his video camera in his hand. I turned on my laptop and plugged his camera in using a USB. The footage we watched was so surreal and once again left us both wondering why we were not dead.

"You were fucking awesome up there Loone, well done mucker!" And he was. Loone kept a cool calm head and when we listened back to the video, it didn't sound like we were in a life-or-death struggle, my orders to him and his answers were clear, concise and calm, as though this was a training scenario at OPTAG. He grinned at me.

"Aye Nay danger mucks, aw in a day's work, eh?" Captain Dinsmore was passing by our tent and stuck his head in.

"Mac can I have a word?" he asked. I put my weapon parts down on my cot bed and stepped out my mozzie net, following Si. We stopped at the HESCO next to Company HQ.

"G2 (Intelligence) says that you were facing a reinforced unit of Taliban fighters and possibly some foreign fighters too, the compounds you tried to get into were storing a Dushka machine gun, recoilless rifle and a mortar not to mention loads of ammo. That's why they didn't want you getting in there, if you had it would have been tea and medals all round!" He grinned.

"Boss, I'm just glad we're all out in one piece."

As he turned to walk away, he said, "Oh, one more thing. The guy who RPG'd you? His name is Abdul Bari, bit of a Taliban big shot around here." I whistled and shook my head. "He's a fucking good shot Boss!" I kept thinking about how if the sand had not been soft under my feet, any one of the three RPGs fired at me could have killed me and by the law of averages I should be dead.

Day 122

Saturday 9th August: Musa Qa'leh DC

We were warned off for a further operation to the south of Musa Qa'leh. Considering how successful we had been last time in giving the enemy a bloody nose, this would be interesting. Would they reinforce? Or would they decide that discretion was the better part of valour and disappear into the Green Zone?

It was anyone's guess of course, but we had noticed that the fields in the area that had once grown poppies were now growing maize. Given the hot weather and the irrigation of the fields, the maize crop had sprung up in height. Each stalk was at least six feet tall, much taller than your average highlander. To me this meant that if we used surprise, deception and stealth, a lot of our future fights would take place at very close quarters; how close, we would soon find out.

No sooner had we prepped ourselves for a mission to the north of Musa Qa'leh, we were told it had been scrapped. The ANA, with whom were due to do a combined operation, had cancelled theirs, so instead it was decided that we would go north again and try to push the FLET in the area of the village of Towghi Keli.

It always seemed to me that the Green Zone to the north of the DC seemed thicker than the south side, so with the maize fields flourishing it would almost be like jungle or bush warfare. So, we started putting Minimi gunners as our point men, as by this stage the Army had not yet brought the combat shotgun into service.

It would be tours like Op Herrick 8 where the British Army was forced to rethink its equipping of combat troops in Helmand. This would include everything from weapons to camouflage.

Day 123

Sunday 10th August: Musa Qa'leh DC

Once again, our Company operation was cancelled today as the Company was struck with a severe case of viral D&V. As a previous victim of it, I could totally sympathise with the afflicted. There were so many that the Battlegroup MO (Medical Officer) had to get more tents erected to house all the sick men. We received signals intelligence to suggest that the enemy were suffering too, the Taliban had put a temporary hold on offensive operations for a few days, so I felt a lot better knowing they were struck down by the dreaded lurgy.

I made sure that we took water to the boys as they would be suffering badly with dehydration. August in Afghanistan is close fifty degrees most days and when you already can't keep fluids down or up, dehydration can be a killer.

The tented camp looked like a Crimean War hospital, with sweating soldiers rolling about on their cot beds in agony from stomach cramps. Some men were so bad they had to have beds with holes cut into them and a bucket underneath as they couldn't even make it to the toilet. The stench of sickness was overpowering. Having had it I knew you had to let the body's immune system go to work and ride the sickness out, as long as you tried to remain hydrated you would get through it.

We still had ground to dominate and patrols to conduct, so that's what we did. We cobbled together patrols from those who had not been affected by the D&V outbreak and we continued to dominate the areas around the DC.

I had been given the task of heading to the 82 Northing to provoke a response from the enemy. So, I actually made it my mission to be seen, within reason of course. I didn't want to risk getting the lads shot up. From the minute we left the DC were being dicked, and we knew we would, but as soon as we got into the Green Zone I began to use deception tactics I had learned as a young patrol commander in Northern Ireland. I would go into cover as a three-section patrol and then come out of cover as a two-section patrol after splitting my third section down. This was designed to confuse the watching enemy; they knew we worked in three distinct groups, so if they couldn't see the third group of soldiers, they would get nervous and wonder where they had gone. It was a great deception as the Taliban never really counted how many soldiers were in each group, so at an opportune moment I would find cover again and break back out into three sections again, which would send the ICOM into a frenzy.

John my interpreter thought it was hilarious listening to the maddened Taliban commander berating his lookouts for being sloppy and asking where all the ISAF troops were. Just when they thought they had us pinged again, I would do something else or change my patrol direction.

As we patrolled, I took the opportunity to talk to the locals as we went. They were more friendly towards us and were willing to talk more openly. Word had gotten around that we were not afraid to fight and did not retreat at every chance and use our heavy stuff to influence the battle. Sometimes it was necessary, but mostly we preferred a stand-up fight and the Afghans respected that and they would only support the team they knew were winning – at this stage of the tour it was definitely us.

We began to hear that the Taliban were reinforcing their units with foreign Jihadists, we thought in preparation for Ramadan in September. The locals told us that there were Russians, Arabs and Pakistanis, as well as other foreigners in the area; mostly to the north of Hajji Rashid gardens, in the villages of Big and Small Kats.

Despite all the ICOM chatter we received, and John made it clear they could see us, nothing happened. We were not engaged at all; I couldn't help but think that this was because of the deception measures I was putting into place.

We returned to the DC and I was able to inform Battlegroup HQ of what had happened by sticking in a patrol report that had the information we had gained and I also believe SIGINT (Signals Intelligence) had recorded the ICOM chatter in the hope they could triangulate the position of the Taliban commander and drop him a nice thousand-pound precision-guided gift from us all.

Day 124

Monday 11th August: Musa Qa'leh DC

Today was a kind of a chill day for most of my Platoon. The lads were able to relax, sleep, play cards or watch movies on their laptops. But for me it was also about battle prep. Si had given out a warning order that we were heading south for real this time, as the ANA had decided it was okay to go out and play.

From experience we figured that the ANA would only stay out till around lunchtime and then sack it off and go home. Despite the pleading and cajoling of their OMLT advisors they would still not full embrace the offensive spirit that was prevalent within the British Infantry.

I would be the reserve Platoon commander and the Company would be the reserve element for the operation, with the ANA taking the lead supported by the Mastiff Company.

We also had some guests arrive in the form of a 3 PARA element. While we would be going south, they would operate to the north. Their arrival was heralded by the deep thumping of Chinook rotor blades and this obviously drew our attention.

3 PARA were operating out of Kandahar Airbase, the Disneyland of Afghanistan. Three decent meals a day, proper accommodation, access to lots of PXs (military shops) for all the countries who had troops at Kandahar, a boardwalk with coffee shops and burger restaurants.

We watched as quad bikes flew down the path from the HLS to the vehicle park, where we all stood gawking. It occurred to me that the only thing missing from this picture was 'Ride of the

Valkyries' playing in the background. To them we must have looked like refugees as we stood there in our boxer shorts and flip flops, each man having lost so much weight and looking malnourished, staring like Third-World refugee children. By comparison, when the dust settled from the multitude of quad bikes, we saw that the Paratroopers were all well fed with fairly nice shiny combats, whereas ours were bleached almost white by the sun and sweat. They had the sleeves on their shirts rolled up to mid forearm and their helmets were covered in hessian strips, reminiscent of the Paras of World War Two in Normandy and Arnhem. But most incredible of all, most of them had beards. One of the Jocks squinted at the Paras who for the most part growled back.

"Ho mate!" he called out. When the Paras ignored him, he got louder. "HO MATE!" he called louder. The nearest Paratrooper looked disdainfully in our direction.

"What the fuck do you want?" he snarled.

"Ho mate, huv you guys no got any hot runnin' water at Kandahar? Is yer plumber aff sick?" He knew full well that they certainly did have the luxury of hot and cold running water. We were only excused shaving when we were out on patrol, but as soon as we returned to the DC, the stubble came off.

"Fuck off!" the Para replied and flew off towards the vehicle park in a cloud of dust and petrol fumes.

"Nay danger ya dobber!" the Jock called to the Para as he roared off. "I dinae ken how the've brought aw they bikes man!" the Jock laughed. "Everybody kens ye cannea use 'em in the Green Zone!" He was right. We had access to quad bikes, but where they were going the quad bike was pretty useless. Which is why we had to carry everything on our backs.

As we trudged back to our area after the 'excitement' of the Paras arrival, Goody grabbed a few us with a view to going across to the Paras and helping them out with a ground brief of the area they would be working in. As we approached a group of commanders, they caught sight of us and began chuckling.

"Awright guys?" Goody asked. "We thought ye might like a groond brief eh this area? We've been fighting here fer a few months noo, so we kinda ken the area." The Paras, none of whom seemed to be wearing any rank, looked down their noses at us.

"Fuck off mate, we don't need any help off you fucking hats!" one of them spat. We all shrugged and turned around.

"Fuckin' retards!" Goody spat back. "We'll see how they get ohn when the shite hits the fan!"

We all shook our heads because if we had been in the same position, no matter where the advice had come from, we would have willingly accepted it.

Day 125

Tuesday 12th August: Musa Qa'leh DC

We continued our battle prep for the southern operation, which included a ROC drill, Rehearsal of Concept. In other words, we would be walking and talking through how each phase of the operation would go and what part each of us would play in it. We liked to include all the members of the Company because as they say, 'A picture paints a thousand words' and indeed the ROC drill did exactly that.

This was nothing new in the British military way of thinking but I'm sure it was an idea first brought about by Canadian commanders during the Great War, who were almost responsible for how modern battle prep is conducted. For example, when the Canadians were given the task of assaulting Vimy Ridge, they did a detailed air and ground reconnaissance of their target and trained for weeks with the attacking formations on ground similar to Vimy Ridge behind the lines. They made scale models of the target and went through step by step every unit's part in the plan until they were ready for H-Hour. And of course, Vimy Ridge was an outstanding success for the Canadians because everyone knew the target and the ground and every soldier knew his part in the plan of attack. This method of pre-op planning is still used today and to great effect.

We came to know the area both by patrolling it and by having the ROC drill so that the boys could conduct the operation in their sleep. For the next twenty-four hours we would eat, sleep and breathe this operation and we were ready for it. My kit checks were done as usual and we were checked and re-checked just to make sure we were ready to go, just in case the Op got called early.

The OC's plan had called for a graduated advance south and in this instance, it was ground that would be ideal for the use of quad bikes.

Goody took the chance to use ours, which would have a trailer loaded down with ammunition and counter-measure gear.

The plan as it stood would be to slowly advance and be at PB South by 06:00hrs. The ANA would have left at 05:00hrs to begin the advance to their start line/FUP and we would caterpillar forward behind them as they advanced ready for CASEVAC duties, fire support tasks and extra assault units, should they be required.

We all knew that no plan survives contact was an inviolable truth, and it seemed that Murphy had got up bright and early ahead of the ANA and began imposing his law. We reached PB South at 06:00hrs, which was the ANA's H-Hour (the time allotted to begin an operation or attack). Delta Company arrived to find a lot of semi-naked Afghan soldiers burping and farting over a late breakfast after a nice long lie in who were in absolutely no rush to get out and have a go at the Taliban. We all looked up into the sky and watched as an Apache Gunship circled over the operational area. Goody stood up off the seat of his quad bike, looked up at the Apache, then eyed the ANA dudes still in their PJ's and shook his head.

"Well that's fuckin' useless up there noo int it?" Indeed, the multi-million-pound killing machine had now flown in so many circles I would be surprised if the pilot was not getting air sick. It was effectively useless. All it told the Taliban was that their dicking screen need not have turned up for work that morning, the coalition troops were coming south.

Eventually, after some pleading and cajoling from their advisors, the ANA got moving and to be fair made a good pace heading towards their start line, but we had already started taking bets that they would sack it off around lunch time.

"Nay danger that lot'll last till lunch time man!" one Jock announced.

"Awright!" said another. "Two hundred snout says they dae stay oot till efter lunch time." There was a shaking of hands and a silent prayer that the ANA would indeed get bored, tired or just want to go home midday. But that also meant that Delta Company would then have to push forward and finish the job.

My Platoon stayed in reserve with Goody, which meant we could ditch our ECM kit onto the quad and still remain safe. We swapped it out for more ammo in case we had to resupply the forward Platoons in an area Goody's bike couldn't reach. The Company stayed a tactical bound behind 2 SCOTS Mastiff Company who had a similar task to us, and they at least could provide mobile heavy fire support to the ANA if they needed it. They had their .50 Cal machine guns, 40mm grenade machine guns and Jimpies.

We could hear the fighting going on all morning and despite expectations, the ANA not only held their ground, they also pushed forward to dislodge the Taliban from their fighting positions. We heard the buzz of spent rounds flying over our heads and could hear mortar fire, but that was aimed primarily at the ANA.

As the sun got higher and the fighting stalled, we decided to take over some compounds as defensive positions in the heat of the day. Still, rounds buzzed over our heads from Taliban firing points hundreds of metres to the south. We knew we weren't the intended targets, but we still had to be careful.

It came over the radio that the enemy were holding the ANA at a standstill to our south and an F-18 fighter was coming in to drop a bomb on the position held by up to fifteen insurgents. I had to witness this as I hadn't seen a bomb being dropped yet so close.

I chose a vantage point and watched; above us was the faint sound of a fighter plane's engine. We all looked but couldn't see it but suddenly the pitch of the engine changed, which suggested it was diving.

We all watched excitedly in the direction of the enemy position. There was a strange silence that made us wonder whether the plane had called off its attack when suddenly a large cloud of black smoke rose into the air above the target. Then came the ominous 'Boom' and the concussion.

"Fuck me Goody! That was massive!" I called as the boys around me began cheering and giving thumbs up to the pilot, who by now was probably on his way back to Kandahar air base for a nice hot shower and a brew, probably coffee. Goody looked over his shoulder at me and grinned evilly. "Two thousand pounder mucker, they're fucked in that compound." The battle damage assessment had said six fighters were under the bomb when it went off, six less AKs to be firing at us tomorrow.

As we moved past the compound that evening there was still smoke boiling out of the destroyed building. I watched as stray dogs who had been picking through the ruins began fleeing with well-cooked body parts. "Good puppies!" I called out to them but was rewarded with a 'stay away' growl.

As we settled in for the night, a local elder from Dagyan came in under a flag of truce and spoke to Si about the day's events. He informed us that thirteen Taliban had been killed in the day's fighting and eleven were wounded, some might not survive the night. He also informed us that the Taliban were fleeing back to Pakistan with their wounded and whatever dead they were able to recover, to try and get reinforcements.

If what the old man was saying was true, then the enemy had been dealt a major blow by the ANA and US air power.

We had a quiet night with not even ICOM chatter and to top it all off the ANA stayed out too, so one of the boys was now down two hundred Pine lights.

After a restful night we were informed that the Taliban had laid an IED during the night near PB South, more than likely expecting to hit forces returning from the Dagyan/Yatimchay area. But some sharp-eyed ANA soldier had spotted them laying it and fired at them, though not before the Taliban were able to plant it. A counter IED Team from Bastion were en route to deal with the device, but in the meantime, we would have to redeploy in order to keep eyes on the device. Other than stagging on to keep eyes on the IED, the lads all took the chance to catch up on their sleep and rest.

As the IED team were coming in the ANA pushed south as a diversion. As luck would have it, they found an IED factory, which, after a short gun battle with the enemy, was cleared. Five insurgents were taken prisoner and one was killed, adding to yesterday's very nice tally.

We watched as the EOD operator walked slowly towards the area of the IED, his team had cleared the route for him and marked it so that he knew where his safe lane was. We provided overwatch on likely enemy positions and just like the two-thousand-pound bomb, we couldn't wait to see this IED being detonated.

I watched from the roof of the compound we had occupied. I could just make out the figure of the EOD operator as he moved to rig the IED up. Rather than try to defuse it and recover it, he had decided that the safest bet was to blow it in place. After what seemed like forever, I watched his shape moving through the swirling haze of the afternoon heat. The heat haze made him look like he was dancing, which I found funny.

The word came over the radio for everyone to take cover, the IED was about to be blown up. I looked around and could see everyone had pulled low enough that only their helmets and eyes would have been visible over the wall. There was a bang, then a large cloud rose sharply into the warm blue sky, to be followed by a louder bang and the blast wave of the IED rushed over our heads.

I could only imagine the devastation that IED would have caused had one of us or the ANA actually stepped on it. At this stage of the war IEDs were a threat, but not a very high threat, we were still facing our enemy across the battlefield and trading rounds with them.

As soon as the all-clear was sounded we were given the order to withdraw back to the US PB for the night, where we would stag on and prep for a further push in the morning. We were joined by 10 Platoon, which was great as it meant fewer sentry shifts for the lads and a good restful night.

The next day my Platoon was ordered to push south again to show a presence and if possible, draw a reaction from the enemy. We all knew, though, that after the beating the Taliban had taken over the last few days, they would more than likely have gone into hiding. As we patrolled around the area, we noticed that there were more civilians than normal, which was a good sign, no civvies or civvies fleeing the area was a bad sign. We patrolled without incident passing the time of day with the locals and keeping our eyes peeled for any sign of the enemy.

Our loop finished back at the US PB without being fired at and we then withdrew back to the DC, mission accomplished. But every one of us knew that within twenty-four hours the Taliban would be back in Yatimchay, because you only hold the ground in Afghanistan when you're standing on it.

As we got through the front gate of the DC, Lt Col Nick Borton, the CO of 2 SCOTS who had taken over our battlegroup after the wounding of our CO, was there to greet us with a grim look on his face.

"Sorry lads," he said. "Well done for your efforts down south, but I need Delta Company to head north and finish 3 Para's work." The lads removed their helmets and wiped their brows and began to shake their heads. Colonel Borton didn't explain why we needed to head north and finish the job, but someone related to us how 3 Para had pushed north with their quad bikes towards their objectives – only then realising that actually they couldn't get into the area to resupply their guys or evacuate wounded personnel. Predictably, as fighting erupted, the troops taking the battle to the enemy began to run low on ammunition and couldn't get it resupplied as the quad bikes couldn't get to them. They began to run low on batteries for all their kit and once again, couldn't resupply from their quads. Our source told us that they had lost an interpreter and had a few lads slightly wounded.

They were withdrawn back to Kandahar and we never saw them in Musa Qa'leh again. So, Delta Company had forty-eight hours and we were going to be going back out. This time heading north towards the town of Kats.

Day 131

Monday 18th August: Musa Qa'leh DC

Our period of relative restfulness was coming to an end. Tomorrow we would be pushing back north to conduct further Ops from where 3 PARA had left off and we knew that without a doubt the fighting would be hard.

Both villages of Kats were known to be strong Taliban bases and they were able to extract themselves, and their casualties, out of Helmand fairly rapidly by heading north. And we were the Coalition's furthest north callsigns in Helmand before they hit Uruzgan Province.

Our personnel who had been away on R&R also returned, including the OC who brought some interesting news with him. A few weeks previously, a TV producer had come to visit us as well as some other units in Helmand with a view to following our Company for a documentary with Ross Kemp. It was to be called *Ross Kemp: Return to Afghanistan* and his team were looking for a group of soldiers to follow that would show the people back home just what soldiers fighting in Afghanistan had to go through on a daily basis.

I had seen his first documentary, *Ross Kemp in Afghanistan* and I liked it very much, it was gritty and pulled no punches. Ross was the first journalist to really do this since probably the Vietnam war and the fact that he had no agenda, he just wanted to tell the story of British soldiers fighting the war in Afghanistan, was even more admirable.

It seems that Ross's producer had gone back to him and told him of a company of Scottish soldiers who were fighting the enemy in ISAF's northernmost outpost in Helmand. Ross was up for the challenge of spending time with us and documenting our war.

I had mixed emotions at the thought of TV cameras following us while we fought, it had the power to make your reputation or break it. However, if we carried on the way we had I thought we would be okay. There was always a concern that he and his crew would get in the way and cause complications for the troops on the ground (as it happens, this fear was totally unfounded).

According to sources at Brigade, we seemed to be one of the only companies in the whole of Helmand facing combat on a daily basis and meeting it with force. It was with a mix of trepidation and excitement that I thought about the coming filming.

Day 132

Tuesday 19th August: Musa Qa'leh DC

We had deliberately left our patrol h-hour till the afternoon so that we could avoiding pattern setting. The Taliban knew that regularly our patrols would leave just before first light in order to make the best use of the lower temperatures. But by now our guys had pretty much acclimatised to the heat and were at the stage where mild discomfort was all they felt (within reason).

Generally, at the late afternoon stage of things the Taliban were at prayer or relaxing if there were no ISAF troops on the ground. But the minute we were seen leaving base, the jungle drums would beat and the enemy would be stood to.

My exit got off to a false start. I had managed to get four hundred metres from the DC when one soldier (who will remain nameless) complained that his leg was hurting. I had inherited this soldier, who was not Royal Regiment of Scotland, but I had high hopes as his unit had a good reputation and esprit de corps. So, I was very disappointed that whenever we went out on the ground, he invariably made three to four hundred metres before complaining of some injury or other. I called a halt to the Platoon and informed Goody that we had a casualty and were returning to the DC to extract him as we were still close enough to do so.

"Who the fuck is it?" he asked, the irritation in his voice very evident. When I told him the soldier's name, he growled. "Git that useless c**t back tae camp ASAP three zero Bravo and let's crack on!" As mad as Goody was, I was twice as mad.

Firstly, the operation had to be held up while the soldier was extracted risking the lads who had to wait for us, and it was embarrassing as it was always the same soldier I was having to extract. Always my Platoon, which had begun to grate on me. Also, my lads had to patrol an extra kilometre pretty much in order to extract the injured soldier, then join up with the rest of the Company.

I fumed all the way back to the DC as the rest of the Platoon carried the casualty's kit. The looks on the faces of the lads showed that they were similarly unimpressed by the soldier's injury and did not relish the tab back to the Company. We walked back through the barrier at the DC and were met with some very confused ANA soldiers who wondered what we were doing. I took the casualty to the medical centre, which was in and to the right of the main entrance in what looked like an old car garage.

"Sir," I said to the doctor. "I've had to extract this man from the ground, he's hurt his leg."

"Thanks Sarge, I'll take it from here." With that I turned on my heels and led the Platoon back out the DC and headed north again to RV with the Company. When I arrived back at the Company, I was met by Goody who had a face like thunder. He grabbed me and we walked away from the Platoon.

"Whit the fuck wis that aw aboot?" he asked. I shrugged my shoulders and shook my head.

"Fuck knows Goody, but this isnea the first time this has happened. He's a liability. If you don't have any objections, from now on he stays in the DC and helps camp security in the sangars?" Goody's face brightened.

"Aye, that's a gid idea, ah'v got nay dramas wi that. We cannae dae that everytime he disnae feel like gon oot on the ground!"

I became aware that this may seem like favouritism or one soldier getting an easy ride, but when I looked at my Platoon, I realised that their lives were in my hands and that this soldier was cutting down the chances of me taking them all home in one piece. I was surrounded by a good core of men in my Platoon, they had been battle-tested now and had not shied away. They were the best I could ask for and I knew that our war was not over yet. We still had a few months to go before we were done and could go home to our loved ones. It also struck me that so far, we had beaten the odds. None of us was dead, yes we had taken casualties, but none of them were fatally wounded and I planned on keeping it that way.

As we pushed through the Green Zone towards the Gardens, our hackles were up and we were ready for a fight. The ICOM scanners had told us the Taliban were waiting for us and were setting up ambushes ahead of our advance, but it all proved to be bluster.

I imagined that the enemy had taken such a beating over the last week that they were in no position to mount a serious attack against us, probably more like their usual hit and run harassing shoot and scoot attacks.

We moved into our night defensive locations, the initial compound I was told to occupy proved a bust, there were no good arcs of fire to tie in with the rest of the Company and fields of view were restricted by the trees in the Green Zone around us. I did a quick map study and across the canal was a compound that fulfilled our needs. The canal was about ten feet wide and was very deep. The only crossing points were huge logs that the locals had sawn down and put across the canal. I watched as my lads all weighed down with heavy kit did a precarious, almost comic tightrope walk along the logs and then breathed a sigh of relief when they hit firm ground on the other side.

As soon as everyone was across and still dry, we moved to compound HK7-259 to see if it was any better. Already from the outside it looked good, all the ground to the east was open land, which looked like it had been cultivated. This would ensure that the Company's entire right flank was covered and any attempt by the Taliban to come from that location would be met with a wall of fire.

Our arcs north, east and south were excellent and once we had stood down after last light, I got the guys bedded down and we began our sentry duty on the compound walls. Throughout the night we saw lights to the north and to the east of us, which I reported to Company HQ.

I believed that it was possibly the enemy was forming up or reinforcing for the next day as they would have exactly no doubt as to where we were. This was exactly the same area that 3 PARA had reported seeing enemy fighters heading towards them during their operation.

The night however, turned out to be quiet and no enemy attack was forthcoming, but we did not relax our guard as we knew that we were most definitely in the Taliban's back yard now, and under cover of darkness they would be moving their fighters around in order to try and encircle us, or at least form a barrier to the north to hold us or slow us down.

Day 133

Wednesday 20th August: Compound HK7-259, North of Musa Qa'leh

After a quiet night, we awoke to a crisp cool morning with a slight mist that we knew would burn off as the sun came up. The boys all stood to on the compound walls waiting to see if the enemy had indeed prepared a dawn attack for us.

With an air of nervous anticipation, we all scanned the dry arid ground around us. To the west immediately next to us was the Green Zone and our canal crossing point. I watched as the mist drifted slowly and eerily through the trees. I almost expected to see a group of black turbaned, AK wielding insurgents burst forth through the trees and mist.

But this did not materialise and pretty soon a burst of static in my left ear was followed by the Company signaller informing the Company to stand down. We did stand down but as always, we left soldiers in position at all the compass points of the compound as we were at our most vulnerable after stand down.

Everyone was trying to grab a bite to eat, a smoke and a drink of water or a hot cup of tea while giving their weapons a quick wipe off, clearing any dew that may have formed on them and oiling them, ready for what the day would bring.

Major Calder gave his orders for the day over the radio and we Platoon commanders gave our acknowledgement that we understood his plan. From where we were, we would push west towards the Musa Qa'leh Wadi and then shake out and push north through Hajji Rashid Gardens; no doubt eliciting a response from the Taliban which would then start the day's activities.

I shook the Platoon out into a 'U' shape formation as we were the reserve Platoon and waited for the OC's order to advance. 10 Platoon, under Jim Adamson, led the Company followed by the OC. Then 11 Platoon under Charlie Grant, then the 2i/c and Goody. And finally, my Platoon.

The boys all assumed a low profile as much as they could. As I looked around, I could see some of the boys had taken off their patrol packs and were lying behind them. Some were kneeling up peering through the foliage expecting the enemy to appear at any moment. But most had adopted a tactical sitting position that allowed them to still cover their arcs but didn't strain their back or knees.

I had no choice, I had to adopt the kneeling position in order to watch for the 2i/c's group moving off. As I slowly dropped to one knee, I started to feel the years of tabbing and carrying heavy kit weigh on the small of my back and my knees. Every joint from the waist down burned, cracked and popped. I sounded like a bowl of rice crispies and I could only maintain that position for a short of time as my armour and patrol pack would drag me down.

The morning prayers had ended and we knew at that stage of the morning, with the sun now coming up, that the Taliban would be in

their fighting positions ready to start the activities for the day and we
had steeled ourselves ready for what may come.

We knew that we were truly into the fighting season, every day we
were out we were fighting the enemy and we were making a dent in their
numbers. Hopefully, we would kill enough of them that their will to fight
would be severely degraded.

It was with this thought in mind that I was rudely brought back to
reality by heavy gunfire from up ahead near 10 Platoon. It sounded like
a Minimi with very little AK fire. As it happened 10 Platoon's point man,
Gordon pollock, had been patrolling through a maize field and as he had
exited it, five metres to his front two Taliban fighters had been waiting.
Thankfully for him they were facing in the wrong direction, they hadn't
anticipated us coming through the maize. Gordon was quicker off the
mark and popping his safety catch to fire, he riddled the two fighters
with a burst of 5.56mm from his light machine gun. As the smoke
cleared from his initial burst, he saw the two Taliban lying dead, blood
slowly spreading out in patterns on their dish dashas.

Suddenly, movement to his front caught his eye and another Taliban
fighter, wide-eyed with shock, tried to bring his rifle to bear. Gordon still
had the safety catch off and loosed another burst of fire at the enemy.
Gordon watched as the rounds struck the fighter. With a shriek of agony,
the fighter, severely wounded around the upper leg and hip, limped as
fast as he could into the cover of the nearest building.

The enemy were now fully alert and had realised we were amongst
them, and began to fire in the direction of our Company. I told the lads
to stay low and listened to the beating of my heart as my pulse rate
began to increase. The trees above our heads were being shredded by
incoming AK and PKM fire and occasionally in the near distance I could
hear the familiar 'whoosh' of RPGs incoming. We had poked a stick into
the wasp's nest and now the wasps were pissed. I got the call over the
radio.

"Three zero Alpha this is zero Alpha I want your callsign to assault
compounds HK8-13, 15 and 16 enemy believed to be in all three." I
did a quick map check and got my section commanders together. As we
formed a circle, I spread the map out on the ground in front of me and
grabbed a twig off the floor.

"As you heard, these are the compounds the Boss wants us to take!"
I paused circling the three compounds that were set in an 'L' shape with
a track running south to north between 13 and 15. "We'll start with
compound 13. I want us to go in red (meaning every building would

have a grenade thrown into it to clear it out), don't do anything fucking stupid, clear the buildings then see who's left alive! Loone I want your section on point mate, first assault section."

Loone McCarthy grinned his big pumpkin faced grin and nodded.

"Nay dramas mucks, let's smash these c**ts!"

"Everybody happy with the plan?" They all nodded and went away to brief their sections. As soon as the section commanders let me know they were ready over the Platoon channel, I keyed the handset on my radio to let the OC know we were ready and moving towards our objective.

As we advanced on compound 13, I could still hear AK fire coming down and a lot of it going over our heads was coming from the compounds we were to clear. I listened in to the net as 11 Platoon breached their first compound. They reported that their first grenade had caused a civilian casualty, an old man had a finger blown off in the explosion and he was being given first aid. My headset burst into life and the relaxed posh voice of major Calder drawled in my ear.

"Charlie Charlie One (every unit in the Company), be aware when using grenades, I don't want collateral damage if it can be helped!" I confirmed my understanding of the order but I was more than prepared to use grenades if it meant we killed the enemy, who were clearly occupying the compounds we were assaulting. I could take no chances with my men's lives.

"Better tae be tried by twelve than carried by six eh mucker?" Loone grinned as though he had read my mind. We approached the first compound and I called a stack left against the wall next to the large iron gate and got the lads to fix bayonets, which we would not remove for the rest of the day.

Loone's section formed up with the skill and experience I had come to expect from my Platoon. I ordered the lads to all drop their patrol packs and the reserve section would wait with them. I listened to see if I could hear any noise coming from inside the compound, it was silent.

Had the enemy heard us? Were they waiting to hit us the minute we came through the gate? A thousand thoughts were running through my head, Loone was stood right behind his first man, a grenade clutched in his fist ready to be hurled over the wall. He had removed the matt black clip holding the flyoff lever in place and his trigger finger was curled through the ring pull, he locked eyes with me in anticipation of the order to let the grenade fly. I studied the doorway and decided that if the enemy were indeed waiting for us on the other side their weapons would be trained on the metal gate.

3 Section in cover seconds before being involved in the RPG strike on Davey McGhee.

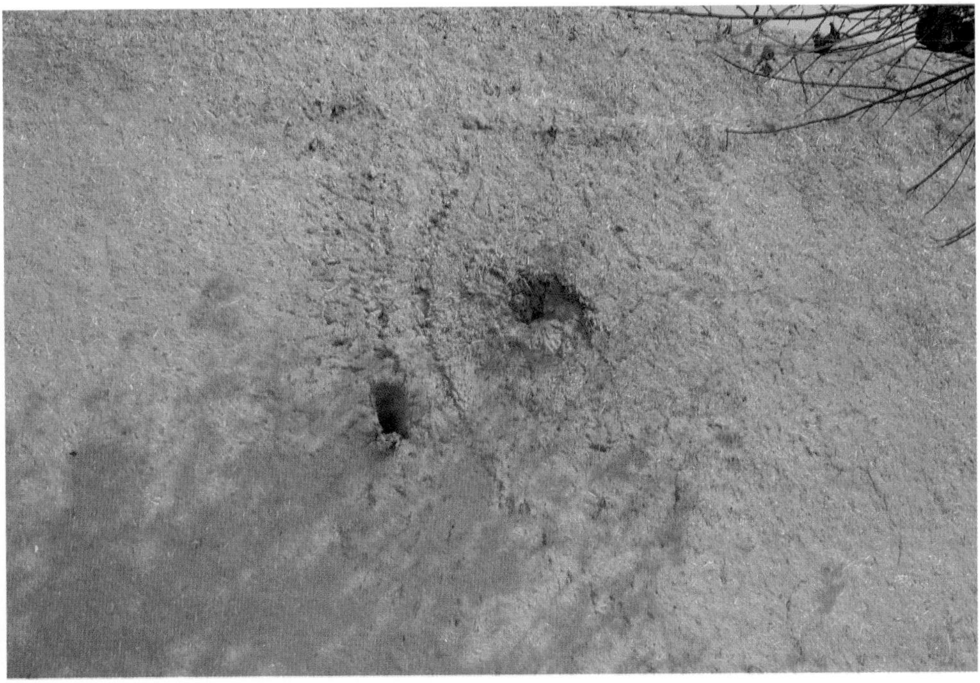

Marks from the RPG strike that severely wounded Davey McGhee.

Medical Treatment Facility (MTF) at Camp Bastion, Afghanistan. The MTF, which is housed in one of the few solid buildings at Bastion, replaced the tented field hospital that had been used since 2003.

The two tier accommodation blocks at Camp Bastion, Helmand, Afghanistan, 2009. In the 2 tours of Afghanistan we would serve, none of the fighting troops would see the inside of this accommodation. (Cpl Steve Blake RLC/MOD)

The move into FOB Keenan. Poppies nearing cultivation told soldiers that the fighting season was near.

D Company in Musa Qa'leh Wadi covering a logistical resupply. In the foreground is the tough little GPMG gunner Scotty McGregor.

Above: Kandahar Airfield, Afghanistan: Members of the 508th Parachute Infantry Regiment prepare for air assault on Musa Qa'leh. (Matt Sanchez)

Left: The Afghan flag is raised over Musa Qa'leh following its recapture on 11 December 2007. (Cpl Wayne K. Pitsenberger, US Army)

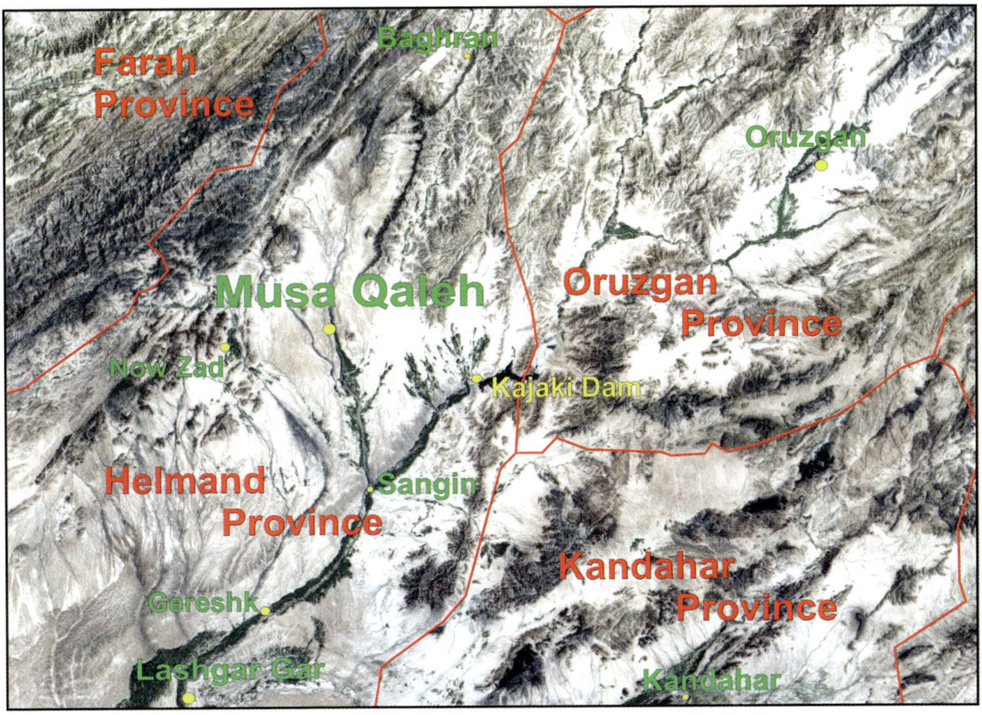

Map showing the Musa Qa'leh area.

The Camp Bastion war memorial, made from 30mm Apache cannon shells and with brass plates inscribed with the names of those who lost their lives in Helmand. This memorial now resides at the National Memorial Arboretum in Staffordshire. (Cpl Daniel Wiepen/MOD)

Above: An F15E drops 2000lb munitions in Afghanistan, 2009. D Company would make much use of close air support during OP Herrick 8, with airframes from various NATO countries answering the call to assist their comrades in Helmand.

Below: Troops retrieve ration supplies, dropped at night by C-130 Hercules aircraft near FOB Edinburgh. (Sgt Keith Cotton RLC/MOD)

Al Lipowski winning the hearts and minds of the locals of Musa Qa'leh by handing out radios. The radios could only be tuned to certain channels that broadcast messages from the Kabul government.

CSM Alan 'Goodie' Goodall, chilling south of Musa Qa'leh.

Left: Davey 'Pods' Poderis, our army reservist who had many tours of duty in both Iraq and Afghanistan under his belt, relaxing with a cup of Afghan chai tea, which is 90% sugar.

Below: Bruce Ewart using a Desert Rose.

Above and below: Davey Pods' miracle helmet.

Left: Geordie Morgan on a sentry position, shortly after being engaged with AK small arms fire from a local child. Geordie was one of our Army Air Corps attachments, who took to infantry fighting like a duck to water.

Below: Falling back after a gun battle in in the Musa Qa'leh Wadi.

Me and Bruce preparing to head out on patrol. Note the differences in camouflage patterns - I am wearing tropical jungle combats which blended better in the Green Zone, whereas Bruce wears desert pattern camouflage which was ideal in other areas. For Herrick 13 we would move to Multi Terrain Pattern (NTP), which would be good for both environments.

Goodie's RPG wound. Goodie would receive shrapnel from the same RPG that wounded Davey McGhee and refused to be evacuated. To me this demonstrated utter selflessness in the greatest traditions of the British Army and was deserving of at least the Mention in Despatches (MiD).

Al Lipowski gives orders prior to an operation north of Musa Qa'leh.

Above left: Colonel David Richmond, who was shot in the leg during an engagement on 12 June 2008.

Above right: Major Nick Calder, a great leader of men. It is thanks to his tactical acumen and leadership that we were able to time and time again defeat the Taliban and get home to our loved ones.

Mastiff after striking a legacy Soviet mine. This shows the durability and survivability of the Mastiff armoured vehicle.

Mount Doom, with ANP officers in the distance.

Chief of the Defence Staff, General Nick Carter. (MOD)

Pete Breen engages Taliban positions near Big Kats.

British troops inspect a downed Mk3 Merlin recovered from an FOB. (US Army)

ISAF troops in a Husky Armoured Vehicle pass Afghan locals on Route Trident in Helmand. (POA(Phot) Sean Clee/MOD)

The last Chinook helicopter flight into FOB (Forward Operating Base) Shawqat, to air lift out UK personnel for the last time. (Cpl Si Longworth RLC (Phot))

Taliban fighters in a captured Humvee after the Fall of Kabul, August 2021. (Voice of America/US Govt)

"Loone, I want you to lob it so that it's just the other side of this gate about three metres into the compound," I called in a low voice. He nodded and I gave the signal to breach, with a sharp tug the grenade pin came free and I watched as his arm raised in an overhand throw and the green ball sailed over the compound wall, the flyoff lever pinged into the air and disappeared.

Every soldier tensed in anticipation of the explosion to come and there was a dull thud followed by the pinging of shrapnel striking things inside the compound. Without hesitation, Loone's section filed into the compound to begin clearing it.

I followed in immediately behind the last man and was greeted by a scene of chaos, as the smoke cleared there was a dead sheep lying next to the compound entrance. Its dark fleece riddled with shrapnel and blood pouring out onto the dry ground, forming dark red pools under its corpse.

Loone set to work clearing the rest of the compound and out the corner of my eye I saw a door open to our front, my safety catch was off and I had brought my rifle into the shoulder and was about to squeeze a round off into the opening door. But as my sight picture formed, I made out an Afghan female wearing a blue head scarf waving her right hand at me, her left hand clutching her neck.

The breath that I had been holding in ready to open fire was released and I rushed forward. In the small room with her were two small children, both girls about four or five years old, the woman must have been around mid to late thirties but it was hard to tell, the harsh environment in Afghanistan aged everyone.

I calmed the children down and lifted the mother's hand away from her neck, a small piece of shrapnel had cut into her neck and she was bleeding heavily. It was horrible proof of the effectiveness of our hand grenades, as the woman had been about ten metres away from the blast area behind a thick wooden door and yet the shrapnel had still managed to hit her.

I quickly rooted around in my kit for a pressure bandage and tore the waterproof pack open with my teeth, popping the grey bandage free. Using hand signals, I was able to get her to release her hand so I could put the bandage on her. She then put her hand back on the bandage to keep the pressure on.

I remembered I still had this compound, and two others, to clear. All were still potentially harbouring Taliban fighters.

"Nige!" I called to Campbell. His head popped up like a meerkat and he came running across to me. "Take care of her mate, will you? I've still got to clear the other two compounds." Nige nodded and took over the treatment, I informed Major Calder that we also had a civvy casualty and were dealing with it. He despatched an Army nurse who had been attached to our Company from the Battle group aid post and she came running through the entry point and began helping Campbell with the mother.

As I looked around her compound, I saw firing positions built up around her walls. Wooden ammunition crates marked with numbers and Cyrillic Russian writing had been stacked up to allow Taliban fighters to fire at us and disappear. The whole area was littered with empty cases that I knew were AK 7.62mm short. I turned back and stalked over to the woman with John in tow.

"John, ask her where the Taliban have gone that were in this compound." John crouched next to the woman who was still being treated by our female medic and relayed my request. I watched intently as she jabbered on and gesticulated with both hands, one of which was covered in her own blood. John shook his head and rose slowly turning towards me.

"She says Sir that she has seen no Taliban around here for many months." He knew it was bullshit, and I knew it was bullshit. I turned to the piled-up boxes of ammunition being used as a firing step and the piles of empty cases and said "What about that lot?" I laughed in frustration, which confused the wounded woman. "I suppose those empty cases fuckin' magicked themselves into her compound!" I didn't press the issue as I had other compounds to take. "John, let's go mate!"

I turned to Loone and told him to leave his section in here to maintain security and look after the Platoon daysacks. Grabbing Geordie Morgan, I headed out the compound and turned left towards my next objective.

As we crossed the track, we watched for any signs that the Taliban were fleeing or coming in to reinforce their embattled colleagues. Again, I called a stack left on the rusting iron door of this compound. Again, I called compound red, acutely aware that we had just fragged a civvy. But I believed the enemy were still in the area.

Periodically, gunfire from the north would crack over our heads. As we stacked, I looked along the line of Geordie's section and saw all the eyes looking back at me. Some lads licked their lips nervously, but all had a grim determination set on their faces. Gloved hands gripped their rifles tightly and where gloves weren't worn, I could see the knuckles on some hands going white. The lad's faces were darkened by a mix of the sun, dirt and cordite from weapons fire.

"Okay Geordie!" I confirmed. "You ready brother?" Geordie caught my gaze and nodded. Behind him, lads were removing grenades from pouches and removing matt black clips. I watched as trigger fingers were inserted into the silver ring pulls on the hand grenades. I gazed up at the lip of the compound wall and was about to give the order to breach when John grabbed my arm.

"Sir, I hear talking!" he said. I raised my hand to halt the boys from grenading the compound and let John get to work. It was then I noticed he was carrying an AK-47. I grinned and shook my head. If any interpreter had the right to carry a rifle it was definitely him, so I let it slide.

John began to shout in Pashtun. I was still preparing to let the grenades fly, should the people on the other side of this gate open fire, or not be who John suspected. After what seemed like an age, the rusty gate creaked open and we were met by an old Afghan man. I peered around the corner of the gate and saw his wife and children sat in a circle before a meal. I breathed out loudly and felt dizzy. It was not lost on me that they were all sat exactly where my grenades would have landed and it was thanks to John hearing their voices that this family was not riddled with shrapnel and I would most likely have been in deep shit!

"Good spot John!" I said gripping his arm. I turned around to Geordie Morgan and told his guys to relax and keep the pins back in their grenades and reattach the matt black clips.

Upon entry to the compound, the old man greeted us like long lost friends and began offering tea to us all, which we graciously accepted. I nodded to Geordie to set up sentry positions on the roofs and then let the guys relax. John stayed and chatted with the old couple and their children while I grabbed Pete Breen and got his section ready to take the next compound.

This one proved to be empty too, but once again we found evidence of Taliban activity, including used medical supplies on the roof of one building. It looked as though someone had been administered blood expander fluids and had to use them all as the bottle was empty and there were empty wrappers for bandages. Bandages that were not British or Afghan.

I settled all my sections into the compounds they had taken and informed Major Calder that my objectives were secure with no more casualties. It turned out that the old man whose family we nearly fragged had an older son with Commander Koka's ANP, a fact he was immensely proud of. I walked alone back to HK8-13 to assess the condition of our civilian casualty. The tall nurse stood up towering over me and looked down.

"She absolutely fine, no serious injuries. Although she should probably get to a hospital and get it cleaned and checked out." I nodded and took my patrol pack off and squatted in the doorway next to the wounded woman.

After calling John back over to the compound, I began to remove a waterproof bag from my patrol pack. Inside it was a stack of US dollars that we were given in case of such incidents or we were required to compensate the locals for any damage caused during our fights. Now seemed like the perfect opportunity to start dishing out the dough.

"Mother!" I said. "Here is some money to help you buy another sheep and get to hospital," I said, pausing to allow John to translate. She waved her hands at me as though she was going to refuse. Until she saw that it was quite a wad of cash, she put her hands together and from what I could gather was thanking me profusely.

I took her hands in mine and apologised for her injury and could she please let us know next time the Taliban were in her area. This way, incidents like this could be prevented. I looked down at my knee pads as I began to pack away the rest of the money and saw that they were covered in blood, I shrugged and stood up to brief the OC by radio on her status.

The OC pushed us further north to take over compounds to rest in for the heat of the day. The one we chose had one very large and very angry occupant in the form of an Afghan Kuchi mountain dog. Needless to say, the lads gave it a wide berth. We had seen how vicious they could be and shooting them was fairly pointless as it just pissed them off. After Richie McCafferty's head shot back in Gereshk, the dog had merely walked away, which bothered me as our 5.56mm rounds were apparently ineffective and they had steel core penetrators in the heads. Just as we were relaxing, my radio blared into life.

"Three zero Alpha, zero Alpha!" the OC called.

"Three zero Alpha send over!" I replied.

"Three zero, I require your callsign to head to an RV point and bring Ross Kemp and his crew to two zero's location, roger so far?" He asked.

"Three zero, so far!" I answered confirming I understood.

"RV point is in the wadi west of compound HK8-3, understood?"

"Three zero understood, I will move in figures one-zero and secure drop off point," I informed Major Calder.

Ross and his crew had not been allowed to come out on the first day of our operation as the doctor did not believe they were fully acclimatised. A review allowed him to come out in the cooler part of the afternoon and he would be deploying by Mastiff from Musa Qa'leh to our drop off point. I would then escort him up to Charlie Grant's Platoon, where he would follow 11 Platoon for the next phase of the patrol.

I gathered my troops together and briefed them up on what we were doing, but I needn't have bothered, the NCOs had passed the info down to the rest of the guys, so all that remained was to brief them on the route. We headed west and patrolled until we reached a series of compounds on a slight ridge overlooking Musa Qa'leh Wadi, a quick map check showed that we were in the right location. I deployed the Platoon into all-round defence and awaited the arrival of the Mastiffs. I didn't have to wait long and detected the sound of heavy engines approaching, soon the vehicles appeared through a gap in the trees and I watched as the 2 SCOTS lads dismounted and provided cover for Ross and his crew leaving the vehicles.

One of the Jocks pointed him in our direction and he strode over to me sticking out like a sore thumb, clad in khaki 5.11 trousers and shirt, with blue body armour and a blue helmet cover on his MK-6A helmet. I walked over to the top of the ridge and thrust my hand out to help him up.

"Welcome to Delta Company Mr Kemp," I grinned. He grinned back and in his cockney accent said "Call me Ross mate," I nodded.

"Fair enough Ross, I'm to take you to one of our other Platoons just to our east. Stay with my last section and if the shit hits the fan? Let us deal with it and follow on if we start running." He smiled and agreed, hanging back with his cameraman with my reserve section.

A part of me was star struck. Here was Grant Mitchell from Eastenders and Henno Garvey from Ultimate Force in the flesh, but also a serious journalist too; so far so good.

Our return to the Company was uneventful and I delivered him into the safekeeping of the pugnacious Danny Carter, a very professional soldier and family man, Ross and his crew could be in no better hands.

No sooner had the Company moved off than we started receiving heavy fire from the north. The rounds were snapping over our heads like hundreds of angry hornets, and the volume of fire was such that it made conversation almost impossible. It was a wall of sound and I watched as the rounds bounced off the tops of compound walls and smashed into trees above us. As the reserve Platoon I had the ANP with me and I pushed my guys into a compound out of the storm of lead, occasionally peeking around the corner to see where the lead Platoons from the Company were.

But from the fire coming in, it was easy to know where they were. As I poked my head around the corner, I became aware of the barrel of an AK behind my right ear and before I could duck my head out of the way, a bright muzzle flash blinded me and I felt the heat and the rounds pass by my face. All heading in the direction the fire was coming from, but also the direction that the rest of my Company were in. I turned around to the firer who was stood right behind me looking sheepish and pointed my finger in his face.

"John. Tell this fucking idiot if he does that again the Taliban will be the least of his fucking problems! I'll shoot the c**t!" John exchanged words with the ANP officer and seeing the look on my face, the copper knew I was deadly serious and slunk off to hide somewhere in the compound.

I peered back out of the compound entrance point again (after checking my back blast) and was met with the most bizarre sight I have ever seen. Directly in front of my compound was another smaller compound and against the wall was an ANP officer performing a little dance with his AK held above his head, the fire from the Taliban had increased and it appeared that this chap may have been the focus for a lot of it.

I watched open-mouthed as bullets began to strike the wall all around him and rather than make him take cover, it spurred him on like applause. He saw me watching and grinned, his eyes wide and bloodshot, his yellow teeth exposed in a dopey grin, I shook my head and tapped the side of my helmet with my index finger. The ANP officer either did not understand me or was too wasted to care, he carried on with his dance. A small audience of Jocks had formed behind me and they were as equally incredulous as I was.

"Whit the fuck is that rocket up tae?" one of the Jocks asked.

"Fuck knows mucker, but I think his audition might get cut short in a bit!" Our personal performance of Afghan Swan Lake was indeed cut short, but by Goody. As I poked my head around the doorway again, I saw him running towards me. Enemy fire still cracking over his head.

"George!" he yelled. "Git yer boys up there noo, the Boss needs yeh." I turned around to my guys and called "Prepare to move lads and stay fucking low, the fire is still fucking heavy out there!" I paused and caught the impatient look on Goody's face. "Let's go … with me!" I yelled, and the Platoon followed on.

We all ran as though facing a heavy storm wind, the enemy fire still searching out targets. This was definitely not one insurgent fighter, the volume of fire was too great, it had to be at least three or four fighters. As I approached where the OC was, I saw our lads lined up on a large dirt bank taking cover. Around them were trees which some were using as cover and fire positions. The OC's group were talking hurriedly into the radios and I could see Bruce consulting his map, which could only mean one thing. Major Calder caught my eye and pointed to the bank.

"I need you over there Sergeant Mac!" He shouted. I gave him the thumbs up and nodded before deploying Loone McCarthy and his guys to the mud bank. The other two sections I merged into one and kept them in cover to act as ammo resupply and casevac teams if required.

I turned back towards the sounds of battle and saw dust being kicked up from the bank all around our troops. The rounds still cracked over our heads and I could see guys kneel and fire at the enemy positions, which were in a compound approximately one hundred metres to our front. I watched as the empty cases span out the sides of the rifles and bounced down the slope, ending up in small piles at the bottom.

Loone slid down the slope and with his helmet below the top of the bank, swung his patrol pack off his back. Strapped to it was the familiar grey tube of a LASM (L72A9 Light Anti-Structures Missile), which he quickly removed. He left his pack to roll down the slope landing in that growing pile of empty bullet cases. He scrambled back up the slope, his boots kicking up dust, and he stopped short of cresting the rise. I watched as he prepared the LASM to fire, pulled off the muzzle and venturi covers, dropping them to the floor. He extended the launcher, which flipped the sights up, pulled the safety switch and he took a deep breath, checked his back-blast area to make sure no one was going to get hit by it and threw it onto his shoulder.

After what seemed like an age, he pressed the large black rubber firing button and in a bright blast of expelled gas and debris. The rocket sped from the front of the tube and hurtled towards the target. Around him lads kept blasting the position with small arms fire, but the fire was being returned. A slight lull after the firing of the LASM was met with a renewed energy from the enemy who were trying to bracket Loone and his rocket position. Bruce's voice came out over the gunfire and he hollered "Get down guys, five-hundred-pounder incoming danger close, get low!" We all did as he said, the guys on the bank slid down into cover and those of us who were behind them dropped to a lower profile.

Then we heard it, the sound almost like a freight train in a tunnel, the loud 'whoosh' expected yet unexpected in its sudden appearance and the violence of the strike. Everything shook. The world became a disorientating blur, leaves were stripped off the trees as shrapnel from the huge precision-guided bomb expanded away from the blast. The concussion of the blast was so fierce that I was thrown off balance and landed on my arse.

Then the world became quiet, no firing, nothing. No AK fire came at us, it was total silence, we all looked around and wondered if the air strike had done its work. Suddenly John's ICOM radio burst into life, the sound making us jump as it was so loud in the sudden quiet after the bombing. On it a man's agitated voice came through, he was screaming something over and over again and I could hear the word 'Allah' being liberally thrown in. I turned to John and squinted. "John, what did he say?" I asked. John grinned and raised his head from the little radio.

"He say Sir, Oh Allah please help me. They are all dead, all dead. Allah send help!" All around John, white teeth were bared in grimy faces as they heard the enemy request for help. After some more begging for salvation, the ICOM went quiet. Which could only mean the Taliban fighter on the other end had succumbed to his injuries.

Bruce would later receive feedback from the pilot who dropped the ordnance and had a bomb's eye view of the strike. There were eight insurgents in the compound when it was struck. Not one of them walked out alive.

As the sun was going down, we had a quick chat with Major Calder and he told us where he wanted us to bed down for the night. I shot a quick glance over at Ross Kemp and his cameraman and couldn't help but smile. His whole front of his kit was covered in mud and he looked like he had crawled there all the way from Musa Qa'leh. We would not see why he got so dirty until the TV programme came out, but I was not surprised. Our compound for the night turned out to be completely inadequate, there was no entrance and no roofs, it appeared to be three walls and a big hole in one side where the west wall had collapsed.

"We can't stay in here lads, there's no protection." Again, I consulted the map and found a smaller but more protected compound at HK8-220, it was cosy and gave us security in the form of a little metal door in the south-east wall. I set the sentries into position and set up my CP in the middle of the compound on a raised structure that could only have been designed to sleep on, and with my Corporals I maintained a radio stag throughout the night. I slept very well wrapped up in my Ranger blanket, glad of a few hours' sleep I wondered what the next day would bring.

Day 134

Thursday 21st August: Compound HK8-220, North of Musa Qa'leh

We awoke as usual before first light. A temporary mist had settled on the area. All the NCOs turned on their Bowman radio sets ready for stand to and they began to post their troops on the roofs of the compound. I conducted a quick radio check to Company HQ and waited. I became aware of the stillness and peace of the surrounding area, only the chirping of birds in the trees around our compound gave any indication that life had not ended overnight.

I looked around at the lads as they squinted into the morning gloom and occasionally looked through their sights for suspicious activity. Here and there on the compound walls a cough would break the stillness and all eyes would be on the soldier responsible, but quiet for the most part, they remained alert, the desert DPM-covered helmets scanning back and forth.

I knelt next to my radio ready for the word to stand down, which eventually came. Almost immediately, the sounds of the call to prayer sounded out across the area and the small villages in the Green Zone surrounding us came to life, the men all heading off to Mosque and the women preparing breakfast.

The smell of wood fires reached our nostrils and the sound of children's laughter lulled us into the sense that peace may have broken out, but we knew it was only fleeting. Once the faithful had said their prayers, magazines would be refilled and placed into old Soviet chest rigs or the pockets of the loose-fitting dishdashas worn by Afghan men. Belts of 7.62mm long would be wrapped around torsos and placed onto the feed trays of PKM machine guns, rockets would be slotted into the front of RPG launchers and hand grenades secreted wherever the owners could put them.

We underwent a similar preparation ourselves. However, no prayer for us, only the smell of cigarette smoke and gun oil. We steeled ourselves for what the day would bring. We had already brought the fight to the enemy yesterday and killed a number of them, but more would fill the gaps. To use a confusing metaphor in this case, Musa Qa'leh was fast becoming a Mecca to foreign fighters, who knew that the fighting here was significant and there was a good chance to become *Shahid*.

We conducted our radio checks just as the Taliban did on their ICOM radios. We drank some water, had something to eat and did ammo checks. We worked out amongst us commanders the order of march for the patrol, our actions on for several scenarios – some that we hoped would never play out, such as actions on casualties or being separated from the rest of the Platoon.

As we were preparing to move out, we were told to remain firm as our plan called for the Mastiff Company to shadow us to the west in Musa Qa'leh Wadi, offering intimate heavy fire support, CASEVAC and ammo resupply, should it be required. We held firm but still had sentries placed at key positions on the compound roof. The sun was now up and with it the temperature, we began to sweat profusely and we hadn't even gone anywhere.

I became aware of the smells coming off me. I looked down at myself, my UBAC shirt was covered in white salt stains which spread out from my shoulders and armpits. The smell of the ammonia from my sweat was quite strong. From my trousers, the smell of sweat and piss. My Blackhawk coyote tan knee pads were splashed with blood, which also left a coppery smell. I had a bit of growth on my chin and my tanned face was grubby and dark. The inside of my helmet smelled strongly of sweat and dirty, oily hair. But my picture of Chanelle Hayes remained unsullied. I grinned as I looked at her, she would not touch me with a barge pole on a good day, never mind reeking! The only things that were clean were my teeth.

My radio earpiece crackled into life and the OC gave everyone the order to move. I was on the left flank of the Company, so I pushed my Platoon almost to where we picked up Ross the previous day, then turned right to begin our advance north. As we passed by local people, I greeted them. "Stari mashe! Salam alikum!" Said with a smile and a wave, sometimes this was returned, sometimes we were ignored. As always, the kids rushed to greet us.

As we paralleled the wadi, the Mastiffs were patrolling slowly in a line with us, their turrets spinning around to cover their arc of fire.

Small Honda motorbikes raced past them throwing up clouds of dust and small stones, sometimes obscuring the massive armoured vehicles, which blended into the background almost to the point they were nearly invisible.

We had gone a few hundred metres when the sound of gunfire to the east reached us, Charlie Grant was in contact. We took cover and began to face the direction of fire, The Platoon had now adopted the prone position and were observing arcs over the top of their patrol packs. I was proud of the fact none of them had to be told to assume all-round defence as it had become instinctive by now. We had learned quickly that it is not always the point section of the point Platoon that come under fire, it can be anyone – Afghanistan had become a three-sixty battlefield.

I listened intently as Charlie reported he was receiving fire from compounds HK8-212 and 211, but that he could handle it. Again, I looked around the lads and could see them fixing bayonets. With a metal on metal sound followed by a distinctive 'click' as the bayonet locked into place. Each soldier who had fixed bayonets gave it a quick twist to ensure that it was firmly fitted as it would be more than a tad embarrassing for the bayonet to fly off in the direction of the Taliban after the first round was fired. And I did not want to have to tell anyone to go and get it back!

The Mastiffs then noticed activity to our north and reported a mortar team setting up ready to drop indirect fire onto us. After a short pause there was a strange sound of a 'click' followed by a loud 'whoosh', much chunkier than the LASM or an RPG.

"Javelin!" I said listening to the noise. I traced the path of the missile as it headed north and seconds later the loud boom of the missile striking its target reached us. We all grinned and nodded as the Mastiff commander's voice came over the radio.

"One-time enemy mortar team neutralised," he informed us, as though he was ordering a pizza.

In the meantime, the enemy had fled in the face of Charlie's assault and the whole Company axis shifted until we were heading east to join 11 Platoon. I was given the task of clearing compound HK8-205 in order to get overwatch onto likely enemy approaches from the east.

As soon as I got in and looked around, I knew it was not going to be viable, there was a lack of elevated positions in which to place sentries to cover the area. And the areas we could get guys up to had no view due to trees growing around the compound.

"Zero Alpha, three zero Alpha!" I called the OC.

"Zero Alpha send over!" came the response.

"Three zero Alpha, my current location is a no go. No coverage of the area and not a great deal of fire positions in this compound, I am moving to check another location."

"Roger." I pushed my Platoon up to compound HK8-210, which on the map looked like a better option. I was keenly aware of the civilian casualty from yesterday's clearance, so I stacked my boys up on the left side of the compound and called a green assault (no grenades). As I turned back to the metal door that was the entrance to the compound, I spotted John my interpreter, AK in hand ready to kick the door in.

"John?" I hissed. "What the fuck are you doing?" he looked at me and stated deadpan.

"I'm going in Sir!" I shook my head and grinned.

"John, no you fucking aren't. We don't speak Pashto, if you get killed who the fuck is going to translate for me?" He smiled and conceded the point before joining me next to the first section.

"Yeh've got tae admire the laddie's baws, but he's aff his nut!" Pete Breen laughed.

"John, call and see if anyone is in will you mate?" Which he did, twice he called and got no answer. So, I gave the go ahead to get into the compound and after a few kicks the door swung open with a sound of grinding rust. The compound was indeed empty and we went room to room just to make sure no one was lurking. Apart from a few goats who were munching on hay and looking at us indifferently, there was no sign of life. We quickly secured the gate and barricaded ourselves in, I set up sentry positions in the compound and allowed the guys to chill out and rest when they weren't on stag.

I found myself an empty room which was nice and cool, out of the heat of the day. I found an Afghan mattress and rolled it out flat with a view to taking the load of my feet. I kept my body armour on, took my helmet off and settled down. I unlaced my Lowe desert boots and pulled them off. My white warm weather issue socks were hot, crusty and sweaty and the pong they were giving off was either good cheese or bad meat.

Then I thought what the hell, I'll go the whole hog and take my socks off, get some air to my stinking feet. For a few seconds, all was right with the world as I laid back on the mattress using my helmet for a pillow.

No sooner had I settled down; a burst of gunfire tore across the top of our compound. 'Fucking arseholes. It's like they knew I was relaxed!' As I got up, I kicked the trigger guard on my rifle with my big toe, which immediately began to pour with blood. I keyed the handset on my radio and sent a contact report to the OC and set about finding out what had happened. I rolled my sock tentatively over my bleeding toe and stuck on my boots. Without doing up the laces I headed out to the northern sentry point where the fire had come from. I could see Geordie Morgan crouching with his head just below the level of the compound wall, looking shocked, maybe bemused. "What happened Geordie?" I called up as I approached his position.

"It was a fookin' wee one aboo-ut ten year old!" he informed me in his Newcastle sing-song. "Wee bastard came oo-ut the maize man, I thought he was carrying a fookin stick until the bastard shot at me!" he growled.

"Did you shoot him back?" I asked. He shook his head.

"Nah man but a threw a grenade at the wee c**t, no sure if I got him though!" I laced up my boots and jumped up to join Geordie before cautiously sticking my head over the top of the compound wall, sure enough there was a big circle of flattened maize where Geordie's L109 hand grenade had exploded. There was no sign of a body so the kid either got away or was off somewhere bleeding to death. I sent a full contact report to the OC, omitting the fact that the only casualty sustained in the contact was my big toe, which was now starting to scab over.

After the eventful afternoon, the area went ominously quiet and we settled in to routine. After about an hour of quiet, the ICOM chatter went insane. Apparently, the Taliban had us surrounded and were just waiting for us to move, then they would hit us with everything they had.

They were bringing more fighters down from Kats and it sounded as though it was going to be all hands to the pump. The Taliban commander in the area was requesting his troops to bring up more 'watermelons', which we believed was code for RPG rounds.

As I listened, I realised it was going to be a very interesting proposition trying to get through. I did not envy the lead Platoon who had to get us out of this.

"Three zero Alpha, zero Alpha." Came the OC's calm voice.

"Three zero Alpha send over."

"Three zero Alpha, I require your callsign to take point and lead us out of the area, we are heading south!"

'Bastard!' This was not what I was expecting and two things ran through my mind; one – Major Calder trusted me to get us out of this encirclement and two – I was expendable and if we got fucked, I'd be too dead to defend myself. I sure as fuck hoped it was the first one.

"Three zero Alpha, understood." Major Calder gave me a no move before time, which meant I could do a map study and brief my sections before we headed off into the teeth of the enemy.

I called to my new South African Corporal Pieter Du Toit who had come to me from support Company: "I want you to take the lead bro." I looked around at all my section commanders and realised the plan I was about to enact would either kill them or lead them to safety. They all looked at me intently.

"My plan lads, is to put in a lot of zig zags and use difficult ground." I paused to let it sink in. "If the lads are complaining about the route and calling me all the c**ts under the sun? We're doing it right!"

We consulted the map and started planning a route, what I learned about deception patrolling in South Armagh was going to come in very handy.

"Loone, make sure that your rear man does not lose touch with 10 Platoon, they're second in the order of march." Loone nodded but said nothing, no words were necessary, to separate from the rest of the Company would be disastrous and could result in one of our Platoons getting encircled and pinned down.

At the allotted time we began to head out, every man in my Platoon understood the important role we had been given in getting the Company out of our Stalingrad situation. The difference between a clean break and a protracted fighting withdrawal lay squarely on my armour-clad shoulders. As planned, we headed south but then I would chuck in a turn to the east, then south, then west. I crossed canals at points where there were no easy crossing points. The lads cursed, the lads got wet, some were cut by branches as they tried to cross the canal and ditches using trees.

I was aware that I needed to take us a route that would keep us away from prying eyes, if the Taliban dicking screen could see us, they could pin us down, but so far so good.

After what seemed like an age there was no enemy fire, no explosions and no RPGs flying into our Platoons, even more reassuringly I began to see signs of human life and human life that was not trying to kill us. Kids were waving to us and groups of women in blue burqas were walking around as if out for a Sunday stroll. I breathed a sigh of relief and I believe I was not the only one holding my breath, my heart rate returned to normal and my case of dry mouth eased. John's ICOM scanner burst into life and a very angry voice began yelling.

"What is he saying John?"

"Sir, he says the Infidels have gone and he says to all his fighters if you see anything shoot at it!" He paused and smiled. "He is very angry Sir." The relief on the faces of everyone in Delta Company was palpable and to my own great relief. I had led the Company out with no one being killed or injured, in fact I couldn't even believe we had gotten out without the Taliban realising it.

As the Company began to consolidate and prepare for the next phase of the operation, I caught sight of Captain Stevie Rae striding towards me purposefully, his face set grimly. Capt Rae was one of, if not the, most respected soldier in the Battalion. He had come up through the ranks and when I had joined 5 SCOTS, he was its Regimental Sergeant Major and had commissioned to Captain not long after. On Operation Herrick 8 Captain Rae had been given a job in the rear, which sat completely at odds with the warrior that he was. So, when the chance came to act as a military chaperone to Ross Kemp and his crew, he took it, knowing that he was coming to one of, if not the, deadliest places in Helmand.

The Captain patiently described the situation to journalists at the time: "The area is extremely dangerous and can go from smiles and a wave to extreme violence in less than a minute, so all the soldiers are switched on and prepared to react to any situation. This is the Wild West and the further you go out from Musa Qal'eh it is the rule of the gun that counts, the Taliban are here and are making themselves known with attacks on Afghan and British forces."

Stevie Rae was a no-nonsense, thoroughly professional soldier with a crazy reputation to back it up so with the look on his face and his gait, I prepared myself for God only knows what. He stopped right in front of me and looked me square in the eye, the steely gaze not leaving me but rather looking straight through my soul. He put his hand on my right shoulder and frowned. "Well done wee man!" he said. I physically sagged in relief. "That wiz an excellent route ye took, good effort!" I let out the breath I was holding and nodded.

"Thanks Sir... I cannae believe we got out under their noses!" For the first time since I'd known him, his face broke into a slight grin.

"Aye, they're no happy," he responded before turning away and heading back to join Ross.

We settled in as the sun began to set and were given compounds to take over for the evening. I was given compound HK8-2 to occupy and as I knocked on the door, I was met with a very angry local gentleman who was gesticulating and gesturing as though his arms were about to fall off. I could see John nodding and frowning, he turned to me and said, "Sir, this man says you cannot come in!" I rubbed my face and groaned; I was in no mood for any bullshit. I pointed at the man and got John to translate.

"He has two fucking choices John!" I paused to allow John to translate; I wasn't sure if there was a Pashto word for 'fucking' but whatever John said to him got his attention. "Number one!" I said holding a single finger up. "I can turf him out in the dark and take his fucking house over!" I paused again to allow John to pass on the good news. "Number two!" I held up two fingers. "He can be a gracious host and let me and my guys in and be given some compensation, his fucking choice!" I growled.

John translated my message and the man seemed to realise that we were coming in whether he liked it or not, at least with option two he would have some coin. The man became animated again and began to shout at John,

"What fucking now?" I asked John in no mood for more bullshit.

"Sir, he says you come in but for one hundred dollars." I was ready to snap but decided to meet him in the middle.

"Seventy dollars or no deal, he finds somewhere else to sleep tonight!" John relayed my response, which judging by the look on the man's face went down like a shit sandwich. Before the man could back out, I nodded to Pete Breen. "Pete clear it out mate, I don't want any nasty fucking surprises."

After hearing our discussion in the growing darkness, Pete was only too happy to oblige and barged past the stunned man, followed closely by what could only be described as a grubby band of dwarf pirates in camouflage. A short while later my headset crackled into life and over the Platoon radio channel Pete let me know the compound was ready for occupation.

The Platoon all filed in and secured the door against any possibility that the compound owner might slip out in the night and lead back some Taliban friends to exact his vengeance. The section commanders, as was standard now, got their guys into defensive positions on the compound building roofs covering arcs of fire.

I had a small stand to period and informed Major Calder that we were secure for the night. After stand down I was so worn out that I collapsed in a heap in a small room on the northern wall of the compound, which could only have been a stable for goats. I passed a warm, stinky night. As it turned out, the owner would have the last laugh, the consequence of sleeping in with the animals is that you pick up bugs, and I had two big fat ticks now enjoying the finest vintage of Chateau McCafferty 1975.

Day 135

Friday 22nd August: Compound HK8-2, North of Musa Qa'leh DC

After morning routine Major Calder informed us that we would be heading to the partnered ANA checkpoint of Satellite Station North (SSN) to wait out the heat of the day. It was ideal as everyone needed a break from stagging on in occupied compounds.

We were welcomed by the Royal Irish senior in charge of the mentoring team and he told us where we could sack out, so as Platoons we were allocated a section of HESCO Bastion wall to prop ourselves against and pretty soon the area began to look like a homeless village as lads went to recycling pallets and grabbed large boxes as shades from the sun.

Weapons were cleaned and ammunition was re-distributed, and the Royal Irish graciously resupplied us with more and allowed us to swap our dead radio and ECM batteries for fresh ones. Only after the admin was taken care of did the lads completely relax, poking out from cardboard boxes were pairs of shoeless feet and the snoring and groaning of sleeping soldiers filled the air. As I looked around, I could see the lads had stripped their kit off and had laid it in neat piles distinguishing their own kit from that of their buddies. Osprey armour was wrapped around patrol packs if it wasn't being used as a mattress/pillow and combat helmets with their faded, torn and grubby desert helmet covers were sat on top, completing the pyramid of protective gear.

The only thing not visible were weapons. These were never more than an arm's reach away from their owners, riflemen spooned or cradled their SA80s as though they were lovers and gunners had their machine guns resting on their bipods next to them. The gleaming brass cartridges on their disintegrating link belts showed that even though the lads were relaxed, their weapons were still good to go should the Taliban attack; which given the remote location of the base, was a strong possibility. But the fact that the Taliban dicking screen would have observed a full other rifle company taking up residence there, would hopefully dissuade them from that course of action. I settled in myself to catch a few z's and use my US Ranger blanket as a sun screen and managed to drop off into a deep sleep. After what seemed like a few seconds I was shaken awake by Major Calder's radioman.

"George!" he said shaking me awake. Bleary eyed I looked up at him, a string of dribble falling off my chin and into the dusty floor.

"Sorry mucker, the Boss wants aww the Platoon commanders on him noo!" He advised me. Rubbing my eyes, I nodded wordlessly and sat up. I retrieved my UBAC shirt from the HESCO Bastion where I had placed it to dry, which in the heat of the day took minutes. I stuck my feet into my desert boots without stopping to lace them up. I retrieved my rifle where I had stacked it against the same HESCO wall and strode off to talk to the OC.

As I approached, I pulled my map out my thigh pocket and my small red notebook, which was normally in the commander's pouch on my armoured vest. I could see him, the 2i/c and Goody poring over his map and I stayed back until I was joined by Charlie Grant, Jim Adamson, Scotty McPhail and Danny Carter.

Once the command team was assembled, we all crouched next to the OC. Major Calder outlined the next phase of the operation, which would involve us pushing back north again, short of the area we withdrew from the day before. This time we would be operating in the HK7 map zone.

As soon as Nick was happy we all knew our parts in the plan, he dismissed us to get our guys ready. Once I had briefed my section commanders on the plan, we did a quick kit check, replenished our water and prepared to move on the OC's order.

We bade farewell to our Royal Irish brothers at SSN and we headed out the main entrance past the Afghan Army guys manning the bunkers. They waved to us as we passed under the watch of their guns and we headed north-west towards the Green Zone and the HK6 map reference.

After entering the Green Zone our senses became more heightened as the chance for close-quarter battle became ever more likely. I passed the word back down quietly to my guys to fix bayonets again. The silence in the greenery was momentarily broken by the sound of metal scraping metal, then the distinctive 'click' of bayonets locking home.

It was not lost on anyone that to the north we had just escaped encirclement by the enemy, and we were about to head back up there. No doubt the Taliban dicking screen would have spotted us, and the enemy would be preparing for our arrival.

At Compound HK6-66 the Company turned north and began to manoeuvre through the fields and around the compounds in the area, trying best to use ground that would confuse the Taliban and render their surveillance useless. As we reached the area near compound HK6-100, a local informed us that the Taliban were hiding out in compound number HK7-251 and there were at least two fighters in there. I informed Major Calder and was given the go ahead to check it out. He advised me to take the ANP detachment that had arrived to assist us. I waited until the four ANP officers made their way to my location carrying a wide assortment of weapons and wearing a motley collection of uniforms and civilian clothing.

We patrolled until we were near the compound and as soon as I identified the correct location, I put my lads down in all-round defence before grabbing John, figuring that this was as good a time as any to allow the ANP to do their job of investigating shit.

"Mate," I said to John. "Take them up!" I pointed to the coppers. "Get them to do a door knock on that compound, if it looks dodgy get the hell out, understand?" John nodded and went to brief the ANP on the plan. "Loone!" I called into the Platoon radio channel, looking around I caught sight of his head rising meerkat-style from the midst of his section.

"Aye mucker!" I pressed the small square button on the side of the green box radio on my vest and after a pause, "Go with these morons mate, make sure they don't kill anyone that doesn't need killing and if the shit hits the fan mucker cover their arses out!" I ordered.

"Aye, nay dramas mucks." He replied, he didn't have to brief his section as they had all heard it, he waited until the ANP and John approached the compound entrance and stayed a safe distance away.

We all watched as the ANP knocked on the door, the stillness of the day broken by the loud clanging of the metal door. They began to shout in Pashto, John seemed to get very nervous very quickly and if John was nervous, it meant something was seriously wrong. Suddenly the ANP all scattered and jumped into a ditch next to the compound.

"Sir! Taliban are in there!" he called to me; his face suddenly pale.

"Loone, frag it and get in there mucker!" I called. I quickly appraised Major Calder of the situation and got ready to make a dynamic entry into a potentially hostile occupied compound.

I looked over at Loone's section now stacked up against the compound and in the gathering gloom I saw him nod and the obvious motion of grenade pins being removed was apparent. The small green balls sailed over the compound wall and after a few seconds came a double 'thud', which told me both grenades had gone off and in the dull light small splinters of shrapnel were visible shooting into the sky like orange fireflies.

This was the point that the ANP got brave again and charged the door, but Loone and his section were already kicking through the door and they found evidence that the Taliban had been there but had withdrawn from the area. The guys thought they had found a blood trail, but this proved inconclusive with darkness falling. We were given the order to withdraw from the area, which we did, falling back through 11 Platoon.

We had to tab back to the wadi as moving through the Green Zone at night was proving to be a deadly proposition given the emerging IED threat. Also, to use white light to check and clear potential IEDs would have taken forever and would have drawn the Taliban to us like a moth to a flame.

So, as it got darker, I ordered the lads to halt and fix night vision equipment into place before the light completely left us. I took my patrol pack off and retrieved my head-mounted night vision goggle, a single tube with adjustable focus, which locked into a bracket on the front of my helmet. I swung the device down over my left eye, suddenly the whole world came into a sharp light green focus, with patches of darker green and black. My right eye adjusted to the new view of the area and quickly began to work with my left eye, I scanned around at my lads and saw them doing similar things.

Those who had sights to put on weapons did so, night sights were gently slid onto sight rails and a gentle 'click', made sure that the sight was set to the firer's eye relief. As soon as the Company acknowledged we were all ready to go, the OC gave the order to move and we patrolled off.

Given the darkness it was inevitable that someone would stumble and hurt themselves, Taff Owen unfortunately stumbled in a ditch and twisted his ankle quite badly. I informed Goody about this and we organised for the Mastiff Company to meet us in the wadi and help extract our casualty.

Given the fact that darkness had now fallen, the Mastiff crews were having difficulty identifying our callsign. I looked around me and saw that we were on the edge of a triangular patch of the wadi on the eastern bank and were in the cover of trees, I could see the Mastiffs in the wadi, so I informed Goody that I was switching on my IR strobe on the back of my helmet.

The 'Firefly', as it was called, was a green plastic strobe with an IR filter that went across the light source and it allowed you to be identifiable using white strobing light and IR light. It was approximately the size of a Nokia 3310 mobile phone and had a small black switch on the front of the device. Once flicked upwards it starts a small clicking noise within the device that tells you it's working. And if you remove the IR shroud, you get blinded by a fucking great big flash. So, if you did it at night, you could kiss your night visual adjustment goodbye.

I wore the device on the back of my helmet for a number of reasons. As a Platoon Sergeant operating in low light or night conditions, I could switch it on in the event of a contact. That way, fast air and attack helicopters could see me and my Platoon and it would still leave my hands free to operate my weapon or 51mm mortar, give first aid to the wounded and also give anyone with NVGs a visual reference as to where my Platoon was. Secondly, when in the Platoon commander role, I could direct the battle my Platoon was fighting and use my radio and weapon while leaving my hands free and it would make me visible to any air platforms circling overhead. Luckily enough the Taliban did not have night vision in great quantities and even then, this prestige item was only given to commanders.

The average fighter on the ground did not possess this capability, as for the foreign fighters I couldn't say. There were rumours that the Chechen fighters in Helmand were the best equipped of all the Taliban order of battle. I could imagine this was due to the amount of kit taken from the Russians during the two forays the Russians made into Chechnya and having seen Chechen rebel videos on the internet, it was easy to see why. Their skill at ambushing Russian troop and resupply convoys meant that invariably a large quantity of material fell into insurgent hands and it could be used to great effect elsewhere, such as Afghanistan.

I reached over the back of my helmet with my left hand and switched on my Firefly, I was rewarded with a quiet 'tick-tick-tick' in my ears, it was working. Goody had informed the Mastiff commanders that I was flashing IR Strobe and for them to confirm they had it. They didn't!

I couldn't understand why as I had direct line of sight to them, even with it on the back of my helmet, the IR light would almost be blinding. Just in case I wasn't going mad and hearing things, I took my helmet off and immediately recoiled as the bright IR flash hit my NVG covering my left eye. I screwed up my eyes and muttered, "Well that fucking works!" I was left with a bright after-image on my retina that eventually went away. Thankfully, closing my right eye as I'd been taught as a young soldier in training, meant that I did not lose all night visibility. I put my helmet back on and turned my body so that my back was to the Mastiff Company. As I looked around, I could see the Platoon in all-round defence covering arcs.

The NVG had rendered my view clearly as though it was daylight and the detail I could make out was outstanding. I watched as heads swivelled left and right covering arcs.

I could see the faint glow on the faces of other soldiers wearing NVGs on the left side of their faces. Weapons were gripped in a manner that showed me they were ready to use and all my machine gunners were in the prone position facing back towards the Green Zone, their patrol packs placed on the ground to their left-hand side, giving them slight protection. As I glanced around my gunners, I could see the metallic glint of ammo belts snaking out the top of their packs, ready to grab in the event of a reload.

Still the Mastiffs could not identify my strobe light and I huffed in frustration. I grumbled to no one in particular, "Next they'll want me to send up a fucking flare, then we'll all be humped!" I keyed the handset on my PRR. "Three three Alpha, three zero Alpha!" I called. Goody answered. "Go ahead three zero Alpha." I paused and decided how I was going to phrase this.

"Three zero Alpha, switching to white light for identification of my callsign, over!" Goody didn't even pause.

"Roger three zero Alpha, if they retards cannae see that they need their fuckin' eyes tested!"

I reached back over my shoulder and flicked the IR shroud off and the area was suddenly bathed in the intermittent white light thrown out by the strobe, we needed to get this CASEVAC done and very quickly. The bright strobing effect would have been obvious to everyone around, including the enemy.

"Three zero Alpha this is three three Alpha over!" Goody called back.

"Three zero send." I replied.

"They finally picked yeh up, git that daft Welsh c**t to the wagons mucker!" I responded and immediately flicked the strobe off and replaced the IR filter. I turned to see the Mastiffs had changed course and were heading towards my location. I turned to the CASEVAC party who were half carrying, half dragging Taff Owen and his kit towards the edge of the wadi.

"Lads, let's get this done sharpish so we can get out of here!" I hissed at the group coming towards me, I decided to meet them halfway and led the CASEVAC party out to the armoured vehicles. As we got closer, the back doors of one vehicle creaked open and a head popped out.

"Chuck him in here!" called the soldier, his shape barely visible in the dark cavern of the troop compartment. The back of the vehicle was bathed in a soft glow from the taillights and the smell of diesel fumes clogged our nostrils as we halted at the rear of the wagon.

"Watch yer step Taff!" I called to him as the lads brought him to the back doors. There was a tiny metal step that let you get into the back of the Mastiff, but even without a dodgy ankle it was a climb.

The lads supporting him released him and let him grab onto the Mastiff doors for support, I watched through my NVG as he winced when the injured foot touched the floor. He immediately shifted legs and hopped onto the metal steps.

A hand reached out from the back of the Mastiff and pulled Taff in, there was a flurry of activity as the CASEVAC party launched his kit into the vehicle after him, then the doors slammed shut and we turned away racing back to the rest of the Company. The vehicles manoeuvred back out into the wadi and disappeared south leaving us to the quiet darkness, Taff would be in and showered before we even got to the DC.

We then formed a Company patrol snake and moved into the wadi, heading south back towards the DC, the patrol back was uneventful, and I watched as the distant glare of lights got closer and the DC became more visible. We began to make out the shapes of the communications dishes and masts which decorated the roof of the HQ building, desert camouflage camo nets covered some of them to try and disguise their shapes, but it was obvious what they were to even the most casual observer.

I could make out small slashes of light where the window of HQ had not been fully blacked out by cardboard ration boxes and duct tape. As we got closer to the main gate, I could make out the distinct cherry glow of cigarette ends and hear the muted chatter of ANA soldiers on duty at the main gate.

The smell of Afghan tobacco wafted over us and as we passed through the barrier into the DC. The ANA looked at us with a mix of surprise and bored indifference. Surprise that ISAF were out after dark and indifference because we were not a threat, but even if we had been, judging by their demeanour they would not have been able to react anyway.

The only saving grace was that the front entrance, the barrier and the ANA were covered by a Brit in an elevated HESCO bunker position with a 7.62mm machine gun and whatever personal weapon he or she carried. We filed wearily into the DC and paused outside the HQ building.

"Delta Company!" Goody shouted. All heads turned and ears strained over the noise of generators that powered the HQ building. "The chefs have put scran oan fer us, drap yer kit aff at yer pits and head tae scoff!" he continued.

We all shouted and nodded that we understood and began to trudge back to our tents and as soon as we dropped our gear off at our bedspaces, we headed back over to the cook tent, rifles slung over our backs, machine guns carried by their carrying handles. Most were too tired to talk, but here and there in the dinner queue small conversations struck up and we looked ahead into the dull lighting of the cookhouse and wondered what delights awaited us at the hot plate. It's fair to say if you weren't expecting much, you'd still be disappointed. The meal, if it could have been described as such, was noodles (without a sauce) and something indescribable that was tough and chewy!

As I sat down with my lads to eat, Ross Kemp and his team came in and started filming the scene and getting everyone's response to the meal; a lot of the comments did not make it onto the programme.

After the meal, we weren't finished. I had to do a kit check of my Platoon and make sure we had all our serial-numbered equipment. It was easy enough in the dark to put something down and forget about it, or if you misjudged where you put something it may fall out of your kit, especially when transitioning from day to night optics. After I was satisfied that all kit was accounted for, the lads began to strip and clean their weapons. I headed over to the HQ tent to let Goody know 12 Platoon was hundred per cent. As soon as that was done I headed back to my bedspace to begin cleaning my rifle. After all weapons were clean, we grabbed our solar showers and headed towards the wooden shower frames to clean up. I decided to stop and have a piss.

In Afghanistan you have two methods of evacuating your waste: the cut-down oil drums to shit in that are filled with fuel and then burned, or you also have what is called a 'Desert Rose', the name is misleading as they smell anything but sweet, imagine a piece of grey plastic plumber's pipe dug into the ground with a soakaway underneath and perched at an angle so that you can pee in. Now given the fact that the vast majority of soldiers in Delta Company were short arses, the genius who put them in had built them at an angle where the only way I could piss was standing on my tip toes. These Desert Roses had been baking in the heat of the Afghan summer for months, so the smell was indescribable. If the soakaway was ineffective (which they generally were) brown stains began to appear at the base of the desert rose and of course where midgets such as myself missed the mark, there were brown patches of piss in the dust that no manner of kicking hid. You were left with the overpowering waft of ammonia.

About 02:00hrs we finally all got to bed, but luckily tomorrow was a rest day. Hopefully!

Day 136

Saturday 23rd August: 12 Platoon Tent, Musa Qa'leh DC

We relaxed today as the lads were still knackered after our night patrol back from the Green Zone, the vast majority slept in and as they were not needed for anything. Who was I to disturb them? I enjoyed the chance to not be wearing body armour or pretty much any clothing at all to be honest. As the lads began to stir, we all got showered and shaved and took the chance to wash our filthy combats.

As there were no washing machines at the DC, for obvious reasons, all our stuff had to be hand-washed. There were large tubs of army laundry powder set near to six-foot tables and large white plastic bowls served as our wash basins for both shaving in and doing laundry.

Every soldier was issued with two white netting laundry bags that we used to keep our dirty laundry in until we could get it clean. If there had been a laundry facility on the base, it would have been a case of slinging the bag and contents into the washing machine and let the machine do its magic. However, at Musa Qa'leh we were the washing machines, so using the wash basins, G10 dhobi dust and a large scrubbing brush, we set to work cleaning our clothes, which we would then hang up on washing lines made of green army string or hang it about our tents, where the Afghan heat would dry it quickly.

You had to replace the water in the bowl after each item as the water took on a beige tinge with dirty soap bubbles and when you emptied the water out, you were left with a small layer of wet dusty granules at the bottom of the basin. You never got the kit fully clean, but it was better than not washing it at all.

Pretty soon Delta Company's accommodation began to take on the look of a gypsy encampment, washing hanging on every spare space and semi-naked people wandering around. If we had to leave Delta Company lines for whatever reason, we would have to put uniform on. Which was fair enough, but generally within our own area, army boxers, flip flops and dog tags were the order of dress. Though of course we were all acutely aware that mess etiquette demanded that 'The cummerbund sash is worn pleats up, and is of the same cloth as the bow tie and lapels.'

Once I was satisfied that I had sorted my admin out for the day, I settled down to watch some DVDs I had brought to country with me. My favourite show at the time was 'Family Guy' the hit American cartoon TV series. Soon Bruce joined me in my mozzie net and we were chuckling away, we had gotten through a couple of episodes before a shadow fell over us and I looked up to see Stevie Rae standing in front of my bedspace, Bruce and I stood up out of respect.

"Sarn't Mac," he said. "Would you mind Ross filming your Platoon and doing a few interviews?" he asked.

"Not at all Sir," I said, a little shocked.

Ross came into our tent and just explained to us how the interview would go. He was not going to talk to us one at a time, but rather as a group, which I thought was really good. His cameraman flitted around getting some shots of our tent, including a mock-up road sign I had hand-drawn, depicting an RPG round inside a red warning triangle, with the legend '12 Platoon, warning, RPGs have right of way'. After our three-sided ambush in the wadi, I saw it as a kind of attempt at humour.

After he got the shots he needed, Ross grouped us all together and began to ask us a series of questions, things like what we thought about our enemy etc, then out of the blue he asked a question that I was not prepared for.

"What has been the most emotional part of the tour so far?" he asked. I felt my throat close and my mouth go dry. We all agreed that losing Davey McGhee had been really tough on us all, as he was a good little soldier and one of our best lads. The death of Jimmy Johnston weighed heavily on the lads too.

But all I could think about was Jon Mathews' goofy smile and the last time I had seen him alive. The nights I had seen the quiet, well mannered, well-spoken friend sitting in a corner of a Colchester pub, nursing a pint of Guinness in one hand and a book in the other.

I guessed it hadn't truly hit me he was dead. As I began to recall and talk about it, unbidden tears started to form in my eyes and I felt ashamed and embarrassed at such an obvious display of emotion, which I was sure would no doubt be broadcast all over the world. I ducked my head and watched the tears drop onto the floor leaving little dark pools in the sand. Ross put his arm around my shoulders and asked his cameraman to cut and once I had recomposed myself, we carried on the interview.

The lads felt really bad for me, but no one judged me for my show of emotion.

"It shows yer human mucker!" said Loone McCarthy.

"Aye mate," I said. "But ah feel a right dick greetin' on tv."

We enjoyed a few more days off before receiving orders for our next operation, which would be another patrol to the north of the DC. This time we would start with a taxi ride to our AOR, which beat walking any day, and unusually this would only be a one-day patrol, also good. Even so we would still take enough kit for three days because the situation could always change and something could happen that would require us to stay out longer than we were briefed. This operation was to try and identify firing positions for Chinese 107mm rockets that were being fired at the DC.

Luckily enough, this was a rare occurrence. But when it did happen, the mortar alarm would blare out through the DC and we, whatever form of dress we were in, had to head to a large HESCO building that served as a bunker against indirect fire attacks such as mortar and rockets. We would don our helmets and body armour, carry our weapons and race into the bunker, sit on the floor in the dark cool bunker and wait for the attack to be over.

The problem with rocket attacks is, there is fuck all you can do but sit and wait. The firing points are generally too far away for us to hit, so you sit and wait like a desert camouflaged turtle, hoping that today is not the day a rocket lands directly on the bunker you're sat in. I would take a book with me or just sit down in the sand and close my eyes, but you could hear when the rockets were overhead and you kind of got an idea from the sound they made where they were going to land.

The Taliban never had an accurate sight system for their rockets, rather they would prop them on a bank or compound wall, then point them in the right direction, set them off and hope they struck their targets. They always overshot, directly over our compound and the US Marines. They never dropped short.

This was great for us, but the only people who suffered were the poor locals who were on the receiving end of the overshoots. The enemy definitely killed or injured more civilians with their wild rocket fire than any ISAF or ANSF personnel. If we could find these assholes and kill them, hopefully it would put a stop to the rocket attacks and the civvy casualties.

The normal pre-patrol admin started, ammo resupplies, warning orders, 'O' Groups etc and we pored over the maps to ID the area of the operation. We knew that the rockets had to be coming from somewhere near or in Hajji Rashid Gardens, as the rockets always came from the north.

I thought that if we were to assault the village of Kats, we would find not only the rocket crews but possibly more of the large missiles. Our mission was to push north to Satellite Station North in Mastiffs and then patrol out into the Green Zone, harass the enemy, mount up and get back to the DC.

Day 139

Tuesday 26th August: Musa Qa'leh AO

We had mounted up into our respective armoured vehicles and began preparing for the lift to our drop-off. It was only as we were leaving the DC that the gunner caught my eye, well, the bottom half of the gunner as that was all that was visible. The gunner was of short stature and it was definitely not a male posterior.

All our heads turned to check it out and I slid forward slightly so that I could see up through the hatch. I was right, the bottom did in fact belong to a female soldier. Apparently, due to the lack of 2 SCOTS personnel available to crew the Mastiffs through sickness and R&R the Mastiff Company had requested soldiers used to working with heavy vehicles and the RLC had no shortage of personnel willing to come out and crew the armoured personnel carriers.

The gunner must have felt the six pairs of eyes burning into her rear. She dropped down from the hatch and glared at us. Quickly she disappeared back up into the hole.

We had been travelling about ten minutes when we heard the distinctive sound of the .50 calibre machine gun above us being cocked. We all looked at one another, we couldn't believe that only now was she making ready! Hopefully, the Taliban would not attack our vehicles.

The rest of the journey north was without incident and we all managed to close our eyes for about thirty minutes, as there is really nothing you can do as dismounted infantry in the back of an armoured vehicle. I tried as much as I could to track our progress through the very limited visibility but soon gave up and closed my eyes, resting my chin on the front plate of my body armour.

All too soon, the vehicle stopped, and the commander informed us that we were at our DOP (Drop Off Point). I jumped down from the back of the vehicle and allowed my eyes to adjust to the sunlight after being in the dark, close, dusty confines of the Mastiff. We were not far from the partnered checkpoint at Satellite Station North. As we pushed west the patrol was uneventful. We had the usual ICOM chatter, but we didn't realise it was not aimed primarily at us.

As part of our patrol the US Marines would be conducting a joint patrol with the ANA from SSN in order to draw attention away from us. They certainly did that because as we reached our first objective, we could already hear the rapid chatter of small arms fire, followed by the flat bangs of RPG explosions and the sharper cracks of the US Marine M16s and M4s; sporadically rounds would fly over our heads and shoot off to the west.

The Mastiff callsigns who had dropped us off had remained in the area to provide intimate support to the Marines and ANA. We could now hear the rise in pitch of the return fire headed into the Taliban positions, a Javelin team on one Mastiff had Positively ID'd enemy fighters, a four-man team which they were preparing to engage.

The crescendo of fire continued until a loud 'fwoosh' was heard over the battlefield and even though we were some distance from the fight we could hear it clear as a bell. Somewhere to our northeast, after a loud explosion there followed the silence which normally told us that the enemy were dead.

Roshan Tower then called up to notify us that they had spotted a large group of insurgents carrying what appeared to be rockets and mortar barrels; at the same time the Mastiff callsign began taking more incoming RPG fire. We could hear the rockets screaming into the armoured position and the bangs of detonations, followed rapidly by the lazy 'chug-chug-chug' of .50 cal machine guns on the Mastiffs engaging.

Roshan Tower decided to get involved, too, and began taking out the Taliban IDF teams as they scuttled around the Green Zone in teams of four. The .50 calibre heavy machine guns from the tower were backed up by their rapid-firing little sisters. I didn't know how many Jimpies or 50 cals were up at the tower but they were firing a shit load of lead to our north and as I glanced up to the west I could see the red and white Roshan phone mast sticking up proudly against the sky on top of a sheer cliff line. I watched as ruby tracers began to arc into the trees to our north.

This was definitely an unusual occurrence for D Company, being out on patrol and not being on the receiving end of Taliban fire. But we knew that our mission had been successful, enemy indirect fire teams had been identified and neutralised. This would hopefully take the pressure off the DC and stop innocent civvies being killed by mortar and rocket attacks.

We began our withdrawal as it started to get dark and were in the DC just before last light. We all thought that if the rest of the tour went like this, the chances of us making it home alive were so much better.

Day 140

Wednesday 27th August: Musa Qa'leh DC

Today began one of the most audacious operations of the war in Afghanistan, Operation Oqab Tsuka (Pashtun for Eagle's summit). After a thorough Reconnaissance and weeks of planning and rehearsal, the British Army were moving a brand-new turbine from Kandahar all the way up to Kajaki Dam.

The Kajaki Dam was built between 1951 and 1953 by an American firm called Morrison-Knudsen and in 1975 a USAID project built two 16.5 megawatt powerhouses for the dam, with a third being planned. Two would only ever be built, as in 1979 Afghanistan was invaded by the Soviets, all the contractors working on the dam left and the third turbine was never built.

Kajaki was the prime example of the paradox that is Afghanistan, beautiful to the eye with its clear blue-green waters and mountains but extremely deadly. Insurgents from Chechnya, Pakistan and other supportive countries were waiting for the chance to strike at any time.

The dam became an area of strategic importance and value. To that end, the Soviets garrisoned the dam and built posts on the hills surrounding it. There were a large number of mines planted by Russian troops in the surrounding area, which covered likely Mujahideen approach routes and staging points for attacks on the dam.

In 2008 not much had changed apart from Soviet troops had been replaced by British troops, the Observation Posts remained and sadly, so did the mines. On 5th September 2006 a unit of British Paratroopers from 3 Para would be caught in one of the so called 'Legacy minefields' left by the Soviets. By the end of the day seven Paras would be severely wounded and one, Cpl Mark Wright, would tragically lose his life.

The massive convoy which would stretch an astonishing four kilometres had to run a gauntlet of hostile territory and potential enemy attack. The plan called for all units within Helmand based on or near the route the convoy was likely to take to strike out on deception operations to draw the Taliban away from it and hopefully get it through without incident. If Operation Oqab Tsuka was successful, it would be a boost for ISAF forces and prove to the Afghan government that Britain was serious in its pledge to support Afghanistan's redevelopment.

Along the route, British and American Special Forces had been dropped with a view to clearing out identified high-value targets and pockets of hardcore insurgent fighters. Air cover from Harrier jump jets, Dutch, French and American aircraft and unmanned drones were giving twenty-four-hour intimate air support. Apaches buzzed menacingly overhead waiting to destroy anything that posed a threat to the convoy. Thirteen Chinook helicopters containing Paratroopers from all three Para Battalions leapfrogged one another ahead of the convoy to hit the Taliban, to ensure they couldn't mount a cohesive attack at any one point of the route.

We, for our part, were required to push north into our most notorious Taliban stronghold, Kats. If the enemy were going to mount an assault on the convoy, it was a good bet it would come from here. It was a staging point, C2 hub and rest area for local Taliban and foreign fighters. If we could get in there and disrupt their plans, so much the better.

We received orders that we would be pushing out to the east mounted on Mastiffs, giving the enemy the impression that we were heading elsewhere. Then, before last light we would swing west again, going into a desert leaguer for the night before striking out at first light for Kats and enemy contact.

Al Lipowski had returned to D Company and I gladly relinquished the mantle of Platoon Commander back to its rightful owner. Which was just as well really, as my guts were playing silly buggers again, nowhere near as bad as my bout of viral D&V but just enough to let me know my bowels were keeping me on their toes.

For this patrol Ross Kemp and his cameraman would follow my Platoon, so I made sure Ross was briefed and was happy with which vehicle he was going on and who he would follow. And, to his credit, he was good as gold.

"No problem mate," he said with his trademark grin. "I'll stay back out your way." That night I had to make quite a few trips to the toilet, but I was determined that in no way was I missing this Operation. They would have to CASEVAC my dehydrated, shit-covered cadaver before I went sick again. Taking dioralite solution in my water bottle and drinking lots of fluid helped stave of the dehydration element, I just had to not shit myself in the back of the Mastiff as it was going to be a long journey out.

Day 141

Thursday 28th August: Musa Qa'leh DC

I got the Platoon together on the vehicle park next to the DC headquarters building and ran through some final checks before we mounted up in the vehicles, making sure each group knew which wagon they were in, tying in with the vehicle commanders and finally squeezing in. I looked across at Ross and his crew and marvelled at how they looked like they were carrying about the same weight in kit as we were.

Talking to Ross, he told me that he carried his cameraman's spare batteries and tapes, so I took the chance to lift his rucksack into the vehicle to gauge its weight. He was definitely not lying, his pack was just as heavy if not heavier than ours, so he gained even more kudos amongst the lads when I told them. One of the Jocks couldn't help himself.

"Ah thot he wiz jist a big poofy actor annaw, no carrying any kit at aww, surely they c**ts have got somedy tae carry their kit fer them?"

Once we were all secured inside the Mastiffs, we waited until we were given the order to move. Then with a roar, the engines of the Mastiff kicked in and we lurched forward driving out the DC into the wadi before heading south then east away from Musa Qa'leh.

Given that we would be in the vehicles for quite some time, I took the chance to read a book I kept in my daysack and grab a few winks. But throughout my journey, the ever-present gurgle emanated from my bowels and the cramping pain let me know that something unpleasant was birthing itself. I closed my eyes as best I could and let the bouncing and rocking of the vehicle as it trundled along put me to sleep.

After what seemed like hours, we got the call from the vehicle commander that we were coming up on the desert leaguer and would need to deploy sweepers to check for IEDs, which we did. I watched as lads exited their vehicles and carefully swept the ground that their vehicle would drive on and then set up for the night.

Sunsets in Afghanistan were amazing, gazing north I could see the light fading from blue to orange as the sun set. The feature we called Mount Doom was high above us like its namesake volcano in Mordor, menacing in the growing darkness. We were in an area where a Soviet paratrooper base had been during their occupation, and it was covered with mines. Then, the Taliban had supposedly set up an observation point to keep the whole area covered, so chances were, they knew we were already here.

The Mastiff crews would carry out the watch during the night and this allowed my lads to get some sleep, as tomorrow we would be going into a potential hornet's nest.

I decided that I would have to go for a crap now, before it got too dark. One of the 2 SCOTS lads handed me a wooden ammo crate with no end panels on it and pointed me in the direction of the latrine hole which had been dug. It was under cover of the Mastiff's gunner, in order to protect its users while they were in a state of vulnerable undress.

I approached the hole but smelled it before I actually caught sight of it in the gloom. There was a persistent buzzing of flies as they chowed down. 'Brilliant. What a way to go, covered in shit and flies.'

I positioned the upended ammo crate over the hole, taking care not to dunk it in the growing pile. I stripped off my body armour, dropped my trousers and boxers before perching on the box in a most undignified manner. With a gurgle and a vicious explosion, I emptied myself. As I gazed up again at Mount Doom, I couldn't help wondering if someone had me in their sights at this exact moment and were being gentlemanly enough to let me finish before filling me with holes.

After what felt like an eternity and, what sounded like chunky soup being fired out of a water pistol, I stood up. The wooden crate had cut off circulation to my feet, nearly making me keel over into the fresh deposit. I managed to catch myself before I toppled and retrieved a pack of paper hankies that came in the ration packs for such work. I had to use a whole packet, but luckily enough I had the foresight to keep a roll of bog paper in my patrol pack. Cautiously, I pulled up my pants and combat trousers and shrugged on my body armour. I had painted the inside of the box a nice shade of taupe with green marbling. Feeling slightly guilty that someone would have to use this after me, I attempted to clean it off, with a small degree of success, but the smell and stain still lingered. Sheepishly, I handed it up to the gunner on top of my Mastiff, hoping he would not stick his nose too close to it. I just hoped that I was the only one that needed to use it for the rest of the night and my paint job would not be discovered until it was too late.

I looked at the guys from my vehicle and saw that they had all fallen asleep. I made an attempt to wash my hands and then drank some more water to top me up, before stretching out my body armour and curling up on top of it, my daysack as my pillow and my rifle in my arms.

Day 142

Friday 29th August: Desert Leaguer East of Kats

After what felt like only a few minutes, I was shaken awake by one of the Mastiff crew.

"Time tae git up fer stand to mucker!" he whispered. I sat bolt upright, rubbed the sleep and grit from my eyes and looked around. I made sure that my lads were stirring and Ross and his cameraman too, we got up and got our kit on ready for stand to as the sun was coming up behind us.

I was surprised that we had passed such a quiet night, I had expected the Taliban to make a show of force to let us know we might be there, but it was still his AO. No mortar fire, no sniper fire and no RPGs, maybe they were saving it all for when we got into Kats itself.

After stand down, the Boss went for a final brief with Major Calder and I got the guys prepped for the day's activities. Pieter Du Toit, my South African Corporal had offered to carry the Jimpy for this Op and he was relishing the chance to use it. Pieter had come to us from support Company to help fill in when we had very few NCOs, he was a tall man who was loyal and totally dependable. One of the very few South Africans in 5 SCOTS. When I was in the Royal Scots I had served with a number of South Africans and had come to respect their fighting Boer spirit, they were very good soldiers.

We gave our weapons a light oiling, grabbed some food and topped up our water bottles and camelbaks from Jerry cans on the Mastiffs. Before long we were mounted up and heading east towards our drop-off point. We were to be dropped next to a large, prominent compound, HK8-102, patrol west into Kats, then north hoping to get a response from the enemy. As desert gave way to lush greenery to our front, my bowels let me know that they had woken up, too.

I decided that there was no time like the present; the enemy were not firing at us yet as it was too early because morning prayers had not begun and the ICOM was nice and quiet. I took the chance to drop my trousers. I removed my daysack and placed my rifle against it, just within grabbing distance should the Taliban make an appearance. It was with some relief that I voided my bowels in a loud and extremely violent manner. As I looked to my right, I could see Ross and his cameraman laughing as they filmed me in my moment of vulnerability, I grinned and called over.

"Not sure the Great British public want to see me drop my arse out mate!" I eventually finished and got ready to move off, leaving a horrid pile topped with G10 ration pack toilet paper, like an ogre's birthday cake. There is still a picture somewhere on the Sky TV website of me kneeling down, a packet of ration pack bog roll sticking out my trouser pocket.

The lead Platoons headed off leaving us as the reserve with Ross Kemp lingering with my group, me and my 51mm mortarman. I looked around and pricked my ears up, something wasn't right.

"Ross, What's wrong with this picture?" I asked him, he knotted his eyebrows and looked around.

"No civvies!" he exclaimed. He was absolutely right, not only were there no visible signs of life but there was also no noise, no call to prayer, not even any smoke that would signal people beginning their day by cooking breakfast and making a hot cup of chai.

The whole area was eerily quiet and that could mean only one thing. The Taliban had warned the locals about a pending fight and they had all fled north or west across the wadi.

We patrolled on to our objective, every man's nerves on edge and their senses heightened. We were definitely going to get into a fight today and this whole area would become a killing ground.

As I moved between the compounds, I saw that most of them were covered in battle damage and evidence of heavy fighting, there were some strikes on the buildings that looked like Apache 40mm cannon hits. Then I realised that this was the enemy's HQ in the north of Musa Qa'leh and since 2006 it had seen some heavy fighting. There were still no signs of life, but there was the undertone of violence humming in the air.

The Company stopped short of its objective, we had a compound on our right-hand side and a high maize field on our left. I gazed to the left; I could make out the distinct shape of Roshan Tower dominating the area.

"Shall we have a bet?" I asked to no one in particular. I saw the OC's head look round and grin.

"I'll take that action," he said.

"Time of first contact Boss," I looked at my watch. "07:30 I reckon."

"07:20!" the OC chimed in.

"07:45!" Ross joined in. We all began to relax and silence began to take hold of the column, sweat began to gather on my nose. The sweat rag I had under my helmet caught most of the sweat that would have run into my eyes and stung them.

I checked my watch, 07:35, well that was my time shot and I let out a deep breath. Maybe the Taliban had withdrawn from the area, maybe they knew about the Kajaki Dam turbine move. The jungle drums had beaten and they had their forces in place ready to attack the convoy and we were just an annoyance that they would deal with later.

Just as I let myself relax, a heavy calibre bullet came out the maize and flew over our heads. It sounded like it may have been a stray .50 calibre round or an ND from a Dushka. I looked at my watch and grinned, nodding to the OC.

"07:45, Ross well done." I turned to Ross and the look on his face suggested that he was not thrilled at being the winner of our little bet. No one else opened fire as no one could determine the location from which the random shot had been fired.

So, we continued on with our patrol and headed north. Moving parallel to us were 10 Platoon and further east of them was 11 Platoon and as we pushed further into the enemy's territory, they brought up the fighters that we had been expecting. 10 Platoon were engaged and I could hear the fight raging and over the radio Jim Adamson was giving quick battle orders to his guys. The return fire was devastating.

We moved up to try and prevent a flank attack and as we rounded the corner of a compound, I looked up a slope between two compounds which looked like it was used as a drainage or irrigation channel and suddenly I noticed movement and what appeared to be something breaking through a wall at the top of the slope.

"Movement right!" I called. "Take cover." I brought my rifle to bear on the hole that was getting bigger and flicked my safety catch to fire. Suddenly something inside my head made me hold my fire and thankfully I did.

I noticed the pattern of desert DPM uniform appearing at the hole and then the tall frame of Jim Adamson. I put my safety back on and waved to let him know we were there. He spotted me and waved back with a big grin on his face. I stood the guys down and Stevie Rae who had been perched on my shoulder observing, patted me on the back and walked off to re-join Ross and his cameraman.

Not long after Jim broke through the wall, we heard over the radio that 10 Platoon had a man down. Pte Johnston (wee Jonno) had been shot, but he had been shot in the big toe. We couldn't for the life of us figure out why the hell he had been hit in the toe but after a while it kind of made sense. If he had been in the prone, which he was, the Taliban fighter on the other end must have been aiming for his head, but at the last minute pulled the shot, striking Jonno in the boot.

We would later see footage on Ross Kemp's programme from a helmet camera, of Jonno being fireman-lifted to the waiting Mastiffs, who were also providing CASEVAC and fire support.

We pushed further north and we, too, came under fire. As we rightly thought, the Taliban would try to flank us. But they hadn't figured on 12 Platoon being there and we ran smack bang into each other.

My forward section began to engage fighters who had appeared in a group of compounds to our front, they had not seen us until it was too late and the lads began to unleash hell. Enemy fire, wild and erratic, began to crack harmlessly well over our heads, but they were not so lucky. Our fire was more accurate and the enemy could be seen pulling back, dragging what appeared to be dead and wounded comrades.

We pushed up to try and catch them, but they had disappeared through a small copse near HK8-212. I pushed my guys into cover and pointed out arcs of fire so that they could cover a small track running east to west and wait to see if the enemy made an appearance. They didn't, so we continued our advance, pushing through a set of compounds. As we exited through the north end of one compound, Loone and I started to receive small arms fire from a small group of trees to our west. Without hesitation, knowing there were no friendlies in that direction, we began a rapid fire into the area. Nobody fired back again, whether we had hit and killed them or they had fallen back on fear of death, we didn't know. But they did not fire again.

We made the conscious decision to now clear all the compounds we came to with grenades and small arms fire. We knew there were no civvies in this area at all, the only humans we were likely to encounter would be the ones who were trying to kill us.

As I advanced with my reserve section, I could hear my boys up ahead making steady progress through the compounds, I could tell how far they had gone by the distinctive thud of grenades exploding followed by the crack-crack-crack of SA80s. We were hitting them badly and they were falling back as fast as their legs could carry them.

We consolidated in a large, very pleasant compound and I had to do a double take when I saw the compound owner's furniture. His tables and chairs, and a bridge crossing a little stream in the middle of his compound, were made of Chinese 107mm rockets.

"Boss, I think we may have found where our chief IDF guru lives." I said pointing the bridge out to Al, his eyes widened and he said, "I hope to fuck they aren't live!" Before we could make a detailed check of them, we began receiving PKM fire from a compound to our north. Quickly, we advanced to the north wall of the compound and I pushed Pieter Du Toit onto the top of the wall with his Jimpy.

Being a tall lad, he could easily see over the top of the wall from his position and engage the enemy. I was pissed off now that the enemy were fleeing, we were all ready for a scrap. Every rifle now had a bayonet fixed to it, every UGL had a 40mm round in it and we were ready to sweep the Taliban out of their own safe haven.

"Sergeant Mac!" Al called.

"Aye Boss!"

"I'm pushing Loone's section forward to clear the next compounds," he informed me. I nodded. I was all set for him to go, Pieter was in a position to provide machine gun support and I had the 51mm mortar ready. My plan for that was to fire HE rounds in depth to hopefully cut off or kill any fleeing fighters.

"Pieter!" I called up to him. "You see anything brass it to fuck!" He nodded and settled in, the butt of the 7.62mm machine gun in his shoulder, his eyes on the sights. I watched and as soon as I saw the guys leave our compound, I got him to open fire, but suddenly he had a stoppage. I didn't want the assault section going forward with no fire support and with a bit too much venom in my voice, (which I did apologise for and did regret afterwards) I shouted "Get that fucking gun cleared *now*!" I could see what was causing the stoppage, where Pieter had rested the gun on the compound wall he was blocking the ejection port on the bottom of the machine gun, so the empty cases were backing up into the gun. I pointed it out to him and quickly he had the gun cleared and was firing again.

I turned my attention to the 51mm mortar. We had laid out all the HE rounds we had between us in a neat row and I now gave my mortarman a target indication and checked the bubble on the sight system. When the bubble was level in the system, I tapped him on the shoulder and he pulled the lanyard to fire the light mortar. With the first round went some of my hearing, reload, 'thud', another bit of my hearing. 'Thud', tinnitus and completely deaf.

As I was firing in depth, Loone's section began to clear into the next compound and I could just vaguely hear the L109 hand grenades exploding in the neighbouring compound. I kept up my fire to the north, hoping that he had forced a few of them out into my fire.

With the ANP in tow, Loone managed to kick the compound door in and began to clear the buildings and courtyard. My mortarman looked up at me and I could make out the words "Rounds complete!" by lip reading. I nodded and probably a bit louder than I meant to, I ordered "DISMOUNT MORTAR!" In my radio earpiece I was starting to make out a few words, but the unmistakeable "prisoner" I definitely heard, and minutes later Loone's guys and the ANP dragged a confused and very scared fighting age male into our midst. He was around twenty-five years old and looked around with a look of sheer terror. He spoke in Pashtun, which John translated.

"He is asking Sir if he knows anyone here, please don't let the police kill him!" The ANP officers did actually look like they were ready to gut this guy, they knew he was Taliban and we knew he was Taliban.

"Bring him over here Loone," I called. Loone dragged him toward me and I sat him down. The ANP Sergeant stalked over to him and through John told me "This guy is Taliban!" And, to reinforce the point, he pulled back the prisoner's shirt. There was a pronounced bruise on his left shoulder. "See! He been firing a Pika (PKM) at us, let me kill him Sir!" The Police officer said. This frightened the prisoner even more and I thought he would keel over dead. I gave him some water and told him not to worry. We would not kill him. We reported our prisoner up to HQ at DC and we were told to take him with the ANP to a pickup point on the Musa Qa'leh Wadi.

"Nice knowing you kid!" I said to him, knowing he wouldn't understand me. I figured that the minute he went into the hands of the ANP he was a dead man. They were not known for their kindness to detainees. But unfortunately, as part of the process of allowing Afghan forces to stand on their own two feet, we had to allow them to go through their processes, however unsavoury they might have been to us. This man would have to be investigated and go through the Afghan courts, which we knew were corrupt anyway. If this detainee even made it that far.

The ANP handcuffed the guy and with us as escort, headed west towards a pickup point on the east bank of the wadi. It was a shaded little grove of trees set into the wadi, there were three ANP Ford Ranger pickup trucks, full of heavily armed ANP waiting for our prisoner.

As we handed him over, we couldn't help but wonder at his fate. We watched as he was manhandled into the back of a Ranger and driven off at high speed, the blue grey pickups disappearing in a cloud of dust.

We made our way back to the rest of the Company and quickly began our extraction to our pickup point. The Mastiff Company were already waiting for us. We already knew our assigned vehicles that we had come in on, so as each vehicle came into the pickup point, the D Company lads jumped on and the vehicles left to take up a more tactical position, freeing the pickup point up for the next one.

As the lads in my vehicle jumped on, we breathed a sigh of relief. Another day survived, even with some heavy fighting thrown in. I took off my helmet and sweat rag, rubbing my face and head. I could feel the adrenaline leave my body. I couldn't completely relax so I put my helmet back on and waited till we had all completed our pickup and were heading east back into the desert.

"How do you think that went George?" Ross asked me.

"I think it went well mate; it was just like a raid. Straight in, job done back out again!" We had surprised the enemy in his own territory, and

I had no doubt we had killed and wounded a good many of them and captured another, who would hopefully spill the beans on his mates.

The journey back to Musa Qa'leh went by with no incidents and before we knew it, we were back into the DC, tired but happy with the way things had gone and could rightfully give ourselves a pat on the back. I did a full kit check on the lads next to their beds using AFB 115 (a green book with a list of kit and serial numbers). I had made each of the lads sign for their kit so that they could take ownership of it. Satisfied that nothing was missing I told the lads to get on with weapon cleaning and then personal admin.

Before I could relax, I had to get an ammunition resupply from Goody so I could top up what we had used. I had fired nearly two full magazines of 5.56mm and used up all our 51mm HE mortar bombs. My hearing had still not returned from firing ten HE bombs from the mortar and I began to fear that it would never come back, or at least have significant hearing problems for the rest of my life.

As a postscript to our operation, the Taliban suspect that we captured was released despite all the evidence against him by the Afghan court system without charge. Due to 'lack of evidence'! It was obvious to us that someone had come along and paid for the man's release and we had no doubt he would be back behind his PKM machine gun firing at us before long, only next time hopefully he would not surrender.

Day 143

Saturday 30th August: Musa Qa'leh DC

Our post-operative admin consisted of what is known as a 'board of officers'; even in a war zone equipment accountability does not take a holiday, the board of officers is primarily aimed at the quartermaster's department and the Company quartermaster Sergeants.

Officers from different companies or organisations would come and inspect your unit's equipment and, in the case of this board of officers, it was our Bowman signals equipment. They didn't really care about the cleanliness of the items, but we gave them a wipe off anyway and made them ready for inspection. All the board wanted to know was, did we have all the equipment we had signed for that was on our account, if not where was it? I could imagine that doing a board of officers in Afghanistan would have been extremely difficult. Most probably, in some incidents radio equipment would have been destroyed or lost in the chaos. In some cases, equipment must be denied to the enemy, in other words, if you can't carry it out, it gets destroyed in place.

It was while we were going about our business that a bizarre occurrence took place. Two white Toyota pick-ups carrying men bearing white flags were ushered through the main gate but held in the outer perimeter before a small group of them were ushered into the base under guard. This drew attention from everyone on camp, especially as the men were blindfolded. Thinking nothing more of it and passing it off as a meeting of village elders, we carried on our business.

For two days we conducted our administration and began to prepare for more operations. We were being tasked with another patrol to the north of Musa Qa'leh, back into the area of Haji Rashid gardens and the 83 Northing. This would be another Mastiff drop off and a foot patrol through the Green Zone.

2 SCOTS had sadly gone, their tour of duty was over, and they had been replaced by 1 QDG, the Queen's Dragoon Guards. Known as the Welsh Cavalry. We were interested in seeing how they operated in comparison with our infantry brothers, given that armoured warfare was their bread and butter.

As we were receiving our orders Nick Calder briefed us on what occurred with the elders who had come into the DC. Apparently, they were not elders, but low-level Taliban commanders. They had come in under a flag of truce to request a ceasefire during the upcoming Holy period of Ramadan. Lt Colonel Borton had told them, "Yes, we will observe a ceasefire during Ramadan, but we will NOT stop patrolling, if your fighters shoot at our men, we will fight them back. It is up to you to keep the peace."

He knew full well that the Taliban in the area were just playing for time, they were not stupid, they knew Delta Company's time in Helmand was almost done. The PIRA knew exactly the time a Battalion was due to rotate out of theatre and would normally test the incoming units, the Taliban were the same. They could tell by the increased amount of Chinook helicopter activity in area normally meant a unit changeover.

The Taliban had taken a beaten during our time so far and I think they were hoping the ceasefire would see us gone from Helmand and they could test the new unit, but what they hadn't figured on was that we were not finished yet and we were not about to give them any breathing space.

Day 145

Monday 1st September: Musa Qa'leh DC, 1st day of Ramadan

The plan of action was to drop off in the Musa Qa'leh Wadi adjacent to the Gardens, patrol into the Green Zone, take over compounds and use them as patrol bases. We would then use them to conduct Platoon-level patrols out into the area to confuse and harass the Taliban, showing them that we were not gone and were not going.

We mounted up in the chilly morning dawn, my Platoon being in the rear of the column. The lads were acutely aware that the tour was nearly finished, but equally, they knew the job was not yet done until we landed back in the UK. The drive north was uneventful, but we were under no illusions that the enemy would be awake, the dickers would be informing them that we were coming and would give the enemy a direction of travel and how many vehicles were in our column. It did not take the brains of Alan Turing to guess at our numbers; if there were a certain number of soldiers in each vehicle they could quite accurately guess at our strength, give or take a couple of soldiers.

I watched through the front window of the Mastiff as we moved slowly up the wadi, the shingle and stone of the wadi bed gleamed white with morning fros; there was a definite turn in the weather and you could see your breath. There was a chill inside the vehicle and if you touched the sides of it, it was freezing.

I watched the other vehicles ahead as they advanced in column, the top cover gunners only visible part was the top of the helmet, until the turret that protected them swung round to cover arcs, you could see the gunner from the waist up. I often thought it was a vulnerable spot to be in, but then I had done it myself on Snatch Land Rovers in Northern

Ireland and I would do it again, even as a Sergeant on my second tour of Afghanistan on my Mastiff.

I checked my map and realised we were nearing the drop-off point, so I woke up the lads that were dozing and informed them we were nearly there. We arrived but the vehicle commander told us to stay on board for some reason, as I looked out it became apparent why.

They were taking one Mastiff into the drop-off point, emptying it and then calling the next one in, which would take ages. We sat for maybe twenty minutes waiting for our turn, by which time the Taliban were not only fully awake, but they were also set up to attack us.

As if they had read my mind, mortar rounds began dropping into the drop-off point, sending up clouds of black smoke and shrapnel. Goody and Nick were livid and ordered us all to get off the vehicles and get into the cover of the Green Zone, where we would be harder targets. The Taliban were more interested in the Mastiffs; so much for a Ramadan ceasefire! I tapped our Mastiff gunner on the leg and yelled up through the hatch.

"We're getting out mate! Safer than getting blown up in here." And quickly we exited the vehicles, slamming the door shut and locking them with the long handles on the outside. I looked around me and could see that pretty much I was the last vehicle in the convoy that would be dropped off and we weren't quite there yet. The lads in my wagon gathered around me and looked to me for instructions, I nodded to the treeline just to our right.

"Come on boys, follow me, we'll tie in with the rest of the Company as soon as we get into the trees, the rest of the Company is a bit further up to the north."

We sprinted as fast as we could to the treeline with mortar rounds still slamming down on the drop-off point, I could make out the shapes of other lads from the Company also moving into the cover of the trees.

We clambered up a slight slope and into the relative safety of the treeline, I watched as the Mastiffs began an elaborate dance to get them out. Luckily, other than some scorched paint and a lively introduction to the 83 Northing, the Mastiffs got away without casualties.

But for us, our problems had just been confounded. It transpired that our radios had the wrong encrypted fill for us to talk to the DC, however we luckily still had comms through our fire support team. The HQ at the DC wanted us to wait where we were so that crypto could be brought up to us and all the Company radios could be filled. Bruce who was talking to the DC relayed this request to Nick, who instantly saw the stupidity of making a rifle company with no comms wait in a drop-off point that had just been mortared by the Taliban. His reaction was delivered with his usual calm.

"Tell them to fuck off!" those of us who were nearby began to laugh and Bruce smirked. His face turning red.

"Do you want me to use those exact words?" Nick was happy that as a Company we could talk to each other and the FST could talk to the DC, so at least there were some comms to the battle group.

We would carry on with our move to take over our patrol bases and then send a Platoon back to a drop-off point, where we could get the fill and take it back to the security of our compounds and fill everyone's radios undercover.

The compound chosen for our patrol base was huge and it was owned by a very cantankerous old man who told us that we were not coming in. But we told him in no uncertain terms that we were not asking to take over his compound, he could leave or stay, but we were taking it over. Given the location of the compound, we figured that he was in some way involved with the Taliban and it would not have surprised us if the enemy had used this as a patrol base at some point. Most people north of the 83 Northing had dealings with the Taliban whether they wanted to or not, they were in an unfortunate position. But we had a job to do and no one was going to stand in our way.

After pissing and moaning about us taking over his compound, he settled down when he realised that we were not going to budge and sloped off quietly about his business mumbling under his breath and wringing his hands and no doubt hating ISAF for invading his peace. I can imagine he was not so reticent towards the Taliban.

The lads all got settled in and prepared for the next three days, which would see us pushing out into the local area and try to get a response from the enemy. We had a psyops team with us, and the message they were pushing out to the Taliban was "Go home, be with your families for Ramadan. Put down your guns and turn from violence, go home!" If they didn't, we would be there to meet them with force.

We didn't rest on our laurels and first out the gate was 10 Platoon, they had literally just left when they started receiving fire from compounds HK8-94 and 8-94. They responded by hammering the enemy positions with fire and then calling in 81mm mortar fire and 105mm artillery from FOB Edinburgh. We could hear the rounds soaring overhead before landing with a solid 'crump' on the enemy, spot on target. They began reinforcing their line and 10 Platoon called in more artillery fire to hit their approach route.

Part of my Platoon stood to as a QRF were pushed off our compound onto a flank to stop the enemy from coming in behind 10 Platoon. We formed an all-round defence position around a group of irrigation ditches and waited, I could hear the sounds of fighting slowly start to die down as 10 Platoon's fire forced them out their positions. Taking a leaf out the Taliban's book, Jim Adamson tried to outflank the enemy. But they withdrew. All the while this was going on, we could hear the sound commander's loudspeaker still broadcasting the message, which seemed to piss the Taliban off even more and they vented their rage by firing in the general direction that the broadcast was coming from.

In front of my position was a large maize field, with the crop at least ten feet high and there was a dirt path between the crop which farmers no doubt maintained as a fire break, or it was part of the irrigation project for the fields. I heard rustling to my front and as I was already in the prone position, I flicked off my safety catch and watched through the SUSAT to see what was coming. I expected it to be at least one Taliban fighter but walking along the track between the maize was a large, grey dog-like creature.

I had to do a double take, surely I was not getting enough sleep? Or was I in the middle of a mental episode? I watched transfixed as this animal, which may have been a jackal, padded towards me, then stopped. I took my eye off my sight and put my safety catch back on and watched as the creature raised its head, no doubt now catching my scent.

It looked at me and for a moment our eyes locked, and we held each other's gaze for what seemed like a few seconds before the creature turned and walked calmly back the way it had come. I still couldn't believe it, I hadn't seen an animal like it in Afghanistan and it didn't look like a Kuchi mountain dog, it was too slender and not as hairy, and was grey, I didn't know whether wolves lived in Afghanistan, but it certainly looked to be canine. I was brought back by Al Lipowski informing me that we were heading back into the compound. So, we quickly peeled right and headed back into the security of our walls.

The rest of the day followed this pattern with the Company sending out small patrols to piss off the enemy. As I was sat talking to the sound commander who was in charge of the psyops unit, I had a brainwave. One thing Scottish troops are known the world over for are bagpipes. Everywhere we have fought, pipers have gone with us and piped us into battle, generally throwing the fear of God into the enemy. Why should this visit to Afghanistan be different? From Waterloo to the Somme, the strains of bagpipes have charged Scots troops with a power and fighting spirit unknown anywhere else.

"Bagpipes Boss!" I said out loud, more to myself than anyone else. The officer in charge of the speaker's eye lit up.

"Great idea Sarge," he said. I did a quick canvas of my lads and low and behold, Scotty McGregor had an iPod on him with bagpipe music on his playlist. We quickly rigged it up to the speaker system and pretty soon the clear tunes of 'The Barren Rocks of Aden' and 'Blue Bonnets o'er the Border' began to flood over the Green Zone.

As I looked around, I could see big grins smiling back at me from under combat helmets and the lads all straightened their backs. We were all feeling the same, the hairs on our arms and the backs of our necks stood on end.

The music had the exact effect on the Taliban I thought it would, our compound and the sound commander began to draw the attention of the enemy and they opened fire with a heavy weight of small arms fire. Rather than discourage us, it made us all the happier, as now we were able to identify their firing points and smash them with a combination of small arms fire and mortars, which quickly silenced the enemy positions.

The sentries on the roof tops were identifying groups of armed men moving around our compounds, sporadically our Minimis and Jimpies began to rattle out a wall of lead which killed quite a few of the would-be attackers before they even got to our compounds.

But sadly, all good things do not last; the sound commander's speaker system died, and it put a temporary hold on our bagpipe band Afghan tour. But the damage to the Taliban had been done and they withdrew their casualties back to the north. Or at least the ones they could get to, that were not directly overwatched by our fighting positions.

It was not long after the sound commander equipment died that the enemy began surging towards our location, heavy small arms fire was received and the Taliban began firing RPGs at our positions too. Once identified, the gun positions on the compound roofs began engaging. John Axcell had set himself up on a compound roof near Gordon Pollock, who was hitting Taliban fighters just a stone's throw away from his position. John was in the process of calling in mortar fire when rounds began striking the wall and roof around him and Gordon. Then the call came around that everyone dreaded.

"Man down, man down!" Gordon had been hit by the enemy and at this stage his status was unknown. Andy Pettiford assessed and treated Gordon as soon as he was able to roll off the roof. At a glance, Gordon was a very lucky boy, he had taken shrapnel from a ricochet that had hit either the compound wall, or the bipod of his weapon. He was bleeding profusely from his injuries but they were not life threatening. It fell to my Platoon to conduct the CASEVAC to Musa Qa'leh Wadi and onto the Mastiffs. I picked an escort team for Pollock. As he was walking wounded, we were merely there to protect him until he was extracted, or to give further treatment if required, should he collapse due to blood loss. Andy had stuck him with morphine, so the pain would hopefully be subsiding. We waited until Goody gave us the green light and I headed off west towards the wadi, Gordon safely cocooned within my CASEVAC party.

The enemy were only focused on the location we had left, not us, bigger fish to fry and all that. So unimpeded we were able to get Gordon safely onto the Mastiffs who bore him back to the DC and then Role 3 at Camp Bastion. In the gathering gloom my team and I moved back to compound 67 to continue with the task at hand.

As the sun was setting a group of civilians approached the OC's compound under a flag of truce. After a quick Shura with Nick, he passed the word around that the locals had requested a ceasefire to take away the now decaying corpses of the Taliban fighters we had killed, as they were starting to scare the local children and as we knew, Muslims had to be buried before sundown. This was granted.

It was always noticeable how quickly the enemy dead began to decay in Afghanistan as the heat was very fierce out there and I could imagine the decomposing effects on the dead were almost immediate.

If you have never smelled death before, or even if you have, nothing quite prepares you for how strong the smell of death is in the heat of Helmand; it sticks in your nostrils for quite some time and takes a long time to get rid of. Even now in the heat of summer in the UK, I only have to smell a food bin with rotting meat in it and see bluebottles hanging around the bins to take me back.

As darkness fell, we all settled in and listened to the night noises of Helmand, we prepared ourselves for possible night attacks, but nothing materialised. We figured that a combination of the bloody nose we had given them that day, and the fact that they were probably suffering from the effects of not eating properly due to Ramadan, kept them away.

Day 146

Tuesday 2nd September: Compound HK8-67, North of Musa Qa'leh

This morning we were slated to go out on a local disruption patrol, which would force the Taliban to fight us or fuck off out of the area. We were to head east towards the village of Towghi Keli, which we knew from the past was a known enemy fighting position and we would always get some kind of incoming fire.

As we patrolled through the Green Zone east, we were cautious, all eyes were on a swivel and every potential firing point was swept by muzzles and rechecked through SUSATs. There was a definite tension in the air as we headed to our objective. We were nearing the end of our tour and so far, we had been lucky. We had not become complacent however, the level of combat activity in Musa Qa'leh prevented that. If you dropped your guard the enemy would exploit it to their advantage.

As we patrolled, we sent LOCSTATS and SITREPS, informing not only the DC of our location, but more importantly the OC. If we got in the shit, the rest of the Company were our QRF and they needed to know exactly where we were at every stage.

We stopped to talk to a few locals and pass the time of day. One old man told us that he knew of a location where there were Taliban holed up for Ramadan and were resting for the day. He told us that the compound they were in contained a shop, this made sense as we knew of a low-level Taliban commander who had a compound which contained a shop. We informed the OC of our finding and he advised us to approach it with caution.

We had to cross a patch of open ground in in order to approach the compound, designated HK8-57, which was actually in the middle of a set of compounds running west to east. 59, 58 and 57 looked as though they could be combined into one larger compound, with 59 being the largest one of the cluster.

We stood off a fair distance to watch the compound before we knocked on the door. John went in with the Boss and I could hear him yelling into the compound and before long the door squealed open and an old man ushered us in. Still cautious of an ambush, the Platoon moved into the compound and straightaway I placed sentries up on the roof in order to cover the surrounding area.

Inside the compound we were confronted with a scene of domestic calm, a woman and some kids were milling around inside. The kids were fascinated by us, coming over to stare at us, we let them look through our sights and have a look at our kit, the lads also dished out sweets. The old man and the woman kept an aloof distance from us. Through John, the Boss questioned the old man to find out if there were Taliban fighters in the area. We received the usual standard reply.

"We haven't seen the Taliban; we haven't seen them for months." I laughed and said to the Boss, "We didn't receive any messages and we certainly didn't eat this delicious plump breasted pigeon!" We left empty-handed and patrolled back to our checkpoint unmolested.

After a rest and some water, we stood to as QRF as the Company were still mounting Platoon-sized patrols into the area in order to dominate the ground. The sound commander continued his broadcast, which drew the attention of the enemy, who began once again to shoot in our direction.

The crack and thump going past the compound walls was continuous, we were obviously doing something right and I could imagine the enemy were starting to get rather pissed off with our broadcasts. A combination of hunger and tiredness was making them sloppy; for every burst of fire they aimed at us, they received accurate small arms and indirect fire, which no doubt killed and injured more of their fighters, losses they could not afford.

Nick Calder decided that just before last light he wanted our Platoon to go out and form a standing patrol on likely enemy approach routes to our temporary base. We pushed out again slightly to the east and took cover in all-round defence in some irrigation ditches and waited for the excitement to settle down.

I fully expected the enemy to try and attack us before last light as we had pissed them off over the last few days with our bagpipes and our psyops broadcasts. But as I lay there in the gathering gloom, I didn't see any signs of the enemy making towards us. Just when I was beginning to think nothing would happen, a Sea King helicopter buzzed over the area heading from the south-west to the north-east, and it was flying pretty low. I thought the pilot was either lost, mad or had been told to make a low flyover near our location to elicit a response from the enemy: this he certainly received.

I pulled my handheld camcorder from my patrol pack and began filming the Sea King as it flew along and suddenly fire began to erupt to our north, all aimed at the helicopter as it flew away. But that was as far as it went, the Taliban commander did not seem willing to commit his forces in our direction as it was not in his best interests, the helicopter made an easier and more tempting prestige target. We watched as the Sea King turned and flew away lazily to the west, no smoke belching from it or any fires visible, but I can imagine that the crew went back to Bastion with a very nice war story.

We slowly picked ourselves up as it got darker and began to patrol back into the compound patrol base, again checking our arcs to make sure that the Taliban were in fact not making their way to our location. The night passed uneventfully with the ICOM chatter suggesting an attack, but our gun positions on the roof were always ready. Each soldier had night sights and access to both infrared and normal rocket flares which would illuminate the enemy in the event of a night attack.

Claymore mines were also set up on likely enemy approaches. I really liked the Claymore mine as it was a versatile weapon, it had avoided the ban on land mines as it had to be set off by a soldier, unlike traditional mines that exploded when stepped on. The Claymore had first come to prominence in the jungles of Vietnam, where it had been used on defensive positions by US forces and was an excellent piece of kit for initiating ambushes. The mine itself was a green box that was slightly curved to allow a good killing arc when it exploded, it was set off by means of an electric detonator which was slotted into the top of the mine and a clacker handheld device attached to the mine via a cable reel. The mine contained high explosives and embedded into them were about seven hundred and fifty steel ball bearings, so when the mine was set off it was essentially a large shotgun. The noise of the explosion would cause an instant shock, never mind the fan of ball bearings coming at you in an invisible cloud.

If the shit really hit the fan, we had artillery from FOB Edinburgh ready on preregistered targets that could land within seconds of a fire mission being called. Given the high volume of traffic on the ICOM scanners, the Company stood to until 2300hrs. All the safeties off our Claymores and fingers itchily stroking the triggers on their weapons ready for the word or action on the part of the enemy.

We all watched the world through our NVGs, those of us with helmet mounted night vision goggles wiped the sweat from our eyes as the rubber eye cups caused us to perspire even more. Our eyes played tricks on us as we imagined we saw enemy troops lurking in treelines or sneaking through bushes towards us, but a quick rub of the eyes or just a blink, told it was an optical illusion. We continued to study the world in its murky hues of green, the sounds of crickets and other insects chirping in the background suggested all was well. If it had suddenly went silent, we would have expected the enemy to be near. In the distance a dog barked, which pricked our ears up again, but after a while the dog went quiet and no attack materialised.

The Taliban commander once again had an attack of common sense and had decided to postpone his assault at least until the morning. With that we all stood down and went into night routine, cooking and eating an evening meal before heading off to sleep.

The next morning, the expected attack unsurprisingly did not happen and after stand to, we made our way to a pick-up point where the Mastiff Company took us back to the DC. All the way home we listened to the ICOM and realised the Taliban did not know we had left.

On return to the DC we had a Company photograph taken with Ross Kemp, which would signify his time with us was up, We thought he got more than he bargained for coming out with us. We would not realise just how good the documentary would be until we were given a private screening by Ross back in Canterbury after the tour.

The documentary entitled *Ross Kemp: Return to Afghanistan* would give the British people an idea of what our men were facing on a daily basis and in my mind would cement Ross's reputation as a serious journalist and war correspondent.

Day 148

Thursday 4th September: Musa Qa'leh DC

No rest for the wicked, no sooner had we returned from our northern operation, we were given a warning order to head back there to Satellite Station North, where we would be using that checkpoint as a patrol base.

It would seem, that the powers that be felt that the ANA were not pulling their weight and not dominating their AO or patrolling as aggressively as they should be. I found this highly strange as the Afghan troops at SSN were mentored by the Royal Irish. But there were a few little, unmentored checkpoints in the area and I could theorise you would need a fucking big crowbar to get the Afghans out of their holes to patrol the area. I would not fully appreciate or understand the frustrations associated with trying to mentor Afghan security forces until I had to do it myself a year later mentoring units of the ANP.

Late afternoon, the Company set off from the front gate of Musa Qa'leh DC and at staggered times would head towards the northernmost ANA checkpoint that would be our base camp for the next few days. As usual, the lads were alert and were watching for all possible methods of attack and any suspicious activity.

We were now starting to see the increase in use of IEDs as a form of attack but sadly for the local Afghan civilians it was they, not us, who felt the devastating effects of what would come to be known back home as 'roadside bombs', a term that made its way across from Iraq, where this attack method was more prevalent and generally used against coalition vehicle and foot patrols in areas such as Basra and Baghdad.

Here in Afghanistan it was lucky that the enemy did not have the level of sophistication that their Iraqi Jihadi brothers had. But still, an IED, no matter how basic, does not distinguish between combatant and non-combatants and we would see pressure plate IEDs of varying sizes explode with destructive force.

As we observed a beautiful Afghan sunset to our west, we moved though familiar treelines and groups of compounds that we had patrolled and fought over for the last few months. As commanders, many of us no longer needed to check our maps when heading to certain locations, their place and references would be seared into our minds for some time to come. We crossed ditches and bun lines, walked through maize fields and crossed small streams and canals. Given how hot our feet got inside our boots, it was a relief to walk through the cool water, then have it drain out your boots. The only downside was that they dried very quickly, and your socks became filthy and crusty and the boots hardened.

I knew that soon we would be at SSN and this was where we went firm to allow an interval between Platoons getting into the checkpoint. That way, we weren't just a big gaggle of bodies. We stopped in the gathering twilight next to compound HJ11-11, which we knew shielded us from the open ground and graveyard to the west of Satellite Station North. I listened as 11 Platoon began to cross the open ground and suddenly fire erupted from the south and I could see red tracers lacing up into the sky heading north.

We'd never been hit this close to Satellite Station North before. Had the enemy somehow managed to infiltrate past the ANA mentored checkpoint and were now roaming with impunity in the Royal Irish back area? We couldn't imagine that happening, knowing exactly how good and professional that the Royal Irish were.

"Zero Alpha, this is two zero Alpha!" came Charlie Grant over the radio.

"Send over!" the OC responded.

"Do we have anyone that can speak to those fucking ANA assholes to the south?" Charlie asked. "That's who's fucking shooting at us!" he informed the OC. Typical, the unmentored ANA checkpoint slightly further south had spotted movement and rather than checking to see who it was, opened fire. Luckily ANA marksmanship was shit and much like their Taliban cousins, they had a tendency to favour quantity over quality. But everyone went firm until we could get someone at Satellite Station North to tell the morons to stop shooting at us.

When it was our turn to cross the graveyard to SSN I called Wullie Rankin over the Platoon channel on my radio.

"Wullie, if those fucking cretins shoot at you? Fucking hit that sangar with a LASM!" I wasn't taking any chances; it could be that it was an honest mistake, or they had genuinely turned from the government and we had a green on blue situation.

After what seemed like an age, we got moving across the graveyard, I kept glancing to the right down to where I could just make out the shape of the ANA checkpoint, which must have only been platoon-sized. I waited for another burst of gunfire and who knew if this time they would get the range and be on target? I would be extremely irritated to survive this long only to be killed or injured by our own allies.

As we arrived into SSN, the Royal Irish senior NCO in charge of the checkpoint was most apologetic as we came in and in a thick Ulster accent told us "The fucking eejits are probably off their tits on weed!" We laughed and completely sympathised with him, how can you mentor and advise guys that don't listen and don't really care?

"How the fuck can we be mistaken for anything other than ISAF mate?" I asked.

"Feck knows mate, they'll shoot at fecking anything!" We picked our usual spot on the walls around Satellite Station North and bedded in for the night, the lads were glad of the rest as we didn't have to provide sentries, but none of us really let our guard down.

Despite the fact that this checkpoint was mentored we still could not trust the ANA, no one could ever know what frame of mind they were in at all, so you always slept with one eye open and your rifle very close to hand.

Day 149

Friday 5th September: Satellite Station North, Mentored ANA Patrol Base

We were to begin in earnest; our patrol today would take us into the village of Towghi Keli. This village was very familiar to us as a hub of Taliban activity. There was always ICOM chatter coming out of the area and we knew that there were a few low-level Taliban commanders in the village.

We believed that this village was probably a FOB for the Taliban so that they could keep an eye on the ANA and the Royal Irish. Of course, when we came into the area, the level of chatter went up as it was not a normal occurrence and the dicking screen went into overdrive.

We set off north as we left the checkpoint. Skirting the graveyard, we headed through the tight maze of compounds that comprised this unfriendly village. I started to notice that the further we got into the village, people were starting to flee. This was not a good sign; I informed the OC that we had people leaving the village fleeing south and that I was going to stop a few and find out what the score was. An elderly man on a big wagon came to a halt as I raised my hand, behind him more people were approaching on foot.

"What is going on? Why are you leaving in such a hurry?" I asked him through John. The man looked extremely nervous and kept glancing back over his shoulder into the village, he rattled off a sentence in Pashto complete with the obligatory hand signals. John turned to me and frowned.

"He says fighting is about to start Sir. Whenever you turn up, the Taliban want to fight!" I was just about to key my radio and let the OC know what was going on, when the rattle of small arms fire sounded off to the west, where the other two Platoons were.

As though to confirm the presence of the enemy, two RPGs flew over our heads. I tutted impatiently and turned to Tam Meighan who was crouching nearby with his section.

"Well, looks like we're about to get busy!" He turned to me and grinned nervously. I turned back to the man I was dealing with and handed him back his documents and allowed him and the other civilians with him to head south.

The contact report came over the radio that 11 Platoon had spotted three males acting suspiciously to their front and as soon as the males spotted his section, they dived into the cover of an alleyway and very soon heavy small arms fire was directed at them. This was met with a more robust and accurate return fire. They then began to push forward and assault compounds HK7-224 and 225 where the three males had been seen diving into. The enemy however had melted away into the surrounding countryside, no doubt moving to fall back positions.

My Platoon pushed up on the flank to support the other two Platoons and hopefully flush the enemy out into the open, or at least push them into the other lads. Then as we were approaching compound HK8-57, just north of 11 Platoon's contact point, Wullie Rankine the point section commander spotted a fighting-age male lurking on the corner of the compound and moved to challenge him.

At this stage I was kneeling behind a mound of dirt just to his south, when we heard the familiar sound of a burst of fire from an AK, the rounds cracked over our heads not causing any harm, just a few sets of soiled pants in the point section. As I reached Wullie's section, I found him ashen-faced and sweating profusely.

"Fuck me!" he announced dead pan. "The fucking arsehole jist grabbed a fucking gat fae behind the wall!" I grinned.

"Did ye git him or no?" I asked.

"Naw mate," he replied. "Ammo tried tae hit im wae the LASM!" I was about to ask if Ammo hit him, but the scorch mark in the dirt just short of the compound told me he hadn't. A full contact report was sent back to the OC and we carried on patrolling, albeit with a lot more caution.

It wasn't long before Nick decided we had hit our LOE (Limit of Exploitation) and decided we should patrol back towards SSN. I'm still not sure to this day how the information came about, but as we patrolled south, my Platoon was tasked to conduct a search of compound HK8-17. We knew from old that it was a frequently used firing point for the enemy, in fact we had killed three Taliban in that area before and the enemy were creatures of habit and normally used the same firing points.

As we approached the compound, we began to feel the hairs on the back of our necks stand on end. The compound was a few hundred metres south-west of where we had been contacted and it was in the middle of a field; we had to cross bushy open ground with little cover. I was keenly aware that if the shit flew, we would have to go forward into the enemy or fall back to compound 18 and suppress 17 with our guns. I pushed in with the reserve section as the Boss made entry into the compound with Wullie's section.

We conducted a thorough search of the place, not finding a living soul, but when I got onto one of the roofs to check for firing points, I was surprised to find an empty plastic bottle that had contained blood expander fluid and a lot of blood-stained dressings. Also, a lot of empty cases which looked like they could be from an AK, small, dark-grey casings which almost looked like 5.56mm but were wider. Whoever had been on this roof had been severely wounded and would have been unlikely to survive. We also found what we believed to be a number of IED component parts, including dual tone multi frequency phones. We passed this info up to the OC and he decided that this gave sufficient grounds for us to put an ambush in on the area, as clearly it was being heavily used by the enemy, our discovery had reinforced that idea. As we began to withdraw, the ICOM which had been quiet up till now began to inform the enemy to stand down and that one fighter had been killed in the exchange of fire with our Company and a number of them wounded.

The next day it was planned that 10 Platoon would conduct an ambush operation in the area we had located as the firing point with med kit and IED components. They would've inserted in the early hours of the morning, knowing that come first light and after morning prayers, the enemy would begin their operations. What they wouldn't know was that a Platoon of heavily armed Jocks would be lurking in the maize, ready to unleash hell upon them.

But the weather and mother nature had other ideas. A change in the temperature meant that the entire area was heavily misted in, so much so that even the imposing feature of Mount Doom was invisible to us. When this happened, it meant that there was a no-fly plan put in place. The knock-on effect for us on the ground was that we couldn't patrol anywhere, if CASEVAC couldn't be guaranteed. Fast air and attack helicopter capability would also be hampered, so support would have to come from the artillery in FOB Edinburgh, that was assuming the Fire Support team could see the target, so the decision was taken out of our hands and we were not to leave Satellite Station North until the clag had cleared.

For two days we waited, yet the clag didn't clear, and we were starting to run out of our own supplies and were relying on the generosity of our Royal Irish hosts. On Monday the 8th, Nick decided to risk heading back to the DC so that we could sort our admin out and begin prepping for the next operation. We figured that if we couldn't see that far, then neither could the Taliban and their dicking screen would be severely compromised. The patrol south passed without incident and before we knew it, we were back home in the DC.

I began to wonder how cold it was back home, as the weather in Helmand had started to get chillier as the days passed.

Day 154

Wednesday 10th September: Musa Qa'leh DC

We had been given orders for a two to three-day patrol to the south of our AO, using PB South as a jumping off point. But we would wait until the afternoon before deploying, this would help with any pattern setting that may have been happening with our deployments and would hopefully see us into PB South before last light.

A huge explosion in the wadi to our south-west, followed by heavy small arms fire got everyone's attention. We suspected an ambush as this was definitely an MO of the Taliban but reports came in that an ANA supply convoy had hit an IED and the cab had been completely destroyed, one of the occupants had lost an arm and the other two had been badly fragged and burned. Unfortunately for any bystanders, the ANA standard response was for survivors to begin spraying the area in the hope that they hit the bomber or any dickers in the vicinity. But normally all that happened was innocent civvies took the fire.

A tragic event also fell out of this IED strike. IEDs were becoming more and more prevalent now, not just in our area, but all over Helmand. The counter IED task force had a team on site that were used to clear devices or suspected devices. Their high threat operator was a seventeen-year veteran by the name of Warrant Officer Class 2 Gary 'Gaz' O'Donnell GM, who had been decorated for bravery previously with the George Medal for his work clearing IEDs in Iraq.

Gaz and his team had headed out to the site of an IED that had been discovered by a high risk search team, Gaz had gone out to clear the IED and as he cleared what he believed to be the whole IED, his elbow struck a pressure plate that had been part of a daisy chain. WO2 O'Donnell GM, a legend within the counter IED community, lost his life that day and the looks on the faces of the young PWRR soldiers from the Warrior Company sent to recover him told of a scene of horror.

Gaz would be awarded a posthumous bar to his George Medal for the IEDs he had already cleared in Helmand and he had no doubt saved many lives, both ours and the local civilians.

With this put to the back of our minds, we patrolled out, but with a more sombre feeling than normal. The journey south was uneventful, even the usual ICOM chatter was missing and we got into PB South, bedding down for the night.

Throughout the night we could hear sporadic gunfire to our south, most of it sounded like American weaponry. We spoke to the Royal Irish mentor team in PB South and asked them what was going on out there. We stood on vantage points such as the roof to see if we could get a handle on it, but the senior advisor shrugged and said "It's unmentored, the ANA decided to go out on an ambush!" This was the first time we had heard of the ANA in Helmand doing anything by themselves. They relied heavily on their NATO allies as they knew that we could always bail them out with artillery and air support.

For an ANA unit to go out on an ambush unpartnered was a big deal. But the ANA concept of an ambush was clearly different to ours. If we opened fire during an ambush, it was an overwhelming volume of fire which would be directed into an area which, by design or by accident, the enemy would wander into. We would not stay in position and sporadically fire into the dark, once an ambush opened fire it was essentially sprung and compromised. You might have time to search those enemies you've hit for intelligence information or to collect weapons, but generally you bugged out sharpish in case the enemy were following up.

We watched as ruby tracers arced up into the starry sky. Flares would shoot up into the air before exploding into a bright white triangle of light that would give troops time to identify enemy personnel and hopefully, for the uninitiated and untrained, it would confuse them and destroy their night vision.

Once you are exposed to bright light in the dark, it can take fifteen minutes or so to get your night vision back. It is always taught to us in training that you don't look directly into the flare or white light, you close one eye as this will help restore your night vision quicker on the flare burning out.

After a while the lads all got bored and began to disperse back to where they had laid their kit to settle in for the night. I could hear the low chatter of the boys as they talked in hushed voices, even though we were in a semi-safe environment, the lads still felt it necessary to whisper amongst themselves and with good reason. On previous tours of Helmand, the Taliban had sneaked up to checkpoints and listened in to see if they could hear chatter or see obvious lights, if they could, they would lob grenades over the HESCO walls.

Occasionally I could hear muted laughter and see the orange glow of cigarette ends burning briefly in the dark. I sat with my back against my patrol pack and used my body armour as a mattress, I had unrolled my American grey digital camouflaged Ranger blanket from the side of my patrol pack and settled in to try and sleep before the patrol tomorrow. I drifted off to the sounds of distant gunfire and the chuckling of my Platoon.

Day 156

Thursday 11th September: PB South, Musa Qa'leh AO

The significance of the date was not lost on anyone, it was the day that my job as a British soldier changed for ever. 9/11. I cast my mind back to September 11th 2001, I was posted to Northern Ireland as part of 1st Bn The Royal Scots, Reconnaissance Platoon, operating out of Ballykelly Army base, north of the city of Londonderry. But on that day, I was home on leave in Colchester.

I watched the World Trade Center in New York in flames and a jumbo jet flying into the side of the already burning building. I found myself rising to my feet completely dumbfounded and shocked by what I was seeing, I listened to the panicked commentary of the newscasters and watched as the picture swapped from the burning World Trade Center to the streets of New York where NYPD officers were trying to shepherd the public to safety and the FDNY fire trucks were racing towards the scene.

What the world had thought was initially a tragic accident would be revealed to be a highly coordinated and planned terrorist attack, the Muslim terror group known as Al Qaeda (The Base) led by the Mujahideen veteran of the Soviet Afghan war, Osama Bin Laden claimed responsibility. Planes had been hijacked and flown to the pre-arranged targets including the Pentagon, the United States Military's HQ outside Washington DC.

As the days went by it became apparent that Bin Laden was seeking sanctuary in Afghanistan, under the protection of the Taliban regime. The Taliban who followed the age-old custom of the 'Pashtunwali code' were obliged to give comfort and support to anyone who requested their protection.

Within a short space of time Western special forces were en route to the area, using staging points such as Uzbekistan to the north as jumping-off points for operations into Afghanistan. We had allies in Afghanistan during this period, known as the Northern Alliance, who up until 9th September 2001 had been commanded by the charismatic Soviet Afghan Mujahideen veteran known as 'The Lion of the Panjshir' Ahmad Shah Massoud.

Massoud had taken his forces north to Mazar-e-Sharif during the Afghan civil war, when the Taliban came to power, as he was a moderate Muslim who had no desire for the kind of country the Taliban had in mind. His forces had kept the Taliban out of Northern Afghanistan throughout the 1990s, but it would appear that the Taliban and their Al Qaeda allies knew what would happen after the attacks of 9/11, so took steps to remove the one man who could unite the whole of Afghanistan with the backing of the West.

Massoud would be assassinated by Al Qaeda militants disguised as a Belgian news crew. During the interview, the camera equipment that was rigged with explosives detonated, fatally wounding Massoud. He would die in a helicopter evacuating him to an Indian field hospital in Tajikistan. One of the assassins would die in the explosion, the other would be wounded, captured, then shot while trying to escape.

Every soldier knew then that our job had taken a sharp turn into newer and deadlier territory. For those of us based in Northern Ireland, the effect was almost immediate. For decades the Irish American communities in New York and Boston had actively funded and supported PIRA activities and attacks on British soldiers in Northern Ireland and the British mainland, which had seen the deaths of not just hundreds of soldiers but also thousands of innocent civilians. Now Americans in those cities had just experienced what the British people had been facing for nearly four decades; funding and support for the Provisional Irish Republican Army (PIRA) dropped literally overnight, forcing Republican terror groups to rethink their strategies now that their bank account was closed.

What followed was a sweeping invasion by Western forces including the main NATO powers who had lost citizens during the 9/11 attacks. As predicted, the Taliban and their Al Qaeda allies could not stand up to the awesome firepower of those forces and melted into the countryside and into their sanctuaries in Pakistan, where the government had turned a blind eye to their activities or actively supported them. What then happened was a brutal counter insurgency war. Al Qaeda militants and Jihadists from around the world flocked to Afghanistan to join the war against non-believers.

These militants would vary in their levels of skill and experience from those who only just knew how to use an AK and were motivated purely by religious zeal, to battle-hardened and experienced Chechen fighters who had fought their own brutal war against the Russian government. Many of them had served in the old Red Army before the breakup of the Soviet Union.

Fast forward to 2006, the British Army would go into the lawless Helmand Province in force in order to restore the rule of law and destroy anti-government factions. We would send a woefully understrength and under-equipped force into the lion's den in that year, on what would come to be known as Operation Herrick.

16 Air Assault Brigade would spearhead the combat mission in Helmand, assisted by soldiers from Denmark and Estonia. But it was quickly realised that a brigade numbering approximately six thousand troops would not be enough to dominate a province of twenty thousand square miles, which was about a quarter of the size of the UK, with a population of approximately 880,000. Then the Platoon house tactic of dominating the ground meant that certain units became fixed in location and surrounded by a hostile population and sometimes numerically superior forces; meaning they became bogged down and in some cases, they could not send out foot patrols into their area of operations.

Our brothers in the Royal Irish Regiment had held Musa Qa'leh in 2006. But due to political shenanigans had been forced to endure an ignominious withdrawal from Musa Qa'leh, being escorted from the town by the Taliban; a scene which still conjures up emotions of rage and betrayal within the ranks of the Royal Irish who fought hard to secure the town and lost comrades in doing so.

The town would be held by the Taliban until December 2007 when Operation Mar Karadad, a joint ANA/ISAF combat operation, would be launched to re-take the town, which had become the Taliban's main drug trafficking hub and would be the only town in Helmand fully occupied by the Taliban.

As we prepared ourselves for the patrol that day, we wondered whether the enemy would realise the significance of the date and try to force more fighters into the area. I had heard it said from a few sources that whoever held Musa Qa'leh, held Helmand Province, as it was key terrain and had vital ground on both sides.

As we prepared to leave to go on patrol, we were told to stand down. The ANA ambush was still on the ground and as it was unpartnered, no one wanted to take the risk of being fired on by jumpy ANA soldiers. So, we waited and waited and waited.

Pretty soon the temperature began to rise. Then we were given the go ahead to conduct our patrol. The patrol was extremely tiring, lads became irritable as the heavy kit they carried began to chafe and dig into already tired shoulders. Legs began to cramp up despite the fact that the boys were drinking fluids and taking electrolytes. We stumbled along like tired zombies as the heat sapped our strength; it was becoming a dangerous proposition. Men were so tired that they could only focus on the ten metres in front of their noses and looked forward to a moment where they could flop down in the shade of a tree, bush or compound wall, out of the glaring sun.

I had a Lance Corporal attached to me from Battalion HQ, Norrie Stevenson, a senior, older soldier who was from the Regimental Police detachment. He had come to me to help bolster numbers. I watched him closely as he had suddenly gone bright red and had stopped sweating.

"Holy fuck Norrie!" I called. "Are you awright mucker!" I asked. But he had gone beyond the line of reason now and was incoherent. I saw that he was getting dangerously hot, maybe even suffering from heat stroke. I immediately stopped my Platoon, which they were grateful for and told Goody what was going on and asked for immediate CASEVAC for Norrie. For Norrie Stevenson to have struggled, it must have been really hot, he was a tough old buzzard who worked really hard.

I evacuated him to the waiting Mastiff Company to our west in Musa Qa'leh Wadi after stripping him of all his kit other than helmet, body armour and rifle. It became apparent quite quickly why the heat had hit him so bad as I lifted his patrol pack, it weighed an absolute ton, more so than any of our kit.

He was carrying unnecessary kit, but he had not been out on patrol with us before, being part of the CO's rover group (bodyguard and escort detail to the Battalion commander). We had long ago learned to carry only what was important on us. If we couldn't eat it, drink it, fire it or use it to patch someone up, we didn't take it, but Norrie did not have that experience behind him patrolling and fighting in the heat of an Afghan summer.

I had to admit, I too began to feel a bit lightheaded, even though I had drunk two bottles of Camp Bastion's finest bottled water and nearly the full contents of my camelbak. We had stopped at a UN-built well to refill our bottles and camelbaks, which nearly descended into a brawl between our guys and the ANP. Whereas we were trying to replenish our water stocks before carrying on with our patrol, the Afghan police thought it would be a good chance to crowd the well and wash their feet, faces and hands. We grabbed the ANP commander and told him that in no uncertain terms, his officers better get the fuck out of the way as they were not getting drinking water, they were having a mother's meeting. For the hot, tired and angry Jocks this was a step too far and the ANP were swept out of the way with threats to blow off certain of their body parts that they might quite like to keep hold of.

We got going again and after an uneventful patrol, we headed back towards the DC. I had spoken to Goody at PB South and he had agreed with me that the Company was not getting enough rest between operations. The lads were tired and, in some cases, still suffering the after-effects of illness. It would not have been so bad had we been getting fed properly at the DC between patrols. But unfortunately, we were not. We knew that it was not only radio batteries and ECM batteries that needed charging, ours did too. There was only so long the human body could take the beating that ours were before our immune systems began to fail and we would become susceptible to all manner of bugs and diseases.

I was informed by Goody that after our next OP on the 13th of September, the Company would get a straight four days' rest. Until then, we were planning for the next set of patrols, which would see the Company face some fierce fighting.

Day 158

Saturday 13th September: Musa Qa'leh DC

After less than twenty-four hours stand down, we were back out again. This time we were heading to Satellite Station North which we would be using as a base of operations before heading out into the Green Zone and the Gardens to hit the Taliban again north of the DC. We began to feel bad that we had not shown them enough attention and we were sure that they had missed us. Our patrol up to SSN was uneventful; the Taliban were definitely taking Ramadan seriously and we wondered if they were so tired and hungry that they wouldn't bother to attack us for the whole month.

As we approached the spot where we would cross the open ground to get to the patrol base, we were concerned that the ANA in the checkpoint to our south would open up again. Tentatively, we moved across the open ground near the graveyard, paying close attention to our arcs of fire, especially our arcs to the south. Luckily the ANA did not open fire, thus negating the need for us to destroy their bunker. We let out the breath we had been holding as we entered the chicane that was the entry point to Satellite Station North and began to relax.

Once we had got settled in, the OC outlined his plan for the next few days, the Company would send out Platoon-level ambushes on known Taliban routes and areas. Leaving the patrol base before first light and being in position for sunrise, knowing that this was when the enemy began moving fighters into their forward positions, especially if they knew we were in the area. They were about to get a nasty surprise over the next few days.

Our maps had changed; the compound numbers stayed the same but the prefixes had changed. I wondered if this was due to some compromise of the present maps, due to one being lost? Or were they changed for the new Brigade coming in, as we were now a mix of Operation Herrick 8 and 9? Our Mastiff Company and the Warrior Company were Herrick 9 and we were still Herrick 8.

12 Platoon was to be the first ambush patrol out the next morning, leaving at 01:30hrs and the rest of the Company would act as our QRF. I had done ambushes on training exercises and commanded them on my leadership courses, but I had never actually formed an ambush party before and began to run through it in my head as Al Lipowski and I briefed up the Platoon. I borrowed some extra claymore mines from the Royal Irish lads to put in with the killing group.

An ambush party is broken down into several key groups, The left and right cut off are the groups that give advanced warning of the enemy's approach and when the ambush is initiated, they will atack anyone attempting to flee from the ambush. The killing group is normally commanded by the Platoon commander and will consist of the bulk of the Platoon, he will normally have right next to him a group including a number of machine gunners and his claymore-firing devices known as clackers (from Vietnam), which are small green plastic handles which you squeeze, which sends an electrical charge down the command wire, setting off the mine. If these are daisy chained together or set up correctly covering the killing area, they are devastating, not only against infantry targets but also against soft-skinned vehicles. I had set them off and used them while I was on Platoon Sergeant's Battle Course in Malawi in 2006. The noise they made was really loud, I could not even imagine being on the receiving end of two or more Claymores, the effect must be catastrophic.

I had read accounts by American soldiers who had used them in Vietnam, and they had testified to the shock and destruction caused by the detonation of a claymore mine during ambushes. The stillness and quiet of the jungle immediately ended by the booming of claymores and the patter of steel ball bearings hitting metal weapon parts and equipment. American Recon units told of how a Claymore would cut a person off at the legs, chest or head depending on how close they were to the mine, reducing a patrol to so much offal.

The Boss would decide his method for kicking off the ambush, he could start it with the claymores and that would be the signal for everyone in the killing group to unleash hell to their front including hand grenades. Or he could choose to position himself between two of our gunners and as soon as the enemy were in the killing area, a tap on the shoulders of the gunners would start them hosing down the killing area, instantly causing everyone else in the killing group to follow suit.

Lastly would be my group. As Platoon Sergeant I would form the rear protection for the ambush party, it would be me and possibly one or two more soldiers and my 51mm mortar. We would cover the rear and prevent the enemy from sneaking in behind the ambush party, we would also act as a rally point for the Platoon as it withdrew from contact, with me conducting a head count of the troops as they passed me by, my party leaving the area last.

I would also act as a CASEVAC team, should we suffer dead and wounded in the ambush party. I could also be used for prisoner of war handling, if the Boss had decided to send out search parties to gather intelligence and search enemy dead, any live fighters could be brought back to me and I would secure them, give first aid and be responsible for their evacuation.

Once Al was happy with the composition of the ambush party, we looked at where we were going to mount the ambush and how we would get in, go through some actions and then we rehearsed getting into the ambush, initiating the ambush and then extracting back to safety again after the chaos had ended. And it would be chaos.

Ambushes in training were chaotic enough, but this was real and there was a good chance we would have lead coming back at us and there would be carnage amongst the enemy fighters expected to walk into our killing area. Only when we were happy as a Platoon did the Boss and I let the lads stand down and get some rest.

But I couldn't really sleep, I began running the scenarios through my head and the what ifs. I ran through my CASEVAC plan again in my head, my POW procedure, my actions on contact with enemy. I ran through my ammunition states, I made sure I had illumination rounds for my 51mm mortar, to give the guys more light to kill by, smoke rounds to cover the withdrawal and HE bombs to drop back into the ambush site, just in case the Taliban decided to fight through or follow us up.

I had made sure the boys had enough ammo, especially my gunners. I made sure guns and rifles were well oiled, we couldn't afford any stoppages in the ambush party, batteries were changed on night vision goggles and Israeli pressure bandages and tourniquets were accessible to everyone.

I made sure my patrol medics had their med packs and lightweight stretchers all prepped ready for a CASEVAC. I pored over my map again and ran through my list of what ifs again, only when I couldn't keep my eyes open did I slump back against my patrol pack and allow sleep to take me. We had been lucky so far, I hoped that the luck would hold out.

Day 159

Sunday 14th September: Satellite Station North, Mentored ANA Checkpoint

We were shaken awake by the watchkeeper from the Royal Irish at 00:30hrs, I stretched and yawned before sorely rising to my feet. I looked around at the rising, groaning forms of my Platoon. They looked like an army of the dead instead of the battle-hardened Platoon of fighting men that they were.

We didn't have time for a fully cooked breakfast, and I was sure the Platoon was glad of the extra sleep. We snacked on fruit or brown biscuits all washed down dry throats with tepid water. Some ate a boil in the bag breakfast cold and some just did not eat at all; we were keenly aware of the deadly ambush that we were about to mount and the area we were mounting it in. It was very familiar ground to us and we knew the enemy used it as a transit route between Kats and the invisible front line. There was a good chance that the enemy would trigger our ambush come first light.

After we had packed away and completed our limited admin, I did a quick kit check on the guys and made sure that those given the Claymores had the bulky square green canvas bags draped over their shoulders.

As we had made safe coming into Satellite Station North, we now had to make ready and I watched in the dark as the gunners knelt and pulled machine gun butts into their groins before pulling back the cocking handles on their Minimis or Jimpies. The riflemen all tilted their rifles to the right, reaching over the SUSAT with their left hands and pulled the teardrop-shaped cocking handles on their SA80s to the rear firmly, then released them sharply, allowing the bolt to rush forward, picking up a 5.56mm round from the magazine and forcing it into the chamber.

Everyone checked their safetys before stepping away from the HESCO wall against which they had made ready, this was done so that should someone have a lapse in concentration due to tiredness, the accidentally discharged round would go into the HESCO wall and not into a fellow soldier. The days of complacent negligent discharges had gone though, we had left that behind us in FOB Keenan. Every soldier in the Company was aware of the state of their weapon, all the time and if they weren't? Well the magazine came off and the chamber of the weapon was cleared, just to be on the safe side.

The Minimi gunners had a small pouch of one hundred rounds fixed onto their light machine guns, which was an initial contact belt. My Jimpy gunners had a 50-round belt of 7.62mm fixed to their guns, with someone always next to them ready to feed more rounds into the gun as necessary.

Additionally, those who had the 40mm underslung grenade launchers (UGL) fitted to their rifles slotted a small HE grenade into the chamber of the grenade launcher. The grenades looked like small fat bullets, but they packed a devastating punch when used by a competent grenadier, my guys no longer needed to use the sights on the UGL but could gauge the angle required to hit the target by glancing at the area, this was a skill born only of experience earned in combat.

We checked one another over to make sure nothing rattled. A head count was done and, as soon as I was happy that the Platoon was formed up and ready, I reported to Al and whispered in his ear that we were ready to go. We all dropped our night vision goggles over our left eye and began to move off slowly.

Moving out of Satellite Station North we hand-railed the HESCO wall of the checkpoint to the right heading west. Around us nothing stirred, it was a quiet morning with the moon still up and the stars visible, through our night vision goggles it was almost like broad daylight.

As we pushed west we could see the little material streamers attached to the grave markers in the graveyard outside the checkpoint, no one moved and the only sounds audible were dogs barking in the distance and the shuffling of twenty-three pairs of booted feet as a trained pack of hunters moved out to their hunting ground.

I watched through my NVG as the lads covered their arcs, weapons held at waist-belt level, ready to be used if the enemy came upon us at close quarters. Small squares of silver glint tape sewn to the arms of our combat clothing glowed brightly through the night sights, these would only be glowing when looked at through NVGs.

Occasionally the Platoon would stop to allow Al Lipowski to do a nav check or to go firm if we heard suspicious noises or saw something odd. The last thing we wanted was to be compromised even before we had gotten into our ambush location.

The Platoon automatically dropped into herringbone formation, covering all arcs of fire. Behind me, the reserve section covered the rear as well. Our objective was a maize field south of the compound, now designated Q5C-17, which was a large, lone compound in the middle of several tracks that criss-crossed the area. We knew from experience that this compound was used by enemy forces as a forward operating base and would likely contain fighters resting up for Ramadan.

We approached the area from the south and used the maize fields and shrubbery as cover to allow us to get into position. We moved into a stop short point a few hundred metres away from the objective and allowed the groups to get ready to move forward into the ambush site.

We knew it would not be long before it got light and the civilian population would begin their daily routine and going to prayers. Our ambush site would be on the boundary of the Q5A and Q5C compound grids and would be covering a track running north to south at the south-west corner of compound 17.

So far so good, we had gotten in without meeting any civpop or having to fight our way in past Taliban patrols, which we knew were out there during the silent hours. The large compound to our east was surrounded by trees and bushes. We scanned the tops of the walls looking for tell-tale signs that the enemy had left sentries in position, the glint of moonlight off metal parts, the silhouette of human heads sticking up over the compound walls or the sound of snoring from the rooftops.

Satisfied that none of this was in evidence, the ambush party filed in, left cut off, right cut off, and killing group last. The only sound that the Platoon made was a slight 'swish' as bodies brushed against maize stalks or other foliage, but other than that they were extremely quiet and I was very impressed, I couldn't hear the earlier sounds of barking dogs, which meant they had probably got bored and settled back to sleep.

I remained about eighty metres to the rear of the ambush site and began laying out my team facing west. I laid out a collection of mortar bombs on top of my daysack, ready in case illumination was needed. I also laid out 1.5-inch rocket flares which could be used in conjunction with the mortar illumination.

I heard over the Platoon radio channel as the cut offs reported that they were in location and ready. Not long after that the claymores went out and over the Company radio channel Al Lipowski let the OC and the comm centre at the DC know "Ambush set!" The next communication would no doubt be a contact report and even the guys at the DC would hear go down and the other Platoons from D Company would be rolling out ready to exploit and assist our ambush.

As we settled in, I began to think of the times I had done ambushes. In Northern Ireland my job had entailed training for 'Reactive Ops', which were essentially ambushes but with the emphasis on capturing the intended target not killing them, but still having the ability to kill if the enemy fired upon you.

They were normally over quite quickly owing to a disease known as 'Exerciseitis' which meant that no one fully appreciated the length of time spent in an ambush location. It was all timed and choreographed, but generally the command 'Ambush set!' was followed by snoring as bored soldiers, who were sleep-deprived anyway, left in the lying position for longer than five minutes, dropped off to sleep.

Here in Afghanistan, or certainly in this ambush, there was none of that, the lads were keyed up and adrenaline had begun to kick in. I for one listened to my heart beating in my chest and wondered if it was so loud that it would give the game away.

In training the ambush goes well, the 'enemy' all fire a few token shots and then fall over dying, with none of the friendlies being killed. But here, there was a real possibility that if you fell asleep or didn't kill the enemy with your first wall of fire, they could recover from their shock and try to kill you back. It was the basic human instinct for survival, like a wild animal caught in a trap. 12 Platoon had been caught in a few hairy incidents that could have been classed as ambushes and knew what it was like to be on the receiving end of that wall of fire.

No one slept, everyone was sweating and dry-mouthed despite the cool predawn air. Everyone's senses were heightened, eyes strained through night vision scopes and goggles, watching for the shapes of armed men walking down the track to their front, waiting for that hellish first burst of fire that would be the signal to lay waste to anything in front. Eyes began to play tricks, swaying maize stalks became insurgents sneaking towards them, sticks began to take on the familiar shapes of AK barrels, but the lads dare not rub their eyes in case any movement gave them away.

The ambush would almost be up close and personal, they would see, hear and smell the men they were about to kill and that was a very daunting prospect. Up till now we had seen our kills in the sights of our weapons. Here we would almost be able to reach out and grab them.

We lay in position for what seemed like forever, backs became stiff and cramp had started to set into limbs. But to move would be to draw attention.

Fairly soon it started to get light and we knew now that the chances of the ambush being sprung were gone, the enemy could have been moving via a different location or may have missed them as they inserted before our ambush patrol had gotten into position.

Whatever the case, we did not spring our ambush and with a mix of relief and disappointment the killing group reeled in its claymores and the cut offs on order collapsed back into the killing group before coming back to me. My bombs, mortar and flares were packed away and I knelt up ready to receive the ambush party to do a head count.

My rear protection group were still in the prone covering their arcs and would do so until we patrolled off. I looked at the boys as they came through my location, they all looked tired and sore, but they were still maintaining their stealth, no one knew we were in this location yet, and if we could keep it that way, so much so the better. But word would soon get around that ISAF forces were operating at night and could just appear from anywhere, given the fact as well that we were all short arses, we could hide in places that your average six-foot guardsman or even your six-foot ANA soldiers could not, which gave us a distinct advantage.

We stayed close together in herringbone formation in the maize field and I reported to Al that the Platoon was all present, then we headed back towards Satellite Station North. Night vision devices had been removed and stowed away and we were back in daytime routine. As we walked away into growing daylight, the sounds of the call to prayer filled our ears, we passed the faithful heading to prayer and farmers carrying the tools of their trade about to tend their fields. Many would show their devotion by praying at the sides of their fields before beginning their backbreaking day-long toil.

We arrived back into Satellite Station North to the sight of the rest of the Company standing down. They had been ready to come to our aid had the shit hit the fan, but as they saw us trudge through the red and white barrier at the checkpoint, they grinned at us and began to strip off their body armour, helmets and daysacks.

I made the Platoon safe and then did a quick kit check to make sure we hadn't left anything out in the ambush site. I reported to Goody before I could relax and I told him that all kit and all soldiers were accounted for.

"Nay dramas mucker, git the heed doon and I'll shout yeh if ah need yeh!" he said. I dropped my kit into a neat pile where I had been sleeping and stripped to the waist. I looked at my own physique and the lads around me, we had lost a shit load of weight, the Op Herrick diet is still the best one I have ever done.

Day 160

Monday 15th September 2008l: Satellite Station North

That morning it was 10 Platoon's turn to act as the ambush callsign, they were given an area slightly further north than my ambush site, but nevertheless it was on a well used track system that we knew the Taliban used to move fighters between Kats and the northern end of Musa Qa'leh itself.

11 and 12 Platoons would remain in SSN to act as a reaction force in case 10 Platoon struck it lucky and were able to spring their ambush. We sat kitted up ready, and for all intents and purposes it seemed as if 10 Platoon's ambush was going to go the same way as ours, until a Dutch F-16 fighter jet that had been allocated to us for air cover informed Bruce: "Widow 59, Tell your callsign on the ground I can see twelve men heading down the track towards their position, they appear to be armed!" Bruce relayed the message to Jim Adamson, who acknowledged as though Bruce was giving him a weather report.

This was definitely not going to go the same way as my Platoon's ambush, twelve armed men heading straight into 10 Platoon's killing area. Everyone's lethargy suddenly disappeared and we moved to the front gate of Satellite Station North and began to slowly patrol north. The next part of the story was related to me by men who were in the ambushing party.

In the killing area, 10 Platoon watched as the group of men walked in front of them on the track which was slightly raised. In the group was

Brian McAllan, a soldier I had served with previously in the Royal Scots. Brian watched as what appeared to be the point man walked in front of him and then stopped, Brian watched him as he turned around looking at the area. Brian was unsure whether the enemy fighter had sensed that 10 Platoon were there or just had a bad feeling, but either way it was going to be the last feeling this fighter would ever have.

At first glance Brian could not see a weapon, but as the fighter turned to face Brian directly, he saw the barrel of an AK underneath the man's clothing, then the fighter locked eyes with Brian and saw him, but too late. The fighter's eye widened and he tried to bring his weapon to bear, but Brian was already on one knee, safety catch off and he fired, watching as the bullets struck the fighter in the torso, punching him backwards and out of Brian's line of sight.

The ambushing party opened fire on the survivors and the survivors recovering from their shock returned fire. Bullets whipped through the maize over the heads of 10 Platoon, leaves and bits of corn rained down on the heads of the ambushers. Jim Adamson calmly radioed his initial contact report.

We could hear the gunfire, punctuated by the thuds of hand grenades. In the killing area the enemy began to fall, dead or fatally wounded. The killing group began lobbing L109 grenades into the killing area, to try and hit those survivors hiding from view and those attempting to flee north, some trying to drag their wounded with them.

One enemy fighter managed to get into a compound and lay down fire on the killing group, but one soldier grabbed a LASM from the daysack of one of his buddies and sent its 66mm warhead racing into the gun position, killing its occupant and destroying the machine gun.

The enemy were not done yet though, and RPGs began exploding overhead and landing near 10 Platoon's location. They were so close in fact that one of 10 Platoon's privates received a piece of RPG frag in his leg. It was not serious, after self-help he returned to the fight. The Taliban were getting their shit together and were starting to try and reinforce their fighters now locked in a life-or-death struggle.

At this point 11 and 12 Platoon were racing as fast as we could towards the ambush site; we were conscious that now there could be friendly casualties. The ambush was closer to enemy territory than to us, so they could get reinforcements quicker to their fighters than we could to 10 Platoon.

Before leaving for Afghanistan the Battalion had emphasised three areas that we would train heavily on for the tour that would definitely save our lives. Fitness, firearms and first aid. The fitness would now come into the fore, in the British Army we train very hard when it comes to running or marching when loaded down with heavy kit and on our command course we have fitness tests in full kit that require you to run or march with full infantry fighting gear. The Brecon two, three and five milers are run on Section Commanders, Platoon Sergeants and Platoon Commanders battle courses in Brecon in Wales over rugged terrain. Luckily the terrain in Helmand was not as hilly or rugged as Wales, but it did have its own hazards and now I felt like I was doing a Brecon two-miler. I yelled to the lads to move, our brothers were fighting to our north and the enemy was nowhere near finished.

"They need us up there boys, no fucker slows down or stops, keep fucking moving!" I yelled. The fire fight to our north was still raging and as I glanced in that direction, I heard the strangest noise: 'zzziiip… thump'. I watched and listened in amazement as bullets from the ambush site, their energy spent, zipped over our heads or landed at our feet.

Without thinking I stooped and picked up a round that had thudded down in front of me, it was a Russian 7.62mm short, the shape not distorted or damaged. A perfect bullet head, just all of its energy dumped, and its flight path had brought it down around the relieving Platoons.

"Holy shit," I said to no one in particular. "Did you fucking see that?" I dropped the expended round and carried on running.

Before long we were up near 10 Platoon and the fighting had pushed into the compounds further to our north. It had become apparent though that the enemy were now reinforcing and were trying to flank our Company. 12 Platoon were ordered onto the left flank covering towards the wadi area. As we moved up, Bruce called over the radio: "Guys the F-16 is coming in low, he's spotted fighters to our north; he's going to strafe them!" I looked to the north of the ambush site where I could just make out a treeline running from west to east and some kind of commotion. The Dutch fighter screamed in low from behind us and I watched as smoke puffed up near the cockpit. There came the sound of 'brrrrrttt' as its M61 Vulcan cannon roared. (The sound of the German MG 42 general-purpose machine gun of World War Two was likened to ripping cardboard and known as 'Hitler's buzzsaw'. The M61 sounds a bit like that, but at 6,000 rounds a minute as opposed to 1,200, it's a whole different proposition.) I followed the sound and watched in awe as the treeline I was watching took a burst of fire and I could see some bodies fall and some being flung into the air; the Taliban had tried to withdraw but they were not outrunning the Vulcan cannon.

Pockets of smoke were still lingering in the area, both from 10 Platoon's ambush site and from where the F-16 had strafed the Taliban, I watched on as our troops swarmed over the area. 11 Platoon pushed right towards compound 180, which was the first in a chain of compounds forming a long crescent south-west to north-east.

I could hear the 'thud' of grenades being lobbed into likely enemy positions and the rattle of SA80 rifle fire as enemy fighters were forced out of cover and harried into the open, trying to flee north. I could only imagine the desperation that they must be feeling, like a hare caught between groups of chasing hounds. The distinct 'whoosh' of RPGs could be heard off to our east and clouds of dark smoke appeared where the Taliban were trying to air burst their warheads over 10 and 11 Platoon's positions.

I turned back to my Platoon, who were pushed around the corner of compound 185. There was a low wall, a ditch and then an expanse of open field stretching towards the wadi. We would push north paralleling the compounds until we reached Q5C-196 and 197 where we would hold the area and prevent the Taliban from trying to catch us in a pincer. We already knew that this would be their tactic. They always tried to flank us, but now, rather than getting in behind us, they generally ran into our flanking callsigns and had to withdraw under heavy fire, sometimes leaving their dead.

Immediately, as predicted, we ran into Taliban reinforcements, the crack and thump of AK fire smacking over our heads and as I looked up above me, the compound walls puffed and bullet holes appeared where the rounds were striking. Chunks of dirt and clouds of dust rained down on our heads, quickly the lads took cover and began to scan for likely enemy positions.

"Where did that come from?" Tam Meighan yelled, but no one could answer.

"Tam!" I yelled trying to get his attention as I knelt behind the cover of the wall. "It came from over there!" I made a chopping motion with my hand to the west. The noise made by a weapon being fired has two stages, the 'crack' and the 'thump'. The crack is the bullet passing you by and the thump is the position of the firer. I had narrowed it down to a single area, but no one could identify the shooter.

Suddenly more fire cracked over our heads and I knew I had him.

"Watch my tracer!" I screamed at the top of my lungs, before rising to a half crouch. I lifted my rifle till my eye met my sight and suddenly there it was zoomed in, a lone tree, surrounded by low scrub and bushes, the magazine that was fitted to my rifle was always full of tracers for just this eventuality. I pressed the safety catch switching it to fire and squeezed the trigger rapidly, sending accurate rapid fire into the suspected enemy firing point. I watched as the tracer rounds struck in and around the tree, which was about one hundred and fifty metres away. I could make out the strikes of the bullets on the trunk of the tree and the bright red glow of tracer as it lodged into the bark and burned out. Then I saw a fighter in a grey dish dash with what appeared to be a green chest rig running back to the north, his AK held in both hands, his legs pumping.

I got my sight pointer over him and began to engage, I watched as the tracer followed him and struck him. He did not go down until about my fifth round struck him. He fell, disappeared and then didn't get back up. I lowered the rifle out of my shoulder and breathed deeply, what felt like an hour had literally been seconds.

After that, the firing stopped, and we continued up until we got into compound 195, which seemed the best suited to our task. No sooner had we put troops on the roof of the compound, they began to receive heavy fire from the north-west and north-east.

11 Platoon hit the men to the north-east, and we hit the men to the north-west. The volume of fire we were receiving was staggering. There was at least one PKM machine gun out there trying to hit us, but the enemy were not having it all their own way and I could hear the lads on the roof calling out targets to one another.

"RPG gunner, two o'clock of fallen wall!" This would be followed by the rattle of Minimi fire punctuated by the 'thoomp' of a 40mm UGL round. Seconds later a sharp crack would be heard in the distance where the grenade had landed. "Enemy down!"

"PKM eleven o'clock of treeline!" 'thoomp'. "Enemy down!" I set up my 51mm mortar ready to hit anything or to at least flush out the enemy that the lads couldn't see, but from the sounds of things they had it sewn up.

"Two zero and three zero, be aware fast air inbound five-hundred-pound ordinance ready to drop," The OC advised us, the Dutch pilot had clearly felt he needed to give the Taliban more love and had lurked in the area in case we needed him. I passed the information over verbally and over the PRR channel. "Keep low on the roof lads, five-hundred pounder coming into the north!" I received the acknowledgement from the lads on the roof and I stood with bated breath in the centre of the compound, waiting for the bomb to hit.

We could just make out the sound of the plane circling overhead. Then the engine pitch changed, so we knew the plane was diving, but then there was an ominous silence, followed by what sounded like a train passing by, then an almighty 'BOOM' which shook the ground under us. Even from inside the compound I could see the pall of black smoke rising into the air to tour north.

The firing had stopped, and the battlefield fell into a weird silence, no gunfire, no screaming, nothing. Just nothing. The guys on the roof kept scanning and kept watching, but there was nothing. If there had been any survivors from the air strike, they were not firing, perhaps scared that the plane would come back and finish the job. But I reckoned that whoever was under that bomb when it went off was completely obliterated.

"All callsigns this is zero Alpha, withdraw back to the south, order of march, one zero, two zero, three zero!" The OC ordered. We waited until the other Platoons confirmed they were moving, then we left our compound and began heading south.

I checked my watch and was surprised that it read 09:30hrs, it was amazing how time became distorted during firefights. We felt as though we had been out there all day, but in actual fact we had only been fighting for about four hours, nearly five. I made sure I was amongst the last out of our compound and left with my reserve section.

The move south went very quietly, the enemy had taken a hell of a beating that morning; my Platoon alone had killed between six and ten enemy fighters, never mind the guys killed by 10 Platoon in the ambush and by the Dutch F-16 and Charlie Grant's guys out on the right flank.

The Taliban would no doubt be consolidating and licking their wounds back up in Kats, I hoped that their morale had taken such a dip that they would not have the will to fight. We pushed through maize fields and across irrigation ditches, crossing streams and weaving between compounds, trying to make our route as unpredictable as possible.

The lads were all dirty and their kit stained black with gunpowder carbon, our faces were blackened and dirty. White marks ran down our skin showing the passage of sweat down from under our helmets, hands were black and grimy, the knuckles just visibly white through the muck, but every set of eyes had a grim determination and focus in them, despite the beating we had given the Taliban, no one was relaxed, no one would switch off until they were safely back in Satellite Station North.

Many of us has parched lips as we had been so focussed on the battle we had forgotten to drink, and it was only now with the sun getting hotter that we began to realise how thirsty we were. Some sipped from camelbak bladders in their patrol packs, others emptied the clear bottles with their blue and white labels from Camp Bastion.

We reached the area of compound Q5A-239, when Al Lipowski called a halt over the Company radio net. He informed everyone that a local had informed him of an IED in our path to the south, on the track next to compound 244.

Quickly a cordon was put in and we went into overwatch locations while a counter IED team was called in from the DC, this was lucky as we would have had to wait forever if the team had to come from Bastion, but most major patrol bases had an IED disposal team that could be transported out.

I thought back to my days in Ireland when we had suspected IEDs. We would normally have had to dig in on a cordon for days to give the IED team a soak period and allow them to gather all the info required to dispose of the bomb. But that was Ireland, which was a more permissive environment, we did not have that luxury in Afghanistan. Yes, there was a chance that PIRA would take pot shots at your cordon and where we were in South Armagh, they were known to have talented snipers. However, they were unlikely to form up and try and assault your cordon locations. They definitely wouldn't try to suicide bomb you. The Taliban on the other hand definitely would, so the less time spent on the ground in the same location the better.

Eventually the ammo tech from the IED team went forward to exploit the device and we all waited for a loud explosion, but it never came. The bomb disposal officer had decided to diffuse it and see what forensics could be gained from it.

We had been extremely lucky that day, if any of our sections had stepped on the device, it would have killed that entire section. Recovered from the ground were twenty-two metres of det cord, four 82mm recoilless rifle rounds, an 81mm mortar bomb that had clearly been an ISAF blind, and a legacy Russian mine. The explosion would have been devastating. 12 Platoon were chosen to escort the Counter IED team back to a pick-up point on the eastern bank of the Musa Qa'leh Wadi, near compound Q5A-241.

As we moved down the slope to the pick-up point, Al Lipowski tripped over on his ankle severely twisting it, forcing him to be evacuated with the IED team back to the DC. Once again, I was back in charge of the

Platoon. For how long I didn't know, maybe until the end of the tour. But for now, my concern was getting the lads back to Satellite Station North and a good night's sleep.

We reached SSN just after last light and the lads flopped down along the wall they had been using as bedspaces for the last few days and within seconds we were all unconscious and snoring away. The next day we patrolled back to the DC and looked forward to a few days' rest.

Day 162

Wednesday 17th September: Musa Qa'leh DC

Waiting for myself and Al Lipowski back at the DC was a package we had not expected to receive. In conversation it turned out that he and I were fans of the popular tabletop wargame, Warhammer 40,000. Some weeks ago, Al had written a letter saying how the war had affected our ability to enjoy our beloved game and could the company Games Workshop please find it in their hearts to send us a few old copies of their monthly magazine, *White Dwarf*. GW came up trumps for us, we didn't get magazines, what we got was a copy of their latest boxed game and a set of paints, which if we'd had to buy would have cost us at least a hundred pounds, it looked like my rest days were going to be busy with painting.

We started four days of rest and it was very much welcome, but even on those days off we didn't stop working. This stand down was a chance to clean weapons and give them a thorough going over, especially our machine guns, which had seen a lot of action.

The spare barrels also needed a good de-gunging and all the weapons needed to be well oiled. Pretty soon all our tents smelled of gun oil and carbon, our hands were so black from scrubbing weapons that I wondered if we would ever clean it off.

Bruce Ewart and I were sat down to dinner that evening when we heard a single gunshot, we had no idea what it was but thought it was most likely to be a negligent discharge from a tired or complacent soldier. We were right, a quick investigation revealed that a US Marine had an ND inside a shipping container right next to the recently established

TV room. We could only count our blessings and be thankful that no one was killed or injured. It would be sod's law to survive everything we had so far to be killed by accident, not a very soldierly way to go at all.

The TV room had recently been added with a nice big telly to watch the Olympic Games, better late than never I suppose. But then we were never in the DC to appreciate it, so it was only those personnel based in the DC who got the benefit.

With the down period came boredom, and with boredom people started to get on each other's nerves. I was sat watching a movie on my laptop one night when I heard a commotion in the tent opposite mine where some other lads from the Platoon were quartered.

There was a lot of shouting and threats of violence, nothing really unusual in Afghanistan but not normally directed at each other. I could distinctly make out the voice of Big Smudger and another soldier who will remain nameless. The commotion started to get more heated and as I stood up to see what it was all about, Tam Meighan came running into my tent flustered.

"George, Smudger is going to kill Bloggs." I came out of my tent into the walkway that separated the rows of tents only to be greeted by Bloggs fleeing big Smudger's tent and Smudger giving chase. Smudger was bollock naked after obviously just being out the shower.

He gained on Bloggs quickly before grabbing him and nearly throttling him.

"What do we do George?" Tam asked. I pointed at Smudger and frowned.

"There's no fucking way I'm getting in the way of that thing mate, it'll take my fucking eye out!" Smudger Smith was blessed with the biggest cock I had ever seen on a human being and at present, said appendage was flapping about like an albino mammoth trunk. Eventually after a minute or so of homo-erotic light throttling, I decided I had seen enough. More than enough, probably more traumatising than any contact.

"Smudger!" I shouted. "For fuck sake let him go mate!" and against my better judgement I got between Smudger and Bloggs. I got them separated and sent them on their way. I never found out what caused the argument, but the fight was both hilarious and psychologically scarring in equal measures.

We had begun winterizing the tents for the arrival of the Royal Gurkha Rifles who would be our relieving unit for OP Herrick 9. I would not appreciate just how cold and miserable Afghanistan could be until I did a winter tour myself and fully understood the need for winterization.

We also were given our dates for leaving Afghanistan, I would fly out of the DC on 24th October, be in Cyprus on decompression on the 25th and would be landing back in RAF Manston in Kent on the 28th of October at approximately 15:00hrs. The end was in sight, all I had to do was survive and not do anything stupid that would prevent my lads from getting home alive; just over four weeks to go.

Winterizing the tents actually made them seem cooler, we had to add white insulating layers inside the tents and make sure there were no holes that would cause leaks. Doors had to be put on too, before we had lived comfortably in the outer shells of the large tents with the sides rolled up. But this would not be possible in the winter, heavy rain and freezing temperatures would prevent that.

D&V was doing the rounds again and a lot of the lads from around the Company had been put in the death tent including a few lads from 12 Platoon. I myself had picked up a bug and at 02:30 had the shits and was puking, but luckily nowhere near as bad as I had before. The problem with viral D&V was that it spread very easily and very quickly, taking down groups of soldiers in one fell swoop. It didn't help that almost all of us were undernourished and our bodies were worn out. Our immune systems were doing their best to fight off some horrible bugs, some people's immune systems (like mine) were fairly good at fighting off the bugs, but others looked as though they were at death's door.

I was able to manage breakfast and then at lunch we were all stood in line waiting to be fed, in front of us were some QDG from the Mastiff Company. In that group of soldiers was a young blonde lad whose face was familiar to some of us, but we couldn't quite put our fingers on it until one of the Jocks piped up from the line.

"Here you, ya wee poof! Geez a song!" He ordered, then it twigged. The lad had been a contestant on a reality TV programme trying to find talented singers and this lad clearly still smarting from not winning the competition had become somewhat sensitive about it and began to hunt for the offending Jock in the line.

Before long there was a dusty scuffle and fists were flying in the scoff queue. The NCOs from both D Company and the QDG managed to intervene and separate the groups of fighting soldiers and seconds later the line moved on towards the hot plate as though nothing had happened. It has always been said that when soldiers have no one to fight they'll fight each other, which is why having your Army constantly on operations is not a bad thing.

We received orders on the 19th for our next operation, given the success of 10 Platoon's ambush, it would be another one. But this time the entire Company would be involved in a 'U' shape, with my Platoon forming the right leg of the 'U' facing east.

We had been informed that the ambush would be conducted in the area of Q5C with my Platoon covering towards compounds 175 and 176. The other Platoons would cover a prominent crossroads just north of compound 192. As Al Lipowski's ankle was still bad, I would be stepping up again as the Platoon commander.

HUMINT had told us that after 10 Platoon's ambush the previous week, the Taliban had been extremely cautious when passing maize fields on patrol. They shone torches into the area and then opened fire on the fields if they were not sure or scared; this was a good sign, psychologically we were getting to them. They were like kids walking past a spooky house or a graveyard at night whistling to keep their spirits up or drive away the fear. If they believed that every maize field contained a Jock Platoon ready to ambush them, their nerves would be constantly on edge.

The date for our ambush would be 21st September, ironic in the fact it was supposed to be ISAF peace day! The hippies had finally made it to Afghanistan, I somehow couldn't imagine there was a Taliban peace day.

On the 20th we conducted our ROC drill talking through everything from the route out to the route back after the ambush was concluded. We left no stone unturned and tried to plan for all eventualities. I got my Platoon together and ran through our part in the ambush. We would leave the DC in vehicles and drop off in the Mande Wadi west of Roshan Tower, patrol up to the high ground the tower was on and wait till the early hours of the morning. Then we would find a route down the cliff face and into the Green Zone on the west bank of Musa Qa'leh Wadi, at which point my Platoon would conduct a route clearance across the wadi and form a bridgehead on the eastern bank. As it would be in the dark, I stocked up on IR glow sticks in order to make the path visible to the following Platoons. Once again, the fate of the Company and the success of the mission was initially in the hands of 12 Platoon.

Once across the wadi, 10 Platoon would lead the Company into the area and we would move into our respective ambush locations. Our orders dictated that should the ambush not be sprung, we would take over the nearest compounds and prepare for fighting patrols into the local area. For 12 Platoon this meant 175 and 176 which were compounds of a decent size on the eastern side of the maize field we would be lurking in. They would cover the area south of Kats, the whole of it known to be an enemy stronghold.

I ran through the composition of my killing group and cut offs. Pieter Du Toit would command my left cut off and Pete Breen would command my right cut off, right next to me in the killing group would be two Minimi gunners and the signal to open fire would be me simultaneously tapping them on the shoulder and the initial burst of fire would signal everyone to open fire.

Looking at the map, if anyone did walk into our killing area, the fighting would be extremely close quarters, no more than fifteen metres. We would see our enemies very clearly.

Day 166

Sunday 21st September: Musa Qa'leh DC

I conducted the pre-deployment checks on the Platoon prior to mounting up on the Mastiffs. There we no claymores on this ambush, but I had filled my dump bag with spare L109 hand grenades. If the enemy went to ground in either the ditch to our front or were in compounds 175 and 176, I would probably have to blow them out of their hidey holes. They would no doubt do exactly the same as they had done with 10 Platoon on the 15th and try to get into compounds; if that was the case it was our job to ensure they didn't leave alive.

We mounted up into our respective vehicles and strapped in, with the amount of IED strikes now happening, we couldn't take the risk of being injured if the vehicle tipped or we were thrown around the inside. Previously we hadn't bothered with the seat belts in the Mastiffs, which may have been a bit complacent of us, but then we only had to worry about small arms and RPG fire. Over the last month however an upsurge in IED laying in the wadis had seen strikes on not only military vehicles, but of course civilian traffic. Many innocent people had lost their lives or limbs after striking Taliban IEDs. This was turning the locals against the Taliban, against all their insurgent ethos. The Taliban had taken to marking their IEDs with little red flags or pieces of cloth, to help locals identify them, but surprise surprise, it also allowed us to identify them, thereby rendering the tactic useless.

We trundled along at a nice even pace heading west towards FOB Edinburgh and Himal OP, passing through small groups of compounds where the people barely noticed the vehicles; just another ISAF patrol heading to who knew where. I watched the legs of the gunner as they spun round in a three-sixty-degree arc, the gunner looking out for any threats.

Clouds of dust came in through the top hatch of the Mastiff filling our nostrils and mouths with dry sand, which made you need to spit every five seconds or blow your nose; the result of which was a rather disgusting green sandcastle at your feet on the floor of the Mastiff. We dropped in our predetermined drop-off point and went firm until all the Company had deployed and shaken out, at which point we patrolled off north up a ravine, which kept us out of view.

When we got to the top of the ravine, we went firm in all-round defence and as I looked to my west, in the distance I could see a Bedouin tribe camped out in the wadi. Their traditional tents were all set up and their camels were staked to the ground. I could see cooking fires rising up from the tents for the evening meal. But the Company had already hunkered down, settling in for last light.

The enemy would not see our position and they definitely wouldn't see us leave or our direction of travel, given that it would be dark by the time we set out. A further deception was the fact that we would be crossing the Musa Qa'leh Wadi again, west to east. If the enemy had seen our drop-off point or knew of it, they certainly wouldn't be expecting us to double back across the wadi, especially given the fact that we would have to go down a sheer cliff.

I told the section commanders to rotate their guys through the sentry positions and get as much rest as they could before we moved off, it would be an arduous crossing with the potential for IED strikes. I wanted my guys fresh, as it would be us clearing the way for Delta Company.

Day 167

Monday 22st September: Desert Lie Up West of Musa Qa'leh DC

As quickly and quietly as a rifle company could, we woke up and rubbed the sleep out our eyes and in the moonlight we moved off. No one had removed any part of their kit in the lie up apart from maybe helmets, I had thrown my Ranger blanket over me to stave off a slight chill in the air and quickly rolled it up before strapping it to the side of my patrol pack.

We moved past Roshan Tower, ensuring that we had informed the troops from the PWRR that we were in the area and that we were moving to their west, which would prevent a blue-on-blue scenario. The moon gave the night sky a dark blue tinge but made it easier for us to navigate and through night vision goggles it was like broad daylight.

Once again, marvelled at the beauty of Afghanistan at night. Look at the mantle of stars too long and their sheer numbers made you dizzy. As we approached the cliff face north of Roshan Tower, Nick sent out a recce party to try and locate a path down into the Green Zone. After a little while, the recce party returned and said they had found a goat path which would suit our purpose, but we had to be careful as it was loose dirt underfoot and very steep.

I watched the snake of troops marching towards the start of the goat path and disappear. I could make out the distinct pattern of their desert combats in light and dark greens, the bright green glow on faces showed where the lads were wearing their NVGs and some of them had left mockingbird IR beacons switched on, so you could see the bright flashes on their kit.

These beacons were only visible through night vision devices and allowed us to see the other Platoons and prevent any chance of separation. I got to the goat path and could see why caution was advised, I stood at the top of the cliff and looked down.

Through my NVGs I could make out compounds on the ground beneath the cliff and they looked frighteningly far away as we were so high. I could also see the twinkling of individual lights in the compounds that had electricity. I could make out the shapes of fields and treelines, it was almost like looking down on a map.

The path itself was very tight and not designed for heavily armed troops wearing body army or heavy kit, I felt my sides scrape against the 'V' slit in the cliff that allowed us to get down onto the path. Below me I could see the lads descending very gingerly, at any minute expecting to slip and fall taking those below them off the cliff and into the Green Zone below. At that point I wished I had talons to dig into the dirt and hold me steady. One wrong step could take me and those immediately below me into a long death tumble, there would be nothing to stop us.

I began sweating harder now, occasionally having to raise my NVG and wipe the sweat from my eyes.

Eventually, the Company was back on the firm ground of the Green Zone west of the Musa Qa'leh Wadi and we set off towards it. We soon came to the crossing point and the OC called my Platoon forward. I had already got the metal detectors out as we went firm, knowing that as soon as we pushed forward, we would need to clear the wadi as quickly as possible and get the Company over so that we were not compromised.

I had told the lads that I would stay at the front with the clearance team and act as their close protection. Once we had cleared far enough, the rest of the Platoon would follow a tactical bound behind. Once again, I realised that what I was doing was potentially stupid. If I was killed that would leave the Platoon leaderless, but I was determined to set the example and stayed with the lads who had the riskiest job, and that was the two lads in front with the detectors.

I had with me a large batch of IR glow sticks and every time the lads cleared an area, I would break one and drop it, being careful to drop it in the arc the detector had covered. I would throw one left, leave a gap, one right, leave a gap, one left and so on.

We were halfway across the wadi when I started to hear music, it wasn't just coming from one location either. I could hear the faint sound of Afghan or Arab-sounding music. Across the wadi in front of me, in a compound behind me, and faintly to the north and my left across the wadi. I began to wonder whether I had truly lost the plot or had just not had enough sleep until I felt a tap on the shoulder.

"Sir!" John whispered in my ear. "That is Taliban music, the enemy are very near!" He was extremely nervous, and John was not a man to be overly dramatic. If he was nervous, then there was a good reason to be. This was info I felt the rest of the Company needed to know.

"Zero Alpha, three zero Alpha," I called over the radio to Nick Calder.

"Zero Alpha send," I paused knowing what I was about to say was going to come off as mental and no doubt raise a few eyebrows for anyone listening to the transmission.

"Three zero Alpha, I have what sounds like music to my east, north-east and south-west. My interpreter tells me it's Taliban music." After a slight pause, Nick came back on the net.

"Roger three zero, thanks for the info, proceed as planned."

"Roger out," I acknowledged.

We pushed on conscious that we were potentially surrounded by the enemy, but from what John had told me they would not be up for a fight.

We hit the far bank of the wadi and secured it and as I turned around to watch the rest of the Company follow, through my night vision goggle I could see the distinct path of IR glowsticks that I had laid for the Company to follow.

On a clear night like this, there was no way they could deviate from the cleared path. Looming out of the green darkness I could make out the shapes of 11 Platoon followed by 10 Platoon. They pushed past my Platoon, stopping only to do a map check.

I watch Jim Adamson through my NVG gathering his command team around him and there was a dim glow as a filtered torch lit up his map, it was more obvious through the NVG as the device picked up ambient light, but to the naked eye it was barely visible.

After a quick brief to his Platoon, they left heading east towards the FRV (Final rendezvous point) before deploying out to our ambush locations. 12 Platoon followed behind in reserve, we tagged on the end of 11 Platoon and began patrolling through the area.

We nipped between compounds and crossed darkened fields and irrigation ditches, all clearly visible through the NVG. As we got into the FRV we all went static and we paused to see if we had been compromised; we hadn't. No gunfire rang out, no tracer landed in our midst and there were no panicked screams of Taliban fighters caught on the hop and trying to withdraw.

I looked around and saw that we were in a muddy clearing in the middle of a large maize field, I faced my Platoon to the east as that was where we would be going. Quickly I set up the order of march, left cut off, killing group and right cut off. Wullie Rankine would stay at the rear but didn't require a big rear protection group as just behind him would be Goody and his party, including Andy the medic.

On the signal from the OC, I pushed the Platoon forward and with a gentle rustle of kit brushing the maize, we moved into position. As I got down on my belly in the maize field I heard and felt Pete Breen's section coming up to my rear then pushing right into position.

I looked to my front and could see literally within spitting distance compounds 175 and 176. We tried as best as we could to blend into the maize and took off our patrol packs as added protection, a kind of sandbag in front of us. I was now well aware how close the enemy were likely to be if the ambush was triggered, if some survived like 10 Platoon's ambush, this could very well descend into hand-to-hand combat.

In front of our ambush position was a large earth bank, behind which was a ditch and then the compounds, which were about thirty metres away. I settled into position but quickly felt the hard-packed earth under my elbows, making it slightly uncomfortable.

This was not such a bad thing because, even as tired as I was, there was no way I could sleep given the pain in my elbows. My neck soon began to ache as the position of my head meant I had to look up at an angle and my helmet kept resting on the back of my body armour. I had to work hard to stop myself from moving, but I did eventually.

Not long after I had settled, I passed onto the OC that 12 Platoon was in position and that the ambush was set. To my left and right I could make out the dark shapes of my Minimi gunners, hunched behind their light machine guns, the butt pulled into the shoulder and their fingers resting on their triggers. Given the closeness of them I could feel the tension in their bodies, they were coiled ready for the tap on the shoulder that would unleash the carnage. Nige Campbell to my left and Granty to my right.

As I lay in the darkness, I could feel the blood start to pump, here I was waiting for heavily armed enemy insurgents to walk into my killing area and I would unload hell at them from my Platoon. But if they survived, they would be turning their guns onto us. 10 Platoon, on return to base after their ambush, had found bullets lodged in rocket flares and patrol packs and the kit inside had been riddled with bullets. That was how close the fighting had become.

I became aware of my heartbeat as it thumped through my chest, body armour and into the ground beneath. I could feel the blood pulsing in my ears and suddenly became overcome by the paranoid feeling that the sound of my very heartbeat would be loud enough to compromise the ambush.

Time went by slowly and quietly. But at some point in the night to our north-west, behind my ambush, a single shot rang out. I risked a glance over my shoulder, I could make out the faint trace of a torch light near the compounds in front of 10 Platoon. 'Fuck,' I thought. 'The Taliban have followed their new tactic and fired into maize fields they weren't sure about.'

The OC whispered over the radio asking if anyone had opened fire. We all replied in the negative, no one knew where the fire had come from, nor the torch light.

The ambush settled down again and I began to think my eyes were playing tricks on me. To my front I thought I could see the distinct shapes of people moving and the shape of a PKM gun barrel held at high port, I blinked, and the shapes were gone! Had I really seen five or six insurgents passing in front of me or were they figments of a tired brain?

As first light appeared, it became apparent that the ambush would not be triggered and that we would have to move forward into the compounds and take them over. It would be fun trying to get my cold tired limbs to move. Slowly and painfully, I pushed myself up onto my knees and then stood up. My section commanders closed in on me for a brief. I had only managed to get out "Were going into these compounds..." before fire erupted from our north-east. Bullets whip cracked over our heads and the 'whoosh' of RPGs was deafening as they raced over our heads, harmlessly exploding to our rear.

I looked at Pete Breen and knotted my eyebrows, shook my head and sighed. "Gonnae no dae that?" He grinned and made a funny face at me.

"How?" he asked, mimicking the lighthouse keepers from the Scottish sketch show *Chewin' the Fat*.

"Jist gonnae no!" I replied. Despite the amount of fire coming down on us, the Platoon broke out into fits of laughter. (This won't mean much to a lot of readers, but those who do get it can feel culturally superior.) Quickly, we got ourselves together and took cover behind the earth bank in front of our ambush site.

We began to identify where the fire was coming from and began to return fire. I watched the lads just behind the firing line, the Minimi gunners were traversing their weapons left to right, cutting the greenery to their front down. Underneath each Minimi gunner was a gathering pile of brass and black disintegrating link.

Momentarily the firing from the enemy stopped. We had either pinned them down, or hopefully, killed them. The firing resumed shortly after, but not to our front, the enemy had decided that they would try and probe the other Platoons. But judging by the fire being returned by 10 and 11 Platoons, they were giving the Taliban the same reception as we were.

After an hour or so, the firing died away and silence returned to the Green Zone. I watched smoke rising from the barrels of the Minimis and quickly the gunners cocked the working parts to the rear and lifted their feed trays in order to allow the guns to cool down.

Those who needed to, changed their barrels. Fresh belts of 5.56mm link were laid out. We watched and observed waiting for the enemy to reappear, but they didn't, the peace and quiet remained.

After a soak period the OC decided that we had done enough damage to the enemy and we began to withdraw to our south by Platoons, leapfrogging one another until we were a safe distance from the area and then we began to patrol back to the DC.

Day 168

Tuesday 23rd September: Musa Qa'leh DC

While we were on our Company ambush, an ANA callsign had come across an IED. Luckily, they had not driven over/stepped on this one, which was a win for everyone. If we could exploit it, we could find out where the components and explosives were coming from. We could even build up a picture of bomb makers in the area as IED specialists build their own devices in their individual style, so it would become apparent if we were dealing with one expert or a whole group.

We were tasked with conducting cordon operations for this clearance. I stepped across to become CSM for the day as Goody did not come out. Given our numbers, it wasn't a full Company I was working with anyway. R&R, sickness and injury were still a factor, but nevertheless I liked to think it would look good on my command CV for the future.

We were back in the Gardens for this one as the Taliban had clearly been laying IEDs on the paths they thought we would take. But where we could, D Company tried to stay off tracks and obvious features that would likely be a spot for IEDs.

Again, it was something that the British Army had learned in our war against the Provisional IRA in places such as South Armagh, Tyrone and Fermanagh. All rural communities where IEDs were placed to catch out security force personnel. The threat from what would come to be known as 'roadside bombs' meant that in South Armagh you just could not travel by road. The threat of command-detonated bombs meant that helicopter and foot insertions were the only options. And foot patrols were not of course without danger. There was a threat from highly trained snipers with Barratt sniper rifles supplied from America that forced us to adopt certain tactics. The bomb layers counted on people being lazy and always choosing the path of least resistance. So you had a difficult choice to make, rip the ball bag out your combat trousers crossing a barbed wire fence, or lose your legs/life crossing an obvious gate or fence crossing. We opted for the tough ground, sometimes even against all logic. On open ground we used deception plans to fool the enemy dicking screen, but over the years we could build up a pattern and get forensic evidence from bombs that had been made safe by ATO.

We were starting to realise that in Afghanistan, forensics was just as important as it had been in Northern Ireland. However, the construction of some of the IEDs in Helmand would mean that brave bomb disposal operators would lose their lives trying to make these devices safe in an attempt to gather evidence.

As we settled into our compounds to cover the Counter IED task force as it moved in to clear the device, we became aware of heavy fire to our east. Our US Marine brothers had received fire while patrolling in Towghi Keli, near Satellite Station North and had responded in true Marine Corps fashion. By blitzing the shit out of the Taliban firing points.

We could hear the deeper, chunkier reports of the AK versus the sharper cracks of the Marine M4s and M16s. Occasionally the sound of the firefight would be punctuated by RPGs and the flat 'bang' of AT-4s and M72s, the Marines were not pissing about.

We listened to the fireworks and in the distance could see dark smoke rising into the air over the tops of trees and high compound walls. It was given an odd dimension by the heat shimmer, which made it look as though the smoke was dancing.

"Thank fuck it's no us this time!" Pete Breen piped up, I nodded.

"Yer no wrong buddy!" I answered. I didn't want to jinx it by adding 'Not long left to go!' But I think everyone was thinking the same thing.

We noticed that the local farmers had started harvesting the maize crops. Some were quicker than others, which left a patchwork of square fields and tall maize to cover our movements. It would make patrolling up north here over the next few weeks that bit hairier, our cover from view was going.

We were approached at some point by the old fellow who told us about the IED on 15th September. We had obviously earned his trust in a big way as he felt comfortable talking to us in broad daylight. He came into our compound and sat with us taking through John and we shared our food with him.

In my admin pouch on my armour, I carried a wad of US dollars. Somewhere in the region of four hundred bucks and I made a move to get some out. I felt that this was a good way to spend it, reward someone who deserved it.

"Sir," I said through John. "Can I offer you this as a thank you?" I paused, removing one hundred from a clear bag I kept it in. He smiled at me and put his right hand over his heart and waved the money away.

"No thank you, it is a kind gesture, but getting rid of the bombs and the Taliban is payment enough for me!" I suddenly felt embarrassed and hoped that I had not offended this kindly gentleman. But clearly, I had not, for he stayed sat with us and then confirmed something that John had told me.

"Yesterday Sir, there were lots of foreign fighters in this area." John announced as the old man spoke. "Many Arabs, Russians (Chechens) and Pakistanis. They were playing music to keep their spirits up!" The old man continued. "The commander in this area is very tired, he has been losing many fighters in battles with you, his fighters are tired, too, and hungry from Ramadan, their morale is very low."

I smiled at the thought of this. Way back when we came to Helmand, we were told by the units we were relieving that the Taliban were invisible – and invincible – ghosts. But after four weeks in Musa Qa'leh, we had proven this theory wrong. We had not only seen them; we had killed them and now we were aware that their morale was on its arse and that was due to the aggressive fighting spirit of the Jock. I hoped that in a compound somewhere to our north, there was a Taliban commander talking to his new fighters.

"Those ISAF guys are fucking nails, we fire everything we can at them and they won't die, they are invincible!"

He also informed us that there was one man laying all the IEDs in this area and he was using children to carry his components for him because he knew that we would not kill kids unless they fired at us first.

I cast my mind back to the poor Para lads who had been killed by the young boy with the wheelbarrow full of dried poppy stalks and then the kid who tried to kill Geordie when he was on stag with an AK. They were being used by evil people who sold them a lie about killing British and American soldiers.

The Afghan security forces were viewed with even more disdain than us, they as Muslims should be fighting for the Taliban. They should be fighting against, not with ISAF. In the enemy's eyes the ANA and ANP were nothing more than traitors. But a lot of the ANA came from places under Taliban domination, or in the case of those from the north of the country, had actively resisted the Taliban government as the Northern

Alliance under Ahmed Shah Massoud, and they were in no hurry to see a return to the type of Islam touted by the Taliban. Public executions, beating of men for not having a beard, beating women for walking around without a chaperone or just showing a patch of skin.

This old gentleman had proved to be a very useful font of intelligence and I was sure that battlegroup headquarters would be interested to hear what he had said and wondered if other agencies could develop him as an asset. That would be extremely useful as he lived slap bang in the middle of the Taliban front line.

Once the IED had been cleared, we absorbed the team into our Company and returned to the DC, arriving just before it started to get dark.

Day 170

Thursday 25th September: Front Gate, Musa Qa'leh DC

After a rest day my Platoon was back out on the ground and this time the reason was a great one, it would mean that the end was in sight. We were out to dominate the ground for the RiP (Relief in Place); going out were our Celtic brothers from the Royal Irish Regiment, coming in were the Rifles.

As we were nearing the gate, we heard a massive explosion coming from the direction of the bazaar in the centre of Musa Qa'leh. I halted the Platoon at the gate until we could get further information, we weren't sure if we were walking into an ambush that may have been sprung way too early by a Taliban ND, an IED or some other Afghan factor i.e. ANA/ANP.

The Op's room was getting mixed and confused messages about an ANP officer firing an RPG at a civvy, deliberately or accidentally no one could tell. There was no word on casualties, but I couldn't help thinking that you can't fire an RPG, especially in a bustling area such as Musa Qa'leh, without casualties being caused.

And as if to reinforce the point, a white Toyota Corolla pulled up outside the front and a group of men got out carrying a man who, by the look of him and the way his friends were carrying him, was seriously wounded. I sent a soldier away to the medical centre to grab the Doc.

In the meantime, my Platoon, and specifically young Nige Campbell, got stuck in to helping the man. He was covered in blood and had severe frag injuries all over him and a particularly nasty head wound, the last time I had saw anyone that badly hurt was wee Davey McGhee.

Looking at the amount of blood he had lost and his pallor, it did not look good. He could be going into shock, his levels of response were extremely low and I reckoned that if he wasn't evacuated soon, he would certainly die. Whoever had initially treated him however, had the presence of mind to stick an IV drip into his arm and get fluids into him to try and help replace the blood loss he had suffered.

Behind us I could hear the Doc approaching with a stretcher and a group of medics, they were all wearing bright blue rubber gloves and were observing the situation as they approached. Nige briefed the Doc on what had occurred since the casualty had arrived at the gate and he quickly took control of the situation and they spirited the wounded man away into the DC to begin treatment. His friends looked stunned and stood in silence covered in blood as we headed away on our patrol.

The rest of the patrol was not as exciting as the start, we moved north paralleling the Musa Qa'leh Wadi with a view to dominating the ground. We used the old Taliban trench systems along the east bank of the wadi that they had used to try and prevent ISAF from retaking the town on Op Herrick 7. There was no ICOM chatter and no enemy fire, so after a while we were ordered to collapse task and move back towards the DC.

As we got back to the DC, we were warned off for a patrol to Chardeh, south-west of Musa Qa'leh, the next day. It would be a Mastiff drop off, once again to support the RiP. We had visited Chardeh irregularly over our time in Musa Qa'leh. The area was dominated by the ANA so they mostly conducted patrolling there. But once in a while we made an appearance, just to let the enemy and the locals know that ISAF had not gone away. Also, the patrol tomorrow would require us to cover the area where the OMLT would be RiPing out from, PB South West primarily, which was on the western side of the wadi.

The next day, as we trundled along in the Mastiffs, I couldn't help feeling it was slightly odd that we were heading in this direction, considering our combat focus and the main enemy locations seemed to be to the north and south of the DC itself, where clearly the enemy were trying to dominate the town.

Chardeh was a small cluster of compounds directly west of Yatimchay on the west bank of the wadi. It was screened by greenery, making it a perfect spot from which to attack any forces moving through the wadi heading south.

I was pretty sure this was the area from which I had been RPG'd my first day as Platoon commander in August and was quite aware of the potential for fighting in the area; the Platoon were spoiling for a scrap if it meant getting back at the insurgent who attacked us in the wadi. As it happened the patrol passed without incident, we essentially went for a nice walk in the sun crossing the wadi before heading north back to the DC.

Upon our return we were informed by Nick Calder that we were to lose a section per Platoon to assist with the RiP. One section would go to Satellite Station North, one to the US PB and one to PB(SW). We were also warned off for a patrol to the Bagni Wadi area east of Musa Qa'leh to support the RiP. The duration and timings for us losing our sections had not been confirmed but we expected all sub-units to be back in on 30th September.

Day 172

Saturday 27th September: Musa Qa'leh Area of Operations

The move of our sections to the ANA patrol bases did not go ahead. But rather than rest on our laurels, we continued to conduct Platoon-level deterrence and domination patrols around the Musa Qa'leh area to cover the RiP.

We waited at the Op's building in the chill morning air, doing our final pre-patrol checks, making our weapons ready and shrugging on our heavy packs. I went inside to give the watchkeeper my flap sheet so that the Operations room knew the composition of my patrol.

I suddenly noticed that new signs had appeared all over the place, red circles with a red line through them and a picture of an RPG in the middle. Underneath written in English, Pashto and Dari were the words 'No loaded RPGs in the Op's room'. At least if the ANP guys couldn't read the signs, the picture left them in no doubt.

The duty officer noticed me looking at the signs. "No sense surviving all the shit out there Sergeant, to be killed accidentally by some fuckwit with a loaded RPG!" he exclaimed in his issued Sandhurst accent. I grinned and nodded.

"Fuckin' sod's law that Boss isn't it? I'd come back and haunt the entire ANP!" The ANP that were likely to kill you by accident, as Green on Blue attacks (Afghan forces deliberately killing NATO personnel) hadn't really happened in significant enough numbers to make the news, so it stood to reason that it would be one of those guys that blew us up by accident. It was one of them who had blown up the café in the bazaar.

"Thanks to those fucking arseholes no choppers are flying into the DC to resupply us," the duty officer continued as though reading my mind.

"Not that the RAF need an excuse to avoid fucking flying!" I said, handing him my flap sheet. He eyed it carefully and nodded.

"Absolutely Sergeant, take care out there!" I grinned, gave him a thumbs up and spun out on my heels back to my waiting Platoon – but it was not what you could really call a Platoon anymore. Most of our reservists had gone back to the UK, their commitment fulfilled. It was a shame as I would have liked to have finished the tour with all my lads, but I understood that we would all be ripping out at various times over the next few weeks.

Outside the sun was coming up and the lads were finishing their last cigarettes or drinking water. I dug into a grimy utility pouch on my vest and pulled out a wrapped army boiled sweet. I tried to peel the wrapper off the little red sweet, but it seemed to me made of super glue. No matter how hard I tried, bits of the wrapper still stuck to the boiley so I gave up and popped it into my mouth, sweet and wrapper together.

"Loone!" I called.The stocky Highlander looked up from his map and grinned. "Let's head out mate." He quickly briefed up his section and they began to move out. A dusty, heavily laden single file trudged out through the HESCO bastion chicane towards the front of the DC. I fell in behind them and signalled to my second section to follow on.

As I headed out of the front gate, a tactical bound behind the point section, I began to take in the sights and smells of the day. Somewhere near the DC a cockerel crowed, setting off others in the distance. The smell of cooking fires drifted on a light breeze and I could see small pillars of smoke rising from areas around the DC. People went about their business heading towards the centre of Musa Qa'leh to trade or just talk to friends over tea. We patrolled south, parallel to the Musa

Qa'leh Wadi and had to cross through the largest cannabis field I had ever seen.

I was quite naïve with regards to drugs but was informed by someone that these were in fact perfect specimens. The cannabis plants were more like trees and indeed a lot of them were taller than me. As we walked through it, the plants brushed our kit, leaving everything smelling strongly of weed.

I did remember reading somewhere that before the Soviet invasion when Afghanistan was quite modern and enlightened, hippies had come from the West travelling around India and Afghanistan looking for pure dope and seeing how easily cannabis and opium grew in this country. I was not surprised; it was readily available and really, they wouldn't have had to pay for it as it actually did grow on trees.

As we approached the Bagni Wadi we turned east towards PVCP South, which was an unmentored ANP checkpoint on the south side of Musa Qa'leh town. It was heavily trafficked and there were vehicles of all descriptions racing north to south and south to north. Beige ANA Ford Rangers filled with heavily armed soldiers bounced along the road, throwing up thick, choking clouds of dust and scattered people in their paths. The soldier on the top clung to the M240B machine gun as if for dear life as he was flung around the back. Huge beige Russian UAZ trucks filled with supplies headed south towards the ANA checkpoints and in the middle, Afghan civilians on little Honda motorbikes nervelessly zipped in and out between the bigger vehicles. But a Honda motorbike versus an ANA truck would be a very one-sided affair. A few times I cringed and closed my eyes expecting to see bodies being mangled under the heavy wheels of the big trucks. As we passed the ANP checkpoint at PVCP South, I saw a group of bored looking police officers waving vehicles into a vehicle checkpoint to be searched.

The level of traffic racing through the gap was phenomenal. Considering how tight the road was, it was nevertheless designed for two-way traffic. However, the Afghan highway code, should such a thing exist, did not take into account crazy. Which was the driving style of just about every Afghan on wheels. Two-way traffic became three-way traffic and gave the area a Mad Max vibe. Woe betide anyone who tried to cross the road on foot! I decided that the best way to cross west to east would be to do it in bounds until the entire Platoon was across and safe. It also kept a tactical 'foot on the ground' as we could cover each other's movement.

Once the Platoon was safely across the road, we headed slightly further east until we could find a spot that the entire Platoon could dominate and observe the crossing point. Before we got comfortable however, we had to sweep the area for IEDs. This was done using metal detectors, the operators focused on their equipment while we provided cover. We would be their eyes while they were scanning the ground ahead. Should we come under fire or spot something we would be in a position to engage or warn the detector operator. But the operator wasn't so close that, should he inadvertently activate the IED, others would be killed or injured.

Once I received the thumbs up from the sweep team, I led the guys into our LUP (Lying up point)/Lurk position. But even after it had been swept, I encouraged the lads to do a five-metre check of the area that they were taking cover in. The equipment was reliable and often found what it was looking for, but they were still mechanical devices and prone to failure, whereas the Mark one eyeball never let you down.

Satisfied we were in position and secure, I sent a SITREP back to the DC letting them know we were in overwatch and were ready to protect the RiP teams going about the area. As I watched the ISAF and Afghan vehicles, it became apparent that the level of military traffic was significantly higher.

If I had noticed it, you could be damn sure the Taliban would have noticed it, too. After all they were not stupid men, they were a resourceful, experienced insurgent force who were adept at reading the local tactical situation for their area of influence.

We experienced a similar thing out in Northern Ireland. Because our tours were generally six months long and started and finished at similar times of the year, give or take a few days, PIRA and other dissident groups would know when a new unit was due in to replace the existing one and as such assumed that this unit would be unfamiliar with the geography and tactics of the insurgents.

Therefore, we would see a spike in activity. The Taliban were exactly the same. In Northern Ireland, we countered this by deception. For instance, on my tour of Forkhill in South Armagh in 1999, I was replacing a unit of Royal Marines. For ground familiarisation we team leaders would patrol with the Marines, in order to get a feel for our new area of operations. We could not patrol in tam o'shanters, as this would give away the identity of the unit arriving in theatre, so every time I left Forkhill SF base on patrol, I was wearing a green beret and a combat jacket bearing the Commando dagger and the 3 Commando Brigade tactical recognition flash. I have no idea where they found a marine short enough to lend me his kit, but they did.

In Afghanistan, we didn't wear soft head dress so from a distance every soldier looked the same. The only difference would be in the Tactical recognition flashes on the desert kit of the soldiers. We were 16 Air Assault brigade, with our Sky blue and purple shield bearing a swooping eagle. Our relieving brigade was, ironically enough, 3 Commando Brigade. Their flash a green square with a black commando dagger.

Chances were the Taliban knew we were in the middle of a RiP and would no doubt take the chance to test the new troops, hoping to find a weakness to exploit. They underestimated the fighting spirit of our Commandos.

As we settled in, I watched ISAF snatch vehicles moving from the north to the south. From the direction of Satellite Station North, they were no doubt heading for PB South and the US PB. I watched the top cover guys on the snatch vehicles, their eyes were everywhere. The barrels of their Minimi light machine guns swung to cover their arcs of fire, conscious of how busy the area was.

We knew from the past that the Taliban did not care about causing mass civilian casualties, just to get to ISAF personnel. The ever-present risk of suicide vehicle-borne IED attacks were uppermost in everyone's mind and even I held my breath as the light-skinned Land Rovers crossed the wadi. Every car and motorbike was a potential bomb and preventing them getting too close to the convoy was a tough call. After what seemed like for ever, the large cloud of dust disappeared and with it the OMLT RiP. I let out the breath I had been holding and now began to focus on the fact that I had to get my guys back to base in one piece.

My headset crackled with static and I heard the radio operator back in the DC inform me that the patrol had safely reached its destination and that I was clear to collapse task and head back to the DC. I turned over, rolled onto my left side and looked around at my Platoon. The NCOs all looked into me and I nodded that it was time to move. I could see them talking to their guys, who raised themselves from a prone position to the kneeling still observing their arcs. As soon as I was confident everyone was ready, I gave the order for my lead section to lead off and head back to the DC.

No one relaxed their guard at all. Every soldier's eyes were like birds of prey, scanning for likely threats, watching for a sign that would indicate suspicious activity. John, who was literally my shadow, listened in to the Taliban ICOM scanner on the off chance that the enemy were planning to attack us. No such intelligence came our way and we decided it was more than likely the Taliban were fearful of coming this far south. We had pushed them as far north and south of the DC as we could and had given the town a massive protective zone; the Taliban had not been seen in the local area in large numbers for quite some time.

As we approached the DC main gate, I spotted a group of children playing in the dirt just near the south wall. I noticed a sad, forlorn little girl in a pretty but dirty little blue dress. Her dark eyes stared at me through tangles of long dark matted hair, her little nose was running leaving a trail down her grubby little face. To me she looked about four or five years old and my heart went out to her, the other children were playing together completely indifferent to her. I reached into a pouch on my vest and found a chewy peanut butter energy bar. I held it so that only she could see it and her face lit up into a bright smile. To get to her I would have to go through the big group of kids playing in the dirt, so I took the risk of lobbing it to her, hoping she would catch it.

I watched as the bar sailed in a perfect arc towards her outstretched hand and as it landed in her cupped hands, a sharp-eyed boy who was slightly older, spotted the sneaky throw and made a grab for it but it was already in the little girl's hands.

There was a blur of arms and legs as the boy tried to take it off her, which then started a fight as possibly the girl's siblings had seen what was happening and went to protect her. There was a cartoon cloud of dust with a raised fist and foot occasionally visible. I shrugged and carried on into the base before standing the boys down.

The next few days proved to be uneventful. Today was the start of Eid, the end of Ramadan. This was signalled by celebratory fire and fireworks all over Musa Qa'leh. My patrol was almost in the same area as yesterday, except I decided to set up in a different location in order to prevent patterns from being set.

As we withdrew back to the DC, I couldn't help notice trainer prints in the dirt that looked almost like a known brand of trainer complete with the logo. Trainers were very rare in Helmand; most people wore sandals or leather shoes. The only people that wore trainers were the Taliban or their foreign comrades, this allowed them to escape quickly as fighting a battle in flip flops or sandals made escape, even from heavily weighed-down British soldiers, a lot harder.

All major operations in the area were cancelled due to there being a Special Forces Ops box in play. They were going after an HVT (High

Value Target) within the Taliban command structure in our area. A few days later I would find out who it was. The IO (Intelligence Officer) informed me that it was none other than Abdul Bari, the Taliban fighter who had RPG'd me on the 7th of August as I attempted to assault compounds from the wadi. They had successfully taken him out, depriving the enemy of an experienced commander and fighter, as well as a fucking good RPG operator.

The next few days were great as we had a chance to rest, catch up on sleep, read mail, write back and call home. We received packages from some of the TA guys who had already gone home, which was more than welcome, it was nice to know they were still thinking of us. Though I thought, after what we had been through, they would never forget.

I was also advised by Nick Calder that I would need to start wearing Osprey now, apparently a few soldiers from other units had been wearing armour without plates and wearing non-ballistic helmets on patrol. The problem was, if I was killed or injured and the inquest found that I was not wearing issued kit, there would be a chance that the insurance company would not pay out, on a technicality.

I would love to see an insurer deny payment to the family of a soldier killed in action! The tabloids would have an absolute field day. Rather than wait for a set to arrive from Bastion, as I didn't know when that would be, I borrowed a set from Sgt Chris Muir, who was there at the DC in a support role. And with only three weeks left of the tour, I could put up with the Osprey. Even though I did not like the quality of the kit.

Bruce left that day for home and I felt like my right arm had gone. It would be weird not to be sharing packages from home with him and our nightly Family Guy and South Park viewings. But I was pleased for him that he was headed home and was looking forward to having a beer with him when I got back.

I also started having severe pain in my guts and was shitting blood, which is never a good sign. I spoke to the medics and they gave me some medication and told me to keep an eye on it and come back if it got worse.

Our RiP team from the RGR (Royal Gurkha Rifles) had begun to arrive and were checking on all the serial-numbered kit that would be staying in country with them, this was a positive sign and it meant that the end was now truly in sight.

Day 181

Monday 6th October: Musa Qa'leh DC

Our next major operation was in an area designated as Ops box Rattlesnake, north of Musa Qa'leh. The plan was to push north again and clear out a large suspected pocket of enemy fighters known to be residing in the Q5C compound box.

The plan was to move east to north into a desert leaguer and wait for first light before moving into the area and sweeping through the target compounds. With any luck the Taliban would still be on a post-Eid high and would either flee or we would make short work of them.

I had briefed the lads the previous night on the ins and outs of the first stage of the Op, which would involve a move by Mastiff, then the drop-off into the target zone. We were clear on what we had to do and once we had settled into the desert leaguer that night, Major Calder would give us a further brief on the following day's action.

I did not require a kit check on the lads as we had been through this so many times that it was not necessary, only a kit check on return would be needed. I checked my list and my order of march and made sure everyone was in the vehicles they needed to be in. I then mounted my own Mastiff and buckled myself in.

I was becoming accustomed to my new Osprey, but I still didn't like it. The pouches did not fit the Molle loops perfectly, unlike my multicam vest, and the Osprey vest was only secured on the sides by Velcro, and not very good Velcro either. Which meant if you leant forward, there was a very good chance your body armour would come undone, exposing you to a potentially fatal injury. This was only alleviated by attaching carabineers to the Molle on the sides of the vest to hold it in place. Not ideal because if you had to remove it should the soldier be injured; it was a ball ache. Luckily enough by the start of my second tour of Helmand in 2010, these problems would have been ironed out and we were issued with a decent set of body armour.

We trundled along at a nice brisk pace. I watched out the small windows on the back door as the countryside flashed by. I made out compounds, treelines and the occasional motorbike or car passing us by. As we moved away from the built-up areas around Musa Qa'leh, the terrain changed to pure desert and it became impossible to see anything out the back windows due to the huge amount of dust being kicked up by the Mastiffs.

I could only imagine how bad it was for the gunner on top of our vehicle. If the Mastiff in front of us was kicking up as much dust as ours, then he must have been engulfed in a thick ochre cloud of dust, which made goggles and mouth and nose protection essential. To confirm this, thick clouds of dust fell into the troop compartment that we occupied, and I felt it catch in my throat, making us all cough and leaving the nose and mouth full of grit. I had a US digital pattern neck scarf almost like a climber's tube scarf around my neck, which I decided to pull up over my nose and mouth, this eased the problem r and all I had to worry about was getting grit in my eyes.

At the leaguer position the Mastiff guys went forward to clear the position to make sure there were no nasty surprises waiting for us. We could only sit tight and wait for the all-clear before moving into position, where we would stand to and see if we had been followed or whether the Taliban planned to attack us.

We would be ready to repel the attack. We moved into a triangular defensive leaguer with some heavy firepower facing out towards the direction of probable enemy threats. If the Taliban were planning to attack, they must have gotten cold feet.

Before the sun set, we stood to again for last light. Nick got all the commanders together again and gave us the brief for the next day. We would be dropping off in the area of Q5C-140, which was a large patch of open ground covered by compounds north, east and south, with the Green Zone on its western flank. We had become very familiar with this area over the last few months as we were only a few hundred metres away from our old ambush sites, we knew that this area would be heavily occupied by the enemy and we would definitely get a scrap going in there.

The minute we got into the area; we knew that the Taliban dicking screen would know where we were as we weren't exactly inconspicuous. There would be time for fighters to get into position and ammunition to be brought forward to resupply those fighters, who only carried about three magazines per man for their AKs and two or three rockets for their RPGs.

The PKMs, however, always seemed to have quite a few for their weapons. Like our machine guns, the PKMs provided Taliban teams with a great amount of firepower. I had not been attacked by hand grenades by the Taliban, but we knew that it was part of their arsenal as they used them to attack checkpoints, driving by on motorbikes and lobbing them over the walls in the hope they exploded somewhere important.

My Platoon would be tasked with pushing through to compounds 130 and 131, clearing north from there and once we hit an LOE (Limit of Exploitation), to be determined by Nick on the ground, we would radio the Mastiffs and get them to pick us up before shuttling us back south to Musa Qa'leh. Hopefully, with nothing more than a bit of sunburn.

After Nick's briefing I went back to 12 Platoon and gathered the boys around the map and gave them a quick rundown on what we would do the next day. I laid out the order of march and that was all that was needed. As long as the boys knew where we were going and what we would be doing, the rest always fell into place. We all remained flexible though, because of the old saying, 'no plan survives contact'.

As I dismissed the Platoon they all got their gear on ready for stand to. The little cooking fires that had sprung up to cook a hot meal were now extinguished and I could still detect the smell of hexamine cubes that we used to cook our food. The low rumble of the vehicle engines was the only audible sound. We climbed aboard our vehicles and I could see the bright light inside the cockpit that showed the vehicle's navigation display screen. The driver and vehicle commander were silhouetted in the darkness by a halo of light thrown up from the display. I could see the commander talking into his headset and nodding frequently. The driver sat strapped into his seat peering out into the growing darkness. Above me the gunner swung his turret around using his right hand, the left one still gripping the handle on his .50 Cal machine gun. I assumed that this process was being repeated in all the other vehicles too.

We sat ready in case we needed to leave the vehicles to counter-attack or search their dead once the Mastiff gunners had chewed them up. But as the lovely yellow, orange and then red sunset fell into the horizon and darkness took over, no attack came. No Taliban were sneaking up on our position ready to launch RPGs from the darkness that would strike the bar armour on our vehicles, or perhaps they would strike the turret housing the heavy weapons, taking them out and allowing fighters to pour into the gaps made by the rocket fire.

No such attack was forthcoming and after a while the Mastiff commander turned to me and gave me the thumbs up. "Stand down bud!" he said.

"Cheers Boss," I responded before giving my guys the order to stand down over my Platoon radio channel. After dismounting my vehicle and closing the door, I found a nice little fold in the ground that would suit me for a bed. I rolled out my Osprey armour flat, using it as a mattress, my helmet as a pillow and my Ranger blanket to cover me.

As usual the Mastiff crews would cover sentry duty during the night, their lads manning the guns and glaring out into the darkness through night vision goggles. On each turret were rocket flares and smoke grenades, we also had access to 81mm mortar illumination rounds and 105mm artillery illumination rounds, should we require light.

Reveille in the morning was scheduled for 0400hrs, this would give us a chance to stand to, have breakfast and then sort our lives out before mounting up again and heading west to our target location. I wrapped myself up in my Ranger blanket and before long had dropped off into a deep sleep.

At around 2100hrs I was woken up by Private Lenno, one of my team medics, who informed me that Pete Breen was suffering badly with D&V. The medic from the Mastiff Company had given him some anti diarrhoea medication and some dioralite sachets for his water. This meant that there was no way Pete could participate in tomorrow's operation, so I grabbed my rifle and made my way over to his section, I found Tam Meighan and shook him awake.

"Sorry to drop this on you Tam, Pete is sick mate, you need to step up and take the section." Tam sat up, rubbed his eyes in the gloom and nodded his assent. "I'll change the order of march mate; I'll keep you in reserve." I let the news sink in, then I walked away back to my pit and resumed my last position before dropping back into a deep sleep.

Day 182

Tuesday 7th October: Desert Leaguer, North of Musa Qa'leh

I awoke at 0400hrs for reveille and stretched out my stiff limbs. There was a slight chill in the air, I shivered slightly as I pulled the Ranger blanket off me and began to roll it up. I looked around me to see that everyone was engaged in similar activity. As soon as all our kit was packed away and we were in our armour, we mounted up again ready for stand to.

All of our night vision gear was removed from our weapons and helmets and stowed safely into our patrol packs. I listened into the radio for any sign that the enemy were sneaking up for a dawn attack. After a wee while we were given the order to stand down as the sun began to rise.

All along the line of vehicles, I could make out the shapes of my lads in the growing light engaged in various activities. Some were wiping moisture off their weapons that had accumulated during the cold night, some were applying oil, especially to machine guns. Men set about making breakfast and a cup of tea.

I grabbed an MRE (Meal Ready to Eat US military ration) heater, placed an all-day breakfast ration meal into it and poured a little water into the bag. The water would react with the element inside the cooker, which would then heat the meal very quickly and effectively. The MRE cookers were an excellent and innovative piece of kit; if you were in a position where you could not light a fire, an MRE heater would give you a hot meal without giving your position away. I had used these before when I was in Kosovo as a Reconnaissance/Surveillance team leader. When you are in a covert observation post you cannot cook as it will give your position away. The cookers gave us the ability to have a decent hot meal, the only downside with them was you couldn't use the water to make a cup of tea afterwards. But as I was in no mood for tea, this suited me fine.

I grabbed my blue plastic spoon from where I kept it on my armour, ripped the foil packet open with my teeth and began to tuck into breakfast. The meal was very nice but had the consistency of rubber, especially the egg, which made it hard to cut when all you had was a spoon. Nevertheless, I managed to finish the meal before adding the bag to a growing pile in a hole in the ground, which would then be covered over.

As soon as we were all ready to move, we mounted back up onto our vehicles and moved off to our drop-off point. I looked around at the lads in my vehicle, each one was locked in his own thoughts, but not one of them looked at all nervous. I guessed that by this stage of the tour we were all battle-inoculated and this was just another walk in the sunshine that may or may not result in a firefight.

I settled down and closed my eyes for a quick power nap, which would help my focus and keep me sharp for the operation. Before long the squeal of the brakes told me my Mastiff had arrived at the drop-off point. It was not big enough to take us all, so the vehicles came in in packets, disgorging their infantrymen before heading back into the desert to a Zulu muster point. When my time came, I quickly dismounted and identified the rest of the Platoon. We pushed into the nearest cover and waited until the rest of the Company were on the ground. But there was a problem.

Hammy who was our MFC (Mortar Fire Controller) had a problem with his radio, which was not good. As part of the FST (Fire Support Team), his radio would be the one that would summon 81mm mortar fire to support us in the event of contact. It was easier for the mortars to fire for us rather than the 105mm guns at FOB Edinburgh. Due to the danger areas for both weapons and GMLRS (Guided Multi Launch Rocket System) platforms they could definitely not fire for us. They were way too close and should we require GMLRS support, I believe our support fire would come from Kandahar air base.

After what felt like an age, Hammy confirmed that his radio was working, so around 07:00hrs we began our operation. Morning prayers would be winding down and the jungle drums would now be starting to beat. Given the nature of our insertion, it would be hard to disguise where we were.

I listened as the sound of Mastiff engines faded into the distance, they were not leaving the area, rather they would leapfrog in such a manner to our east that they could provide intimate fire support, CASEVAC and resupply if required.

As if on cue the ICOM chatter began, the enemy definitely knew where we were, and we could hear their scouts informing their commander of the location of the 'tanks' which is what they called any armoured vehicle bigger than a Land Rover. The commander told his men to 'prepare the work and bring up more pineapples'; it would seem that we were going to get our fight that day after all.

Pushing on through a tight group of compounds, we came upon two fighting-age males who did not expect to see us. They were unarmed but by the looks of hatred on their faces and their shifty demeanour, they were up to no good. My lead section challenged them and conducted a search, which came up empty. But I didn't want to just let them disappear, I also couldn't shoot them as we had no proof that they were scouting for the Taliban.

I called to John. The big man looked over and then rushed over to join me. "John, can you get the ANP to question them and arrest them if need be?" John trotted over to the trio of ANP officers in their blue grey uniforms, festooned with belts of ammo for the one PKM they had between them and began talking to them.

I watched as the police officers approached the pair of locals and began a discussion, which was very loud with a lot of hand gestures and gesticulating. I nodded for John to hover near the group so he could tell me what was going on, but by the look on John's face I could tell the police officers were not going to hold them and John confirmed this minutes later when he approached me.

"Sir, the police are not going to hold them, there is not enough evidence." At this I frowned but I knew they were right. It would have been nice to arrest on suspicion, but they didn't and as I handed back the ID documents that both men had handed me, the fighting started.

The Mastiff Company started taking RPG fire to our north-east and I could hear the chunky report of .50 Cal machine guns returning that fire as explosions rocked the area. I watched in the direction the Mastiffs and could see clouds of dark smoke rising lazily into the air.

Now and then I could make out the 'thunk-thunk-thunk' of 40mm grenade machine guns lobbing grenades into the enemy; these were very accurate. The only weapon the Taliban had to match it was the Russian AGS-17 automatic grenade launcher. But these were prestige weapons, most of which were relics of the Soviet Afghan war and I could imagine were not well maintained and ammunition could be hard to come by.

I watched in frustration as the two males we had stopped disappeared, no doubt heading to join their friends and fight us. My only ray of sunshine was that if they did, there was going to be a good chance we would kill them.

As we pushed north, north-east towards our objective, I heard the unmistakable sound of firing coming from the area that 10 Platoon were pushing through. This was confirmed almost a split second later by Jim Adamson giving an initial contact report over the net. He reported that the contact was from the Q5F area just to our north-west and he was preparing to assault the enemy position.

We in the meantime had continued our advance, hoping to push the left flank of the enemy and stop them from trying their usual tactic of outflanking and encirclement. As we pushed up into the Q5F area ourselves, the ANP suddenly started acting really strange and began opening fire on compound 50.

I did not order my guys to fire as we hadn't received any fire ourselves, but it didn't hurt to get into cover and observe, as maybe the ANP had seen something that we hadn't. One of their guys began firing RPG rounds at a Mosque, but with little effect.

I knew that the enemy had used Mosques in the past to hide themselves and their equipment as they knew we would not fire on

Mosques unless it was absolutely necessary in self-defence, but the ANP were having a field day. To my west I could still hear the sound of 10 Platoon fighting. I had pushed into a patch of Green Zone next to a small stream by this stage, an idyllic spot even with the sounds of battle filling my ears.

At some point there was a loud explosion to the east, which could have only been the Mastiff Company. Major Calder confirmed that indeed one of the Mastiffs had a mine strike, disabling the vehicle and it would require a Foden recovery vehicle to extract it. Luckily enough, part of the QDG order of battle included a few Foden armoured recovery vehicles, crewed by the men and women of the Royal Electrical Mechanical Engineers (REME). It would still take time to get the area cleared in case of further mines or IEDs then get the vehicle in a state where it could be hitched up to the Foden and then driven out into the safety of the desert. (During 2008, Foden recovery vehicles were withdrawn from service.)

Jim Adamson meanwhile reported that he had ten EKIA and five suspected wounded seen fleeing the area, two POWs and three captured weapons. It was on this note that it was decided to withdraw back to the pick-up point and extract back to the DC.

It was a slow, measured withdrawal as we knew the enemy were out there and we had given them a bloody nose, killing a good number of them and capturing two of their own, the Taliban would want payback, so we expected that they would follow us up and that was exactly what happened.

The Mastiff Company was waiting for us in a pick-up point which was bigger than the drop-off point, allowing all vehicles to get in giving us a rapid extraction. The young officer who was in command of my vehicle was stood on the top of his Mastiff calling down to us to throw our patrol packs up to him so that he could secure them on top and free up space in the vehicle. Given that I had my radio in mine, it was not going on top of the Mastiff and I was in the process of telling him so, when all hell broke loose.

The enemy who had followed us up were now on a high feature south of compound Q5C-84 and 85, which also had a graveyard on it, giving them walls to use as cover. The doors on my Mastiff were open and the lads were piling in when bullets began smacking into the door next to me and pinging off the sides of the vehicle.

I was the last man in and jumped into the vehicle with rounds skipping off the ground under the back of the Mastiff. From the top of the vehicle came a piercing shriek and I realised that the officer had been hit. The gunner dropped into the troop compartment of the Mastiff, followed by the officer. The call had gone out 'Man Down', which told everyone there was a casualty on my vehicle, I grabbed the young officer to assess his wounds.

"Fuck Boss, what happened?" I asked checking him over.

"I don't know Sarge, one minute there was nothing then a loud bang and I felt pain on my face."

In my headset I could hear Goody calling for a SITREP on the casualty and that he was coming over to check on him. But the injury was not serious enough to warrant Goody leaving the security of his vehicle to come through fire to us.

"Three three Alpha from three zero Alpha, casualty is not serious do not come to us!" I called, but the message did not get through and before I knew it the door to my vehicle swung open and I saw a red-faced, sweating Goody stood below me.

"Where's the fucking casualty?" he called over the noise of the incoming fire. I shook my head.

"I tried to tell you Goody, he's not serious!" I yelled over the cacophony. "Git in here before you get hit!" I called to him, not expecting him to head back to his Mastiff. But he slammed the door and raced off back to his own vehicle.

I turned my attention to the young QDG officer, his face was scratched and bleeding in places and it became apparent what had happened. While securing the bags a shot from an AK had struck the shield around the gunner and fragmented hitting him in the face, his scream had been more from shock than pain.

Happy that he was safe, we turned our attention to the enemy. We were still in a vulnerable position and the enemy were still engaging us with heavy fire. The gunner was now turning the full force of his .50 Cal machine gun on the enemy. Behind my head were two GPMGs secured by bungee cords and at our feet were boxes and boxes of 7.62mm ammunition.

"Lads!" I called. "Grab these and get some fire going down." I didn't need to ask for volunteers, the lads were clambering over one another to get to them. Taff Owen and Bloggs flipped open two smaller hatches on the top of the vehicle that allowed them to stick out and return fire.

Soon both GPMGs were sending controlled bursts of fire at the enemy and I could hear the lads confirming hits on target. They were cutting the enemy to pieces. I had opened up boxes of 7.62mm link and was handing it up through the hatches to Taff and Bloggs. The combined weight of fire from a .50 Cal and two GPMGs was sending a wall of fire into the graveyard and high ground occupied by the enemy now overlooking us. The fire from the Taliban had only slightly slackened. I could hear and feel it hitting the side of our vehicle. Suddenly there was an ear-splitting bang and Taff dropped into the troop compartment, a look of shock on his face.

"Are you hit?" I called grabbing him, but Taff couldn't speak. I quickly ran my eyes and hands over him, no blood, that was a good sign. As I checked him over, I saw a scorch mark on the back of his armour. Intrigued I looked up through the hatch and saw a thick gouge on the hatch cover, I suddenly put two and two together.

"Fuck me Taff you are one lucky fucker!" but the look on his face said he didn't feel very lucky.

What had happened was, a round had been fired at Taff with the express purpose of parting his head from his shoulders. The round had gone wide, hit the metal hatch cover and ricocheted past Taff. But so close that it had skimmed the top of his rear body armour plate, leaving a scorch mark in its wake. With everyone now mounted up, we started heading east back into the desert. Taff had now resumed his position behind the GPMG and we sped off in a flurry of dust and a hail of bullets.

We were a very subdued vehicle that headed south back towards Musa Qa'leh, our adrenaline was now spent and some of us had come face to face with our own mortality and were pondering the luck with which we seemed to be blessed; giving grateful thanks for the poor marksmanship of our enemies.

Only on return to the DC and talking about the Op did we realise just how much damage we had caused to the enemy. One of the men we had captured was a Taliban commander for the area, who we believed was called Mullah Chagur. We had killed a number of their fighters. Jim Adamson had performed with such bravery that he would be awarded the Military Cross.

Of all the fighting I had heard to my west, one engagement in particular it would seem was a life-and-death struggle won against the odds. Jim and Hammy, who had been seconded to 10 Platoon, were checking on the dispositions of Jim's sections when they came across a gap in his line, which was next to a stream crossing. Hammy, who had been in the lead, had come across a Taliban fighter and had gone to engage him, Hammy had hit him but then incurred a stoppage. Another enemy fighter had come into view attracted by the fire, he had the drop on Hammy and Hammy had to dive into the water in order to not get hit. He was trying to unjam his stoppage underwater while trying not to get hit by the fighter, now firing into the river trying to kill him.

Jim had come upon this and engaged the fighter shooting at Hammy, killing him stone dead, but another fighter appeared from the cover of a compound with a PKM machine gun and had opened fire on Jim, miraculously missing him. Jim engaged the fighter, hitting him before he himself incurred a stoppage. But the Taliban fighter was not out the game yet and was now turning his machine gun to finish off Jim. Despite being wounded, he had the drop on Jim who had no time to clear his stoppage.

Without thinking, Jim had rushed the Taliban fighter, killing him with his bayonet, which we all had fixed as a matter of course as soon as the fighting started. And a now soggy Hammy rose safe and sound from the river.

Three dead Taliban lay around them and an impressive haul of weapons. Lt James Adamson would be the only man I knew who would be decorated twice for bravery on the same tour, receiving the MiD (Mention in Despatches) and the MC.

Day 183

Wednesday 8th October: Musa Qa'leh DC

During our post Op admin, I decided to check up on Taff Owen. He had been extremely subdued since our return from the Northern Op where he nearly got killed. We looked over his body armour and I could see that in addition to the scorch mark on the back of his armour, we found specks of copper from the round that had hit the hatch behind him.

He didn't really want to talk about the incident yet, and I could imagine that it hadn't yet sunk in what had happened. Once again, I was thankful that the Taliban were such poor marksmen.

What Taff was experiencing was nothing new, but the way the British Army were starting to deal with these events was. A new idea know as TRiM (Trauma Risk Management) was being brought in. Those soldiers who had experienced traumatic events were encouraged to talk about it, if it was a group, then they were encouraged to talk about the incident together. There would then be a soak period after which time the TRiM practitioner would talk to the guys again, then back in the UK. The reasoning behind this was that PTSD wouldn't kick in straightaway, rather it was a slow build-up that would manifest itself in certain ways.

But if the best way to spot the onset of PTSD was by peer checking, only a soldier's closest friends and brothers would notice a change in his behaviour that would send out warning signs. These were normally changes in behaviour pattern or in the soldier's personality, for instance a normally chatty outgoing lad suddenly becoming withdrawn and subdued, or a normally well-disciplined soldier becoming a nightmare back in camp.

Drunkenness, failure to turn up for work, these were all signs that would be flagged as potential areas for concern. Previously, if a soldier had suffered traumatic experiences and had even suggested that he was suffering or there was a problem, it was a career ender and that soldier's name and reputation would have been tarnished with the stigma of mental health issues.

Closer to home, having now fought in combat and seen some of the things I had seen, I noticed those signs in my own father. My father had also been a career soldier, and an Argyll and Sutherland Highlander, too. Serving from the mid 1970s up to 1993, he had served in Northern Ireland when the troubles were at their worst, he had seen friends killed and injured, not only on operations but in training also. My father had been an outstanding soldier and had been tipped for great things, but the beast that was PTSD had festered inside him and there was not a day I remember my father being sober. If he was not away working, then he would spend his day wallowing in a bottle of brandy.

It also manifested itself in violence towards my mother, their relationship had been strained but my father would drink heavily and beat my mother. If TRiM had been a thing when my father had served and mental health not have been such a stigma, my father may have received the help he so clearly needed.

Sadly, my father's reputation and legacy would not be his performance as a soldier and his many course distinction passes, it would be his nightmare behaviour when under the influence of alcohol. With the

TRiM system, hopefully soldiers would know that there would not be that stigma and if they needed help and support, they would get it.

I received my orders for the next operation, this would be a push south-west to have a look at the compound area that we had previously searched on 19th July, where we had located IED-making kit and other suspicious items. We would be forward mounting to PB(SW) where we would overnight before heading out around first light and then surge out into the area to harass and disrupt Taliban activity.

Day 184

Thursday 9th October: Musa Qa'leh DC

It was on this day that the nickname the Taliban had given us would be known. A local national had come to the DC for medical treatment, as he knew it was the best place to come to in order to get decent medical care. As part of our hearts and minds approach to the war, we were obliged to help them and of course our medics had their Hippocratic oath and would never turn away injured people who begged for medical help, even the Taliban.

The LN lived in the area to the north of the DC where we had fought so hard and so recently against the Taliban and as he was sat talking to the doctor during his treatment, he had looked over and saw a group of Delta Company soldiers, he smiled and said: "The Taliban thought the little men had left Musa Qa'leh. With all the helicopters coming and going the Taliban thought they had gone, but then they appeared out of the Green Zone and left it littered with Taliban dead."

When we heard this news it made us smile, the enemy had actually named us, it was not often that a unit had caused so much fear and carnage to its enemies that a nickname was bestowed by that enemy. The little men, this was quite fitting as very few soldiers within Delta Company were over 5'8".

Which when you think about it was perfect for the Green Zone. We were able to move about poppy fields, maize fields and other pieces of cover which helped confound the enemy dicking screen, you can't hit what you can't see and even today whenever someone comments on my height, I smile and think back to Helmand and say "Being short has saved my life more times than I care to think, people shoot at what height they think you are, not what height you actually are!"

In late afternoon the Company geared up and headed out the front gate of Musa Qa'leh DC with a bit of a spring in its step and our new nickname seemed to make the lads walk a little taller. As I exited the gate, I watched the beautiful sunset, the ochre surroundings taking on a grey pallor in the falling light, the sky a rich orange and yellow.

I could hear the call to prayer coming from all over Musa Qa'leh and stepped off, my eyes scanning everywhere as we made the crossing of the Musa Qa'leh Wadi. I looked over and saw Himal OP sat squat on its plateau to my right in the distance, to my left I could see clumps of trees and the odd compound here and there.

Locals were moving sheep and goats around the area and small groups of children were playing in the dust. Life seemed normal and if you didn't know that out there somewhere were pockets of men whose sole purpose and desire was to kill you, this could almost be a peaceful oasis in a dangerous world. People waved or nodded as we passed and did not seem to be afraid of talking to us infidels; I was starting to see the rewards for the actions that we were carrying out. People were not afraid to go about their business, safe in the knowledge that the Taliban did not venture too close to Musa Qa'leh – not any more, not since the little men had arrived.

Our constant domination of the ground and aggressive fighting spirit had seen to it that the enemy no longer had freedom of action and could no longer bully or terrorise the locals as they had done previously, hanging people from the scaffolding they had erected around a damaged minaret. The area seemed to be thriving again and the dark days of Taliban rule were almost a memory.

We arrived in PB(SW) as darkness was falling and began settling in for the night. Unfortunately for me, I chose the wrong spot to sleep in. I had parked myself right next to the generator that the OMLT were using for their Op's room, nothing I did could cancel out the noise. I tried ripping up the anti-fogging cloth that came with the issued goggles and stuffing that in my ears, but that didn't work. I tossed and turned till the early hours of the morning, when my body shut down and I had an hour of sleep.

Day 185

Friday 10th October: PB(SW) Mentored ANA Patrol Base

I stood in the morning pre-dawn gloom shivering in the chill in the air and wrapped my Ranger blanket tightly around me. The lads were also beginning to stir. I felt like I had not slept for weeks, my eyes bleary and my head fogged with tiredness.

I took a sip of cool water from my Camelbak and felt a little better. My nemesis, the generator, was still happily running like a V8. I felt like I had slept with my head in the engine bay of a tank with some sort of engine defect, I shook my head to clear the lack of sleep away and began packing my gear up.

As we were in a friendly location-ish, there was no requirement for the boys to stand to. So we all set about our morning routine, eat, drink, smoke, brush our teeth etc, before final kit checks to head out and down south towards the village of Deh Zohr-e Sofla and our sweep through looking for evidence of the Taliban.

My Platoon was going to be the point Platoon today, which suited me just fine. So, on Major Calder's signal, I pushed my guys out the main gate of the PB and began to head south-west using the ground for cover as much as possible. The area west of PB(SW) was mostly open desert with groups of compounds dotted around forming loose little hamlets, interspersed with high ground that would give attackers and defenders a commanding view of the area.

Unlike our patrols north of the DC, patrolling in this area had hazards of its own, the main one being the large expanse of open ground broken only by compounds forming little islands in an otherwise barren landscape.

As we pushed on, our eyes were everywhere. We checked the distance and any high ground we could see as likely enemy firing points. In the near distance was a small village that we had named horseshoe village due to its shape on the map. It bulged on its southern end and the points were to the north. It was also on a piece of high ground, I needed to get the Platoon up there as quickly as possible and dominate it. This would give Delta Company one huge foot on the ground and the ability to suppress enemy action.

The one thing that was obvious to me at this stage was the lack of people in the area. Nobody was going about their daily business.

The whole area seemed to have been abandoned and from previous experience this was never a good sign.

If the Taliban fighters were local to the area, they would warn the locals that a fight was impending, and this would give the locals time to leave and seek safety and shelter elsewhere. This also worked in our favour as it meant that when, not if, we were engaged by the enemy, we could smash them with no fear of any collateral damage. When it was foreign fighters, they didn't give a shit if the locals were killed. To the foreigners, the collateral fatalities were seen as martyrs. This did not endear the foreigners to the local population, who sometimes viewed them with more hatred than ISAF. They knew that we would strive not to kill civilians. Unfortunately, sometimes in the type of war we were engaged in, civilians were killed, caught in the crossfire between opposing forces. Bombs and artillery dropped on their homes when the Taliban used them as firing points and rest stations, but that has been the nature of counter insurgency warfare for a long time.

I had settled my Platoon into a defensive position and the lads were observing their arcs of fire, when from behind a compound lower down I spotted a dust cloud. That meant movement, and they were not being careful about it either.

I quickly pulled the butt of my rifle into my shoulder, the SUSAT coming up and resting against my eyebrow. Suddenly the area was brought into sharp focus, albeit with a large dark obelisk-shaped pointer in the middle. The heat haze shimmered in my sight and I watched as dark shapes began to materialise.

I alerted the lads closest to me and we began to observe the area, I clicked my safety catch off and began to take the pressure up on my trigger. As soon as the enemy materialised, I would gauge the numbers and allow them to get into the open. Into an area of no return.

I began to regulate my breathing and scrunched up my left eye, the sight post was placed slap bang where the enemy would appear. 'Where was the ICOM chat?' I asked myself, normally they give the game away long before the attack. Was the radio discipline of this Taliban cell better than the rest? I didn't know, but one thing I was certain of, once that enemy patrol exposed itself, I was going to do my level best to wipe it out.

Dark shadows begun to appear at the edges of the compound wall, I held my breath. Sweat was running down the sides of my face. 'This is it; I've got the drop on these c**ts!' I thought to myself.

Around me I could feel rather than see the lads around me tense. The tell-tale clicks of safety catches being pressed off was audible, but only to those of us in the immediate area. A shape homed into view and I let out a breath and a deep sigh, facing me was not a battle-hardened Taliban fighter toting an AK-47 with a chest rig full of magazines and grenades, but rather a small brown and white goat, a piece of dried grass between its lips. It plodded along unaware that it had nearly been riddled with the fire of several rifles and a machine gun.

The sound of bleating reached our ears and following the first little goat was a large group of the animals, all jostling one another in a big gaggle. Following the goats was a tall man in his thirties or forties. I found it hard to tell the age of Afghans, they had such a hard existence that they all looked a lot older than they actually were.

Again, he was oblivious to our unit on top of the hill barely eighty metres away. He was wearing the standard Afghan clothing of loose fitting, light linen trousers and a shirt, perfect for the heat. Over the top of these he wore a brown waistcoat, on his head a light-coloured turban. In his hand he carried a large stick for prodding wayward goats back into line.

The sound of clinking bells began to reach our ears and I turned and saw the boys all relax slightly, slipping safety catches back on. However, we did not relax our guard. Just because he looked like a goat herder did not necessarily mean he was innocent.

The goat herd had been so preoccupied straightening his gaggle of goats out that he hadn't noticed us until he was about thirty metres away. He jumped doing a double take, but then regained his composure. He waved and called over to us a friendly "Salam alaikum!" to which I called "Tsunga ye?" which meant "How are you?" He nodded and waved but continued about his business crossing in front of us heading towards the village of Dand.

As the clinking and bleating faded away into the distance, we focused on the mission ahead. Over two kilometres to our south lay Deh-Zohr-e-Sofla and the potential IED factory and C2 hub for the Southern Taliban Cells in our AO.

Once the Company was re-established, we began moving off towards the target village. I had gone three hundred metres when I heard retching behind me. The spectre of disease had not left us, and I watched as Scotty McGregor began throwing up. Scotty who had given me my bad bout of viral D&V was now sick again and was looking very pale. I was conscious that it was only going to get hotter and we still had a long patrol ahead of us, I needed to CASEVAC him otherwise he would become a heat casualty and that would only make his condition – and ours – worse.

I was in the process of informing Goody that we had a sick soldier when Tom Williamson my little TA cavalryman made a funny noise. Then his face went bright red then pale, he grimaced and caught my eye before remarking with a mix of shock and embarrassment, "George!" He paused and looked behind himself. "I've just shit myself!" he turned around and right enough there was a large wet brown patch on the arse of his combat trousers. In desert kit a shit patch is not going to be that noticeable. But what would be very soon was the odour. Despite the situation, we were rolling around with tears running down our dirty cheeks. The sight of poor Tom trying to walk like John Wayne, with liquid shit now running down his legs, was more than most of us could bear and the laughing must have been obvious as I keyed my radio pressel switch to request a CASEVAC. The whole Platoon had now seen Tom's predicament and were now making farting noises.

Given our proximity to the Musa Qa'leh Wadi, it was easy enough to gingerly walk east and rendezvous with the Mastiff Company, who would take Scotty and Tom back to the DC. But before they went, I made Scotty swap his weapon and ammunition over with one of the other lads from the Platoon. As he was one of my GPMG gunners, I couldn't afford to lose that weapon. The natural choice was big Ammo Armstrong, my Army Air Corps Lance Corporal. He took the machine gun with relish, happy to swap over his rifle and mags for belts of 7.62mm ammunition and spare gun barrels.

After what seemed like no time at all, the Mastiff Company met us and we began to load Scotty and Tom onto the nearest vehicle and I couldn't help but smirk as the young top gunner from the vehicle helped the lads into the vehicle. I watched him wither and his nose wrinkle up as the waft from Tom's soiled trousers hit his nostrils. His face began to take on the look I like to describe as 'a bulldog licking piss off stinging nettles'. The door of that vehicle would probably need to be left open and the wagon aired out for a while. The seats would also require a good cleaning.

Once the CASEVAC had disappeared back north in the direction of the DC, I moved the Platoon off again. We patrolled back down towards Deh-Zohr-e-Sofla, but now due to the CASEVAC, we were no longer the lead Platoon. We had been relegated to the reserve and we patrolled off into the rising heat towards our destination.

Thankfully, no one else fell ill and we met up with the rest of the Company in the village, just in time to take over compounds for the heat of the day. We would also provide cover to 10 Platoon who would search compound 17, the suspected IED factory we had found previously.

We maintained our sentry positions in our compound and rotated through them so that the lads could get something to eat and drink, as well as rest in the shade of the buildings. I kept my ear to the radio, even though I was dozing I had not switched off completely and was chuffed when Jim Adamson reported that his Platoon had found IED components and bomb-making kit, which was bagged and secured ready to be handed over to G2 (intelligence) back in the DC.

As it cooled down, Major Calder decided that we had achieved our mission and it was time to return north. The plan called for the Company to patrol back to PB(SW) where we would relax until the sun started to set, then we would head east into the wadi and then north into the DC.

The patrol back to both PB(SW) and the DC went without a hitch and no more sharting! The only ICOM we received was that the Taliban were preparing to send out a six-man night foot patrol. Whether they did or not was never established, but it was a very tired Delta Company that trudged back into the DC in the gloomy darkness.

After a kit check on the Platoon, I went to check on Tom and Scotty who were both now quartered in the death tent, looking and smelling slightly cleaner. I took some cold water up them as they had done for me when I had the misfortune to be an inmate.

They had the chance now to have a few days to sleep, relax and gather their strength again. I could imagine that they would not have the stomach for food, but we definitely needed to keep an eye on their fluid levels and also drop off any mail that they might have received, as they would definitely need cheering up.

Day 186

Saturday 11th October: Musa Qa'leh DC

We received some very interesting news today from G2. They had a walk-in by a Malik (village elder) from the area of the Hajji Rashid

Gardens, he had been speaking to the Taliban commanders up north and their morale was extremely low. The casualties we had inflicted upon them over our time in Musa Qa'leh had been such that they were willing to talk terms and lay down their weapons. They had requested a Shura with Lt Col Borton with a view to laying down their arms.

This was a very good sign. For me it was a validation for what we had been doing so far having had an impact not only on the enemy but hopefully a positive effect on the local population, too, leading them to believe that they could live in peace and security and do things that they had been unable to do while under the thumb of the Taliban.

Another good sign, especially for us, was the arrival of the Gurkha advance party from 2 RGR. I was being shadowed by a Gurkha Sergeant by the name of Nockul Rai, who, like all Gurkhas, was a very pleasant and friendly chap. He would follow me now getting the lay of the land until his Platoon arrived and he would have at least spent a bit of time on the ground getting to know the area and would have a better understanding than his men, which would help with the continuity between Operation Herrick 8 and Operation Herrick 9.

The deputy commander of 3 Commando Brigade also came to visit us in order to get the lay of the land and do a fact-finding tour of the locations that his units would be operating from. With him he brought his chief medical officer and while the deputy commander was receiving briefings from all the relevant commanders of the sub-units based in Musa Qa'leh, the doctor took the opportunity to walk around camp. When he came to Delta Company's lines, he was extremely shocked by our physical condition. He could be seen shaking his head in bewilderment.

"You men are extremely malnourished!" he exclaimed. "If I was to take a picture of you boys and develop it in black and white, it could almost be a snap shot from the Far East in World War Two, you men literally look like skeletons or prisoners of war!"

He just could not believe it, but it was explained to him that our chefs had produced sub-standard meals, a large contributing factor to our skeletal appearance. We would be out fighting for anything up to four days in the blistering Afghan heat, we would eat 24-hour boil in the bag ration meals and the heavy kit we carried meant that weight dropped off us at an incredible rate. Then upon our return to Musa Qa'leh, all we asked for was food that would replace the calories we had lost in combat. We did not get this and indeed many of the boys were so sick of the poor quality of food that they relied solely on the care packages sent from friends, loved ones and indeed the kind and caring British public who would fill shoe boxes with treats that were so very welcome.

I myself in four months had lost nearly four stone in weight and it was obvious. All our uniforms were hanging off us and our belts were fastened as tight as they could possibly go. As the end neared, the conversation invariably turned to what we would eat when we got back to the UK.

A week or so later, on a relaxing day for the Company. I was sat wondering how many actual contacts the Company had been in during our time in Musa Qa'leh as it had to be a large number given that just about every time we went out on patrol we engaged the Taliban in some sort of firefight. I must have posed the question to Jim Adamson at some point, as he poked his head through the tent and with his boyish grin he said: "That thing you asked me about George?" I nodded. "As it stands mate fifty-two SALTAs!" I whistled, that was a lot of firefights. In Afghanistan we adopted the American contact report format known as SALTA, which stood for Size (of enemy unit), Action (the enemy are taking), Location (of contact), Time (of contact), Action (taken by ISAF).

All ISAF units had adopted this method in order to standardise reporting of engagements with the enemy, so fifty-two SALTAs since arriving in Musa Qa'leh was pretty high. But it also occurred to me that within those fifty-two SALTAs the firefights were never just single shoot and scoots.

Generally, the enemy after the initial engagement would come back at us, try to flank, surround or overrun us. So, the initial SALTA could easily have been the heads up to the headquarters in the DC we were in a fight. But that first contact would initiate maybe four or five sub contacts where the enemy withdrew and then came around to flanking positions. I surmised that you could add perhaps another twenty to thirty contacts onto that number, but at present it stood at fifty-two logged official SALTAs.

Day 189

Tuesday 14th October: Musa Qa'leh DC

I gave a set of orders for what I hoped would be our last operation of the tour. It would consist of the Company forward mounting to Satellite

Station North and operating in the areas surrounding SSN. We would achieve this by conducting Platoon-level local security patrols and Major Calder had designated three Operations boxes for this Op in which we were to conduct our patrols.

Ops box one would be in the area of the desert compounds to the north-east of SSN, Ops box two would be in the area of Towghi Keli north-west of SSN and the last Ops box would be to the south in the area of Kunjak. Then on the 17th we would come back together as a company and surge north into Towghi Keli, which was always an area to get into a fight.

As I gave my orders, I became acutely aware that these areas had all proved hostile in the past and our exit from SSN would no doubt elicit a response from the Taliban. On the plus side as a Platoon, and a small Platoon at that, I could afford to be sneaky and use the terrain to my advantage as we had in the past.

But as I closed my notebook, I looked around at my lads. They looked tired, they had aged since their time in Musa Qa'leh and they could see the light at the end of the tunnel. Their eyes were hollow and every man in my Platoon had the thousand-yard stare, a haunted look that told the story of men who had faced death and survived. Men who knew they should be dead many times over. But due to a twist of fate, a snatched trigger, a nervous shot, the bullet or rocket intended to kill them had gone wide.

Some had killed. Some were okay with that and some I suspect would be seeing Helmand in their dreams for many years to come. I looked conspiratorially over my soldiers before lowering my voice.

"Lads, this is it, we're almost done… I don't plan on doing anything fucking stupid!" I paused and looked around the lads to gauge the response, many nodded, all grinned. "I will not push us into anything that is likely to stop us from getting home."

I left it there, I felt that there was no need to elaborate. These men that were crouched squatting or sat in front of me had become my family and as the oldest amongst them, I felt like a father. And as a father I would never do anything to hurt my children. Getting these boys, my brothers, home in one piece was a goal from the very beginning. But at the end of this tour even more so, our relief was in and more replacements from 2 RGR were coming in every day.

Twenty-three had already arrived, a full Platoon by our standards. Twenty-three Jocks did not leave in their place, but we were being extracted at different times and some of our Company were now into single figures until they were on that chopper back to Bastion.

We welcomed our Gurkha replacements enthusiastically and they were very polite and tried to converse with the Jocks in their broken English and none of our boys apart from Corporal Nawal Rai, who was now a badged Argyll having come from the RGR, could speak Nepalese. Nawal Rai greeted his Gurkha brothers with great excitement, it had been a difficult transition for him to badge over to us, but for his career progression it was important that he had come to us.

I am a double-digit midget. Having read books about the war in Vietnam I had heard these terms used for 'Short timers', soldiers whose tour of duty was coming to an end and who were so 'short' they "Had to tie their bootlaces with a step ladder". Or "I'm so short I need a parachute to get out bed and a chopper ride to get back in it!"

I hoped that this next operation would be quiet, but if it's wasn't, we'd still fight as hard as we did day one and try to kill as many of the enemy as we could.

The rumour from G2 was that a lot of the enemy fighters from our area had left and were heading towards the Lashkar Gah area to stir up trouble and as Lash was the provincial capital, things could get bloody.

Day 190

Wednesday 15th October: Patrolling North of Musa Qa'leh DC

We began our insertion patrol to Satellite Station North, the area was thriving and the locals were going safely about their business. The bazaar and main street of Musa Qa'leh were bustling, but there was no air of fear or threat.

We still couldn't drop our guard because of the ever-present threat of suicide bombers and given that this was such a built-up area, the effects of a suicide bomb would be utterly devastating. Heads were on a swivel, arcs were covered and men patrolled like it was their first patrol in Helmand, not one of their last.

We scanned ahead of us and to the flanks. Observing likely enemy firing points, keeping a particular eye out for areas we knew the Taliban had used previously to hit us from. We knew they were creatures of habit and liked to use pervious firing points as they felt comfortable using them and they knew how to get in and out of them fairly safely. But when they set patterns like this, it was easier to know where they were going and hit them accordingly.

We crossed irrigation ditches, streams and fields which were now being cleared of their crops, which meant cover from view was gone. I did not envy the Gurkhas having to fight over this terrain with no cover and it would not be until 2010 when I did a winter tour of Afghanistan that I would appreciate just how bare arsed and dangerous the terrain would be. But then I would be in a different part of Helmand and in a different role.

We reached SSN without incident and were warmly greeted by the lads from the Rifles who had taken over as the OMLT for the ANA. They were good guys and very accommodating, just as our Celtic brothers from the Royal Irish had been. We settled into our normal areas that we took when we forward mounted at SSN. The cardboard shanty town sprang up fairly quickly and the Company began settling into routine. Apart from my Platoon: we had been given the first patrol task of the operation and we would be heading into Ops box one, Towghi Keli.

I did my radio checks to the Company headquarters, sorted out my order of march and then we set off out of the patrol base before swinging west then north into Towghi Keli. There was no ICOM at all and we formed a Platoon snake and began to move between the compounds and the Green Zone trying to make ourselves difficult to spot.

Those locals we did come into contact with just waved but did not stop to talk, I stopped occasionally for water breaks and to listen out for enemy activity. There was none, so I pushed as far north as I dared before swinging back down through the village and back into SSN.

Sgt Nokul was taking in everything he could that would help benefit his Platoon when they got out on the ground. I made a point of showing him areas that we knew the enemy used regularly to both infiltrate and fire upon us. I hoped that what we were showing him would save his men because as yet we had no fatalities and it was due to a combination of skill and luck that we were all still alive. But the superstitious part of me quickly dismissed this thought from my head.

I did not want to jinx us, not with it being so close to the end and if there's one thing soldiers are, it's superstitious. Probably from Bronze Age Greek warriors, all the way through to the Iraq and Afghan wars. We didn't tempt fate or risk the wrath of the Gods.

As soon as we returned another patrol went out, this time heading south towards Kunjak, they too were able to patrol the area unmolested and didn't even get any ICOM chatter.

We passed a relaxed night under the stars, resting up for the next day's patrolling, this time we would be heading south to Kunjak.

Day 191

Thursday 16th October: Satellite Station North, Mentored ANA checkpoint

After pre-patrol checks, 12 Platoon left the front gate of SSN and swiftly pushed south then west across the open ground south of SSN and into a cluster of compounds that merged into the Green Zone.

It hardly felt like a patrol in one of the most dangerous places on earth, it felt like a stroll through some beautiful countryside but carrying guns. Aggressive rambling. We had not received any ICOM chatter at all, which was nice and refreshing, I decided that even though we weren't receiving ICOM chatter it didn't mean we weren't being observed. So I used compounds to dart between and treelines that would confuse any spotters into thinking that perhaps we were a larger force than we actually were. Looking at the map I spotted a little cluster of compounds that would help conceal us from the east and west.

I could hear the engines of the little Yamaha motorbikes the Taliban used, driving up and down the main tracks. But as yet there was no indication the enemy knew where we were and besides, we had never been contacted in this neck of the woods. It would have been too risky for the Taliban to have patrolled down here, the area was dotted with ANA and ANP checkpoints, mentored and unmentored. If the ANA shot us when they got spooked, then I figured the Taliban would be fair game, too.

As we wound our way through compounds Q4W 52 -57, we walked along a well-used track and I was confident there were no signs of IED laying so I continued cautiously down the track between the compounds.

I decided to stop, check the map and was about to give a LOCSTAT (location status) to Company HQ, when a loud burst of gunfire echoed in the alleyway behind me. I flinched as rounds went over my head and the heads of the point section. The fact that we were in an alleyway made the noise reverberate off the compound walls making it sound like a PKM.

At first I thought an insurgent had stepped out from one of the gateways behind us and opened fire on the Platoon. Just as I was about to key my radio pressel switch and send a contact report, the fire stopped, there was no return fire, just utter silence. I quickly moved back to where the firing had come from and saw young Granty lying on his back covered in dust looking shocked and pale.

"What the fuck happened mate?" I asked, he licked his lips and pointed to an open gate to his left.

"Fucking dug George man!" he answered. I looked into the gateway and grinned.

"I know Afghan dugs are nails, but how the fuck did a dug shoot you?" I asked.

"Bastard jumped oot ohn me man!" he exclaimed. "Ah shot the c**t, but it jist fucked off man." A quick interrogation of Pete Breen's section revealed that as the section had passed the open gate, a massive Afghan Kuchi dog had leaped out on Granty and reacting instinctively, he had swung his Minimi LMG and fired a burst at it.

Unfortunately, the burst not only hit the dog, but also ricocheted off the mud door frame and came back at him, hitting him in the calf. He was lucky, it did not appear to have struck the bone and a quick check of the rest of the lads revealed that no one else had been hit by the burst.

As Pete Breen was patching Granty up, I decided to follow the large blood trail that led into the interior of the compound. But the blood trail just tailed off (no pun intended) and there was no sign of any dead or wounded dog. Once again, I was left to marvel at the toughness of these animals.

We had been warned previously about shooting dogs for this exact reason. Not only were they people's property and in most cases guard dogs, our rounds were pretty useless against them. In this fight, Granty appeared to have come off worse than the dog.

"Zero this is three zero Alpha, man down, I say again man down!" At this point I could imagine that Company HQ had fallen over and spilt their coffee everywhere and in no time I was hit with a battery of questions.

"No, it wasn't enemy action!"

"No, he is not bleeding to death, standby for ATMIST report!"

"Casualty sustained engaging a dog!"

"Yes, a dog Delta-Oscar-Golf!"

"Yes, he does feel like a c**t!"

"No, he didn't at least kill the dog. Dog remains at large!"

As soon as he was fit to travel, he was stripped of all but his protective gear and Pete Breen lifted Granty up onto his shoulders and began carrying him to a CASEVAC point. As we moved, I gave Goody a running report on what was happening and Goody in his usual fashion advised me to "Move my fucking arse to the RV," where he would be waiting with the quad bike to evacuate Granty back to SSN. Pete kept going and did not stop until we had reached the RV point in the vicinity of compound Q4X-7, where a pissed-off Goody had raced on his quad bike alone to pick Granty up. We quickly bundled him and all his gear into the trailer on the quad bike and watched as Goody spun away leaving us in a cloud of dust.

We trudged back along the road towards Satellite Station North, we got back as Granty was being loaded onto a stretcher and Andy Pettiford was keeping an eye on him. Granty was wrapped in a thermal blanket, despite the heat, to stop him from going into shock.

Goody informed us that the Warrior Company were coming to get Granty and take him back to the DC, as for some reason it was the only place a CASEVAC mission would fly into. I had the feeling that the pilots were still a bit nervous flying into Musa Qa'leh, but as Granty's injury was not thought to be life threatening/life changing, the chopper wasn't in such a hurry to come and get him.

I stood at the front gate of SSN with the CASEVAC party and watched as the Warriors raced past the patrol base and disappeared up to the high ground just north of SSN. We all looked at each other in confusion, perhaps this was a screen to cover the CASEVAC party to the north. We weren't sure; suddenly it came over the radio, the Warriors were having trouble locating us. I looked at Goody and remarked sardonically.

"Perhaps they missed the large patrol base surrounded by HESCO Bastion walls?" After a bit of guidance, the Warriors turned around and halted in front of us and the back door of the nearest Warrior opened. By now a group of well-wishers and piss takers had formed around Granty to see him off.

"Here ya wee fanny, the tour's nearly done, ye didnae need to shoot yersell!"

"How ye gonnae explain this tae yer burd? I got shot by a dug!"

"Aye we'll still be hame before ye yah wee fud!"

The banter was all good natured and really everyone was relieved that Granty was alive and we all waved as he disappeared into the back of the Warrior and it sped off south back towards Musa Qa'leh. Granty would still be CASEVAC'd within the golden hour, but we were pissed off that this close to the end of the tour we had taken a casualty.

That evening my Platoon were given the task of pushing out on another patrol to Tamyan Keli and as we were leaving Major Calder approached and said "And for fuck sake, don't shoot anymore dogs Sergeant Mac!"

"Roger Sir!" I replied. "Fuckers don't die anyway!"

We headed out and began to patrol west but as we were moving into our assigned area my lead section spotted a group of armed men moving to our front. Quickly we took cover and set up a firing point, I scanned through my SUSAT and caught the tell-tale US leaf pattern camouflage worn by the ANA.

"What the fuck are those idiots doing here?" I asked no one in particular. I could see no desert pattern camouflage, which meant that this ANA patrol was unmentored. "Zero this is three zero Alpha, I have an Alpha-November-Alpha patrol in my AO, they are clearly unmentored over!" There was a pause on the other end before I heard Major Calder reply.

"Roger three zero Alpha, return to base, we don't need a Green-on-Blue contact!" He knew how twitchy the ANA were and if they spotted my Platoon, rather than clarify our identity, they would have more than likely opened fire on us. So, we quickly and quietly slipped away, leaving the ANA patrol none the wiser.

Day 192

Friday 17th October: Ops Box North of Satellite Station North

Major Calder's plan was to push as far north as practicable and stimulate some ICOM chatter. We were successful, given that we were now operating as a company again and easier to spot.

The ICOM went apeshit, orders were being passed between commanders and "Big things, pineapples and watermelons" were being brought up.

At one point 10 Platoon thought they heard someone whispering into a radio and decided to assault the location. They didn't find any Taliban, but they did find an old hunting rifle, which was confiscated, and an old couple who were acting very suspiciously as though they had someone or something to hide. The rest of the patrol was uneventful and we pushed south again back to Musa Qa'leh DC.

The next day the lads are in high spirits, some of Delta Company have gone back to Camp Bastion for the first leg of the journey home. I am so happy to see the lads getting away and with them they are taking serial-numbered kit back with them. I am more than happy with this as it means it's off my flick, millions of pounds worth of gear was now becoming thousands of pounds worth of gear. That sounded much better to me.

We received a very large box from Ross Kemp and his production team, enclosed was a letter that was nearly thrown out, but I decided to keep it and put it inside my diary (where it still remains today fifteen years later).

The box would appear to have been opened and rummaged through by people back at Bastion before it made its way forward to its intended recipients, Delta Company. I was very touched by Ross Kemp's kindness that I wrote a bluey to him and his team thanking them for their thoughtfulness. This care package was well received by the guys as some lads had nobody to write to or send them packages, so it was a nice gesture.

Day 195

Monday 20th October: North of Musa Qa'leh DC

Today I conducted a joint patrol with the lads from 2 RGR, Major Calder had given me the north of the DC to show the Gurkhas. I took the chance to visit some of the patrol bases and checkpoints. I chose a nice easy route and gave the Gurkhas a guided tour. As we passed by each checkpoint and PB I informed the Gurkhas as to who was there and whether they were mentored or unmentored and little titbits of advice for the commanders when operating in this area.

We were five hundred metres short of Satellite Station North when I spotted the ANA and their Rifles mentors leaving to go on patrol. I halted my patrol and allowed them to carry on, waving to them as they went by.

The enemy were obviously watching them not us, because no sooner had the ANA left SSN, than the ICOM came alive with chatter. They were planning to attack the patrol as it came in range. I knew the patrol they were talking about was not ours as we had received no ICOM chatter until the ANA and Rifles had left SSN.

At this point I decided we'd seen enough and began to steer our patrol back to the south. Suddenly I could hear all hell breaking loose north of SSN and I watched as tracer rose into the sky.

The ANA commander on the patrol must have been in comms with his guys left back in the PB as the Dushka 12.7mm Russian heavy machine guns in the northern bunkers of the base began to let loose a heavy volley of fire with their rapid 'thunk-thunk-thunk'. I felt sorry for the Taliban on the receiving end of that, the ANA heavy machine gunners were giving them a good hammering.

We patrolled back south without further incident and didn't get drawn into the fight still raging, but we could hear it fading into the distance. We returned back to the DC and the Gurkhas had had their first taste of enemy contact, even if it wasn't directed at them.

Day 196

Tuesday 21st October: West of Musa Qa'leh DC

My patrol today consisted of heading west to confirm or deny the presence of suspicious activity in the form of IED-laying or obvious digging in the area of Wasak Keli. We set off into the area designated and began checking tracks there. Then we headed north towards Roshan Tower with a view to using them as resupply routes for the guys at Roshan Tower.

We found no signs of digging in the entire area and speaking to locals they told us that they knew nothing of a Taliban IED layer/facilitator in the area, but we had heard he was using children from the Musa Qa'leh area to carry his IED components. He did this because he knew full well we wouldn't shoot kids.

If we found IED components on them, a slap on the head and threats of being handed over to the NDS (National Directorate of Security), the Afghan secret police, would have made grown men spill their guts. But as it happened, we never came across any kids with IED components on them, so the theory was never tested.

We moved through Wasak Keli and began heading back towards the DC, at that point the ICOM came alive with commanders fighting for the chance to attack us. They knew where we were and they wanted more fighters brought into the area before they attacked.

But we moved into the Green Zone east of Wasak Keli and began heading back to the DC, the enemy attack never materialised and we made it safely back into the DC. We had shown our Gurkha comrades another part of the AO they would be operating in.

That night, I transferred over six thousand pounds to Goody to buy his BMW 316 off him as soon as I got back to the UK. I had always promised myself that one day I would own a BMW and I liked the look of Goody's.

It was a BMW 316Ti, which was fast as fuck, very nice and reliable and well kept. I couldn't wait to get back to the UK and drive it. I would insur it as soon as I got to an internet terminal in Camp Bastion.

Day 198

Thursday 23rd October: Musa Qa'leh DC – The Last Patrol

Today I had the honour of commanding an ad hoc Platoon made up of Jocks from all over the Company. The other two Platoons on the patrol would be Gurkha Platoons, with Jim Adamson tagging along as an advisor to their Platoon commander and Charlie Grant advising the other.

The patrol did not start too well as a piece of our counter measure kit went down and had to be taken back into the DC to be replaced; we could not go any further without it.

As we waited, an old Afghan gentleman approached us requesting medical assistance. He'd had a motorbike crash, looking at the wounds it had been some time ago. His leg was in absolute bits and the path of infection on the limb was quite obvious, his kneecap had also taken a beating and had not set properly. We advised him that he needed to get to a hospital, there was nothing to be done for him with what we had. There was a good chance he was going to lose the leg and if he didn't go to hospital, there was a good chance he would die of septicaemia.

As soon as we were sorted, we moved off. The plan was to go around the AO from south anticlockwise through the Green Zone, back into the DC. The move round to PB(SE) was fairly relaxed and I made sure the Argyll boys were in cover and in no way liable to be hurt if we were opened up on. By contrast, the Gurkha boys seemed to be struggling with the heat and the heavy kit they had to carry. I had to remember that six months ago this was us, but at least we'd had FOB Keenan to allow us to acclimatise.

We were aware that the ANA and their Advisor callsign were out on the ground again, pretty much in the area they had been hit on 20th October. We listened to the ICOM as the Taliban threatened to bring more weapons and fighters to bear. We all thought this was bollocks, they always talked a good fight but recently hadn't been backing it up, until the sounds of a heavy firefight reached our ears. The sound was a thunderous cacophony of gunfire and RPGs outgoing and incoming to the ANA and Rifles unit.

We heard over the radio that the Rifles soldier in charge of the advisor callsign had been hit, Amber 51 Alpha was down, and he'd been hit quite badly too.

"Fuck, they've only just started their tour too!" I said to myself, and looking around me at the faces of the Jocks I could see they were thinking the same thing too. But more importantly, "Let's get this fucking patrol done and get home!" was the unspoken feeling. We heard ATMISTs (Age, Time, Mechanism, Injury, Symptoms, Treatments) and 9 liners (emergency medevac requests) going in for the Rifles lad and concurrently we could hear the Taliban, they knew they had hit someone, and an argument broke out between two low level Taliban commanders.

"Wait till the helicopter comes to pick them up, then shoot it down!" One commented.

"Are you crazy? The dragonfly (Apache gunship) will be with them, as soon as you shoot the dragonfly will kill you!" Said the smarter of the two commanders.

"I don't care. God willing, I will shoot the helicopter down!"

"No you won't, your men will die for nothing!"

"Okay. We wait until the helicopter goes, then we hit the traitors (ANA)."

After what only seemed like seconds, a Chinook helicopter from the MERT flew in low over our heads and disappeared to the north. We could detect the change in pitch of the engines that told us the Chinook was landing; overhead a pair of AH-64 Apache Longbow helicopters stalked. Waiting for someone to be stupid enough to fire at them or the Chinook.

We had used the Apaches to goad the Taliban into attacking us previously as we knew that one of the gunships up there was being piloted by a female Captain and our Psyops team made a great show of informing the Taliban.

"Not only are you being killed by an Infidel, but you are being killed by a female Infidel! She takes great pleasure in killing you as she knows you will not get to paradise if she kills you!" This would piss the Taliban off royally and make them all the more determined to kill us; almost as much as playing the bagpipes to them.

We watched as the Chinook lifted off in the distance from a desert HLS box to the north-east and began to fly away south, back towards Camp Bastion and the Role 3 hospital. We began to take our leave too and began to patrol back towards the DC. I stopped short of the DC to take a breather and was sat next to a young Afghan lad about fifteen years old. I had taken my helmet off to air my head and could see the young lad was staring intently into my helmet.

I twigged, Chanelle Hayes was smiling up at him in her underwear. Afghan men were not used to seeing such things and I was about to put my helmet back on in order to protect this young Afghan male's purity, then I thought, 'Fuck it, he needs her more than I do now!' I reached into my helmet and slipped the bleached, sweat-stained, but still very clear picture of Miss Hayes out of my helmet and handed it to the lad.

He looked at me, looked at the picture and his eyes began to bulge. He was unsure as to whether I was actually giving it to him, but I thrust it at him and he grabbed it like it was a million-pound note and raced away in a cloud of dust. Somewhere in Musa Qa'leh, there is probably still an Afghan male who thinks he has a picture of my girlfriend. If only!

As we patrolled back into Musa Qa'leh, I watched as children with their little UN school bags and books were coming home from school and not just boys, there were little girls amongst the group as well.

I felt my heart surge with pride, we did this, we made it possible. The markets were thriving, the people were safe, and the children felt safe enough to go to school. And more importantly their parents felt safe enough to send them to school.

On return to the DC, everyone breathed a sigh of relief and we made safe our weapons. Beaming from ear to ear, shaking hands with our Gurkha relief and hugging one another, we had made it. We had fucking made it, we'd survived, fuck knows how. I should be dead many times over, but I was still here to tell the tale.

The Gurkha OC made a very good speech thanking us for our assistance in getting his men ready for their upcoming tour. Our OC wished his men the greatest success and luck over the next six months and said he knew that we were leaving Musa Qa'leh in safe hands.

It was a bittersweet feeling that stirred in me as I jumped onto the back of the Chinook that would take us to Camp Bastion and the first leg of our journey home. I strapped myself into the webbed seating and watched as the load master threw a cargo net over our baggage.

The sight of Musa Qa'leh DC shimmering through the heat haze of the Chinook's engines, and possibly tears that had formed in my eyes, was one I will never forget. I looked around at the other Argylls on the helicopter, each one was alone in his thoughts. We had seen war and we had survived it. That was maybe the easy part, coming home would be harder.

My stomach lurched as the Chinook lifted off from the HLS in the DC and through the rear door, I could see Mount Doom and the ANA soldiers on the rooftops of the DC. I could see little palls of smoke in the distance to the north, which showed where small firefights were going on.

I could see the lush Green Zone disappear beneath us to be replaced by nothing but desert and then the rear ramp on the Chinook closed, sealing me in and leaving me with my last visual memory of Musa Qa'leh.

Emotions flooded through me in a rush, we were alive, 12 Platoon were all going home, not all of us were unhurt, but we were all going home.

We landed at Camp Bastion and were rushed to Delta Company's accommodation where we were met by the CQMS, all the rest of our serial-numbered kit was handed in and we emptied our magazines.

Waiting for us were the lads who had left previously, there was a lot of hugging, back slapping and hand shaking. Everyone had the biggest grins on their faces and they helped us empty all the bullets out of our magazines, before long there were metal ammo containers filled to the brim with loose bullets and piles of green plastic bandoliers holding clips of 5.56mm rounds lay in a small mound. We had left hand grenades and other stuff with the Gurkhas.

I felt naked, my rifle had been taken and bundled with other rifles ready for transit back to Canterbury. My bullets were gone, and my Osprey had been handed in, to be replaced once again with the ECBA (Enhanced Combat Body Armour) which we would need to fly to Kandahar.

I had a hot shower and a shave before heading off for my first decent meal at the main kitchen at Camp Bastion. I was struck by how the other half lived, all the buildings were air conditioned, and the Royal Military Police were manning speed traps in camp like they were back in Bulford or Aldershot.

Rear echelon soldiers were having a go at the fighting men due to the standard of their uniforms and a few had to be taken to one side and told to fuck off or they would be killed regardless of rank.

There was a coffee shop, a pizza hut and couples were sitting kissing one another like they weren't on an operational tour. Some of the Bastion troops were even wearing civilian clothing as though they were back in the UK and many of them wondered why the fighting troops felt resentment towards them.

But then I told myself 'I earned my medal in Afghanistan.' The only people at Camp Bastion who really got our full respect were the CASEVAC crews. The American Pedros and all the staff who worked at the Role 3 hospital. We understood that those men and women saw more horrible shit than we did, so they were alright in our book.

We had all kept behind in Bastion one decent set of combats. Tam o'shanters were pulled out of grip bags, dusted off, hackles were bent back into shape and we prepared ourselves for the next phase of our journey, the C-130 ride to Kandahar air base.

Kandahar was again another world; it was the size of a city and troops from all over NATO were based here, the majority American and Canadian. To us coming into Kandahar and being allowed to roam free was like a tribe from the Amazon rainforest, untouched by the modern world, being let loose in London or New York. There was a Burger King, a Subway sandwich shop, a little place that made t-shirts, there was a hockey pitch, basketball courts and the American PXs were like our supermarkets back home.

As we walked towards the boardwalk for a bite to eat, attack alarms sounded, followed by a robotic voice that announced, "Rocket attack, rocket attack!" We watched incredulous as people dived into ditches and under cars, trying to find the nearest cover. We all stopped and listened, where were these rockets? Surely there had to be rockets for there to be a rocket attack.

We all looked skywards, our ears straining to hear the tell-tale noises that would herald the passage of a 122mm or 120mm rocket. We didn't hear a thing, but still the robot warbled on. From underneath a Humvee next to us an American soldier poked his head out and yelled "Hey man, take cover there's a rocket attack. Are you guys nuts?"

"Whit rocket attack ya dobber?" was the response. "Ah cannea hear any rockets man!" The American just looked at us as though we were insane and slid back under the Humvee.

We kept walking and the promised rocket attack never materialised. We met up with more of our boys who had been in the American PX at the time of the attack. We all sat in the now deserted boardwalk, laughing about the rocket attack that never was.

"Ye should'a seen it man, it wiz fucking brilliant," one of the Jocks piped up. "This gadjee starts trying tae pull doon the shutters in the shop, yelling 'git oot git oot we're under attack!'" He chuckled at the recollection. "We aw looks aroond the place, whit fucking attack arsehole? Nay Taliban here man!" He continued. "So, as this dobber's trying tae kick us oot, we're filling oor pockets wae awsorts man!" He grinned handing me a can of American energy drink. "I came oot aboot two stone heavier than ah went in man. Yah dancer!"

After this quick interlude of pillage and pizza we were boarded on a plane bound for Cyprus and mandatory decompression.

Day 200

Saturday 25th October: Bloodhound Camp, Cyprus

It was a weary and somewhat subdued Delta Company that stepped off the buses at Bloodhound Camp, near Episkopi in Cyprus. Most of us just wanted to get home to our loved ones and games consoles/local bars, but the Army had stipulated that all soldiers coming from Afghanistan had to undergo a twenty-four-hour period of decompression.

The Army didn't want us returning straight from a war zone back to normal life and then flip out and kill our significant others, or for me, some moron who cuts me up on the A2070. There was much tired grumbling. "Why the fuck do we have to be here?" and "Kin we no jist go home?" Our baggage was left on our plane at RAF Akrotiri, we had a sleeping bag, wash kit and sports kit, all we would need for our twenty-four-hour stopover in Cyprus.

We stood in ranks facing the old prefab huts that characterised Bloodhound Camp. It was a transit camp for soldiers conducting adventure training on the Island or when the Army Reserve came on exercises such as Lion Sun and Lion Star. It was a very temporary looking place with the most basic of amenities, but we were too tired to care.

After Musa Qa'leh, it was luxury. Right now though, all I wanted was a cold beer and a cheeseburger, I knew that I would have to wait for both for at least a few hours. I stood in the chill morning as the sun started to rise above the camp and wondered what the day held for us; details had been given quickly in Afghanistan, so we had a fair idea of what we were doing. A bit of a day at the beach, BBQ, then in the evening beer and entertainment. Apparently, comedy acts and a band had been booked for us, but no one was really in the mood for it.

We received the fire brief and all the usual safety briefs associated with coming to new accommodation, muster points, actions on etc. Most of it washed over us as it was standard stuff and to be honest, after three beers most of us would be too fucked to care if the place was on fire!

After the briefs we were given a white laundry bag and told to strip out of our combats, these would be taken away and washed for us. Breakfast would be served after we got into our sports kit and then we would be bussed down to the beach for water sports activities and whatever else was available. After stripping off and getting into sports kit, we trudged like zombies up to the main kitchen where a decent full English breakfast would be waiting for us. We sat most of us in silence as we ate our breakfast and had a nice cup of tea or coffee that didn't require long life or powdered milk.

The full English started to have a disastrous effect on most of our digestive systems. Having come from Helmand where we didn't get a decent meal, the richness of the food was a shock. I found the ablutions block and began a very noisy and disgusting evacuation, 'so long breakfast, it was great knowing you!'

Slightly ropey, I headed to the parade square where the coaches were waiting for us. We all boarded and immediately most of us fell asleep. It was only a short hop to the beach, but we slept the sleep of men who were physically and mentally exhausted. We had allowed ourselves now to switch off and rest. No sentry duty, no advance to contact, no risk of someone firing a rocket into your camp.

We wound our way from Bloodhound Camp down the steep, sometimes precarious roads with large drops to the sides. We passed under a tunnel and came out onto Fossil Beach, which was also the location for the services Yacht club, so I expected to see a lot of checked shirts, corduroy trousers, and hear Sandhurst accents.

We trooped off the buses in the car park and took in our surroundings, behind us were rocky hills covered in scrub brush and ahead of us was a cluster of small buildings, above which we could see the masts of small sailing craft. We were led to the beach by a PTI (Physical Training Instructor) who was based there as an adventure training instructor.

We arrived on the beach and were confronted by blue sun loungers and out to sea I could see all the paraphernalia associated with water sports – banana boats, large water slides. As we settled in, we received another brief from the PTI, this time all about water safety and then he advised us that if we wished to participate in any of the activities, we had to take a swimming test.

'I am not the greatest of swimmers and the thought of doing a swimming test didn't' t fill me with enthusiasm. I had attempted selection for the SAS and part of that was a pre-selection phase that included the SF swimming test, which to me was nails, so having to do a swimming test in the sea was not what I anticipated. I had no intentions of participating in the water sports, my plan was to eat cheeseburgers and drink lots of coke, then sleep in the sun. But if I did decide to get in the water at least I could have the option. So, I joined the queue of lads wading into the water and I looked out to sea and listened as the PTI gave us the instructions. We were to swim between two buoys out to sea and it looked bloody far away.

I watched the lads enter the water and then took my turn, I shivered as I entered the water, but quickly I warmed up as the sun was already up over this little piece of Mediterranean paradise. I swam the breaststroke really slowly to the first buoy and my inexperience of swimming started to show, I was huffing and puffing as I reached it.

All I could think was 'Fuck me, I survived six months in Afghanistan to drown on a swimming test in Cyprus.' Luckily enough I huffed and puffed my way around the second buoy and safely dragged my knackered arse out the water and lay down on my sun lounger. That was where I stayed for the whole day, occasionally I went into the little café on site and grabbed a coke, there was a beaten path from my lounger to the café.

Around about lunchtime a barbecue had been organised for the Company and the chefs outdid themselves. The food was immense, and we could eat as much as we wanted, but much to the disappointment of all the troops was not accompanied by any beer, but we made the most of it.

After a few more hours of fun at the beach we were bussed back to the Camp for our night's entertainment. The padre spoke to us about serious issues facing soldiers returning from the combat that we'd faced and told us not to be afraid to talk if we were having trouble adjusting. The biggest take away from his chat was about looking after one another. Spotting signs in one another that we knew would indicate a change in behaviour and may signpost our mates who were not handling the return to normality. We had brought each other home alive together as a team and that job was not yet finished, even months after the deployment we still had to keep an eye on each other. This was where the brotherhood and shared hardships we had faced would be put to the test.

As darkness started to fall, we were taken to a set of bleachers and a stage had been set up in front of them. The beer began to come out and the lads just let loose. The music was great and the comedians were brilliant, most of us had not laughed so hard in the last six months. As we drank more beer we laughed more, cried some and hugged. So glad that we were alive. As I sat on the bleachers looking around me, seeing the boys laughing and joking I couldn't help but feel so proud and so happy that we had all come through it. Some of us were wounded and in our emotional state we thought of those boys; we wept for Jimmy Johnston, I wept for Jon Mathews.

We were predicted to have men killed on the tour and have others with life threatening/life changing injuries. We had lost no one as a company and that was definitely not for the want of trying on the part of the enemy. They had certainly tried but were not successful and for that I was grateful, as I was one of those who had used up their nine lives on this tour.

By all rights I should have not made it out of the ambush that injured Davey McGhee and I should not have walked away from the three-sided ambush that hit us with RPGs, my first day as Platoon commander. But I was here and for that I was thankful, and even more thankful that all my Platoon were alive.

I knew Sergeants who had not been so lucky and would have to live with that, so I counted my lucky stars and smiled as each of my lads caught my eye. We raised our beer cans to one another in mock salutes and continued to enjoy the rest of the night.

The next morning it was a weary, hungover Delta Company that went for a shower, shave and breakfast. Men had cut lips and black eyes; arguments had been settled and we were back to being one unit and we prepared to come home to normal life and peacetime army soldiering.

We changed back into out desert combats, now clean and fresher smelling. We boarded the bus and headed towards RAF Akrotiri and the journey back home to the UK.

Day 103

Tuesday 28th October: RAF Manston, Kent

I sat on the plane on the way back to the UK in a daze, I watched the clouds go past me and couldn't help thinking how anti-climactic it all was. I had just survived some of the fiercest combat that the British Army had ever faced and I was on my way home, I should have been over the moon, but inside, mentally I was still in Afghanistan and quite frankly I missed it already.

Looking around the cabin I could see the lads were either fast asleep or similarly alone with their own thoughts, 'What comes next?' I wondered to myself. How can anyone top what we've just done, how can *we* top what we've just done?

I was glad that we were returning to Manston, which was only a short hop to Canterbury. At least we would not be stuck on motorways coming back from Brize Norton or Lyneham. I looked at my tam o'shanter which had survived in my kit for six months, the green hackle was looking decidedly tired. I considered that this hackle and this cap badge with its St Andrews cross with the lion rampant mounted upon it was making history and a whole new set of battle honours. Even if we never did get 'Helmand Province 2008' embroidered on those flags, we would still be making a formidable name for our Regiment. On Herrick 8 in Musa Qa'leh alone, at one point there were three companies from different Battalions of the Royal Regiment of Scotland fighting side by side. We had a standard to uphold and indeed great traditions of courage and prevailing against the odds.

Queen Victoria who was known to love Scotland had used our soldiers as her shock troops in previous wars and names such as 'Tangiers', 'Minden', 'Waterloo' and more recently 'Gulf 1991' adorned our colours, speaking of a legacy of bravery and professionalism; as well as the dogged determination and spirit that are the hallmark of the Scottish soldier. In my mind we had more than fulfilled our part in the history of not only our Regiment but also of our people.

Before long the pilot announced that we were preparing to land at RAF Manston. My heart leapt excitedly as I felt the plane began to descend. As we dropped out of the clouds, I looked out of the window at the county that had been my home since 2003. The first thing to strike me were the colours, for six months everything had been a dusty drab ochre, only the green of the trees in the Green Zone breaking it up. But now I was seeing reds, yellows and blues. As we crossed over the English Channel, even at this height the geography was familiar, the triangular wedge of Dungeness jutting out into the sea with the power station an obvious landmark.

I watched as the sun glimmered off the surface of the sea, making it sparkle like millions of diamonds. I could make out the grey of the roads and the patchwork quilt of fields that made Kent 'The Garden of England'. Pretty little Kentish villages dotted the landscape and I could imagine the English country pubs below us with their patrons enjoying a pub lunch and a pint, oblivious to the fact that above them travelled hundreds of young men and women who were coming home from the most dangerous place on Earth.

We landed and taxied towards the arrivals terminal and baggage handlers prepared to grab our baggage. A group of white military coaches sat outside the terminal waiting for us. As the door opened on the plane I began to smell not only the fumes of the aviation fuel but also the freshness of being home in the UK and as joined the slow procession of soldiers making their way to the cabin door, I could hear the strains of bagpipe music drifting into the plane over the noise of the engines. As I stepped onto the stairs leading down onto the runway. I caught sight of a piper awaiting our arrival home playing Regimental marches. I felt the hairs on my arms and neck stand up. as I always do when I hear the bagpipes. Even now there is a quality to the bagpipes that when I hear them, my adrenaline spikes, my pupils dilate, my pulse races and the blood pounds in my ears, once again the body is gearing up for combat.

Any Scotsman will tell you, especially if they have been soldiers, that the bagpipes are something more than a musical instrument. To us they are just as much a weapon of war as our SA80 assault rifles and throughout history the bagpipes have stirred soldiers to battle and made them charge through hell to reach their objectives. For us it was a psychological tool against the Taliban, but also a boost for our men, and there is still no sound even today that can match it.

As we passed the main gates of Howe Barracks in Canterbury, I felt happy to be home, knowing that in a few hours I would be enjoying a cold pint and a well-cooked meal courtesy of my local pub in Littlestone-on-Sea. I couldn't wait.

The sight that greeted us was amazing: as we swung round the bend towards the Battalion square, we saw the large gathering through the little line of trees that ringed the parade square. Union Jack flags, Scottish Saltire flags and a multitude of lovingly crafted signs came into view.

The families had been told of our return and had been encouraged to come and greet us. The cheers and shouts from the families was not audible on the bus, but as I watched the smiles and tears of relief on the faces of wives, girlfriends and children. I felt a lump catch in my throat and tears begin to come into the corners of my eyes. I read the signs with love hearts drawn on and slogans such as 'Welcome home daddy' and 'We've missed you'. The sea of flags and signs became even more excitable and as the doors to the coaches opened, loved ones could no longer contain themselves and surged forward to embrace and kiss their returning hero.

I stood back and watched as the married soldiers held their loved one tight, as though if they let them go it would somehow become an illusion. Children were hoisted up and squeezed in almost bone-crushing hugs. I thought to myself, 'How many families up and down the country will not get this opportunity ever again?' I thought of Jon Mathews who left a wife and two children when he was taken from us. I thought of Jimmy Johnson, who left behind a fiancée, a young woman he would never get to marry.

These men were in the prime of their lives. Now, they were just two of the hundreds of young men and women who would be forever young in the hearts of those they loved and whose memories would live on through pictures and stories.

Soldiers who had no one to meet them, like me, took solace in one another and shook hands or embraced one another. Through the crowd I spotted a familiar goofy grin and there was Bruce Ewart. He strode forward and took my hand in his vice-like grip.

"Welcome home buddy," he said. I took a deep breath and smiled back.

"Thanks mate, feels good to be back."

Also present was a familiar face amongst the families going around gauging reactions and speaking to wives and children, Ross Kemp had come to see Delta Company home. When he came and spoke to me, I thanked him very much for the box of goodies he sent to the Company and informed him that he had missed quite a bit of action after he left. He laughed and said he was glad we had all made it back in one piece and asked after everyone who had been wounded. He informed me that at some point he was going to have a special screening of the documentary before it was released on Sky One.

The families would have to wait slightly longer for their loved one to be released into their loving arms as we still had a bit of admin to do. Weapons and equipment would have to be accounted for and the boys would have to get their 253 boxes back from storage.

Goody gave me the keys to my dream car and I loaded my gear into it, still smelling of dust and gunpowder, the camouflage pattern faded by the sunlight and hidden under layers of dust and dirt.

Bruce followed me to the nearest petrol station where I filled her up and began my journey home to my quiet little flat overlooking the sea near New Romney and who knew what future. I wasn't sure I had a girlfriend to go back to and I wasn't sure how I was going to reintegrate back into normal society, but today was that first step. Hot shower, beer, food and hopefully a night of passion...

Epilogue

Delta Company returned to normal life, resumed normal duties. But most of us didn't fully return from Afghanistan. Even now, fifteen years after Operation Herrick 8, there's not a day that goes by when I do not think of Afghanistan and my part in that war.

Prior to our departure from Musa Qa'leh, the Brigade Commander 16 Air Assault Brigade paid us a personal visit and got the Company together in our protective indirect fire bunker. and started his speech with "You men of Delta Company stink!" Okay, not what we were expecting but you can't have everything. With a wry smile the former Special Forces commander continued, "…of success and a job well done!"

He went on to praise the Company for its actions during Op Herrick 8. He announced quite without any agenda, and with sincere honesty, that we were the most battle-hardened and experienced rifle company in his Brigade.

The pace of combat had been ferocious and we had taken the fight to the Taliban in the toughest traditions of Scottish soldiers and had beaten them resoundingly, paving the way for reconstruction and some semblance of peace and security that they had not known in some time.

As I looked around at the guys from Delta Company, I saw the wide grins and humility with which they took the well-deserved praise that was heaped upon them. After that speech every man in the Company walked taller and it was nice to have our service recognised by the most senior officer of our brigade.

Studies would later show that Delta Company had endured some of the most gritty and sustained fighting seen by the Argylls since the

Korean War. And the Argylls had lost an entire rifle company during that war, a forgotten war. This was why in the Argyll order of battle the Rifle Companies went Alpha, Bravo and Delta. Charlie had been lost on Hill 282 in Korea after a US fighter bomber mistook the Jocks for North Korean troops, believing the enemy had stormed the hill and taken it. The following airstrike was described as an inferno, as napalm washed over the hilltop turning soldiers into human torches and leaving the hillside with a burning petroleum stench and the odour of burned meat. This was followed up by a strafing run with .50 calibre machine guns.

The Battalion second-in-command, Major Kenneth Muir, who was leading an ammo resupply party towards the hill, along with a small band of survivors, would hold off the North Koreans who exploited the accidental airstrike. With bugles sounding across the hillside they conducted a human wave assault in what they thought was going to be a one-sided attack that would see them sweep the Jocks off the hill, if there were any left. They did not bank on the hardiness of the Jocks who, even though many were badly wounded, held their ground and stubbornly refused to yield to the numerically superior Communist forces.

Major Muir and Major Ingram would man a 2-inch mortar which they used to hold of the enemy attacks before two bursts of gunfire mortally wounded Muir. His last words were: "The Gooks will never drive the Argylls from this hill." For his courage and leadership in rallying the band of survivors from B and C companies and holding the position against overwhelming odds, Major Kenneth Muir would be awarded a posthumous Victoria Cross.

To be spoken of in the same breath as these legendary Argylls was high praise indeed and we were proud to uphold that dogged and aggressive fighting spirit.

There is a saying that no one returns from war unwounded, and that I believe is true. Many veterans of our war have scars that no one can see, many cannot reconcile with what they've seen or done. For some soldiers, just the general stresses of war have taken their toll on their mental state. In the darkness, or left alone with their thoughts, many struggle. Especially those who were wounded. For them the struggle is not only mental but physical.

Wee Davey McGhee, severely wounded by an RPG South of Musa Qa'leh would suffer during his treatment on return from hospital; still to this day having metal fragments from his body. Almost reclusive. A brilliant young man with a great future as a soldier aged and damaged before his time. His youth stolen from him by the marksmanship of a Taliban rocket operator.

Young Cassidy, wounded by blue on blue artillery fire. Denied the use of his hand by a miscommunication.

Pollock, wounded in both forearms by a bullet striking the bipod of his Minimi would bear the very visible scars of war.

But we were just a small part of the story of those who had gone before us and those who would follow us into Helmand.

We would start to see that upon our return from POTL (Post Operational Tour Leave) certain personality changes became apparent in guys and those who required help would get it. I expected to suffer worse than I did. There were no flashbacks, no strange feelings. Only on fireworks night 2008 would I feel it, lying in bed at 01:00hrs and someone decided to fire a large rocket firework over the top of my flat. I sat bolt upright in bed sweating and for just a second, I was back in Musa Qa'leh Wadi being ambushed on three sides by RPG fire, my girlfriend sleeping next to me oblivious.

The big questions were asked. What do you tell people? How do you explain Afghanistan? The reality of it is, no one really gives a fuck. Unless someone has been there or been directly affected by the war, they really don't care. Society as a whole is apathetic towards soldiers. We are a nuisance when we are not deployed, getting drunk, fighting, chasing the local girls and generally living each day as though it was our last.

What people perceive as the big issues in their lives pale into insignificance for a soldier. I would find myself enraged and found it hard to control my anger when I would hear people complain about what we call first world problems.

"My skinny frapalattemochachinoesspresso is not hot enough! ... There's no Wifi in this place!"

There were young men and women fighting and dying, and the biggest problem for some people was that the latest episode of their favourite TV show had been cancelled. The truth is, you can only talk about something like Afghanistan with people who have shared similar experiences, which is why veterans bond together and look after one another.

Out of that apathy for veterans in the past, certain groups have sprung up. After Vietnam (in fact, after World War Two) many veterans joined motorcycle clubs such as the Hells Angels, which gave them a sense of brotherhood, belonging and comradeship.

After Russia's war in Afghanistan, disaffected Soviet veterans were angry at the dissolution of a country they had fought for, lost brothers for, and that they themselves were seen as an anachronism of the Cold War and part of a chapter best consigned to history. They formed groups that would become the infamous Russian mafias.

I couldn't even tell those I was close to about Afghanistan, you start to talk and see people glaze over and go into screen saver mode, which is normally your clue to shut the hell up. But amongst fellow soldiers and veterans, especially over a beer, stories are retold. Old wounds are healed and the dark humour and banter come to the fore. The humour, humility and attitudes that get you through war. Somehow, being in the right circles can help you stay sane in the peace.

How do you explain to someone who has never been in combat, what combat is like? How do you explain taking another human being's life? How do describe loading a badly wounded boy onto a poncho to then never see him again? You can't.

The struggles get worse when there are no more wars to fight, you are no longer a soldier, you have to reintegrate into normal society and that brotherhood, belonging and comradeship are no longer there. You become another face in the crowd and walk like a ghost among the living. Only you know the stories you hold dear, the experiences that have made you richer and more appreciative of life.

When you are no longer Private so and so, Corporal Whoever 1 section 12 Platoon, Sergeant Blah Platoon Sergeant 12 Platoon, you become Mr Blah. You take the warrior out of the war, but the war will never leave the warrior.

On my return I watched the news every day for news from Afghanistan. I did not have long to wait to hear news of our Gurkha replacements. On the 4th of November 2008, Rifleman Yubraj Rai would be killed by small arms fire South of Musa Qa'leh, only a few weeks after our return.

When I heard where he had died, it conjured up images of Davey McGhee being RPG'd and being caught in that three-sided ambush. I couldn't help but think how lucky we had been, the enemy had tried damn hard to kill us down there and we had denied them every time.

Eleven days later C/Sgt Krishnabhahdur Dura would be killed in an IED explosion that struck his Warrior armoured vehicle west of Musa Qa'leh. In less than a month we'd left Musa Qa'leh two of our Gurkha brothers were dead.

NATO had said that the summer of 2008 was the deadliest summer of the war so far and having fought in it I could very well believe it but more unbelievable was that Delta Company had bucked the odds.

The story of Delta Company did not end there. As with all combat tours, there were the inevitable bravery awards:

Major Nick Calder, Military Cross. For his outstanding leadership of Delta Company.

Lt James Adamson, Military Cross and Mentioned in Despatches. For bravery under fire and saving the life of his MFC.

Corporal Shaun Whitehead, Military Cross. For his leadership under fire.

Lt Colonel Nick Borton from 2 SCOTS awarded the Distinguished Service Order for his outstanding leadership, taking over our battlegroup after the wounding of our commanding officer.

Delta Company was the most decorated company in the Battalion and we wore that badge with pride. We had the best leadership team, our commanders all the way down to section level were phenomenal and I feel proud and privileged to have been part of such an excellent fighting unit as Delta Company 5 SCOTS.

The one thing that brought the plight of the grunts fighting in Afghanistan back to the people at home was Ross Kemp. He kept us alive in the minds of the public to ensure that our sacrifices were not forgotten. We weren't just a gung-ho uniformed group of gun-toting nutters. Behind each skeletal frame, each thousand-yard stare, each gaunt look was a father, a son, boyfriend or husband. We were human and we had seen the worst of humanity that war brings. We had seen the results of modern warfare and inflicted our share of damage. There was generally no animosity towards the Taliban, we respected our foes for their courage and their fighting spirit and as with us, they were fathers, sons and husbands.

I could imagine that there were families in Afghanistan and Pakistan who never knew the fate of their loved ones fighting in the ranks of the insurgents. Modern firepower could render human bodies into nothing more than mulch. Our casualty notification chain was first rate and we always retrieved our dead and wounded from the field, so British families could have that closure.

We had a private screening of *Ross Kemp: Return to Afghanistan*. We sat in the Warrant Officers' and Sergeants' mess at Howe Barracks and watch as our tour, our war came back to us on the large screen. We were nervous as to how it would be received. We need not have worried. The documentary was excellent and when it aired on Sky One, it became an instant hit with the lads of Delta Company becoming household names. Ross Kemp also campaigned for soldier's welfare and veterans' causes, tirelessly working with and endorsing 'Help for Heroes', trying to ensure that our service was never forgotten.

I would leave Delta Company temporarily for a six-month attachment to the Infantry Training Centre Catterick. I was to be a Platoon Sergeant attached to the Queen's Division and in an unusual twist, one of the Corporals in my training team would be Corporal Stu Parker from the 1st Battalion the Royal Anglian Regiment (The Vikings) who had featured in Ross's first outing to Afghanistan.

His unit had suffered a devastating blue on blue attack by a US aircraft, which killed three members of their Platoon and severely wounded two, including Stu. We became the Ross Kemp training team and I embraced this with great enthusiasm.

We were training young potential infantry soldiers. As soon as they finished basic training, some would be bound for the battlefield in Helmand and if I could somehow impart my experience and my knowledge to them, maybe save them, I could consider my job done.

I would learn from my instructors back when I was in training. Most importantly, how not to be like them. I would be patient and supportive. I would be a father figure to my trainees and as long as they were under my care, I would try and get them ready for the horrors they might have to deal with.

After six months, I stood proudly looking at my young charges and wished them all good fortune in their future careers, especially if they found themselves in the dusty heat of Helmand. As I wished them luck I told them to learn from their more senior peers and NCOs, it would hopefully keep them alive.

In my mind there are no finer English soldiers than the men of the Queen's Division and I enjoyed my time training their soldiers, who would fill the ranks of such Regiments as the Royal Anglian Regiment 1st and 2nd Battalions, Princess of Wales Royal Regiment 1st and 2nd Battalions, and The Royal Regiment of Fusiliers 1st Battalion.

I would return to Delta Company in Canterbury to a very different command team and would go on to undertake another tour of duty in Afghanistan during the winter of 2010-2011, where I would see a very different war, working with the ANP.

The kinetic fighting was pretty much over and the enemy was focussing mostly on the placement of IEDs. The Argylls would lose one more man on this tour, the gentle giant Fijian Private Joseva Vatubua, affectionately known as 'Big Joe' to those who knew him. He was killed by an IED placed in the wall of a Mosque near PB 5 in Nahr-e-saraj district south of Gereshk.

Over the months and years I would watch with heartbreak as more Union Jack-draped coffins arrived at RAF Lyneham to be driven through the streets of the lovely little town of Wootton Bassett. When the funeral corteges would slowly parade through the streets, a credit to the wonderful people of that town, whenever a brother or sister was flown home on their last journey the town would come to a standstill and the population would line the streets, with the Royal British Legion forming an honour guard, their standards lowered as a mark of respect for our fallen. I could never watch a repatriation through Wootton Bassett without a tear in my eye. Although the majority of those fallen heroes I didn't know, occasionally the casket would contain the remains of someone I did know, and that was harder.

I believe my experiences in Afghanistan made me a better man; a better soldier and better human being and if I was given my life to live again, I would change nothing. I served in the best Infantry Company in the British Army under some fantastic officers and fellow senior NCOs. I was honoured and privileged to have some of the finest young soldiers and NCOs under my command to whom I would entrust my life again and again. I saw first-hand how the ranks of our Army are filled with the greatest young men and women, those who have the moral courage to stand up when others would cower, raise their hand and say "Aye. I'll join the army." They can stand tall amongst their generation safe in the knowledge that when asked "What did you do for your country?" They can answer with all honesty and sincerity that they answered their country's call to arms and fought in a war that is now largely forgotten by those who have not fought in it or been directly affected by it.

This generation of young men and women have done their country proud and I hope that in some small measure this book will help remind people about what these soldiers have sacrificed and how some are still suffering now.

It never ceased to amaze me that the young men of Delta Company were asked time and time again to kit up and head out into enemy territory – knowing that they would be shot at, knowing there was a chance they could be killed – but they bore it like the heavy burdens they carried into battle, with courage and stoicism.

To those who say there is no glory or honour in war, I say this. You have never fought alongside The Argyll and Sutherland Highlanders.

Index